P9-EGM-751

NORTH AFRICA

SWEDEN
ESTONIA
DENMARK LITHUANIA LATVIA
RUSSIAN FEDERATION
RUSSIAN FED.
REPUBLIC OF IRELAND UNITED KINGDOM NETHERLANDS GERMANY POLAND BELARUS
BELGIUM LUXEMBOURG
CZECH REPUBLIC SLOVAKIA UKRAINE
FRANCE SWITZERLAND AUSTRIA HUNGARY MOLDOVA
SLOVENIA CROATIA ROMANIA
SERBIA
BOSNIA AND HERZEGOVINA BULGARIA GEORGIA
ITALY FYR OF MACEDONIA
PORTUGAL SPAIN ALBANIA GREECE TURKEY
Athens
MOROCCO CYPRUS SYRIA
TUNISIA ISRAEL IRAQ
ALGERIA LIBYA EGYPT JORDAN SAUDI ARABIA

L'viv

Dnister

UKRAINE

Chernivtsi

MOLDOVA

CHISINAU

Prut

Siret

ROMANIA

Braşov   Galaţi

BUCHAREST
Constanţa

Dunărea

Iskŭr

Varna

SOFIA

Burgas

BULGARIA

Néstos

Black   Sea

Kavála
Alexandroúpoli
Thessaloníki

Istanbul

GREECE

Eskişehir   ANKARA

Kızıl Irmak

Vólos

Skiáthos   Lésvos

TURKEY

Aegean Sea

Ewoia

Izmir

Tuz Gölü

ATHENS
Piraeus

Sámos   Kuşadası

Tínos

Konya

Mykonos   Pátmos   Bodrum

Kos   Marmaris

Dalaman   Antalya   İçel

Santorini

Rhodes

Chaniá   Irákleio   Kárpathos

SYRIA
Al-Lādiqīya

E75

Agios Nikólaos

Crete

CYPRUS   NICOSIA

Pafos   Lárnaka

Lemesós

Sea

LEBANON

BEIRUT

Hefa

0 kilometres   200

0 miles   200

ISRAEL

Alexandria   EGYPT

●Dráma   THRACE   ●Komotiní

Kavála●

Alexandroúpoli ●

NORTHERN GREECE
Pages 232–257

AROUND
ATHENS
● ATHENS
ATTICA
Lávrio ●

ATHENS
Pages 62–135

AROUND ATHENS
Pages 140–157

EYEWITNESS TRAVEL

GREECE
ATHENS & THE MAINLAND

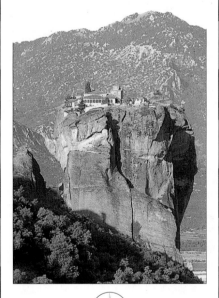

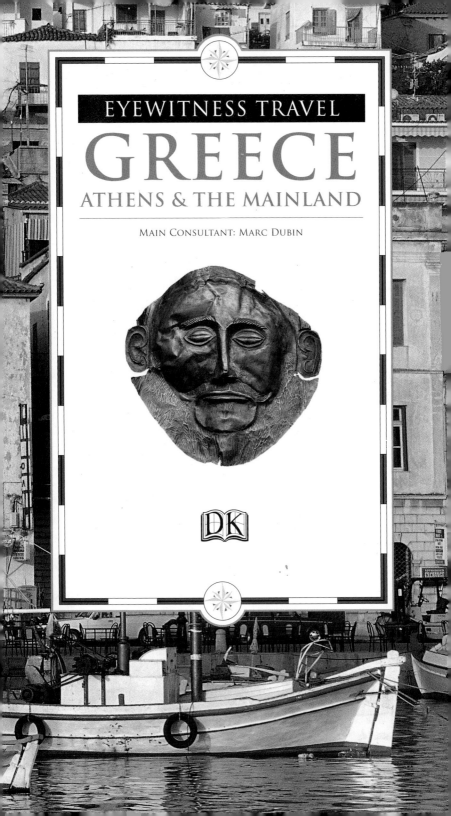

EYEWITNESS TRAVEL

GREECE
ATHENS & THE MAINLAND

MAIN CONSULTANT: MARC DUBIN

DK

LONDON, NEW YORK,
MELBOURNE, MUNICH AND DELHI
www.dk.com

PROJECT EDITOR Jane Simmonds
ART EDITOR Stephen Bere
EDITORS Isabel Carlisle, Michael Ellis, Simon Farbrother,
Claire Folkard, Marianne Petrou, Andrew Szudek
US EDITORS Michael Wise, Mary Sutherland
DESIGNERS Jo Doran, Paul Jackson, Elly King, Marisa Renzullo
MAP CO-ORDINATORS Emily Green, David Pugh
VISUALIZER Joy Fitzsimmons
LANGUAGE CONSULTANT Georgia Gotsi

CONTRIBUTORS AND CONSULTANTS
Rosemary Barron, Marc Dubin, Mike Gerrard, Andy Harris,
Lynette Mitchell, Colin Nicholson, Robin Osborne, Barnaby
Rogerson, Paul Sterry, Tanya Tsikas

MAPS
Gary Bowes, Fiona Casey, Christine Purcell (ERA-Maptec Ltd)

PHOTOGRAPHERS
Joe Cornish, John Heseltine, Rob Reichenfeld, Peter Wilson,
Francesca Yorke

ILLUSTRATORS
Stephen Conlin, Paul Guest, Steve Gyapay, Maltings Partnership,
Chris Orr & Associates, Paul Weston, John Woodcock

Reproduced by Colourscan (Singapore)
Printed and bound by L. Rex Printing Company Limited, China

First American Edition, 1997
08 09 10 9 8 7 6 5 4 3 2
Published in the United States by
DK Publishing, Inc., 375 Hudson Street,
New York, New York 10014

Reprinted with revisions 1998, 1999, 2000, 2001,
2002, 2003, 2004, 2006, 2007

Copyright © 1997, 2007 Dorling Kindersley Limited, London

ISBN: 978-0-75662-636-5
ISSN: 1542-1554

Throughout this book, floors are referred to in accordance with US
usage, ie the "first floor" is at ground level.

Front cover main image: Tholos *at Delphi*

**The information in this
DK Eyewitness Guide is checked regularly.**

Every effort has been made to ensure that this book is as up-to-
date as possible at the time of going to press. Some details,
however, such as telephone numbers, opening hours, prices,
gallery hanging arrangements and travel information are liable to
change. The publishers cannot accept responsibility for any
consequences arising from the use of this book, nor for any
material on third party websites, and cannot guarantee that any
website address in this book will be a suitable source of travel
information. We value the views and suggestions of our readers
very highly. Please write to: Publisher, DK Eyewitness Travel
Guides, Dorling Kindersley, 80 Strand, London WC2R 0RL.

◁ **Morning at Gýtheio harbour in the Peloponnese**

CONTENTS

HOW TO USE THIS
GUIDE **6**

**Black-figure bowl depicting
the god Dionysos**

INTRODUCING
ATHENS AND
MAINLAND GREECE

DISCOVERING GREECE
10

PUTTING GREECE ON
THE MAP **12**

A PORTRAIT OF
MAINLAND GREECE **14**

THE HISTORY
OF GREECE **24**

ATHENS AND MAINLAND
GREECE THROUGH
THE YEAR **44**

ANCIENT GREECE

GODS, GODDESSES
AND HEROES **52**

Tower houses at Vátheia, Inner Máni, in the Peloponnese

Greek salad

Fresco at Varlaám monastery at
Metéora, Central Greece

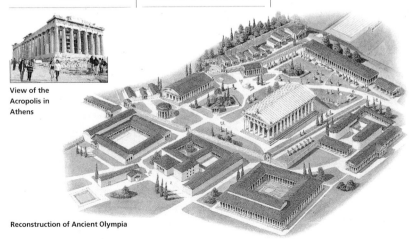

View of the
Acropolis in
Athens

Reconstruction of Ancient Olympia

HOW TO USE THIS GUIDE

This guide helps you to get the most from your visit to Mainland Greece. It provides expert recommendations and practical information. *Introducing Athens and Mainland Greece* maps the country and sets it in its historical and cultural context. *Ancient Greece* gives a background to the many remains and artifacts to be seen. The four regional chapters, plus *Athens*, describe important sights, with maps and illustrations. Restaurant and hotel recommendations can be found in *Travellers' Needs*. The *Survival Guide* has tips on everything from using a Greek telephone to transport.

ATHENS

Athens has been divided into two sightseeing areas. Each has its own chapter, opening with a list of the sights described. All sights are numbered on an area map, and are described in detail on the following pages.

Sights at a Glance gives a categorized list of the chapter's sights: Museums and Galleries; Squares, Parks and Gardens; Churches and Historic Buildings.

All pages relating to Athens have red thumb tabs.

A locator map shows you where you are in relation to the rest of Athens.

1 Area Map
The sights are numbered and located on a map. Sights in the city centre are also shown on the Athens Street Finder *on pages 122–35.*

2 Street-by-Street Map
This gives an overhead view of the key areas in central Athens. The numbering on the map ties in with the area map and the fuller descriptions that follow.

Story boxes highlight special aspects of a particular sight.

Stars indicate the sights that no visitor should miss.

A suggested route for a walk is shown in red.

3 Detailed Information
The sights within Athens are described individually. Addresses, telephone numbers, opening hours and information concerning admission charges and wheelchair access are given for each entry. Map references to the Athens Street Finder *are also provided for orientation.*

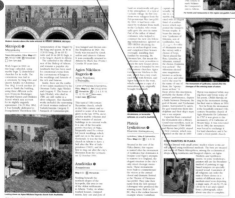

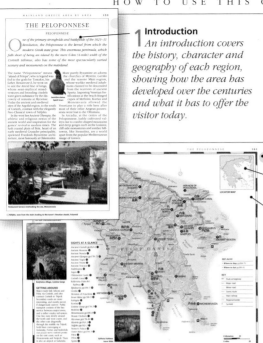

1 Introduction
An introduction covers the history, character and geography of each region, showing how the area has developed over the centuries and what it has to offer the visitor today.

MAINLAND GREECE AREA BY AREA
Mainland Greece has been divided into four regions, each of which has a separate chapter. A map of these areas can be found inside the front cover of the book.

Each region can be identified by its colour coding, shown on the inside front cover.

A locator map shows you where you are in relation to the other regions in the book.

2 Regional Map
This shows the region covered in the chapter. The main sights are numbered on the map. The major roads are marked and there are useful tips about the best ways of getting around the area.

3 Detailed Information
All the important towns and areas to visit are described individually. They are listed in order, following the numbering on the Regional Map. Within each entry there is detailed information on all the major sights.

A Visitors' Checklist provides the practical information you will need to plan your visit.

4 Greece's Top Sights
These are given one or more full pages. Historic buildings are dissected to reveal their interiors. Many of the ancient sites are reconstructed to supplement information about the site as it is seen today.

INTRODUCING
ATHENS AND
MAINLAND GREECE

DISCOVERING MAINLAND GREECE

Four thousand years of civilization and waves of invaders have made Greece a patchwork of history and geography, from the northern snows of Epirus and Macedonia to the fertile plains of Thessaly and Attica and the sun-baked slopes of the Peloponnese. More than half of the Greek

Ancient treasure of Greece

population live in the three largest cities, leaving much of hinterland under-populated and untouched by 21st-century urbanization, with ruins of ancient temples and medieval castles still brooding over the deserted countryside. These pages offer an at-a-glance guide to the highlights of each region.

The ancient Parthenon on the Acropolis, Athens

ATHENS

- **The temples of the Acropolis**
- **Authentic café culture**
- **Treasures of the National Archaeological Museum**

The urban sprawl of Greece's capital surrounds an inner historic core overlooked by the imposing temples of the **Acropolis** *(see pp94–101)* and the hills of Attica. Despite its size, Athens retains a village charm, with little squares shaded by palm trees, cafés and tavernas at every corner and pots of geraniums growing on apartment balconies.

Atop the Acropolis, the Parthenon is a majestic sight. Below it, surrounding the remarkable **Tower of the Winds** *(see pp86–7)* and **Ancient Agora's** toppled columns *(see pp90– 91)* lie the bustling street markets of the vibrant **Monastiráki** district *(see p117)*.

Dotted around the city are tiny churches dating back to its Byzantine heyday, like the delightful **Panagía**

Gorgoepíkoös *(see p105)* located in picturesque **Pláka** *(see pp102–3)*, where tourists and Athenians alike flock to soak up the thriving outdoor café culture.

The **National Archaeological Museum** *(see pp68–71)* with its impressive exhibits is unmissable, but the city also has many smaller museums, such as the **Benáki Museum** *(see pp78–9)* and the **Museum of Cycladic Art** *(see pp74–5)* with its enigmatic relics of Europe's oldest civilization.

AROUND ATHENS

- **Glorious Soúnio**
- **Opulent beach resorts of the Attica Coast**
- **Traditonal tavernas**

The Athens suburbs have spread almost all the way across the upper Attica peninsula, but below the city is the appealing **Attica Coast** *(see p149)*, where a string of luxury resorts stretch south towards **Soúnio** *(see p148–9)* and the soaring columns of

the Temple of Poseidon. The hinterland is much less attractive and largely industrial, however **Ancient Eleusis** *(see pp156–7)* and the spectacular **Monastery of Dafní** *(see pp152–3)* both merit a visit.

Sacred sites, including **Ancient Brauron** *(see p146)*, **Ancient Oropós** *(see p144)*, the ruined Temple of Nemesis at **Ramnoús** *(see p144)* and the evocative battlefield of **Marathónas** *(see p145)* are scattered across the peninsula, and on the east coast is **Rafína** *(see p145)*, a lively harbour with some great fish tavernas.

THE PELOPONNESE

- **Magnificent ancient sites at Olympia and Corinth**
- **Byzantine architecture**
- **Empty beaches and wilderness landscapes**

South of the Gulf of Corinth, the Peloponnese waits to be discovered. A region of

The beautiful Attica Coast at Cape Soúnion

Spectacular clifftop monasteries, Metéora, Central Greece

immense beauty, with a mountainous interior, lush valleys and fine beaches, it is also home to some of Greece's most important ancient cities and temples, including **Ancient Corinth** *(see pp162–5)*, **Spárti** *(see p189)* and **Ancient Messene** *(see p201)*.

Byzantine ruins at Mystrás, Peloponnese

Its greatest strength is its wealth of hidden histories, from the ruins of the last outpost of Byzantium at **Mystrás** *(see pp192–3)* to the spooky Venetian fortress at **Monemvasía**. However, no visit would be complete without heading for the region's key attractions – **Ancient Corinth** *(see pp162–5)*, the overwhelming remains of Agamemnon's capital at **Mycenae** *(see pp178–9)*, the magnificent amphitheatre at **Epidaurus** *(see p184)* with its amazing acoustics, and **Olympia** *(see p170–2)*, birthplace of the Olympic Games. The Peloponnese has more to offer than just ancient ruins. Walkers are drawn to the **Loúsios Gorge** *(see pp174–5)*, a striking canyon where

monasteries nestle in wooded flanks, and dozing in the sun, elegant **Náfplio** *(see pp182–3)* and pretty **Gýtheio** *(see p198)* are simply delightful.

CENTRAL AND WESTERN GREECE

- Ruins of Ancient Delphi
- Breathtaking Píndos mountains
- Traditional Zagórian villages

This vast region spells remote mountain wildernesses and fertile plains. **Ancient Delphi** *(see pp228–31)* attracts droves of visitors but the coastal towns of **Galaxídi** *(see p224)* and **Náfpaktos** *(see p224–5)* also demand to be visited. The Parnassus massif cuts the province off from the plains of Thessaly, and merges with the **Píndos Mountains** *(see p206)*, enclosing breathtaking scenery – much of it within nature reserves that provide refuge for bear and wolf, and a paradise for walkers.

In **Metéora** *(see pp216–17)*, monastaries perch dramatically on clifftops and in **Zagória** *(see p207)*, enchanting hamlets cling to the stark slopes of the Epirus range. **Pílio** *(see pp218–20)*, on the Aegean coast, is a forested peninsula dotted with fishing villages and olive groves. To cap it all, the region has some fine beaches at **Párga** *(see p212)* and **Agios Ioánnis** *(see p220)*.

NORTHERN GREECE

- Thriving city nightlife
- Unspoilt Préspa Lakes
- Splendid monasteries of Mouth Athos

Macedonia and Thrace are Greece's least-explored regions, despite glorious beaches on the **Chalkidikí** peninsula and an array of rewarding archaeological sites. The old Macedonian capital at **Ancient Pélla** *(see p243)* and the temple site of Dion, slumbering beneath Greece's tallest mountain, **Mount Olympos** *(see p241)*, both warrant a visit. **Thessaloníki** *(see pp244-5)*, Greece's second largest city, has two world-class museums, the **Thessaloníki Archaeological Museum** *(see pp246–7)* and the **Museum of Byzantine Culture** *(see p244)*, and its lively nightlife attracts a young crowd.

Inland, ruined Byzantine castles crown hilltops along the line of the Via Egnatia that once connected Rome with Constantinople. The **Préspa Lakes** *(see pp236–7)*, a unique, multi-national nature reserve, has a dazzling array of flora and fauna and attracts an abundance of wildlife. The spectacular monasteries of **Mount Athos** *(see pp252–4)* are off-limits to female visitors but can be viewed by boat from the coast. The gorges of the **Néstos Valley** *(see p255)*, where the river flows through the Rodopi mountains, make for some of the loveliest scenery in Greece.

The gorgeous turquoise sea on the Chalkidikí peninsula, Northern Greece

Putting Greece on the Map

Occupying the southernmost tip of the Balkan peninsula, Greece divides into over 2,000 islands stretching from the Ionian Sea in the west to the Aegean Sea in the east. The mainland has borders with Albania, Bulgaria, Turkey and the former Yugoslav Republic of Macedonia and is home to most of Greece's 10.9 million people, with a third of these in Athens.

KEY

⛴ Main international ferry service

✈ International airport

═══ Dual-carriageway

━━━ Major road

──── Railway line

─ ─ ─ National boundary

◁ **The fortified islet of Boúrtzi, off the coast at Methóni**

A PORTRAIT OF
MAINLAND GREECE

*G*reece is one of the most visited European countries, yet one of the least known. The modern Greek state dates only from 1830 and bears little relation to the popular image of ancient Greece. At a geographical crossroads, Greece combines elements of the Balkans, Middle East and Mediterranean.

For a relatively small country, less than 132,000 sq km (51,000 sq miles) in area, Greece possesses marked regional differences in topography. Nearly three-quarters of the land is mountainous, uninhabited or uncultivated. Fertile agri-cultural land supports tobacco farming in the northeast, with orchard fruits and vegetables grown further south. A third of the population lives in the capital, Athens, the cultural, financial and political centre, in which ancient and modern stand side by side.

Rural and urban life in con-temporary Greece have been trans-formed this century despite years of occupation and conflict, including a bitter civil war *(see p42)* that would surely have finished off a less resilient people. The society that emerged was supported with US aid, yet Greece remained relatively under-developed until the 1960s.

**Fresco from Moní
Frankavílla, Amaliáda**

Rural areas lacked paved roads and even basic utilities, prompting extensive, unplanned urban growth and emigration. It has been said, with some justice, that there are no architects in Greece, only civil engineers.

For centuries a large number of Greeks have lived abroad: currently there are over half as many Greeks outside the country as in. This

Backgammon players at the flea market around Plateía Monastirakíou in Athens

◁ **Leading a mule on the streets of Monemvasía**

The Píndos mountain range, from above the village of Vrysochóri

diaspora occurred in several stages, prompted by changes in the Ottoman Empire late in the 17th century. Most post war emigration was to Africa, the Americas and Australia.

RELIGION, LANGUAGE AND CULTURE

During the centuries of domination by Venetians and Ottomans *(see pp38–9)* the Greek Orthodox Church preserved the Greek language, and with it Greek identity, through its liturgy and schools. Today, the Orthodox Church is still a powerful force despite the secularizing reforms of the PASOK government in the 1980s. The query *Eísai Orthódoxos*

Votive offerings in the Pantánassas convent

(Are you Orthodox?) is virtually synonymous with *Éllinas eísai* (Are you Greek?). While no self-respecting couple would dispense with a church wedding and baptisms for their children, civil marriages are now equally valid in law as the traditional religious service. Sunday Mass is very popular with women, who often use the services as meeting places for socializing much in the same way as men do the *kafeneía* (cafés).

Parish priests, often recognizable by their tall stovepipe hats and long beards, are not expected to embody the divine, but to transmit it at liturgy. Many marry and have a second trade (a custom that helps keep up the numbers of entrants to the church). There has also been a recent renaissance in monastic life, perhaps in reaction to the growth of

Greek priests leading a religious procession in Athens

materialism since World War II.

The subtle and beautiful Greek language, another great hallmark of national identity, was for a long time a field of conflict between *katharévousa*, an artificial, written

Tavernas in the town of Náfplio

form hastily devised around the time of Independence, and the slowly evolved *dimotikí*, or everyday speech, with its streamlined grammar and words borrowed from several other languages. The dispute acquired political overtones, with the Right tending to champion *katharévousa*, the Left, *dimotikí*, with blood even being shed at times.

Today the supple and accessible *dimotikí* is the language of the nation. The art of storytelling is still as prized in Greece as in Homer's time, with conversation pursued for its own sake in *kafeneía* and at dinner parties. The bardic tradition has remained alive with the poet-lyricists such as Mános Eleftheríou, Apóstolos Kaldarás and Níkos Gátsos. The continuous efforts made to produce popular and accessible art have played a key role in helping to keep *dimotikí* alive from the 19th century until the present day.

Both writers and singers, the natural advocates of *dimotikí*, have historically been important to the Greek public. During recent periods of censorship under the dictatorship or in times of foreign occupation, they carried out an essential role as one of the chief sources of coded information and morale-boosting.

DEVELOPMENT AND DIPLOMACY

Compared to most of its Balkan neighbours, Greece is a wealthy and stable country. However, by Western economic indicators Greece is poor and languished

An archaeologist helping to restore the Parthenon

at the bottom of the EU league table until the addition of ten new East European countries in 2004. The persistent negative trade deficit is aggravated by imports of luxury goods, an expression of *xenomanía* or belief in the inherent superiority of all things foreign. Cars are most conspicuous among these, since Greece is one of the very few European countries not to manufacture its own.

Greece still bears the hallmarks of a developing economy, with agriculture and the service sector accounting for two-thirds of the GNP. Blurred lines between work and living space are

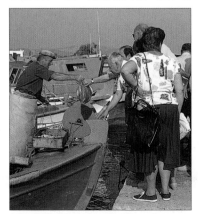
Selling fish at Vólos harbour, the Pílio

Barrels in the Achaïa Klauss winery at Pátra

the norm, with professional brass plates alternating with personal bell-buzzer tags in any apartment block. There is a tenacious adherence, despite repeated campaigns against it, to the long afternoon siesta. As a result, some workers have to endure commuting twice a day.

With EU membership since 1981 and a nominally capitalist orientation, Greece has now overcome its resemblance to pre-1989 Eastern Europe. The state no longer invests heavily in antiquated industries nor is the civil service of today overstaffed as part of a full-employment policy. Instead, recent years have seen a number of improvements: loss-making state enterprises have been sold off, inflation has dipped to single figures for the first time since 1973 and interest rates have fallen. However, the drachma suffered on entry to the ERM and unemployment remains stubbornly high. Tourism ranks as the largest hard-currency earner, offsetting the depression in world shipping and the fact that Mediterranean agricultural products are duplicated within the EU. Greece's historically lenient entry requirements for refugees, and its pre-eminent status in the Balkans, have made it a magnet for Arabs, Africans, Kurds, Poles and Albanians for a number of years. Now protectionist procedures, such as stringent frontier clamp-downs and the deportation of all undoc-umented individuals, have been introduced.

The fact that the Greek state is less than 200 years old, and that this century has been marked by political instability, means that there is little faith in government institutions. Life operates on networks of personal friendships and official contacts. The classic designations of Right and Left have only acquired their conventional meanings since the 1930s. The dominant political figure of the first half of the 20th century was Elefthérios Venizélos, an anti-royalist Liberal. The years following World War II have been largely shaped by the influence of

Statue of Athena standing beside the Athens Academy

Rooftops of Náfplio and Boúrtzi islet from the Palamídi fortress

House in the village of Psarádes, beside the Préspa lakes

two men: the late Andréas Papandréou, three times premier as head of the Panhellenic Socialist Movement (PASOK), and the late conservative premier Konstantínos Karamanlís.

With the Cold War over, Greece looks likely to assert its underlying Balkan identity in many ways. Relations with Albania have improved since the collapse of the Communist regime in 1990. Greece is already the biggest investor in Bulgaria, and after a recent rapprochement with Skopje, it seems poised to be a regional power, with Thessaloníki's port (second largest in the Mediterranean) seen as the future gateway to the southern Balkans.

Man with a shepherd's crook in the village of Métsovo

HOME LIFE

The family is still the basic Greek social unit. Traditionally, one family could sow, plough and reap its own fields, without need of cooperative work parties. Today, family-run businesses are still the norm in urban settings. Family life and social life are usually one and the same, and tend to revolve around eating out, which is done more often than in most of Europe. Arranged marriages and granting of dowries,

though officially banned, persist; most single young people live with their parents or another relative until married, and outside the largest cities, few couples dare to cohabit. Despite the renowned Greek love of children, Greece has the lowest birth rate in Europe after Italy: less than half its pre-World War II levels. Owing in part to the recent reforms in family and inheritance law, urban Greek women have been raised in status. Better represented in medicine and the law, many women run their own businesses. In the country, however, macho attitudes persist and women often forgo the chance of a career for the sake of the house and children. New imported notions and attitudes have begun to creep in, especially in the larger cities, but generally tradition remains strong and no amount of innovation or outside influence is likely to jeopardize the Greek way of life.

Wednesday market in Argos

Byzantine Architecture

Medieval churches are virtually all that have survived from a millennium of Byzantine civilization in Greece. Byzantine church architecture was concerned almost exclusively with a decorated interior. The intention was to sculpt out a holy space where the congregation would be confronted with the true nature of the cosmos, cleared of all worldly distractions. The mosaics and frescoes portraying the whole body of the Church, from Christ downwards, have a dual purpose: they give inspiration to the worshipper and are windows to the spiritual world. From a mountain chapel to an urban church there is great conformity of design, with structure and decoration united to a single purpose.

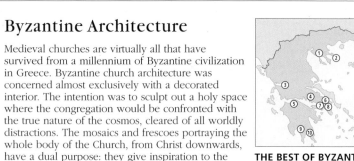

THE BEST OF BYZANTINE ARCHITECTURE

① Thessaloníki *p248*
② Mount Athos *pp252–4*
③ Arta *p213*
④ Monastery of Osios Loúkas *pp222–3*
⑤ Pátra *p169*
⑥ Moní Kaïsarianís *pp150–51*
⑦ Monastery of Dafní *pp152–3*
⑧ Athens *p80, p105, p108*
⑨ Mystrás *pp192–3*
⑩ Geráki *p189*

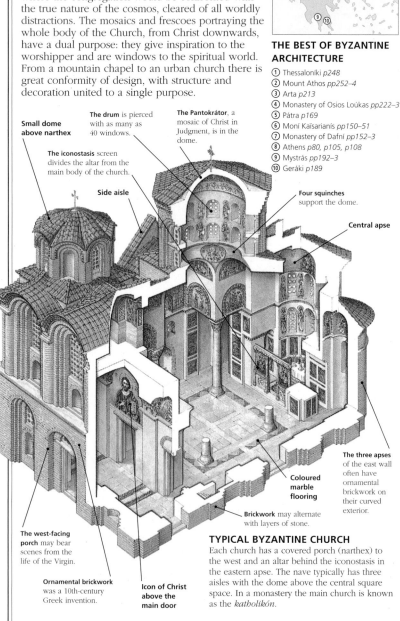

The drum is pierced with as many as 40 windows.

Small dome above narthex

The Pantokrátor, a mosaic of Christ in Judgment, is in the dome.

The iconostasis screen divides the altar from the main body of the church.

Side aisle

Four squinches support the dome.

Central apse

The west-facing porch may bear scenes from the life of the Virgin.

Ornamental brickwork was a 10th-century Greek invention.

Icon of Christ above the main door

Coloured marble flooring

Brickwork may alternate with layers of stone.

The three apses of the east wall often have ornamental brickwork on their curved exterior.

TYPICAL BYZANTINE CHURCH

Each church has a covered porch (narthex) to the west and an altar behind the iconostasis in the eastern apse. The nave typically has three aisles with the dome above the central square space. In a monastery the main church is known as the *katholikón*.

UNDERSTANDING FRESCOES IN A BYZANTINE CHURCH

The frescoes and mosaics in churches' interiors were organized according to a standard scheme. Symbolically, images descended from heaven (Christ Pantokrátor in the dome) to earth (the saints on the lowest level). The Virgin was shown in the semi-dome of the apse, with the fathers of the church below her.

THE VIRGIN MARY

Icons of the Virgin Mary abound in every Orthodox church, where she is referred to as Panagía, the All Holy. Her exceptional status was confirmed in 431 when she was awarded the title Theotókos "Mother of God", in preference to just "Mother of Christ".

Choirs of angels

Windows in drum

Christ Pantokrátor

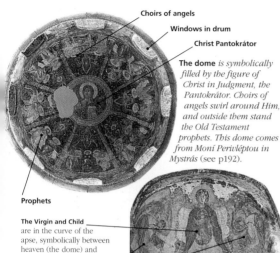

The dome *is symbolically filled by the figure of Christ in Judgment, the Pantokrátor. Choirs of angels swirl around Him, and outside them stand the Old Testament prophets. This dome comes from Moní Perivléptou in Mystrás (see p192).*

Prophets

The Virgin and Child are in the curve of the apse, symbolically between heaven (the dome) and earth (the nave).

Archangels Michael and Gabriel, dressed like courtiers of a Byzantine emperor, honour the Virgin.

The Fathers of Orthodoxy, here in their episcopal robes, defined Orthodoxy in the early centuries.

Upper register of saints

Eleoúsa, *meaning "Our Lady of Tenderness", shows the Virgin Mary brushing cheeks with the Christ Child.*

The Virgin seated on a throne, *flanked by two arch-angels, is a depiction usually found in the eastern apse.*

The apse *is often hidden from public view by an elaborate iconostasis screen, through whose doors only the clergy are admitted. This apse is from Agios Stratigós in the Máni (see p199).*

Lower register of saints

Sand-filled tray for votive candles

The side walls *are decorated in registers. On the lowest level stand life-size portrayals of the saints, their heads illuminated with haloes. More complex scenes portraying incidents from the Gospels or the Day of Judgment fill the upper walls and vaults. This church is at Miliés in the Pílio (see pp218–20).*

Odigítria, *meaning the "Conductress", shows the Virgin indicating the Christ Child with her right arm.*

The Landscape of Mainland Greece

Greece is a land of rugged beauty. The narrow coastal belt is backed by cliffs in places while inland there are massive mountain ranges, gorges and cliffs, the haunt of eagles and vultures. The fantastic array of vegetation, including many species of spring wild flowers, is strongly influenced by the Mediterranean climate of long, hot and dry summers and mild, wet winters. Clearance of forests for agriculture and timber has produced a mosaic of flower-rich fields and areas of shrubs. This shrubland habitat is of two kinds: the dense aromatic bushes of *maquis* and the sparser *phrygana* with lower and more compact plants. Although the country's millions of goats destroy the vegetation with their constant grazing, one of the most romantic sights in Greece is that of flocks being herded through olive groves full of archaeological remains, as at Sparta in the Peloponnese.

Common poppy

Abandoned areas of cultivation soon revert to the wild. Larks and pipits feed and nest here and, in spring, wild flowers and butterflies are abundant.

Phrygana often covers bare slopes and rocky outcrops.

Hilly landscapes *with stately cypress trees standing tall and dark against the steep slopes are closely associated with Greece's archaeological sites. These, including the Byzantine town of Mystrás above, are worth visiting for their wildlife alone and in particular the spring wild flowers that mix rare orchids with daisies, poppies and marigolds.*

Olive trees harbour numerous birds and insects among their silvery-green foliage.

Spring flowers such as poppies and irises have a brief but prolific season.

MAQUIS AND PHRYGANA

Maquis shrubland dominates the landscape in this view of Mycenae. It is a mixture of rockroses and aromatic herbs. The more barren *phrygana*, in the far distance, has clumps of spiny vetches.

Olive groves *are found all over Greece at low altitudes; this one is at Argalastí in the Pílio. In spring, flowers grow in profusion in the shade of trees and attract a wealth of butterflies and beetles. Lizards hunt for insects in the twisted trunks that also provide nesting places for birds such as masked shrikes.*

Wetland areas, *such as the margins of Lake Stymfalía in the Peloponnese, are often used for farming. Usually fairly dry underfoot, they are rich in birds, amphibians and plants.*

WILD FLOWERS OF GREECE

Greece is blessed with an extraordinary wealth of flowering plants. At least 6,000 species grow in the country, quite a few of them found nowhere else in the world. The floral richness is due in part to the country's diversity of habitats, ranging from wetlands, coastal plains and lowland *maquis* to snow-capped mountain tops. The growing period for many plants is winter, the dampest, coolest season, and the flowering periods run from March to early June, and again in September. Coastal areas of the Peloponnese are perhaps the richest in wild flowers.

The wild gladiolus has several varieties that are among the most showy spring flowers.

The tassel hyacinth is aptly named for its appearance. It grows on open ground and flowers in May.

Cytinus hypocistus is a parasite plant found growing close to the base of colourful cistus bushes *(see below)*.

Sage-leaved cistus is widespread in *maquis* habitats. Its colourful flowers attract pollinating insects.

White asphodel is often seen growing on roadside verges in many parts of Greece. Tall spikes of white flowers appear from April to June.

Areas of *maquis* provide ideal habitats for nesting birds such as warblers, serins and hoopoes.

Between the shrubs in open areas of *maquis*, orchids, tulips and other native flowers appear in the spring.

ORCHIDS

One of the botanical highlights of a visit to Greece is the range of wild orchid species that can be found in bloom between late February and May. All have strangely shaped, and sometimes colourful, flowers whose purpose is to attract pollinating insects.

The four-spotted orchid has spots on the flower lip. A plant of open hillsides, it flowers in April.

The naked man orchid has a dense head of pale pinkish flowers and favours open woodland.

The Greek spider orchid looks more like a bumblebee than a spider. It is found in *maquis* in early spring.

THE HISTORY
OF GREECE

The history of Greece is that of a nation, not of a land: the Greek idea of nationality is governed by language, religion, descent and customs, not so much by location. Early Greek history is the story of internal struggles, from the Mycenaean and Minoan cultures of the Bronze Age to the competing city-states that emerged in the 1st millennium BC.

Alexander the Great, by the folk artist Theófilos

After the defeat of the Greek army by Philip II of Macedon at Chaironeia in 338 BC, Greece soon became absorbed into Alexander the Great's new Asian empire. With the defeat of the Macedonians by the Romans in 168 BC, Greece became a province of Rome. As part of the Eastern Empire she was ruled from Constantinople and in the 11th century became a powerful element within the new, Orthodox Christian, Byzantine world.

After 1453, when Constantinople fell to the Ottomans, Greece disappeared altogether as a political entity. Eventually the realization that it was the democracy of Classical Athens which had inspired so many revolutions abroad gave the Greeks themselves the courage to rebel and, in 1821, to fight the Greek War of Independence. In 1832 the Great Powers that dominated Europe established a protectorate over Greece which marked the end of Ottoman rule. Although Greece reestablished itself as a sizeable state, the "Great Idea" – the ambition to recreate Byzantium – ended in a disastrous defeat by Turkey in 1922.

The instability of the ensuing years was followed by the dictatorship of Metaxás and then by the war years of 1940–8, during which half a million people were killed and one in ten was made homeless. The present boundaries of the Greek state have only existed since 1948, when Italy returned the Dodecanese. Now, as an established democracy and member of the European Union, Greece's fortunes seem to have come full circle after 2,000 years of foreign rule.

A map of Greece from the 1595 Atlas of Abraham Ortelius called *Theatrum Orbis Terrarum*

◁ **The beginning of the 1821 Greek Revolution as shown in 1825 by L Dupré**

Prehistoric Greece

Mycenaean gold brooch

During the Bronze Age three separate civilizations flourished in Greece: the Cycladic, during the 3rd millennium; the Minoan, based on Crete but with an influence that spread throughout the Aegean islands; and the Mycenaean, which was based on the mainland but spread to Crete in about 1450 BC when the Minoans went into decline. Both the Minoan and Mycenaean cultures found their peak in the Palace periods of the 2nd millennium when they were dominated by a centralized religion and bureaucracy.

PREHISTORIC GREECE

Areas settled in the Bronze Age

Neolithic Head *(3000 BC)*
This figure was found on Alónnisos in the Sporades. It probably represents a fertility goddess who was worshipped by farmers to ensure a good harvest. These figures indicate a certain stability in early communities.

The town is unwalled, showing that inhabitants did not fear attack.

Cycladic Figurine
Marble statues such as this, produced in the Bronze Age from about 2800 to 2300 BC, have been found in a number of tombs in the Cyclades.

Multistorey houses

Minoan "Bathtub" Sarcophagus
This type of coffin, dating to 1400 BC, is found only in Minoan art. It was probably used for a high-status burial.

TIMELINE

	7000 Neolithic farmers in northern Greece	3200 Beginnings of Bronze Age cultures in Cyclades and Crete	2000 Arrival of first Greek-speakers on mainland Greece
200,000 BC	**5000 BC**	**4000 BC**	**3000 BC**	**2000**

200,000 Evidence of Palaeolithic civilization in northern Greece and Thessaly

"Frying Pan" vessel from Sýros (2500–2000 BC)

2800–2300 Kéros-Sýros culture flourishes in Cyclades

2000 Building of palaces begins in Crete, initiating First Palace period

Mycenaean Death Mask
Large amounts of worked gold were discovered at wealthy Mycenae, the city of Agamemnon. Masks like this were laid over the faces of the dead.

Forested hills

WHERE TO SEE PREHISTORIC GREECE
The Museum of Cycladic Art in Athens (see pp74–5) has Greece's leading collection of Cycladic figurines. The remains at Mycenae are extensive (pp178–80) and the museum at Náfplio (p182) displays finds from this and other Mycenaean sites, as does the National Archaeological Museum, Athens (pp68–71). Excavations at Nestor's Palace (p201) uncovered tablets written in Linear B script. These earliest examples of Greek language can be seen in the museum at nearby Chóra, together with frescoes and pottery from the palace.

The inhabitants are on friendly terms with the visitors.

Cyclopean Walls
Mycenaean citadels, such as this one at Tiryns, were encircled by walls of stone so large that later civilizations believed they had been built by giants. It is unclear whether the walls were used for defence or just to impress.

Oared sailing ships

MINOAN SEA SCENE
The wall paintings on the island of Santoríni were preserved by the volcanic eruption at the end of the 16th century BC. This section shows ships departing from a coastal town. In contrast to the warlike Mycenaeans, Minoan art reflects a more stable community which dominated the Aegean through trade, not conquest.

Mycenaean Octopus Jar
This 14th-century BC vase's decoration follows the shape of the pot. Restrained and symmetrical, it contrasts with relaxed Minoan prototypes.

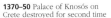

Helen of Troy

1800 BC	1600 BC	1400 BC	1200 BC
1750–1700 Start of Second Palace period and golden age of Minoan culture in Crete	**1525** Volcanic eruption on Santoríni devastates the region	**1250–1200** Probable destruction of Troy, after abduction of Helen (see p54) **1450** Mycenaeans take over Knosós; use of Linear B script	
1730 Destruction of Minoan palaces; end of First Palace period		*Minoan figurine of a snake goddess, 1500 BC*	**1200** Collapse of Mycenaean culture
1600 Beginning of high period of Mycenaean prosperity and dominance			**1370–50** Palace of Knosós on Crete destroyed for second time

The Dark Ages and Archaic Period

After 1200 BC, Greece entered a period of darkness. There was widespread poverty, the population decreased and many skills were lost. A cultural revival in

Silver coin from Athens about 800 BC accompanied the emergence of the city-states across Greece and inspired new styles of warfare, art and politics. Greek colonies were established as far away as the Black Sea, present-day Syria, North Africa and the western Mediterranean. Greece was defined by where Greeks lived.

Koúros *(530 BC)*
Kouroi were early monumental male nude statues (see p70). Idealized representations rather than portraits, they were inspired by Egyptian statues, from which they take their frontal, forward-stepping pose.

Bronze breastplate

MEDITERRANEAN AREA, 479 BC

☐ *Areas of Greek influence*

The double flute player kept the men marching in time.

Bronze greaves protected the legs.

Solon *(640–558 BC)*
Solon was appointed to the highest magisterial position in Athens. His legal, economic and political reforms heralded democracy.

HOPLITE WARRIORS

The "Chigi" vase from Corinth, dating to about 750 BC, is one of the earliest clear depictions of the new style of warfare that evolved at that period. This required rigorously trained and heavily armed infantrymen called hoplites to fight in a massed formation or phalanx. The rise of the city-state may be linked to the spirit of equality felt by citizen hoplites fighting for their own community.

TIMELINE

Vase fragment showing bands of distinctive geometric line patterns

900 Appearance of first Geometric pottery

1100 BC	1000 BC	900 BC
1100 Migrations of different peoples throughout the Greek world	**1000–850** Formation of the Homeric kingdoms	

6th-Century Vase
This bowl (krater) for mixing wine and water at elegant feasts is an early example of the art of vase painting. It depicts mythological and heroic scenes.

Spears were used for thrusting.

Bronze helmets for protection

The phalanxes shoved and pushed, aiming to maintain an unbroken shield wall, a successful new technique.

Gorgon's head decoration

Characteristic round shields

WHERE TO SEE ARCHAIC GREECE

Examples of *koûroi* can be found in the National Archaeological Museum *(see pp68–71)* and in the Acropolis Museum *(p97)*, both in Athens. The National Archaeological Museum also houses the national collection of Greek Geometric, red-figure and black-figure vases. The first victory over the Persians in 490 BC was commemorated by the mound of Athenian dead which still dominates the plain at Marathon *(p145)*. The museum at Sparta *(p189)* contains a bust of Leonidas, the Spartan king, who with his 300 hoplite soldiers was massacred by the Persians at Thermopylae in 480 BC.

Hunter Returning Home *(500 BC)*
Hunting for hares, deer, or wild boar was an aristocratic sport pursued by Greek nobles on foot with dogs, as depicted on this cup.

Darius I *(ruled 521–486 BC)*
This relief from Persepolis shows the Persian king who tried to conquer the Greek mainland, but was defeated at the battle of Marathon in 490.

---

776 Traditional date for the first Olympic Games

675 Lykourgos initiates austere reforms in Sparta

600 First Doric columns built at Temple of Hera, Olympia

Doric capital

490 Athenians defeat Persians at Marathon

800 BC	700 BC	600 BC	500 BC

750–700 Homer records epic tales of the *Iliad* and *Odyssey*

770 Greeks start founding colonies in Italy, Egypt and elsewhere

Spartan votive figurine

546 Persians gain control over Ionian Greeks; Athens flourishes under the tyrant, Peisistratos, and his sons

630 Poetess Sappho writing in Lésvos

480 Athens destroyed by Persians who defeat Spartans at Thermopylae; Greek victory at Salamis

479 Persians annihilated at Plataiaí by Athenians, Spartans and allies

Classical Greece

Trading amphora

The Classical period has always been considered the high point of Greek civilization. Around 150 years of exceptional creativity in thinking, writing, theatre and the arts produced the great tragedians Aeschylus, Sophocles and Euripides as well as the great philosophical thinkers Socrates, Plato and Aristotle. This was also a time of warfare and bloodshed, however. The Peloponnesian War, which pitted the city-state of Athens and her allies against the city-state of Sparta and her allies, dominated the 5th century BC. In the 4th century Sparta, Athens and Thebes struggled for power only to be ultimately defeated by Philip II of Macedon in 338 BC.

CLASSICAL GREECE, 440 BC

▨ Athens and her allies

▨ Sparta and her allies

Fish Shop
This 4th-century BC Greek painted vase comes from Cefalù in Sicily. Large parts of the island were inhabited by Greeks who were bound by a common culture, religion and language.

Theatre used in Pythian Games

Temple of Apollo

Siphnian Treasury

THE SANCTUARY OF DELPHI
The sanctuary *(see pp228–9)*, shown in this 1894 reconstruction, reached the peak of its political influence in the 5th and 4th centuries BC. Of central importance was the Oracle of Apollo, whose utterances influenced the decisions of city-states such as Athens and Sparta. Rich gifts dedicated to the god were placed by the states in treasuries that lined the Sacred Way.

Perikles
This great democratic leader built up the Greek navy and masterminded the extensive building programme in Athens between the 440s and 420s, including the Acropolis temples.

TIMELINE

Detail of the Parthenon frieze

462 Ephialtes's reforms pave the way for radical democracy in Athens

431–404 Peloponnesian War, ending with the fall of Athens and start of 33-year period of Spartan dominance

c.424 Death of Herodotus, historian of the Persian Wars

475 BC	450 BC	425 BC

478 With the formation of the Delian League, Athens takes over leadership of Greek cities

451–429 Perikles rises to prominence in Athens and launches a lavish building programme

447 Construction of the Parthenon begins

Bust of Herodotus, probably of Hellenistic origin

Gold Oak Wreath from Vergína
*By the mid-4th century BC, Philip II of Macedon
dominated the Greek world through diplomacy
and warfare. This wreath comes from his tomb.*

WHERE TO SEE CLASSICAL GREECE

Athens is dominated by the Acropolis and its religious buildings, including the Parthenon, erected as part of Perikles's mid 5th-century BC building programme *(see pp94–9)*. The Marmaria, just outside the sanctuary at Delphi, features the remains of the unique circular *tholos (p230)*. In the Peloponnese, the town of Messene dates from 396 BC *(p201)*; the best-preserved theatre is at Epidaurus *(pp184–5)*. Philip II's tomb can be seen at Vergína in Macedonia *(p242)*.

Votive of the Rhodians

Stoa of the Athenians

Sacred Way

Athenian Treasury

Slave Boy *(400 BC)*
*Slaves were funda-
mental to the Greek
economy and used for
all types of work.
Many slaves were
foreign; this boot
boy came from as
far as Africa.*

Athena Lemnia
*This Roman copy of a
statue by Pheidias
(c.490–c.430 BC), the
sculptor-in-charge at
the Acropolis, depicts
the goddess protector of
Athens in an ideal
rather than realistic
way, typical of the
Classical style in art.*

387 Plato founds Academy in Athens

Sculpture of Plato

337 Foundation of the the League of Corinth legitimizes Philip II's control over the Greek city-states

359 Philip II becomes King of Macedon

400 BC	375 BC	350 BC

399 Trial and execution of Socrates

371 Sparta defeated by Thebes at Battle of Leuktra, heralding a decade of Theban dominance in the area

338 Greeks defeated by Philip II of Macedon at Battle of Chaironeia

336 Philip II is assassinated at Aigai and is succeeded by his son, Alexander

Hellenistic Greece

Alexander the Great

Alexander the Great of Macedon fulfilled his father Philip's plans for the conquest of the Persians. He went on to create a vast empire that extended to India in the east and Egypt in the south. The Hellenistic period was extraordinary for the dispersal of Greek language, religion and culture throughout the territories conquered by Alexander. It lasted from after Alexander's death in 323 BC until the Romans began to dismantle his empire, early in the 2nd century BC. For Greece, Macedonian domination was replaced by that of Rome in AD 168.

Relief of Hero-Worship (*c.200 BC*)
The worship of heroes after death was a feature of Greek religion. Alexander, however, was worshipped as a god in his lifetime.

The Mausoleum of Halicarnassus was one of the Seven Wonders of the Ancient World.

Issus, in modern Turkey, was the site of Alexander's victory over the Persian army in 333 BC.

Pélla was the birthplace of Alexander and capital of Macedon.

BLACK SEA

• Pélla

• Athens

ASIA MINOR

Mausoleum of Halicarnassus

• Issus

MEDITERRANEAN SEA

Ishtar Gate in Babylon

Ammon •

Lighthouse at Alexandria

EGYPT

Alexander died in Babylon in 323 BC.

RED SEA

ARABIA

The Ammon oracle declared Alexander to be divine.

Alexandria, founded by Alexander, replaced Athens as the centre of Greek culture.

Alexander Defeats Darius III
This Pompeiian mosaic shows the Persian leader overwhelmed at Issus in 333 BC. Macedonian troops are shown carrying their highly effective long pikes.

Terracotta Statue
This 2nd-century BC statue of two women gossiping is typical of a Hellenistic interest in private rather than public individuals.

KEY

– – – Alexander's route

◻ Alexander's empire

◻ Dependent regions

TIMELINE

333 Alexander the Great defeats the Persian king, Darius III, and declares himself king of Asia

323 Death of Alexander, and of Diogenes

301 Battle of Ipsus, between Alexander's rival successors, leads to the break-up of his empire into three kingdoms

268–261 Chremonidean War, ending with the capitulation of Athens to Macedon

325 BC	300 BC	275 BC	250 BC

322 Death of Aristotle

331 Alexander founds Alexandria after conquering Egypt

287–275 "Pyrrhic victory" of King Pyrros of Epirus who defeated the Romans in Italy but suffered heavy losses

Diogenes, the Hellenistic philosopher

Fusing Eastern and Western Religion
This plaque from Afghanistan shows the Greek goddess Nike, and the Asian goddess Cybele, in a chariot pulled by lions.

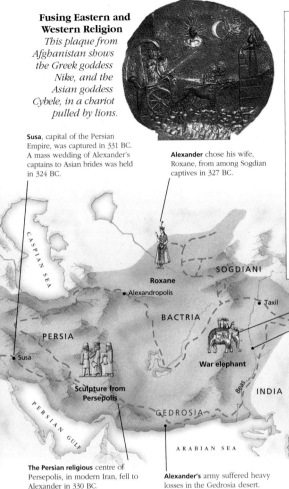

Susa, capital of the Persian Empire, was captured in 331 BC. A mass wedding of Alexander's captains to Asian brides was held in 324 BC.

Alexander chose his wife, Roxane, from among Sogdian captives in 327 BC.

SOGDIANI

Roxane
Alexandropolis

Taxil

Battle elephants were used against the Indian King Poros in 326 BC.

Alexander's army turned back at the River Beas.

CASPIAN SEA

BACTRIA

PERSIA

Susa

War elephant

INDIA

Sculpture from Persepolis

PERSIAN GULF

GEDROSIA

ARABIAN SEA

The Persian religious centre of Persepolis, in modern Iran, fell to Alexander in 330 BC.

Alexander's army suffered heavy losses in the Gedrosia desert.

ALEXANDER THE GREAT'S EMPIRE

In forming his empire Alexander covered huge distances. After defeating the Persians in Asia he moved to Egypt, then returned to Asia to pursue Darius, and then his murderers, into Bactria. In 326 his troops revolted in India and refused to go on. Alexander died in 323 in Babylon.

The Death of Archimedes
Archimedes was the leading Hellenistic scientist and mathematician. This mosaic from Renaissance Italy shows his murder in 212 BC by a Roman.

227 Colossus of Rhodes destroyed by earthquake

Colossus of Rhodes

197 Romans defeat Philip V of Macedon and declare Greece liberated

146 Romans sack Corinth and Greece becomes a province of Rome

225 BC	200 BC	175 BC	150 BC

222 Macedon crushes Sparta

217 Peace of Náfpaktos: a call for the Greeks to settle their differences before "the cloud in the west" (Rome) settles over them

168 Macedonians defeated by Romans at Pydna

Roman coin commemorating Roman victory over the Macedonians in 196 BC

Roman Greece

After the Romans gained final control of Greece-with the sack of Corinth in 146 BC, Greece became the cultural centre of the Roman Empire. The Roman nobility sent their sons to be educated in the schools of philosophy in Athens

Mark Antony

(see p57). The end of the Roman civil wars between leading Roman statesmen was played out on Greek soil, finishing in the Battle of Actium in Thessaly in 31 BC. In AD 323 the Emperor Constantine founded the new eastern capital of Constantinople; the empire was later divided into the Greek-speaking East and the Latin-speaking West.

ROMAN PROVINCES, AD 211

Mithridates

In a bid to extend his territory, this ruler of Pontus, on the Black Sea, led the resistance to Roman rule in 88 BC. He was forced to make peace three years later.

Bema, or raised platform, where St Paul spoke

Roman basilica

Bouleuterion

Springs of Peirene, the source of water

Notitia Dignitatum *(AD 395) As part of the Roman Empire, Greece was split into several provinces. The proconsul of the province of Achaïa used this insignia.*

RECONSTRUCTION OF ROMAN CORINTH

Corinth *(see pp162–6)* was refounded and largely rebuilt by Julius Caesar in 46 BC, becoming the capital of the Roman province of Achaïa. The Romans built the forum, covered theatre and basilicas. St Paul visited the city in AD 50–51, working as a tent maker.

Baths of Eurycles

TIMELINE

A coin of Cleopatra, Queen of Egypt

49–31 BC Rome's civil wars end with the defeat of Mark Antony and Cleopatra at Actium, in Greece

AD 49–54 St Paul preaches Christianity in Greece

AD 124–131 Emperor Hadrian oversees huge building programme in Athens

100 BC

AD 1

AD 100

86 BC Roman commander, Sulla, captures Athens

46 BC Corinth refounded as Roman colony

St Paul preaching

AD 66–7 Emperor Nero tours Greece

Mosaic *(AD 180)*
This highly sophisticated Roman mosaic of Dionysos riding on a leopard comes from the House of Masks, on Delos.

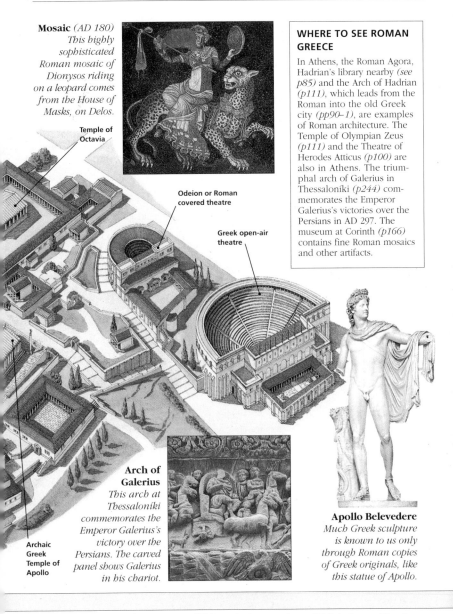

Temple of Octavia

Odeion or Roman covered theatre

Greek open-air theatre

WHERE TO SEE ROMAN GREECE

In Athens, the Roman Agora, Hadrian's library nearby *(see p85)* and the Arch of Hadrian *(p111)*, which leads from the Roman into the old Greek city *(pp90–1)*, are examples of Roman architecture. The Temple of Olympian Zeus *(p111)* and the Theatre of Herodes Atticus *(p100)* are also in Athens. The triumphal arch of Galerius in Thessaloníki *(p244)* commemorates the Emperor Galerius's victories over the Persians in AD 297. The museum at Corinth *(p166)* contains fine Roman mosaics and other artifacts.

Apollo Belevedere
Much Greek sculpture is known to us only through Roman copies of Greek originals, like this statue of Apollo.

Arch of Galerius
This arch at Thessaloníki commemorates the Emperor Galerius's victory over the Persians. The carved panel shows Galerius in his chariot.

Archaic Greek Temple of Apollo

170 Pausanias completes guide to Greece for Roman travellers

267 Goths pillage Athens

323 Constantine becomes sole emperor of Roman Empire and establishes his capital in Constantinople

395 Goths devastate Athens and Peloponnese

390 Emperor Theodosius I makes Christianity state religion

AD 200

AD 300

Coin of the Roman Emperor Galerius

293 Under Emperor Galerius, Thessaloníki becomes second city to Constantinople

393 Olympic games banned

395 Death of Theodosius I; formal division of Roman Empire into Latin West and Byzantine East

Byzantine and Crusader Greece

Byzantine court dress arm band

Under the Byzantine empire, which at the end of the 4th century succeeded the old Eastern Roman Empire, Greece became Orthodox in religion and was split into administrative *themes*. When the capital, Constantinople, fell to the Crusaders in 1204 Greece was again divided, mostly between the Venetians and the Franks. Constantinople and Mystrás were recovered by the Byzantine Greeks in 1261, but the Turks' capture of Constantinople in 1453 was a significant part of the demise of the Byzantine Empire. It left a legacy of hundreds of churches and a wealth of religious art.

BYZANTINE GREECE IN THE 10TH CENTURY

Watch-tower of Tsimiskis

Chapel

Refectory

Two-Headed Eagle
The double-headed eagle was an omnipresent symbol of the power of the Byzantine empire in this era.

GREAT LAVRA

This monastery is the earliest (AD 963) and largest of the religious complexes on Mount Athos *(see pp252–4)*. Many parts of it have been rebuilt, but its appearance remains essentially Byzantine. The monasteries became important centres of learning and religious art.

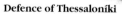

Defence of Thessaloníki
The fall of Thessaloníki to the Saracens in AD 904 was a blow to the Byzantine Empire. Many towns in Greece were heavily fortified against attack from this time.

TIMELINE

578–86 Avars and Slavs invade Greece

Gold solidus of the Byzantine Empress Irene, who ruled AD 797–802

400	600	800
529 Aristotle's and Plato's schools of philosophy close as Christian culture supplants Classical thought	**680** Bulgars cross Danube and establish empire in northern Greece	**726** Iconoclasm introduced by Pope Leo III (abandoned in 843) **841** Parthenon becomes a cathedral

Constantine the Great
The first eastern emperor to recognize Christianity, Constantine founded the city of Constantinople in AD 324. Here he is shown with his mother, Helen.

WHERE TO SEE BYZANTINE AND CRUSADER GREECE

In Athens, both the Benáki (pp78–9) and the Byzantine (p76) museums contain sculpture, icons, metalwork and textiles. The medieval city of Mystrás (pp192–3) has a castle, palaces, houses and monasteries. The churches of Thessaloníki (p248), and the monasteries of Dafní (pp152–3) and Osios Loúkas (pp222–3) contain fine Byzantine mosaics and frescoes, as do the monasteries of Mount Athos (pp252–4). Chlemoútsi (p169), built in 1223, is one of Greece's oldest Frankish castles. There are important fortresses at Acrocorinth (p166) and Monemvasía (pp186–8).

Cypress tree of Agios Athanásios

Christ Pantokrátor
This 14th-century fresco of Christ as ruler of the world is in the Byzantine city and monastic centre of Mystrás.

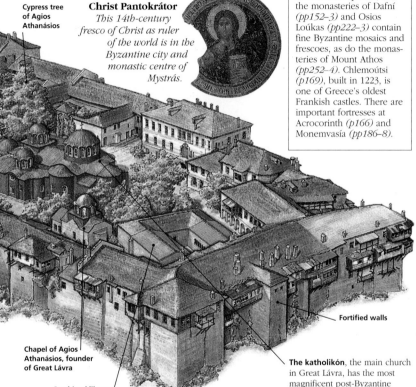

Chapel of Agios Athanásios, founder of Great Lávra

Combined library and treasury

Fortified walls

The katholikón, the main church in Great Lávra, has the most magnificent post-Byzantine murals on Mount Athos.

1054 Patriarch of Constantinople and Pope Leo IX excommunicate each other

Frankish Chlemoútsi Castle

1081–1149 Normans invade Greek islands and mainland

1354 Ottoman Turks enter Europe, via southern Italy and Greece

1390–1450 Turks gain power over much of mainland Greece

1000	1200	1400

Basil the Bulgar Slayer, Byzantine emperor (lived 956–1025)

1204 Crusaders sack Constantinople. Break-up of Byzantine Empire as result of occupation by Franks and Venetians

1210 Venetians win control over Crete

1261 Start of intellectual and artistic flowering of Mystrás; Constantinople re-occupied by Byzantines

1389 Venetians in control of much of Greece and the islands

Venetian and Ottoman Greece

Venetian lion of St Mark

Following the Ottomans' momentous capture of Constantinople in 1453, and their conquest of almost all the remaining Greek territory by 1460, the Greek state effectively ceased to exist for the next 350 years. Although the city became the capital of the vast Ottoman Empire, it remained the principal centre of Greek population and the focus of Greek dreams of resurgence. The small Greek population of what today is modern Greece languished in an impoverished and underpopulated backwater, but even there rebellious bands of brigands and private militias were formed. The Ionian Islands, Crete and a few coastal enclaves were seized for long periods by the Venetians – an experience more intrusive than the inefficient tolerance of the Ottomans, but one which left a rich cultural and architectural legacy.

GREECE IN 1493

Areas occupied by Venetians

Areas occupied by Ottomans

Cretan Painting
This 15th-century icon is typical of the style developed by Greek artists in the School of Crete, active until the Ottomans took Crete in 1669.

Battle of Lepanto *(1571)*
The Christian fleet, under Don John of Austria, decisively defeated the Ottomans off Náfpaktos, halting their advance westwards (see p225).

ARRIVAL OF TURKISH PRINCE CEM ON RHODES

Prince Cem, Ottoman rebel and son of Mehmet II, fled to Rhodes in 1481 and was welcomed by the Christian Knights of St John. In 1522, however, Rhodes fell to the Ottomans after a siege.

TIMELINE

1453 Mehmet II captures Constantinopole which is renamed Istanbul and made capital of the Ottoman Empire

1503 Ottoman Turks win control of the Peloponnese apart from Monemvasía

1571 Venetian and Spanish fleet defeats Ottoman Turks at the Battle of Lepanto

| 1500 | 1550 | 1600 |

1460 Turks capture Mystrás

Cretan chain mail armour from the 16th century

1456 Ottoman Turks occupy Athens

1522 The Knights of St John forced to cede Rhodes to the Ottomans

Shipping

Greek merchants traded throughout the Ottoman Empire. By 1800 there were merchant colonies in Constantinople and as far afield as London and Odessa. This 19th-century embroidery shows the Turkish influence on Greek decorative arts.

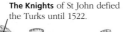

The Knights of St John defied the Turks until 1522.

The massive fortifications eventually succumbed to Turkish artillery.

The Knights supported Turkish rebel, Prince Cem.

WHERE TO SEE VENETIAN AND OTTOMAN ARCHITECTURE

Náfplio contains many examples of the Venetian presence, especially the Naval Warehouse (now a museum) and the Palamídi fortress *(see p183)*. Following a pattern familiar throughout the Balkan states, enormous efforts were made after Independence to remove or disguise all Ottoman buildings. However, in Athens there are small but well-preserved Ottoman quarters in the Pláka district, and the Tzistarákis Mosque (now the Ceramics Museum, *p86*) is also Ottoman. The White Tower in Thessaloníki *(p244)* was built by the Turks in the 15th century. In Kavála *(p255)*, there is an aqueduct built in the reign of Suleiman the Magnificent, and in Ioánnina *(p210)* the Aslan Pasha Mosque.

Dinner at a Greek House in 1801

Nearly four centuries of Ottoman rule profoundly affected Greek culture, ethnic composition and patterns of everyday life. Greek cuisine incorporates Turkish dishes still found throughout the old Ottoman Empire.

1687 Parthenon seriously damaged during Venetian artillery attack on Turkish magazine

1715 Turks reconquer the Peloponnese

Ali Pasha (1741–1822), a governor of the Ottoman Empire

1814 Britain gains possession of Ionian Islands

1650	1700	1750	1800

1684 Venetians reconquer the Peloponnese

Parthenon blown up

1778 Ali Pasha becomes Vizier of Ioánnina and establishes powerful state in Albania and northern Greece

1801 Frieze on Parthenon removed by Lord Elgin

1814 Foundation of *Filikí Etaireía*, Greek liberation movement

The Making of Modern Greece

Flag with the symbols of the *Filiki Etaireia*

The Greek War of Independence marked the overthrow of the Ottomans and the start of the "Great Idea", an ambitious project to bring all Greek people under one flag (*énosis*). The plans for expansion were initially successful, and during the 19th century the Greeks succeeded in doubling their national territory and reasserting Greek sovereignty over many of the islands. However, an attempt to take Asia Minor by force after World War I ended in disaster. In 1922 millions of Greeks were expelled from Smyrna in Turkish Anatolia, ending thousands of years of Greek presence in Asia Minor.

THE EMERGING GREEK STATE

- Greece in 1832
- Areas gained 1832–1923

Klephts (mountain brigands) were the basis of the Independence movement.

Massacre at Chíos
This detail of Delacroix's shocking painting Scènes de Massacres de Scio *shows the events of 1822, when Turks took savage revenge for an earlier killing of Muslims.*

Weapons were family heirlooms or donated by philhellenes.

Declaration of the Constitution in Athens
Greece's Neo-Classical parliament building in Athens was the site of the Declaration of the Constitution in 1843. It was built as the Royal Palace for Greece's first monarch, King Otto, during the 1830s.

TIMELINE

1824 The poet Lord Byron dies of a fever at Mesolóngi

1831 President Kapodístrias assassinated

1832 Great Powers establish protectorate over Greece and appoint Otto, Bavarian prince, as king

1834 Athens replaces Náfplio as capital

German archaeologist Heinrich Schliemann

1830	1840	1850	1860	1870

1827 Battle of Navaríno

1828 Ioánnis Kapodístrias becomes first President of Greece

King Otto (ruled 1832–62)

1862 Revolution drives King Otto from Greece

1874 Heinrich Schliemann begins excavation of Mycenae

1821 Greek flag of independence raised on 25 March; Greeks massacre Turks at Tripolitsá in Morea

1864 New constitution makes Greece a "crowned democracy"; Greek Orthodoxy made the state religion

Life in Athens
By 1836 urban Greeks still wore a mixture of Greek traditional and Western dress. The Ottoman legacy had not totally disappeared and is visible in the fez worn by men.

FLAG RAISING OF 1821 REVOLUTION
In 1821, the Greek secret society *Filikí Etaireía* was behind a revolt by Greek officers which led to anti-Turk uprisings throughout the Peloponnese. Tradition credits Archbishop Germanós of Pátra with raising the rebel flag near Kalávryta *(see p168)* on 25 March. The struggle for independence had begun.

WHERE TO SEE 19TH-CENTURY GREECE
Independence was proclaimed at the Moní Agías Lávras, near Kalávryta *(see p168)*. Lord Byron died at Mesolóngi *(p225)*. Ioánnis Kapodístrias was assassinated at the church of Agios Spyrídon in Náfplio *(p182)*. Pýlos is the site of the battle of Navaríno *(p200)*.

Corinth Canal
This spectacular link between the Aegean and Ionian seas opened in 1893 (see p167).

Elefthérios Venizélos
This great Cretan politician and advocate of liberal democracy doubled Greek territory during the Balkan Wars (1912–13) and joined the Allies in World War I.

1893 Opening of Corinth Canal

1896 First Olympics of modern era, held in Athens

1908 Crete united with Greece

1917 King Constantine resigns; Greece joins World War I

1919 Greece launches offensive in Asia Minor

1922 Turkish burning of Smyrna signals end of the "Great Idea"

1880	1890	1900	1910	1920

Spyrídon Loúis, Marathon winner at the first modern Olympics

1899 Arthur Evans begins excavations at Knosós

1912–13 Greece extends its borders during the Balkan Wars

1920 Treaty of Sèvres gives Greece huge gains in territory

1923 Population exchange agreed between Greece and Turkey at Treaty of Lausanne. Greece loses previous gains

Twentieth-Century Greece

The years after the 1922 defeat by Turkey were terrible ones for Greek people. The influx of refugees contributed to the political instability of the interwar years. The dictatorship of Metaxás was followed by invasion in 1940, then Italian, German and Bulgarian occupation and, finally, Civil War between 1946 and 1949, with its legacy of division. After experiencing the Cyprus problem of the 1950s and the military dictatorship of 1967 to 1974, Greece is now an established democracy and a member of the European Economic and Monetary Union.

1947 Internationally acclaimed Greek artist, Giánnis Tsaroúchis, holds his first exhibition of set designs, in the Romvos Gallery, Athens

1938 Death of sculptor Giannoúlis Chalepás, best known for his *Sleeping Girl* funerary statue

1946 Government institutes "White Terror" against Communists

1957 Mosaics found by chance at Philip II's 300 BC palace at Pélla

1945 Níkos Kazantzákis publishes *Zorba the Greek*, later made into a film

1933 Death of Greek poet, Constantine (C P) Cavafy

1967 Right-wing colonels form Junta, forcing King Constantine into exile

1925	1935	1945	1955	1965

1925	1935	1945	1955	1965

1951 Greece enters NATO

1955 Greek Cypriots start campaign of violence in Cyprus against British rule

1939 Greece declares neutrality at start of World War II

1963 Geórgios Papandréou's centre-left government voted into power

1932 Aristotle Onassis purchases six freight ships, the start of his shipping empire

1948 Dodecanese becomes part of Greece

1960 Cyprus declared independent

1925 Mános Chatzidákis, who wrote music for the film *Never on Sunday*, is born

1958 USSR threatens Greece with economic sanctions if NATO missiles installed

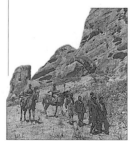

1946–9 Civil War between Greek government and the Communists who take to the mountains

ΟΙ ΗΡΩΙΔΕΣ ΤΟΥ 1940

1940 Italy invades Greece. Greek soldiers defend northern Greece. Greece enters World War II

1944 Churchill visits Athens to show his support for Greek government against Communist Resistance

1981 Melína Merkoúri appointed Minister of Culture. Start of campaign to restore Elgin Marbles to Greece

1993 Andréas Papandréou wins Greek general election for the third time

1973 University students in Athens rebel against dictatorship and are crushed by military forces. Start of decline in power of dictatorship

1994 Because of the choking smog (néfos) central Athens introduces traffic restrictions

1998 Karamanlís leaves office and Stefanopoulos succeeds him

2003 Greek presidency of EU (Jan-Jun)

2005 The Greek Parliament ratifies the EU consitution

1988 Eight million visitors to Greece; tourism continues to expand

1974 Cyprus is partitioned after Turkish invasion

1975	1985	1995	2005

1975	1985	1995	2005

1975 Death of Aristotle Onassis

1990 New Democracy voted into power; Konstantínos Karamanlís becomes President

2002 Euro becomes sole legal currency

2004 Athens hosts the Olympic Games

1974 Fall of Junta; Konstantínos Karamanlís elected Prime Minister

1981 Andréas Papandréou's left-wing PASOK party forms first Greek Socialist government

1997 Athens is awarded the 2004 Olympics

1973 Greek bishops give their blessing to the short-lived presidency of Colonel Papadópoulos

1994 European leaders meet in Corfu under Greek presidency of the EU

1996 Andréas Papandréou dies; Kóstas Simítis succeeds him

ATHENS AND MAINLAND GREECE THROUGH THE YEAR

Predominantly rural, Greece is deeply attached to its locally produced food and wine, and chapels dotting the countryside serve as the focus for culinary, as well as religious, celebrations. Festivals of the Orthodox Church are deeply identified with Greekness, no more so than on 25 March, a date which

May Day wild flower wreath

commemorates both the Feast of the Annunciation and the start of the Independence uprising in 1821. Summer festivals are celebrated widely in rural villages, and expatriate Greeks return from across the globe. Organized arts events are a more recent phenomenon, paralleling the rise of tourism.

SPRING

Spring is a glorious time in Greece. The lowland landscape, parched for much of the year, luxuriates in a carpet of green, and wild flowers abound. But the

25 March, Independence Day

weather does not stabilize until late spring, with rainy or blustery days common in March and April. Artichokes ripen in March, and May sees the first strawberries. The fishing season lasts to the end of May, overlapping with the start of the tourist season. Spring festivities focus on Easter.

MARCH

Apókries, Carnival Sunday *(first Sun before Lent)*. Carnivals take place for three weeks leading up to this climax of pre-Lenten festivities. There are parades and costume balls in many large

cities, and the port of Pátra *(see p169)* hosts one of the most exuberant celebrations. **Katharí Deftéra**, Clean Monday *(immediately after "Cheese Sunday" – seven Sundays before Easter)*. Kites are flown in the countryside.
Independence Day and **Evangelismós** *(25 Mar)*. A national holiday, with parades and dances nation-wide celebrating the 1821 revolt against the Ottoman Empire. The religious festival, one of the most important for the Orthodox Church, marks the Angel Gabriel's announcement to the Virgin Mary that she was to become the Holy Mother.

CELEBRATING EASTER IN GREECE

Greek Orthodox Easter can fall up to three weeks either side of Western Easter. It is the most important religious festival in Greece and Holy Week is a time for Greek families to reunite. It is also a good time to visit Greece, to see the processions and church services and to sample the Easter food. The ceremony and symbolism is a direct link with Greece's Byzantine past, as well as with earlier and more primitive beliefs. The festivities reach a climax at midnight on Easter Saturday. As priests intone "Christ is risen", fireworks are lit, the explosions ushering in a Sunday devoted to feasting, music and dance. Smaller, more isolated towns, such as Andrítsaina and Koróni in the Peloponnese, and Polýgyros (the capital of Chalkidikí), are particularly worth visiting during Holy Week for the Friday and Saturday night services.

Priests in their richly embroidered Easter robes

Christ's bier, *decorated with flowers and containing His effigy, is carried in solemn procession through the streets at dusk on Good Friday.*

Candle lighting *takes place at the end of the Easter Saturday mass. In pitch darkness, a single flame is used to light the candles held by worshippers.*

Banners raised during a workers' May Day rally in Athens

APRIL

Megáli Evdomáda, Holy Week *(Apr or May)*, including *Kyriakí ton Vaíon* (Palm Sunday), *Megáli Pémpti* (Maundy Thursday), *Megáli Paraskeví* (Good Friday), *Megálo Savváto* (Easter Saturday), and the most important date in the Orthodox calendar, *Páscha* (Easter Sunday).

Agios Geórgios, St George *(23 Apr)*. One of the most important feast days in the Orthodox calendar, commemorating the patron saint of shepherds, and traditionally marking the start of the grazing season. Celebrations are nationwide, and are particularly festive at Aráchova, near Delphi *(see p221)*.

MAY

Protomagiá, May Day, *(1 May)*. Also known as Labour Day, this is given over to a national holiday. Traditionally, families go to the countryside and pick wild flowers, which are made

Firewalkers in a Macedonian village, 21 May

into wreaths with garlic. These are then hung on doors, balconies, fishing boats and even car bonnets to ward off evil. In major towns and cities across the country, there are also parades and workers' rallies to mark Labour Day, usually led by the Communist Party.

Agios Konstantínos kai Agía Eléni *(21 May)*. A celebration throughout Greece for Constantine and his mother, Helen, the first Orthodox Byzantine rulers *(see p37)*. Firewalking ceremonies may be seen in some Macedonian villages.

Análipsi, Ascension *(40 days after Easter; usually late May)*. This is another important religious feast day.

The procession of candles *in the very early hours of Easter Day, here at Lykavittós Hill in Athens, celebrates Christ's resurrection.*

Easter biscuits *celebrate the end of Lent. Another Easter dish,* magerítsa *soup, is made of lamb's innards and is eaten in the early hours of Easter Sunday.*

Egg loaves, *made of sweet plaited dough, contain eggs with shells dyed red to symbolize the blood of Christ. Red eggs are also given separately as presents.*

Lamb roasting *is traditionally done in the open air on giant spits over charcoal, for lunch on Easter Sunday. The first retsina wine from the previous year's harvest is opened. After lunch young and old join hands to dance, Greek-style.*

SUMMER

Warm days in early June signal the first sea-baths for Greeks (traditionally after Análipsi, Ascension Day). The peak tourist season begins, and continues until late August; after mid-July it can be difficult to find hotel vacancies in the more popular resorts. June sees the arrival of cherries, plums and apricots, and honey can start to be collected from hives.

Beehives for summer honey production, near Mount Parnassus

The last green leaf vegetables are soon totally replaced by tomatoes, melons and cucumbers. By July much of the Aegean is buffeted by the notorious *meltémi*, a high-pressure northerly wind, which – though more severe on the islands – can be felt along the mainland coast.

Various cultural festivals – programmed with an eye on the tourist audience, but no less impressive for that – are hosted in major cities and resorts. Outdoor cinemas are also well attended *(see p119)*. Urban Greeks retreat to mountain villages, often the venues for musical and religious fairs.

Consecrated bread, baked for festivals

JUNE

Pentikostí, Pentecost or Whit Sunday *(seven weeks after Orthodox Easter)*. This impor-

tant Orthodox feast day is celebrated throughout Greece. **Agíou Pnévmatos**, Feast of the Holy Spirit or Whit Monday *(the following day)*. A national holiday.
Athens Festival *(mid-Jun to mid-Sep)*. A cultural festival encompassing a mix of modern and ancient theatre, ballet, opera, classical music and jazz. It takes place at various venues, including the Herodes Atticus Theatre *(see p119)* and the Lykavittós Theatre *(see p72)*. The Herodes Atticus Theatre, on the slopes of the Acropolis, hosts performances of ancient tragedies, concerts by international orchestras and ballet. The Lykavittós Theatre, spectacularly situated on Lykavittós Hill, with extensive views across Athens, hosts performances of modern music – jazz and folk – as

well as drama and dance.
Epidaurus Festival *(Jun-Aug)*. Affiliated to the Athens Festival, though sited 150 km (90 miles) from the capital at the Epidaurus Theatre *(see p184)* in the Peloponnese, this festival includes open-air performances of Classical drama.
Agios Ioánnis, St John's Day *(24 Jun)*. A day celebrated throughout Greece commemorating the birth of St John the Baptist. However, it is on the evening of the 23rd that bonfires are lit in most areas, and May wreaths consigned to the flames. Older children jump over the fires. This is an equivalent celebration to midsummer's eve.
Agioi Apóstoloi Pétros kai Pávlos, Saints Peter and Paul *(29 Jun)*. A widely celebrated name day for Pétros and Pávlos.

JULY

Agía Marína *(17 Jul)*. This day is widely celebrated in rural areas, with feasts to honour the saint, an important protector of crops.
Ioánnina's Cultural Summer *(through Jul and Aug)*. A wide range of music, arts and cultural events.
Profítis Ilías, the Prophet Elijah *(18–20 Jul)*. Widely celebrated at hill-top shrines, the best known being Mount Taÿgetos, near the town of Spárti. Name day for Ilías.
Agía Paraskeví *(26 Jul)*. There are many big village festivals on this day, but it is particularly celebrated in the Epirus region.

Concert at Herodes Atticus Theatre during the Athens Festival

Agios Panteleímon
(27 Jul). As a
doctor-saint, he is
celebrated as the
patron of many hos-
pitals, and as a
popular rural saint he
is celebrated in the
countryside. Name
day for Pantelís and
Panteleímon.

AUGUST

Metamórfosi,
Transfiguration of
Christ *(6 Aug)*.
For the Orthodox
church this is an important
feast day. Name day for
Sotíris and Sotiría.
Koímisis tis Theotókou,

Girl in national dress
for 15 August
festivities

Pános and Panagiótis.
Pátra Summer Festival
(Aug–Sep). This festival
offers events such as
Classical drama and art
exhibitions, as well as
music concerts in the
Roman theatre.
Vlachopanagía *(19 Aug)*.
This is a day of
celebration in many
Vlach villages located in
the mountainous
Epirus region.
**Apotomí
Kefalís Ioánnou
Prodrómou,**
beheading of John
the Baptist *(29 Aug)*. The
occasion for festivals at
the many country chapels
that bear his name.

AUTUMN

By september most village
festivals have finished. The
sea is at its warmest for
swimming and, though the
crowds have gone, most
facilities are still available.
There is a second, minor
blooming of wild flowers,
and the fine, still days of
October are known as
the "little summer of St
Dimitrios", randomly
punctuated by stormy
weather. Grapes, and
the fat peaches
germádes, are virtually
the only fruit to ripen
since the figs of August,
and strings of onions,
garlic and tomatoes are
hung up to dry for the
winter. The hills echo

with the sound of the
September quail shoot and
dragnet fishing resumes.

SEPTEMBER

Génnisis tis Theotókou, birth
of the Virgin Mary *(8 Sep)*.
An important religious feast
day in the calendar of the
Orthodox church.
Ypsosis tou Timíou Stavroú,
Exaltation of the True Cross
(14 Sep). This is an important
Orthodox feast day, and,
although it is almost autumn,
it is regarded as the last of
Greece's major outdoor
summer festivals.

OCTOBER

Agios Dimítrios *(26 Oct)*.
This marks the end of the
grazing season, when sheep
are brought down from the
hills. Celebrations for
Dimítrios are particularly lively in Thessaloníki, where he
is the patron saint. Name day
for Dimítris and Dímitra.
Ochi Day *(28 Oct)*. A
national holiday, with
patriotic parades in
cities and plenty
of dancing. It
commemorates
the Greek re-
ply to the 1940
ultimatum from
Mussolini calling
for Greek sur-
render: an em-
phatic no *(óchi)*.

Ceromonial dress
on Ochi Day

NOVEMBER

**Ton Taxiarchón Archangélou
Michaïl kai Gavriíl** *(8 Nov)*.
Ceremonies at the many
rural monasteries and
churches named after Arch-
angels Gabriel and Michael.
It is also name day for
Michális and Gavriíl.
Eisódia tis Theotókou,
Presentation of the Virgin
in the Temple *(21 Nov)*. An
important feast day in the
Orthodox calendar, celebrated throughout Greece.
Agios Andréas, St Andrew
(30 Nov), Pátra. A long
liturgy is recited in Pátra's
patron saint in the opulent
cathedral named after him.

Strings of tomatoes hanging out
to dry in the autumn sunshine

Assumption of the
Virgin Mary *(15 Aug)*.
A national holiday, and an
important and widely
celebrated feast day. This is
traditionally a day when
Greeks return to celebrate in
their home villages. It is also
a name day for Mary, María,

Parade in Thessaloníki for Agios Dimítrios, 26 October

View over a snow-covered Herodes Atticus Theatre, Athens

WINTER

Many mountain villages assume a ghostly aspect in winter, with their seasonal inhabitants returned to the cities. Deep snow accumulates at higher altitudes and skiing can begin; elsewhere, rain falls several days of the week. Fishing is in full swing, and at the markets kiwi fruits and exotic greens abound. Cheese shops display a full range of goat and sheep products, and olives are pressed for oil. The major festivals cluster to either side of the solstice. New Year and Epiphany are the most fervently celebrated festivals during winter.

Branch of olives

DECEMBER

Agios Nikólaos, St Nicholas *(6 Dec)*. The patron saint of seafarers, travellers, children and orphans is celebrated at

Women playing cards on Gynaikokratía day, Thrace

seaside churches. Name day for Nikólaos and Nikolétta. **Christoúgenna**, Christmas *(25 Dec)* A national holiday and, though less significant than Easter, it still constitutes an important religious feast day.
Sýnaxis tis Theotókou, meeting of the Virgin's entourage *(26 Dec)*. A religious celebration and national holiday.

JANUARY

Agios Vasíleios, also known as *Protochroniá*, or New Year *(1 Jan)*. A national holiday. Gifts are exchanged on this day and the traditional new year greeting is *Kalí Chroniá* **Theofánia**, or Epiphany *(6 Jan)*. A national holiday and an important feast day. Blessing of the waters ceremonies take place by rivers and coastal locations throughout Greece. Youths dive to recover a cross that is thrown into the water by a priest.

Gynaikokratía *(8 Jan)*, Thrace. Matriarchy is celebrated by women and men swapping roles for the day in some villages of Thrace.

FEBRUARY

Ypapantí, Candlemas *(2 Feb)*. An Orthodox feast day all over Greece, at a quiet time, prior to pre-Lenten carnivals.

Diving for a cross at a blessing of the waters ceremony, 6 January

NAME DAYS

Most Greeks do not celebrate birthdays past the age of about 12. Instead they celebrate their name day, or *giortí*, the day of the saint after whom they were named when baptized. Children are usually named after their grandparents, though in recent years it has become fashionable to give children names deriving from Greece's history and mythology. When someone celebrates their name day you may be told, *Giortázo símera* (I'm celebrating today), to which the traditional reply is *Chrónia pollá* (many years). Friends tend to drop in, bearing small gifts, and are given cakes and sweet liqueurs in return.

The Climate of Mainland Greece

Summer visitors

The mainland climate varies most between the coastal lowlands and the mountainous inland regions. The mountains of western Greece and the Peloponnese get heavy snow in winter, rain during autumn and spring, and hot days in summer. The Ionian coast has milder temperatures, but is the wettest part of Greece. In Macedonia and Thrace rainfall is spread more evenly across the year, with the North Aegean exerting a moderating influence on coastal temperatures. Around Athens, temperatures are hot in summer and rarely drop below freezing in winter, when rainfall is at its greatest.

NORTHERN GREECE

°C (F)	Apr	Jul	Oct	Jan
max	26 (79)	38 (100)	28 (82)	16 (61)
min	4 (39)	17 (63)	7 (45)	-4 (25)
☀	8 hrs	12 hrs	6 hrs	4 hrs
☂	41 mm	22 mm	57 mm	44 mm
month	Apr	Jul	Oct	Jan

CENTRAL AND WESTERN GREECE

°C (F)	Apr	Jul	Oct	Jan
max	27 (81)	40 (104)	33 (91)	16 (61)
min	2 (36)	15 (59)	5 (41)	-6 (21)
☀	8 hrs	11 hrs	5 hrs	3 hrs
☂	80 mm	19 mm	80 mm	84 mm
month	Apr	Jul	Oct	Jan

ATHENS AND AROUND ATHENS

°C (F)					
Average monthly maximum temperature	26 (79)	39 (102)	30 (86)	18 (64)
Average monthly minimum temperature	6 (45)	19 (66)	11 (52)	1 (34)
Average daily hours of sunshine	8 hrs	12 hrs	7 hrs	4 hrs
Average monthly rainfall	23 mm	6 mm	51 mm	62 mm
month	Apr	Jul	Oct	Jan

THE PELOPONNESE

°C (F)	Apr	Jul	Oct	Jan
max	25 (77)	36 (97)	28 (82)	15 (59)
min	1 (34)	11 (52)	4 (39)	-4 (25)
☀	8 hrs	12 hrs	7 hrs	4 hrs
☂	62 mm	20 mm	82 mm	127 mm
month	Apr	Jul	Oct	Jan

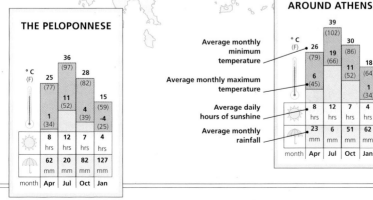

NORTHERN GREECE

CENTRAL AND WESTERN GREECE

ATHENS AND AROUND ATHENS

THE PELOPONNESE

ATHENS

ANCIENT GREECE

Gods, Goddesses and Heroes

The greek myths that tell the stories of the gods, goddesses and heroes date back to the Bronze Age when they were told aloud by poets. They were first written down in the early 6th century BC and have lived on in Western literature. Myths were closely bound up with Greek religion and gave meaning to the unpredictable workings of the natural world. They tell the story of the creation and the "golden age" of gods and mortals, as well as the age of semi-mythical heroes, such as Theseus and Herakles, whose exploits were an inspiration to ordinary men. The gods and goddesses were affected by human desires and failings and were part of a divine family presided over by Zeus. He had many offspring, both legitimate and illegitimate, each with a mythical role.

Hades and Persephone *were king and queen of the Underworld (land of the dead). Persephone was abducted from her mother Demeter, goddess of the harvest, by Hades. She was then only permitted to return to her mother for three months each year.*

Poseidon, *one of Zeus's brothers, was given control of the seas. The trident is his symbol of power, and he married the sea-goddess Amphitrite, to whom he was not entirely faithful. This statue is from the National Archaeological Museum in Athens (see pp68–71).*

Zeus was the father of the gods and ruled over them and all mortals from Mount Olympos.

Eris was the goddess of strife.

Clymene, a nymph and daughter of Helios, was mother of Prometheus, creator of mankind.

Hera, sister and wife of Zeus, was famous for her jealousy.

Athena was born from Zeus's head in full armour.

Paris was asked to award the golden apple to the most beautiful goddess.

Paris's dog helped him herd cattle on Mount Ida where the prince grew up.

Dionysos, *god of revelry and wine, was born from Zeus's thigh. In this 6th-century BC cup painted by Exekias he reclines in a ship whose mast has become a vine.*

A DIVINE DISPUTE

This vase painting shows the gods on Mount Ida, near Troy. Hera, Athena and Aphrodite, quarrelling over who was the most beautiful, were brought by Hermes to hear the judgment of a young herdsman, the Trojan prince, Paris. In choosing Aphrodite, he was rewarded with the love of Helen, the most beautiful woman in the world. Paris abducted her from her husband Menelaos, King of Sparta, and thus the Trojan War began (see pp54–5).

Artemis, *the virgin goddess of the hunt, was the daughter of Zeus and sister of Apollo. She can be identified by her bow and arrows, hounds and group of nymphs with whom she lived in the forests. Although sworn to chastity, she was, in contrast, the goddess of childbirth.*

Happiness, here personified by two goddesses, waits with gold laurel leaves to garland the winner. Wreaths were the prizes in Greek athletic and musical contests.

Helios, the sun god, drove his four-horse chariot (the sun) daily across the sky.

Hermes was the gods' messenger.

Aphrodite, the goddess of love, was born from the sea. Here she has her son Eros (Cupid) with her.

Apollo, *son of Zeus and brother of Artemis, was god of healing, plague and also music. Here he is depicted holding a lyre. He was also famous for his dazzling beauty.*

THE LABOURS OF HERAKLES

Herakles (Hercules to the Romans) was the greatest of the Greek heroes, and the son of Zeus and Alkmene, a mortal woman. With superhuman strength he achieved success, and immortality, against seemingly impossible odds in the "Twelve Labours" set by Eurystheus, King of Mycenae. For his first task he killed the Nemean lion, and wore its hide ever after.

Killing the Lernaean hydra *was the second labour of Herakles. The many heads of this venomous monster, raised by Hera, grew back as soon as they were chopped off. As in all his tasks, Herakles was helped by Athena.*

The huge boar *that ravaged Mount Erymanthus was captured next. Herakles brought it back alive to King Eurystheus who was so terrified that he hid in a storage jar.*

Destroying the Stymfalian birds *was the sixth labour. Herakles rid Lake Stymfalia of these man-eating birds, which had brass beaks, by stoning them with a sling, having first frightened them off with a pair of bronze castanets.*

The Trojan War

Ajax carrying the body of the dead Achilles

The story of the Trojan War, first narrated in the *Iliad*, Homer's 8th-century BC epic poem, tells how the Greeks sought to avenge the capture of Helen, wife of Menelaos, King of Sparta, by the Trojan prince, Paris. The Roman writer Virgil takes up the story in the *Aeneid*, where he tells of the sack of Troy and the founding of Rome. Recent archaeological evidence of the remains of a city identified with ancient Troy in modern Turkey suggests that the myth may have a basis in fact. Many of the ancient sites in the Peloponnese, such as Mycenae and Pylos, are thought to be the cities of some of the heroes of the Trojan War.

Achilles binding up the battle wounds of his friend Patroklos

GATHERING OF THE HEROES

When Paris *(see p52)* carries Helen back to Troy, her husband King Menelaos summons an army of Greek kings and heroes to avenge this crime. His brother, King Agamemnon of Mycenae, leads the force; its ranks include young Achilles, destined to die at Troy.

At Aulis their departure is delayed by a contrary wind. Only the sacrifice to Artemis of Iphigéneia, the youngest of Agamemnon's daughters, allows the fleet to depart.

FIGHTING AT TROY

The Iliad Opens with the Greek army outside Troy, maintaining a siege that has already been in progress for nine years. Tired of fighting, yet still hoping for a decisive victory, the Greek camp is torn apart by the fury of Achilles over Agamemnon's removal of his slave girl Briseis. The hero takes to his tent and refuses adamantly to fight.

Deprived of their greatest warrior, the Greeks are driven back by the Trojans. In desperation, Patroklos persuades his friend Achilles to let him borrow his armour. Achilles agrees and Patroklos leads the Myrmidons, Achilles's troops, into battle. The tide is turned, but Patroklos is killed in the fighting by Hector, son of King Priam of Troy, who mistakes him for Achilles. Filled with remorse at the news of his friend's death, Achilles returns to battle, finds Hector, and kills him in revenge.

King Priam begging Achilles for the body of his son

PATROKLOS AVENGED

Refusing Hector's dying wish to allow his body to be ransomed, Achilles instead hitches it up to his chariot by the ankles and drags it round the walls of Troy, then takes it back to the Greek camp. In contrast, Patroklos is given the most elaborate funeral possible with a huge pyre, sacrifices of animals and Trojan prisoners and funeral games. Still unsatisfied, for 12 days Achilles drags the corpse of Hector around Patroklos's funeral mound until the gods are forced to intervene over his callous behaviour.

PRIAM VISITS ACHILLES

On The Instructions of Zeus, Priam sets off for the Greek camp holding a ransom for the body of his dead son. With the help of the god Hermes he reaches Achilles's tent undetected. Entering, he pleads with Achilles to think of his own father and to show mercy. Achilles relents and allows Hector to be taken back to Troy for a funeral and burial.

Although the Greek heroes were greater than mortals, they were portrayed as fallible beings with human emotions who had to face universal moral dilemmas.

Greeks and Trojans, in bronze armour, locked in combat

ACHILLES KILLS THE AMAZON QUEEN

Penthesileia Was the Queen of the Amazons, a tribe of warlike women reputed to cut off their right breasts to make it easier to wield their weapons. They come to the support of the Trojans. In the battle, Achilles finds himself face to face with Penthesileia and deals her a fatal blow. One version of the story has it that as their eyes meet at the moment of her death, they fall in love. The Greek idea of love and death would be explored 2,000 years later by the psychologists Jung and Freud.

An early image of the Horse of Troy, from a 7th-century BC clay vase

Achilles killing the Amazon Queen Penthesileia in battle

THE WOODEN HORSE OF TROY

As was Foretold, Achilles is killed at Troy by an arrow in his heel from Paris's bow. With this weakening of their military strength, the Greeks resort to guile.

Before sailing away they build a great wooden horse, in which they conceal some of their best fighters. The rumour is put out that this is a gift to the goddess Athena and that if the horse enters Troy, the city can never be taken. After some doubts, but swayed by supernatural omens, the Trojans drag the horse inside the walls. That night, the Greeks sail back, the soldiers creep out of the horse and Troy is put to the torch. Priam, with many others, is murdered. Among the Trojan survivors is Aeneas who escapes to Italy and founds the race of Romans: a second Troy. The next part of the story (the *Odyssey*) tells of the heroes' adventures on their way home to Greece.

DEATH OF AGAMEMNON

Klytemnestra, the wife of Agamemnon, had ruled Mycenae in the ten years that he had been away fighting in Troy. She was accompanied by Aigisthos, her lover. Intent on vengeance for the death of her daughter Iphigéneia, Klytemnestra receives her husband with a triumphal welcome and then brutally murders him, with the help of Aigisthos. Agamemnon's fate was a result of a curse laid on his father, Atreus, which was finally expiated by the murder of both Klytemnestra and Aigisthos by her son Orestes and daughter Elektra. In these myths, the will of the gods shapes and overrides that of heroes and mortals.

GREEK MYTHS IN WESTERN ART

From the Renaissance onwards, the Greek myths have been a powerful inspiration for artists and sculptors. Kings and queens have had themselves portrayed as gods and goddesses with their symbolic attributes of love or war. Myths have also been an inspiration for artists to paint the nude or Classically draped figure. This was true of the 19th-century artist Lord Leighton, whose depiction of the human body reflects the Classical ideals of beauty. His tragic figure of Elektra is shown here.

Elektra mourning the death of her father Agamemnon at his tomb

Greek Writers and Philosophers

Playwrights Aristophanes and Sophocles

The literature of Greece began with long epic poems, accounts of war and adventure, which established the relationship of the ancient Greeks to their gods. The tragedy and comedy, history and philosophical dialogues of the 5th and 4th centuries BC became the basis of Western literary culture. Much of our knowledge of the Greek world is derived from Greek literature. Pausanias's *Guide to Greece*, written in the Roman period and used by Roman tourists, is a key to the physical remains.

Hesiod with the nine Muses who inspired his poetry

EPIC POETRY

As far back as the 2nd millennium BC, before even the building of the Mycenaean palaces, poets were reciting the stories of the Greek heroes and gods. Passed on from generation to generation, these poems, called *rhapsodes,* were never written down but were changed and embellished by successive poets. The oral tradition culminated in the *Iliad* and *Odyssey* (see pp54–5), composed around 700 BC. Both works are traditionally ascribed to the same poet, Homer, of whose life

nothing reliable is known. Hesiod, whose most famous poems include the *Theogony*, a history of the gods, and the *Works and Days*, on how to live an honest life, also lived around 700 BC. Unlike Homer, Hesiod is thought to have written down his poems, although there is no firm evidence available to support this theory.

PASSIONATE POETRY

For private occasions, and particularly to entertain guests at the cultivated drinking parties known as *symposia*, shorter poetic forms were developed. These poems were often full of passion, whether love or hatred, and could be personal or, often, highly political. Much of this poetry, by writers such as Archilochus, Alcaeus, Alcman, Hipponax and Sappho, survives only in quotations by later writers or on scraps of papyrus that have been preserved by chance from private libraries in Hellenistic and Roman Egypt. Through these fragments we can gain glimpses

of the life of a very competitive elite. Since *symposia* were an almost exclusively male domain, there is a strong element of misogyny in much of this poetry. In contrast, the fragments of poems discovered by the authoress Sappho, who lived on the island of Lésvos, are exceptional for showing a woman competing in a literary area in the male-dominated society of ancient Greece, and for describing with great intensity her passions for other women.

HISTORY

Until the 5th century BC little Greek literature was composed in prose – even early philosophy was in verse. In the latter part of the 5th century, a new tradition of lengthy prose histories, looking at recent or current events, was established with Herodotus's account of the great war between Greece and Persia (490–479 BC). Herodotus put the clash between Greeks and Persians into a context, and included an ethnographic account of the vast Persian Empire. He attempted to record objectively what people said about the past.

Thucydides took a narrower view in his account of the long years of the Peloponnesian War between Athens and Sparta (431–404 BC). He concentrated on the political history, and his aim was to work out the "truth" that lay behind the events of the war. The methods of Thucydides were adopted by later writers of Greek history, though few could match his acute insight into human nature.

Herodotus, the historian of the Persian wars

An unusual vase-painting of a *symposion* for women only

The orator Demosthenes in a Staffordshire figurine of 1790

ORATORY

Public argument was basic to Greek political life even in the Archaic period. In the later part of the 5th century BC, the techniques of persuasive speech began to be studied in their own right. From that time on some orators began to publish their speeches. In particular, this included those wishing to advertise their skills in composing speeches for the law courts, such as Lysias and Demosthenes. The texts that survive give insights into both Athenian politics and the seamier side of Athenian private life. The verbal attacks on Philip of Macedon by Demosthenes, the 4th-century BC Athenian politician, became models for Roman politicians seeking to defeat their opponents. With the 18th-century European revival of interest in Classical times, Demosthenes again became a political role model.

DRAMA

Almost all the surviving tragedies come from the hands of the three great 5th-century BC Athenians: Aeschylus, Sophocles and Euripides. The latter two playwrights developed an interest in individual psychology (as in Euripides' *Medea*). While 5th-century comedy is full of direct references to contemporary life and dirty jokes, the "new" comedy developed in the 4th century BC is essentially situation comedy employing character types.

Vase painting of two costumed actors from around 370 BC

GREEK PHILOSOPHERS

The Athenian Socrates was recognized in the late 5th century BC as a moral arbiter. He wrote nothing himself but we know of his views through the "Socratic dialogues", written by his pupil, Plato, examining the concepts of justice, virtue and courage. Plato set up his academy in the suburbs of Athens.

His pupil, Aristotle, founded the Lyceum, to teach subjects from biology to ethics, and helped to turn Athens into one of the first university cities. In 1508–11 Raphael painted this vision of Athens in the Vatican.

Aristotle, author of the *Ethics*, had a genius for scientific observation.

Euclid laid the rules of geometry in around 300 BC.

Plato saw "the seat of ideas" in heaven.

Epicurus advocated the pursuit of pleasure.

Socrates taught by debating his ideas.

Diogenes, the Cynic, lived like a beggar.

Temple Architecture

Temples were the most important public buildings in ancient Greece, largely because religion was a central part of everyday life. Often placed in prominent positions, temples were also statements about political and divine power. The earliest temples, in the 8th century BC, were built of wood and sun-dried bricks. Many of their features were copied in marble buildings from the 6th century BC onwards.

Pheidias, sculptor of the Parthenon, at work

TEMPLE CONSTRUCTION

This drawing is of an idealized Doric temple, showing how it was built and used.

The pediment, triangular in shape, often held sculpture.

The cella, or inner sanctum, housed the cult statue.

The cult statue was of the god or goddess to whom the temple was dedicated.

Fluting on the columns was carved *in situ*, guided by that on the top and bottom drums.

A ramp led up to the temple entrance.

The stepped platform was built on a stone foundation.

The column drums were initially carved with bosses for lifting them into place.

TIMELINE OF TEMPLE CONSTRUCTION

Detail of the Parthenon pediment

700 First temple of Poseidon, Ancient Isthmia (Archaic; *see p167*) and first Temple of Apollo, Corinth (Archaic; *see p162*)	**550** Second temple of Apollo, Corinth (Doric; *see p162*)	**520** Temple of Olympian Zeus, Athens, begun (Doric; completed Corinthian 2nd century AD; *see p111*)		
		6th century Temple of Artemis, Ancient Brauron (Doric; *see pp146–7*)		
700 BC	**600 BC**	**500 BC**	**400 BC**	**300 BC**
	460 Temple of Zeus, Olympia (Doric; *see p171*)		**4th century** Temple of Apollo, Delphi (Doric; *see p229*); Temple of Athena Aléa, Tegéa (Doric and 1st Corinthian capital; *see p177*)	
7th century Temple of Hera, Olympia (Doric; *see p170*)	**447–405** Temples of the Acropolis, Athens: Athena Nike (Ionic), Parthenon (Doric), Erechtheion (Ionic) (*see pp94–9*)		**440–430** Temple of Poseidon, Soúnio (Doric; *see pp148–9*)	
	445–425 Temple of Apollo, Bassae (Doric with Ionic; *see p177*)			

The gable ends of the roof were surmounted by statues, known as *akroteria*, in this case of a Nike or "Winged Victory". Almost no upper portions of Greek temples survive.

The roof was supported on wooden beams and covered in rows of terracotta tiles, each ending in an upright *akroteria.*

THE DEVELOPMENT OF TEMPLE ARCHITECTURE

Greek temple architecture is divided into three styles, which evolved chronologically, and are most easily distinguished by the column capitals.

Doric *temples were surrounded by sturdy columns with plain capitals and no bases. As the earliest style of stone buildings, they recall wooden prototypes.*

Triangular pediment filled with sculpture

Guttae imitated the pegs for fastening the wooden roof beams.

Triglyphs resembled the ends of cross beams.

Metopes could contain sculpture.

Doric capital

Ionic *temples differed from Doric in their tendency to have more columns, of a different form. The capital has a pair of volutes, like rams' horns, front and back.*

Akroteria, at the roof corners, could look Persian in style.

The frieze was a continuous band of decoration.

The Ionic architrave was subdivided into projecting bands.

The Ionic frieze took the place of Doric *triglyphs* and *metopes.*

Ionic capital

Stone blocks were smoothly fitted together and held by metal clamps and dowels: no mortar was used in the temple's construction.

The ground plan was derived from the megaron of the Mycenaean house: a rectangular hall with a front porch supported by columns.

Caryatids, *or figures of women, were used instead of columns in the Erechtheion at Athens' Acropolis. In Athens' Agora (see pp90–91), tritons (half-fish, half-human creatures) were used.*

Corinthian *temples in Greece were built under the Romans and only in Athens. They feature columns with slender shafts and elaborate capitals decorated with acanthus leaves.*

The pediment was decorated with a variety of mouldings.

Akroterion in the shape of a griffin

The cella entrance was at the east end.

The entablature was everything above the capitals.

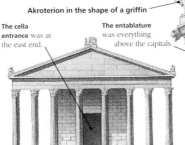

Acanthus leaf capital

Vases and Vase Painting

Donkey cup

The history of Greek vase painting continued without a break from 1000 BC to Hellenistic times. The main centre of production was Athens, which was so successful that by the early 6th century BC it was sending its high-quality black- and red-figure wares to every part of the Greek world. The Athenian potters' quarter of Kerameikós can still be visited today *(see pp88–9)*. Beautiful works of art in their own right, the painted vases are the closest we can get to the vanished paintings with which ancient Greeks decorated the walls of their houses. Although vases could break during everyday use (for which they were intended) a huge number still survive intact or in reassembled pieces.

This 6th-century BC black-figure vase *shows pots being used in an everyday situation. The vases depicted are* hydriai. *It was the women's task to fill them with water from springs or public fountains.*

The white-ground lekythos *was developed in the 5th century BC as an oil flask for grave offerings. They were usually decorated with funeral scenes, and this one, by the Achilles Painter, shows a woman placing flowers at a grave.*

The naked woman holding a *kylix* is probably a flute-girl or prostitute.

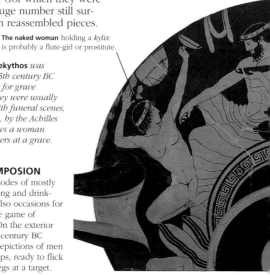

THE SYMPOSION
These episodes of mostly male feasting and drinking were also occasions for playing the game of *kottabos*. On the exterior of this 5th-century BC *kylix* are depictions of men holding cups, ready to flick out the dregs at a target.

THE DEVELOPMENT OF PAINTING STYLES
Vase painting reached its peak in 6th- and 5th-century BC Athens. In the potter's workshop, a fired vase would be passed to a painter to be decorated. Archaeologists have been able to identify the varying styles of many individual painters of both black-figure and red-figure ware.

The body of the dead man is carried on a bier by mourners.

The geometric design is a prototype of the later "Greek-key" pattern.

Chariots and warriors form the funeral procession.

Geometric style *characterizes the earliest Greek vases, from around 1000 to 700 BC, in which the decoration is in bands of figures and geometric patterns. This 8th-century BC vase, placed on a grave as a marker, is over 1 m (3 ft) high and depicts the bier and funeral rites of a dead man.*

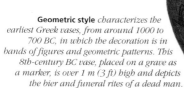

Eye cups *were given an almost magical power by the painted eyes. The pointed base suggests that they were passed around during feasting.*

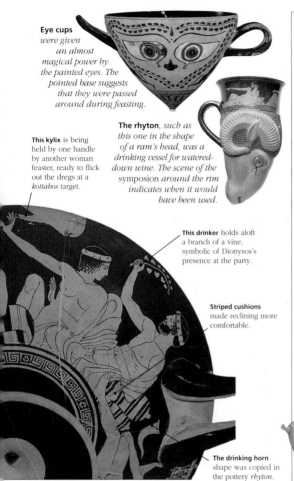

This kylix is being held by one handle by another woman feaster, ready to flick out the dregs at a *kottabos* target.

The rhyton, *such as this one in the shape of a ram's head, was a drinking vessel for watered-down wine. The scene of the symposion around the rim indicates when it would have been used.*

This drinker holds aloft a branch of a vine, symbolic of Dionysos's presence at the party.

Striped cushions made reclining more comfortable.

The drinking horn shape was copied in the pottery *rhyton.*

Black-figure style *was first used in Athens around 630 BC. The figures were painted in black liquid clay on to the iron-rich clay of the vase which turned orange when fired. This vase is signed by the potter and painter Exekias.*

Red-figure style *was introduced in c.530 BC. The figures were left in the colour of the clay, silhouetted against a black glaze. Here a woman pours from an oinochoe (wine jug).*

VASE SHAPES

Almost all Greek vases were made to be used; their shapes are closely related to their intended uses. Athenian potters had about 20 different forms to choose from. Below are some of the most commonly made shapes and their uses.

The amphora *was a two-handled vessel used to store wine, olive oil and foods preserved in liquid such as olives. It also held dried foods.*

This krater *with curled handles or "volutes" is a wide-mouthed vase in which the Greeks mixed water with their wine before drinking it.*

The hydria *was used to carry water from the fountain. Of the three handles, one was vertical for holding and pouring, two horizontal for lifting.*

The lekythos *could vary in height from 3 cm (1 in) to nearly 1 m (39 in). It was used to hold oil both in the home and as a funerary gift to the dead.*

The oinochoe, *the standard wine jug, had a round or trefoil mouth for pouring, and just one handle.*

The kylix, *a two-handled drinking cup, was one shape that could take interior decoration.*

ATHENS
AREA BY AREA

Athens at a Glance

Athens has been a city for 3,500 years but its greatest glory was during the Classical period of ancient Greece from which so many buildings and artifacts still survive. The 5th century BC in particular was a golden age, when Perikles oversaw the building of the Acropolis. Within the Byzantine Empire and under Ottoman rule, Athens played only a minor role. It returned to prominence in 1834, when it became the capital of Greece. Today it is a busy and modern metropolitan centre.

• ATHENS

The Kerameikós *quarter* (see pp88–9) *was once the potters' district of ancient Athens and site of the principal cemetery, whose grave monuments can still be seen. Tranquil and secluded, it lies off the main tourist track.*

SEE ALSO

• *Where to Stay* pp264–7

• *Where to Eat* pp284–8

• *Getting Around Athens* pp324–7

The Agora (see pp90–91), *or market place, was the ancient centre of commercial life. The Stoa of Attalos was reconstructed in 1953–6 on its original, 2nd-century BC foundations. It now houses the Agora Museum.*

The Tower of the Winds (see pp86–7) *stands beside the Roman forum, but this small, octagonal building is Hellenistic in style. The tower – built as a water clock, with a compass, sundials and weather vane – has a relief on each side depicting the wind from that direction.*

The Acropolis (see pp94–101) *has dominated Athens for over 2,000 years. From the scale of the Parthenon to the delicacy of the Erechtheion, it is an extraordinary achievement.*

0 metres	500
0 yards	500

◁ The Parthenon on the Acropolis, viewed from the Hephaisteion

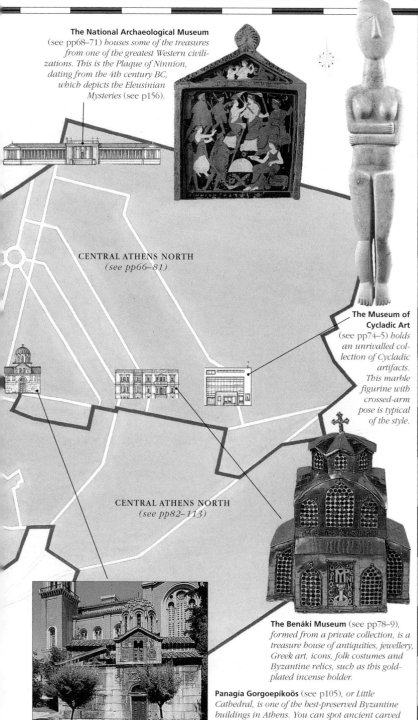

The National Archaeological Museum (see pp68–71) *houses some of the treasures from one of the greatest Western civilizations. This is the Plaque of Ninnion, dating from the 4th century BC, which depicts the Eleusinian Mysteries (see p156).*

CENTRAL ATHENS NORTH
(see pp66–81)

The Museum of Cycladic Art (see pp74–5) *holds an unrivalled collection of Cycladic artifacts. This marble figurine with crossed-arm pose is typical of the style.*

CENTRAL ATHENS NORTH
(see pp82–113)

The Benáki Museum (see pp78–9), *formed from a private collection, is a treasure house of antiquities, jewellery, Greek art, icons, folk costumes and Byzantine relics, such as this gold-plated incense holder.*

Panagía Gorgoepíkoös (see p105), *or Little Cathedral, is one of the best-preserved Byzantine buildings in Athens. You can spot ancient carved reliefs reused in the walls of this tiny church.*

CENTRAL ATHENS NORTH

Inhabited For 7,000 Years, Athens was the birthplace of European civilization. It flourished in the 5th century BC when the Athenians controlled much of the eastern Mediterranean. The buildings from this era, including those in the ancient Agora and on the Acropolis, lie largely in the southern part of the city. The northern half has grown since the early 1800s when King Otto made Athens the new capital of Greece. When the king's architects planned the new, European-style city, they included wide, tree-lined avenues, such as Panepistimíou and Akadimías, that were soon home to many grand

Icon of the Archangel Michael, from the Byzantine Museum

Neo-Classical public buildings and mansion houses. Today, these edifices still provide elegant homes for all the major banks, embassies and public institutions, such as the University and the Library.

The chic residential area of Kolonáki is located in the north of the city centre, as is the cosmopolitan area around Patriárchou Ioakeím and Irodótou. These streets have excellent shopping and entertainment venues. Most of Athens' best museums, including the National Archaeological Museum, are also found in this area of the city. For information on getting around Athens, see pages 324–7.

SIGHTS AT A GLANCE

Museums and Galleries
Benáki Museum pp78–9 ⑩
Byzantine Museum ⑦
City of Athens Museum ⑫
Museum of Cycladic Art pp74–5 ⑧
National Archaeological Museum pp68–71 ①
National Gallery of Art ⑤
National Historical Museum ⑬
Theatrical Museum ⑪
War Museum ⑥

Squares, Parks and Gardens
Exárcheia and Stréfi Hill ②
Lykavittós Hill ③
Plateía Kolonakíou ⑨

Churches
Kapnikaréa ⑭

Historic Buildings
Gennádeion ④

KEY

Ⓜ Metro station

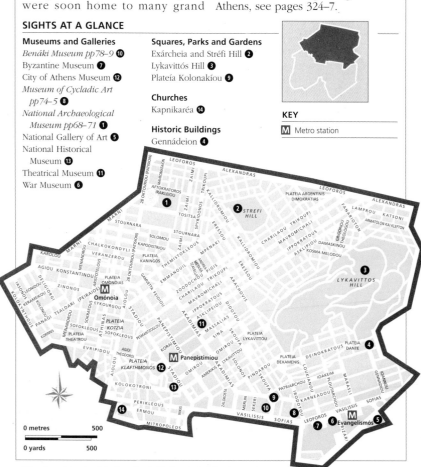

0 metres   500

0 yards   500

◁ The elegant façade of the Neo-Classical University building (see p81)

National Archaeological Museum ❶
Εθνικό Αρχαιολογικό Μουσείο

Hellenistic bronze head from Delos

Opened In 1891, this superb museum, often known simply as the National Museum, brought together a collection that had previously been stored all over the city. New wings were added in 1939. The priceless collection was then dispersed and buried underground during World War II to protect it from possible damage. The museum reopened in 1946, but it took a further 50 years of renovation and reorganization finally to do justice to its formidable collection. With the combination of such unique exhibits as the Mycenaean gold, along with the unrivalled amount of sculpture, pottery and jewellery on display, this is without doubt one of the world's finest museums.

Neo-Classical entrance to the National Archaeological Museum on Patission

GALLERY GUIDE

On the ground floor, Mycenaean, Neolithic and Cycladic finds are followed by Geometric, Archaic, Classical, Roman and Hellenistic sculpture. Smaller collections of bronzes, Egyptian artifacts, the Eléni Stathátou jewellery collection and the Karapános collection are also on the ground floor. The first floor houses a collection of pottery.

Dipylon Amphora
This huge Geometric vase was used to mark an 8th-century BC woman's burial and shows the dead body surrounded by mourning women. It is named after the location of its discovery near the Dipýlon Gate in Athens' Kerameikós (see pp88–89).

Bronze collection

Sculpture garden

Main entrance hall

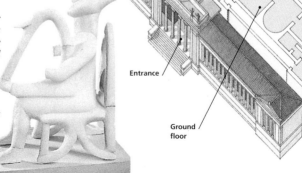

Harp Player
The minimalist Cycladic style of sculpture flourished in the 3rd millennium BC and originated in the Cyclades. The simple lines and bold forms of the marble figurines influenced many early 20th-century artists, including the British sculptor Henry Moore.

Entrance

Ground floor

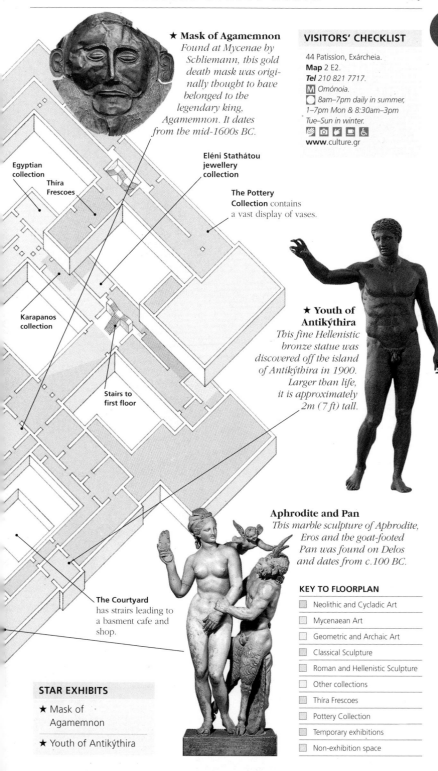

★ **Mask of Agamemnon**
Found at Mycenae by Schliemann, this gold death mask was originally thought to have belonged to the legendary king, Agamemnon. It dates from the mid-1600s BC.

Eléni Stathátou jewellery collection

Egyptian collection

Thíra Frescoes

The Pottery Collection contains a vast display of vases.

Karapanos collection

★ **Youth of Antikýthira**
This fine Hellenistic bronze statue was discovered off the island of Antikýthira in 1900. Larger than life, it is approximately 2m (7 ft) tall.

Stairs to first floor

Aphrodite and Pan
This marble sculpture of Aphrodite, Eros and the goat-footed Pan was found on Delos and dates from c.100 BC.

The Courtyard has strairs leading to a basment cafe and shop.

KEY TO FLOORPLAN

- Neolithic and Cycladic Art
- Mycenaean Art
- Geometric and Archaic Art
- Classical Sculpture
- Roman and Hellenistic Sculpture
- Other collections
- Thira Frescoes
- Pottery Collection
- Temporary exhibitions
- Non-exhibition space

STAR EXHIBITS

- ★ Mask of Agamemnon
- ★ Youth of Antikýthira

Exploring the National Archaeological Museum's Collection

Displaying its treasures in chronological order, the museum presents an impressive and thorough overview of Greek art through the centuries. Beginning with early Cycladic figurines and continuing through the Greek Bronze Age, the exhibits end with the glories of Hellenistic period bronzes and a collection of busts of Roman emperors. High points in between include the numerous gold artifacts found at Mycenae, the elegant Archaic *koûroi* statues and the many examples of fine Classical sculpture.

Mycenaean head of a sphinx

NEOLITHIC AND CYCLADIC ART

The dawning of Greek civilization (3500–2900 BC) saw primitive decorative vases and figures. This collection also contains terracotta figurines, jewellery and a selection of weapons.

The vibrant fertility gods and goddesses, such as the *kourotrópos* (nursing mother) with child, are particularly well preserved. Of exceptional importance are the largest known Cycladic marble figurine, from Amorgós, and the earliest known figures of musicians – the *Flute Player* and *Harp Player* both from Kéros. Later finds from Mílos, such as the painted vase with fishermen, reveal the changes in pot shapes and colour that took place in the late Cycladic Bronze Age.

Neolithic clay vases with simple painted decoration

MYCENAEAN ART

It is not difficult to understand the allure of the museum's most popular attraction, the Hall of Mycenaean Antiquities, with its dazzling array of 16th-century BC gold treasures. Other exhibits in the collection include frescoes, ivory sculptures and seal rings made out of precious stones.

From the famous shaft graves *(see p180)* came a procession of daggers, cups, seals and rings as well as a number of regal death masks, including the justly famous *Mask of Agamemnon*. Two superb *rhytons*, or wine jugs, are also on display: one in the shape of a bull's head, made in silver with gold horns, and one in gold shaped like a lion's head. Equally rich finds from sites other than Mycenae have since been made. These include two gold bull cups found at Vafeió, in Crete, a gold phial entwined with dolphins and octopuses (excavated in a royal tomb at Déntra), clay tablets with the early Linear B script from the Palace of Nestor *(see p201)* and a magnificent sword from the Tomb of Stáfylos on the island of Skópelos.

Mycenaean bronze dagger, inlaid with gold

THE DEVELOPMENT OF GREEK SCULPTURE

Sculpture was one of the most sophisticated forms of Greek art. We are able to trace its development from the early *koûroi* to the great works of named sculptors such as Pheidias and Praxiteles in Classical times. Portraiture only began in the 5th century BC; even then most Greek sculptures were of gods and goddesses, heroes and athletes and idealized men and women. These have had an enormous influence on Western art down the centuries.

The Volomándra Koúros *was discovered in Attica and dates from the mid-6th century BC. The highly stylized* koúroi *(statues of naked youths) first appear in the mid-7th century BC. Derived from Egyptian art, these figures share a common pose and proportions. Clothed* kórai *are the female counterpart.*

The Marathon Boy *(340 BC), like many other Greek bronzes, was found on the sea floor. The dreamy expression and easy pose of the figure are characteristic of the works of Praxiteles, the leading late Classical sculptor. An example of the "heroic nude", it shows a great naturalism and perfect balance.*

For hotels and restaurants in this region see pp264–7 and pp284–8

GEOMETRIC AND ARCHAIC ART

Famed for its monumental burial vases, such as the *Dipylon Amphora*, the Geometric period developed a more ornate style in the 7th century BC with the introduction of mythological and plant and animal motifs. By the 6th century BC the full artistry of the black-figure vases had developed. Two rare examples from this peri-od are a *lekythos* depicting Peleus, Achilles and the centaur, Cheiron, and the sculptured heads known as *aryballoi*.

Warrior from Boiotia, early 7th century BC

CLASSICAL SCULPTURE

The collection of Classical sculpture contains both fine statues and a selection of grave monuments, mostly from the Kerameikós. These include the beautiful *stele* (c.410 BC) of Hegeso *(see p88)*. Classical votive sculp-ture on display includes parts of a statue of the goddess

This "valedictory stele" (mid-4th century BC) shows a seated woman bidding farewell to her family. The figures express a dignified suffering found in many Greek funerary reliefs.

Hera, from the Argive Heraion in the Peloponnese, and many statues of the god-dess Athena, including the *Varvakeion Athena*, a reduced copy of the original ivory and gold statue from the Parthenon *(see p99)*.

ROMAN AND HELLENISTIC SCULPTURE

Although a large number of Greek bronzes were lost in antiquity, as metal was melted down in times of emer-gency for making weapons, the museum has some excel-lent pieces on display. These include the famous bronzes *Poseidon* and the *Horse with the Little Jockey*, both found at Cape Artemísion on Evvoia, and the *Youth of Antikýthira,* found in the sea off that island. Another of the best known sculptures is the *Marathon Boy.*

OTHER COLLECTIONS

The museum also houses several smaller collections, many donated by private in-dividuals. Among these is the glittering **Eléni Stathátou jewellery collection**, which covers the Bronze Age through to the Byz-antine period. The **Karapános col-lection**, which is composed mainly from discoveries made at the site at Dodóni *(see p211)*, contains many fine bronzes, including *Zeus Hurling a Thunderbolt.* Also on display are small decorative and votive pieces, and strips of lead inscribed with questions for the oracle at Dodóni.

Gold Hellenistic ring from the Eléni Stathátou collection

Other collections include the recently opened **Egyptian collection** and the **Bronze collection** which comprises many small pieces of stat-uary and decorative items discovered on the Acropolis.

Hellenistic bronze known as the *Horse with the Little Jockey*

THIRA FRESCOES

Two of the famous frescoes discovered at Akrotíri on the island of Thíra (Santoríni) in 1967, and originally thought to be from the myth-ical city of Atlantis, are displayed in the museum. The rest are on Santoríni. Dating from 1500 BC, they confirm the sophistication of late Minoan civilization. The colourful, restored images depict boxer boys, and animals and flowers symbolizing spring time.

POTTERY COLLECTION

The strength of this vast collection lies not only in its size, but in the quality of specific works, repre-senting the flowering of Greek ceramic art. The real gems belong to the 5th century BC when red-figure vases and white-ground *lekythoi* became the established style *(see p60)* and were produced in vast numbers. Expressive painting styles and new designs charac-terize this period. The most poignant pieces are by the "Bosanquet Painter" and the "Achilles Painter" who por-trayed young men by their graves.

View northeast to Lykavittós Hill from the Acropolis

Exarcheía and Stréfi Hill ❷

Εξάρχεια
Λόφος Στρέφη

Map 2 F2 & 3 A2. Ⓜ *Omónoia.*

Until recently, the area around Plateía Exarcheíon was renowned as a hotbed of anarchist activity. Prior to the invasion of students, Exárcheia was a very attractive area and the 19th-century Neo-Classical buildings still stand as testament to this. Today, the area is picking up again and although parts of it are still rather run-down, an influx of new gentrification has brought many fashionable cafés, bars and *ouzerí* to the area. Themistokléous, which leads off the square down to Omónoia, is pleasant to wander along; the local food stores and small boutiques make a refreshing change from the noisy bars. Plateía Exarcheíon is especially lively at night when the outdoor cafés and the open-air cinema, the Riviera, in the streets that climb towards Stréfi, attract many visitors.

Every year a demonstration takes place on 17 November, marking the date in 1973 when many students were killed by the Junta *(see p43)* during a sit-in.

The nearby park of Stréfi Hill, with its intriguing maze of paths, is quiet and peaceful by day but comes to life at night when its cafés are full. Stréfi Hill is one of the many green areas in Athens that provide welcome relief from the noise and grime of the city, particularly in the oppressive heat of summer.

The restaurant on Lykavittós Hill, overlooking Athens

Lykavittós Hill ❸

Λόφος Λυκαβηττού

Map 3 C3. **Funicular:** *from Ploutárchou, 8:45am–12:45pm Mon–Wed & Fri–Sun, 10:30am–12:45pm Thu.*

The peak of Lykavittós (also known as Lycabettus) reaches 277 m (910 ft) above the city, and is its highest hill. It can be climbed on foot by various paths or by the easier, albeit vertiginous, ride in the funicular from the corner of Ploutárchou. On foot, it should take about 45 minutes. The hill may derive its name from a combination of the words *lýki* and *vaino*, meaning "path of light". The ancient belief was that this was the rock once destined to be the Acropolis citadel, accidentally dropped by the city's patron goddess, Athena. Although it is without doubt the most prominent hill in Athens, surprisingly little mention is made of Lykavittós in Classical literature; the exceptions are passing references in Aristophanes's *Frogs* and Plato's *Kritías*. This landmark is a favourite haunt for many Athenians, who come for the panoramic views of the city from the observation decks that rim the summit.

The small whitewashed chapel of **Agios Geórgios** crowns the top of the hill. It was built in the 19th century on the site of an older Byzantine church, dedicated to Profítis Ilías (the Prophet Elijah). Both saints are celebrated on their name days (Profítis Ilías on 20 July and Agios Geórgios on 23 April). On the eve of Easter Sunday, a spectacular candlelit procession winds down the peak's wooded slopes *(see p45)*.

Lykavittós Hill is also home to a summit restaurant and café and the open-air **Lykavittós Theatre**, where contemporary jazz, pop and dance performances are held annually during the Athens Festival *(see p46)*.

Gennádeion ❹
Γεννάδειον

American School of Classical Studies,
Souidías 61, Kolonáki. **Map** 3 C4.
Tel 210 723 6313. Ⓜ Evangelismos.
🚌 3, 7, 8, 13. 🕐 9am–5pm
Mon–Fri (to 8pm Thu), 9am–2pm Sat.
🔴 Aug, main public hols.

The Greek diplomat and
bibliophile, Ioánnis
Gennádios (1844–1932),
spent a lifetime accumulat-
ing rare first editions and
illuminated manuscripts. In
1923, he donated his collection to the American School
of Classical Studies. The
Gennádeion building, named
after him, was designed and
built between 1923 and 1925
by the New York firm Van
Pelt and Thompson to house
the collection. Above its
façade of Ionic columns is an
inscription which translates as
"They are called Greeks who
share in our culture" – from
Gennádios's dedication speech
at the opening in 1926.

Researchers need special
permission to gain access to
over 70,000 rare books and
manuscripts and no items are
allowed to be removed from
the library. Casual visitors
may look at selected exhibits
that are on show, and books,
posters and postcards are for
sale at the souvenir stall.

Exhibits in the main reading
room include 192 Edward
Lear sketches purchased in
1929. There is also an eclectic
mix of Byron memorabilia,
including the last known
portrait of the poet made
before his death in Greece in
1824 (see p149).

The imposing Neo-Classical
façade of the Gennádeion

National Gallery of Art ❺
Εθνική Πινακοθήκη

Vasiléos Konstantínou 50, Ilísia.
Map 7 C1. **Tel** 210 723 5937.
Ⓜ Evangelismos. 🚌 3, 13.
🕐 9am–3pm Mon, Wed–Sat,
10am–2pm Sun. 🔴 main public
hols. 🅿 ♿

Opened in 1976, the National-
Gallery of Art is housed in a
modern low-rise building
which contains a permanent
collection of European and
Greek art. The ground floor
stages travelling exhibitions
and opens out on to a sculpture garden. The first floor,
with the exception of five
impressive works by El Greco
(1541–1614), is devoted to a
minor collection of non-Greek,
European art. Alongside
works of the Dutch, Italian
and Flemish schools, there
are studies, engravings and
paintings by Rembrandt,
Dürer, Brueghel, Van Dyck,
Watteau, Utrillo, Cézanne and
Braque, among others. These

include Caravaggio's Singer
(1620), Eugène Delacroix's
Greek Warrior (1856) and
Picasso's Cubist-period Woman
in a White Dress (1939).

A changing display of Greek
modern art from the 18th to
the 20th century is featured
on the second floor. The 19th
century is represented mainly
by numerous depictions of
the War of Independence and
seascapes, enlivened by portraits such as Nikólaos Gýzis's
The Loser of the Bet (1878),
Waiting (1900) by Nikifóros
Lýtras and The Straw Hat (1925)
by Nikólaos Lýtras. There are
many fine works by major
Greek artists including Chatzimichaïl, Chatzikyriákos-Gkíkas,
Móralis and Tsaroúchis.

War Museum ❻
Πολεμικό Μουσείο

Corner of Vasilíssis Sofías & Rizári,
Ilísia. **Map** 7 C1. **Tel** 210 725 2975.
Ⓜ Evangelismos. 🚌 3, 7, 8, 13.
🕐 9am–2pm Tue–Sun. 🔴 main
public hols. ♿

The War Museum was
opened in 1975
after the fall of
the military dic-
tatorship (see
p43). The first
nine galleries
are chronologi-
cally ordered,
and contain
battle scenes,
armour and
plans from as far   **Spartan bronze**
back as ancient   **helmet**
Mycenaean
times through to the more
recent German occupation of
1941. Other galleries contain
a miscellany of items
including a selection of
different uniforms and
Turkish weapons.

There is a fine display of
paintings and prints of leaders
from the Greek War of Independence (see pp40–41),
such as General Theódoros
Kolokotrónis (1770–1843).
His death mask can also be
seen in the museum. A sizable collection of fine oils and
sketches by the artists Floras-
Karavías and Argyrós vividly
captures the hardships of the
two world wars.

Modern sculpture outside the National Gallery of Art

Museum of Cycladic Art
Μουσείο Κυκλαδικής Τέχνης

Opened in 1986, this modern museum offers the world's finest collection of Cycladic art. It was initially assembled by Nikólas and Dolly Goulandrí and has expanded with donations from other Greek collectors. The museum now has an excellent selection of ancient Greek and Cypriot art, the earliest from about 5,000 years ago. The Cycladic figurines, dating from the 3rd millennium BC, have never enjoyed quite the same level of popularity as Classical sculpture. However, the haunting simplicity of these marble statues has inspired many 20th-century artists and sculptors, including Picasso, Modigliani and Henry Moore.

Cycladic marble head

LOCATOR MAP

Third floor

Second floor

Red-Figure Kylix
This 5th-century BC drinking cup depicts a boxing match between two young male athletes, supervised by their instructor.

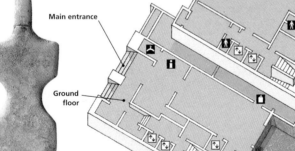

First floor

Main entrance

Ground floor

Violin-Shaped Figurine
This 13-cm (5-in) high, Cycladic, white marble statuette is thought to be a stylized human figure. Most figurines of this shape come from Páros and Antíparos.

Stairs to toilets

Walkway leading to Stathátos Mansion

GALLERY GUIDE
In the main building, the Cycladic collection is on the first floor. Ancient Greek art is on the second, and the third shows Ancient Cypriot art. The fourth floor houses the Charles Polítis collection. The Greek art collection of the Athens Academy is in the Stathátos Mansion.

STAR EXHIBITS
★ Cycladic Figurine

★ White Lekythos

★ Cycladic Figurine
This "Folded Arm" type statue of a woman is 39 cm (15 in) tall. It has only four toes on each foot and a swollen abdomen, indicating pregnancy.

Terracotta Figurine
This elegant figure of a woman is one of many that were thought to have been produced at Tanágra, in Boiotia, Central Greece. It dates from 330–320 BC.

VISITORS' CHECKLIST

Neofýtou Doúka 4, Kolonáki (entrance to Stathátos Mansion at Irodótou 1). **Map** 7 B1. **Tel** 210 722 8321. 🚌 3, 7, 8, 13. ⏱ 10am–4pm Mon, Wed–Fri, 10am–3pm Sat. ⛔ main public hols. 🎫 📷 ♿ limited. 💻 www.cycladic.gr

KEY

⬜	Shop and ticket office
⬜	Cycladic art
⬜	Ancient Greek art
⬜	Ancient Cypriot art
⬜	Charles Polítis collection

Fourth floor

Stairs and lifts connecting all floors

★ White Lekythos
This fine clay lekythos (funerary vase) is an example of white-ground vase painting (see p60) and was used to contain embalming oil. It depicts a mourning woman taking offerings to a grave, and dates from c.450 BC.

Bronze Askos
This elegant Hellenistic bronze wine jar dates from the 2nd century BC. The jar is so named because of its resemblance to the shape of a goat skin, or askos.

Entrance to main building via walkway

The first floor houses temporary exhibitions.

The original porch is the entrance to the Stathátos Mansion.

The ground floor is home to the Greek art collection of the Athens Academy. The glass conservatory-style roof at the back makes this a very light and airy floor.

STATHATOS MANSION
The "new" wing of the Museum of Cycladic Art was opened in 1992. It is housed in this elegant Neo-Classical building, once the home of Otto and Athína Stathátos. It was designed and built by the architect Ernst Ziller in 1895.

The lower ground floor has a café in the courtyard between the two buildings.

A 14th-century icon of St Michael in the Byzantine Museum

Byzantine Museum ❼

Βυζαντινό Μουσείο

Vasilíssis Sofías 22, Plateía Rigíllis, Kolonáki. **Map** 7 B1. **Tel** 210 721 1027. Ⓜ Evangelismos. 🚌 3, 8, 7, 13. ⏰ 8:30am–3pm Tue–Sun. ⬤ main public hols. 📷 ♿ ground floor only.

Originally called the Villa Ilissia, this elegant Florentine-style mansion was built between 1840 and 1848 by Stamátis Kleánthis for the Duchesse de Plaisance (1785–1854). This eccentric woman, wife of one of Napoleon's generals, was a key figure in Athens society during the mid-19th century and a dedicated philhellene.

Collector Geórgios Sotiríou converted the house into a museum in the 1930s with the help of architect Aristotélis Záchos. They transformed the entrance into a monastic court, incorporating a copy of a fountain from a 4th-century mosaic in Dafní (see pp152–3).

Following extensive renovations, the museum reopened in summer 2004 with a new open-plan, split-level exhibition space built underground, below the courtyard. The museum's collection is now divided into two sections and laid out in chronological order: section one, *From the Ancient World to Byzantine*, traces the rise of Christianity, while section two, *The Byzantine World*, runs from the 6th century AD up until the fall of Constantinople in 1453.

Section one is dominated by fragments of ornamental stone carvings and mosaics taken from basilicas, sarcophagi, and early

Funerary stele showing Orpheus with his lyre

religious sculpture such as the *Shepherd Carrying a Lamb* and *Orpheus Playing a Lyre*, both of which illustrate the way in which the Christian church absorbed and adapted pagan symbols. Section two presents an array of icons, frescoes and precious ecclesiastical artifacts. Fine pieces to watch out for include the Treasury of Mytilene (a horde of 7th century gold and silver jewellery, coins and goblets discovered in a sunken ship), the Double-sided Icon of St George and the Mosaic Icon of the Virgin (both dating from the 13th century). There are also some magnificent frescoes that were rescued from the Church of the Episkopi and are cleverly displayed in the positions they would have been in in the church, which was based on a cross in square plan with a dome and narthex.

There are plans to open a café, ticket office and cloakroom in the villa, though this is unlikely to be realised before summer 2007.

The *Episkepsis*, from the Byzantine Museum, depicting the Virgin and Child

ICONS IN THE ORTHODOX CHURCH

The word icon simply means "image" and has come to signify a holy image through association with its religious use. Subjects range from popular saints such as St Andrew and St Nicholas to lesser known martyrs, prophets and archangels. The image of the Virgin and Child is easily the most popular and exalted. Icons are a prominent feature in the Greek Orthodox religion and appear in many areas of Greek life. You will see them in taxis and buses, on boats and in restaurants, as well as in homes and churches. An icon can be in fresco, a mosaic, or made from bone or metal. The most common form is a portable painting, in wax-based paints applied to wooden boards treated with gesso. The figures are arranged so that the eyes are clearly depicted and appear to be looking directly at the viewer of the icon. These works, often of great artistic skill, are unsigned, undated and share a rigid conformity, right down to details of colour, dress, gesture and expression (see pp20–21). The icon painter is careful to catch every detail of a tradition that stretches back hundreds of years.

Puppet Theatre from the Theatrical Museum

Museum of Cycladic Art ⑧

See pp74–5.

Plateía Kolonakíou ⑨
Πλατεία Κολωνακίου

Kolonáki. **Map** 3 B5. 🚎 *3, 7, 8,13.*

Kolonaki Square and its neighbouring side streets are the most chic and sophisticated part of Athens. The area is often missed by those who restrict themselves to the ancient sites and the popular flea markets of Monastiráki. Also known as Plateía Filikís Etaireías, the square is named after a small ancient column (*kolonáki*) found in the area. Celebrated for its designer boutiques and fashionable bars and cafés, smart antique shops and art galleries, sumptuous *zacharoplastéia* (pastry shops) and *ouzerí*, it revels in its status as the city's most fashionable quarter *(see p116).* The lively pavement cafés around the square each attract a particular devoted clientele. At one there may be rich kids drinking *frappé* (iced coffee) perched on their Harley Davidson motorbikes. Another, such as the *Lykóvrissi*, will be full of an older crowd of intellectuals sipping coffee and discussing the ever-popular subject of politics.

Benáki Museum ⑩

See pp78–9.

Theatrical Museum ⑪
Μουσείο και Κέντρο Μελέτης του Ελληνικού Θεάτρου

Akadamías 50, Kéntro. **Map** 2 F4. **Tel** *210 362 9430.* Ⓜ *Panepistimio.* 🚎 *3, 8, 13.* ⏰ *9am–2pm Mon–Fri.* ⚫ *Aug, 17 Nov, main public hols.* ♿ *limited.* 📷

Housed in the basement of a fine Neo-Classical building, this small museum traces Greek theatrical history from Classical times to present day. There are displays of original posters, programmes, costumes and designs from productions by influential directors such as Károlos Koun. There is also a colourful puppet theatre. The dressing rooms of famous Greek actresses such as Eléni Papadáki and Elli Lampéti have been recreated to give an insight into their lives.

City of Athens Museum ⑫
Μουσείο της Πόλεως των Αθηνών

Paparrigopoúlou 7, Plateía Klafthmónos, Syntágma. **Map** 2 E5. **Tel** *210 324 6164.* Ⓜ *Panepistimio.* 🚎 *1, 2, 4, 5, 9, 11, 12, 15, 18.* ⭕ *9am–4pm Mon & Wed-Fri, 10am–3pm Sat-Sun.* ⚫ *main public hols.* 📷

King Otto and Queen Amalía (see p40) lived here from 1831, until their new palace, today's Voulí parliament building (see p112), was completed in 1838. It was joined to the neighbouring house to create what was known as the Old Palace.

The palace was restored in 1980 as a museum devoted to royal memorabilia, furniture and family portraits, maps and prints. It offers a delightful look at life during the early years of King Otto's reign.

Exhibits include the manuscript of the 1843 Constitution, coats of arms from the Frankish (1205–1311) and Catalan (1311–88) rulers of Athens, and a scale model of the city as it was in 1842, made by architect Giánnis Travlós (1908–1985). The museum also has a fine art collection, including Nikólaos Gýzis's The Carnival in Athens (1892) and a selection of watercolours by the English artists Edward Dodwell (1767–1832), Edward Lear (1812–88) and Thomas Hartley Cromek (1809–73).

Perikles, from the Theatrical Museum

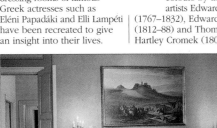

Upstairs sitting room recreated in the City of Athens Museum

Benáki Museum ⑩
Μουσείο Μπενάκη

This outstanding museum was founded in 1931 by Antónis Benákis (1873–1954), the son of Emmanouíl, a wealthy Greek who made his fortune in Egypt. Housed in an elegant Neo-Classical mansion, which was once the home of the Benákis family, the collection contains a diverse array of Greek arts and crafts, paintings and jewellery, local costumes and political memorabilia that spans over 5,000 years, from the Neolithic era to the 20th century.

Flag of Hydra
The imagery symbolizes the island of Hydra's supremacy in sea warfare as it was Greece's most powerful naval community.

Lecture hall

Bridal Cushion
This ornate embroidered cushion comes from Epirus and dates from the 18th century. It depicts a bridal procession, with ornamental flowers in the background.

Second floor

Roof garden

Auditorium

★ Detail of Wood Decoration
This intricately painted and carved piece of wooden panelling comes from a mansion in Kozáni, in western Macedonia. It dates from the 18th century.

Atrium

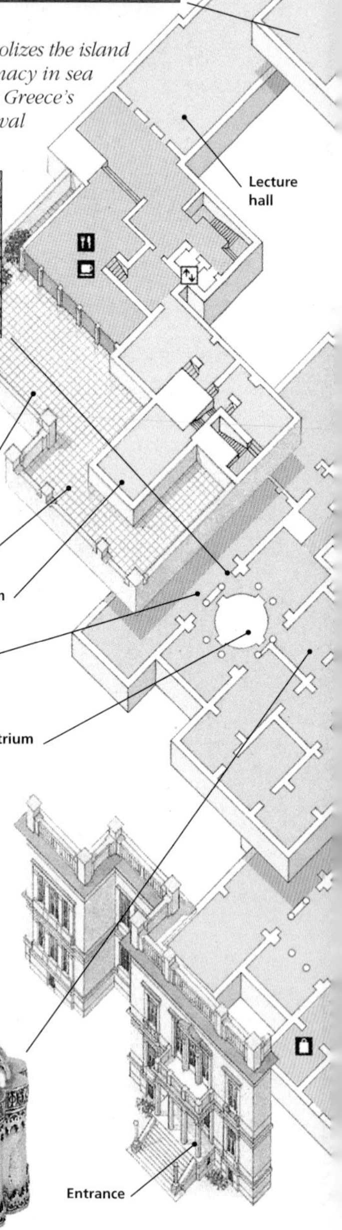

Silver Ciborium
Used to contain consecrated bread, this elegant piece of ecclesiastical silverware is dated 1667 and comes from Edirne, in Turkey.

KEY TO FLOORPLAN

- ☐ Ground floor
- ☐ First floor
- ☐ Second floor
- ☐ Third floor
- ☐ Non-exhibition space

Entrance

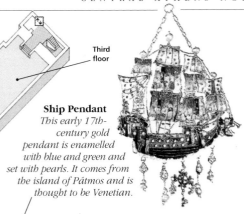

Third floor

Ship Pendant
This early 17th-century gold pendant is enamelled with blue and green and set with pearls. It comes from the island of Pátmos and is thought to be Venetian.

GALLERY GUIDE

The ground floor collection is arranged into different periods and ranges from Neolithic to late-Byzantine art and Cretan icon painting. The first floor exhibits are organized geographically and are from Asia Minor, mainland Greece and the Greek islands. There is also a collection of ecclesiastical silverware and jewellery. The second floor displays items relating to Greek spiritual, economic and social life, and the third floor concentrates on the Greek War of Independence (see pp40–41) and modern political and cultural life.

First floor

Ground floor

★ Icon of St Anne
The icon of St Anne was painted in the 15th century. She is carrying the Virgin Mary as a child, who is holding a white lily, symbol of purity.

Bowl from Paphos
Dating from the 13th century AD, this colourful bowl originates from Cyprus. The dancing figure is holding rattles.

★ El Faiyûm Portrait
This Hellenistic portrait of a man, painted on linen, dates from the 3rd century AD.

STAR EXHIBITS

★ El Faiyûm Portrait

★ Icon of St Anne

★ Detail of Wood Decoration

Neo-Classical façade of the National Historical Museum

National Historical Museum ⓭

Εθνικό Ιστορικό Μουσείο

Stadíou 13, Sýntagma. **Map** 2 F5. **Tel** 210 323 7617. Ⓜ Sýntagma. 🚌 1, 2, 4, 5, 9, 10, 11, 18. ⬭ 9am–2pm Tue–Sun. ⬤ main public hols. 🎫 free Sun.

Designed by French architect François Boulanger (1807–75), this museum was originally built as the first home of the Greek parliament. Queen Amalía laid the foundation stone in 1858, but it was 13 years later that it became the first permanent site of the Greek parliament. The country's most famous prime ministers have sat in the imposing chamber of the Old Parliament of the Hellenes, including Chárilaos Trikoúpis and Theódoros Deligiánnis, who was assassinated on the steps at the front of the building in 1905. The parliament moved to its present-day site in the Voulí building on Plateía Syntágmatos (see p112) after the Voulí was renovated in 1935.

In 1961, the building was opened as the National Historical Museum, owned by the Historical and Ethnological Society of Greece. Founded in 1882, the purpose of the society is to collect objects that illuminate the history of modern Greece. The museum covers all the major events of Greek history from the Byzantine period to the 20th century in a chronological display. Venetian armour, traditional regional costumes and jewellery and figureheads from the warships used during the Revolution in 1821 are just some examples of the many exhibits on show.

The collection also focuses on major parliamentary figures, philhellenes and leaders in the War of Independence, displaying such items as Byron's sword, the weapons of Theódoros Kolokotrónis (1770–1843), King Otto's throne and the pen that was used by Elefthérios Venizélos to sign the Treaty of Sèvres in 1920. The revolutionary memoirs of General Makrigiánnis (1797–1864) can also be seen. Among the numerous paintings on view is a fine rare woodcut of the Battle of Lepanto (1571), the work of Bonastro.

Outside the building is a copy of Lázaros Sóchos's statue of Kolokotrónis on horseback, made in 1900, the original of which is in Náfplio (see pp182–3), the former capital of Greece. There is a dedication on the statue in Greek, which reads "Theódoros Kolokotrónis 1821. Ride on, noble commander, through the centuries, showing the nations how slaves may become free men."

Statue of General Theódoros Kolokotrónis

Kapnikaréa ⓮

Καπνικαρέα

Corner of Ermoú & Kalamiótou, Monastiráki. **Map** 6 D1. **Tel** 210 322 4462. Ⓜ Monastiráki. ⬭ 8am–2pm Mon, Wed, 8am–12:30pm & 5–7pm Tue, Thu, Fri, 8–11:30am Sun. ⬤ main public hols.

This charming 11th-century Byzantine church was rescued from demolition in 1834, thanks to the timely intervention of King Ludwig of Bavaria. Stranded in the middle of a square between Ermoú and Kapnikaréa streets, it is surrounded by the modern office blocks and shops of Athens' busy garment district.

Traditionally called the Church of the Princess, its foundation is attributed to Empress Irene, who ruled the Byzantine Empire from AD 797 to 802. She is revered as a saint in the Greek church for her efforts in restoring icons to the Empire's churches.

The true origins of the name "Kapnikaréa" are unknown, although according to some sources, the church was named after its founder, a "hearth-tax gatherer" (kapnikaréas). Hearth tax was imposed on buildings by the Byzantines.

Restored in the 1950s, the dome of the church is supported by four Roman columns. Frescoes by Fótis Kóntoglou (1895–1965) were painted during the restoration, including one of the Virgin and Child. Much of Kóntoglou's work is also on display in the National Gallery of Art (see p73).

The dome and main entrance of the Byzantine Kapnikaréa

Athenian Neo-Classical Architecture

Neo-Classicism flourished in the 19th century, when the architects who were commissioned by King Otto to build the capital in the 1830s turned to this popular European style. Among those commissioned were the Hansen brothers, Christian and Theophil, and also Ernst Ziller. As a result of their planning, within 50 years a modern city had emerged, with elegant administrative buildings, squares and tree-lined avenues. In its early days Neo-Classicism had imitated the grace of the buildings of ancient Greece, using marble columns, sculptures and decorative detailing. In later years, it evolved into an original Greek style. Grand Neo-Classicism is seen at its best in the public buildings along Panepistimíou; its domestic adaptation can be seen in the houses of Pláka.

National Bank, built in the 1890s

Schliemann's House *(also known as Ilíou Mélathron, the Palace of Ilium, or Troy) was built in 1878 by Ziller. The interior is decorated with frescoes and mosaics of mythological subjects. It is now home to the Numismatic Museum* (**Map** 2 F5).

The National Theatre *was built between 1882 and 1890. Ernst Ziller used a Renaissance-style exterior with arches and Doric columns for George I's Royal Theatre. Inspired by the Public Theatre of Vienna, its interior was very modern for its time* (**Map** 2 D3).

The National Library *was designed by Danish architect Theophil Hansen in 1887 in the form of a Doric temple with two side wings. Built of Pentelic marble, it houses over half a million books, including many illuminated manuscripts and rare first editions* (**Map** 2 F4).

Athens Academy *was designed by Theophil Hansen and built between 1859 and 1887. Statues of Apollo and Athena, and seated figures of Socrates and Plato, convey a Classical style, as do the Ionic capitals and columns. Inside the building, the Academy hall has beautiful frescoes that depict scenes from the myth of Prometheus* (**Map** 2 F4).

The University of Athens *was designed by Christian Hansen. This fine building, completed in 1864, has an Ionic colonnade and a portico frieze depicting the resurgence of arts and sciences under the reign of King Otto. A symbol of wisdom, the Sphinx is connected with Athens through the Oedipus legend (see p221). Oedipus, who solved the riddle of the Sphinx, later found sanctuary in enlightened Athens. Other statues on the façade include Patriarch Gregory V, a martyr of the War of Independence* (**Map** 2 F4).

CENTRAL ATHENS SOUTH

Southern Athens is dominated by the Acropolis and is home to the buildings that were at the heart of ancient Athens. Pláka and Monastiráki still revel in their historical roots as the oldest inhabited areas of the city, and are full of Byzantine churches and museums. Nestling among the restored Neo-Classical houses are grocery stores,

Relief from Panagía Gorgoepíkoös

icon painters and open-air tavernas. In the busy streets of Monastiráki's flea market, food vendors, gypsies and street musicians provide the atmosphere of a Middle Eastern bazaar. Southeast of Plateía Syntágmatos are the National Gardens, the city centre's tree-filled park. For information on getting around Athens, see pages 324–7.

SIGHTS AT A GLANCE

Museums and Galleries
Greek Folk Art Museum ⑯
Jewish Museum of Greece ⑰
Kanellópoulos Museum ⑧
Kyriazópoulos Folk Ceramic Museum ①
Municipal Art Gallery ④
Museum of Greek Popular Musical Instruments ⑩
University of Athens Museum ⑨

Ancient Sites
Acropolis pp94–101 ⑦
Ancient Agora pp90–91 ⑥
Kerameikós pp88–9 ⑤
Temple of Olympian Zeus ⑱
Tower of the Winds pp86–7 ②

Churches
Agios Nikólaos Ragavás ⑬
Mitrópoli ⑫
Panagía Gorgoepíkoös p105 ⑪
Russian Church of the Holy Trinity ⑲

Historic Districts
Anafiótika ⑭

Markets
Flea Market ③

Squares and Gardens
National Gardens ㉑
Plateía Lysikrátous ⑮
Plateía Syntágmatos ⑳

Historic Buildings and Monuments
Kallimármaro Stadium ㉓
Presidential Palace ㉒

Cemeteries
First Cemetery of Athens ㉔

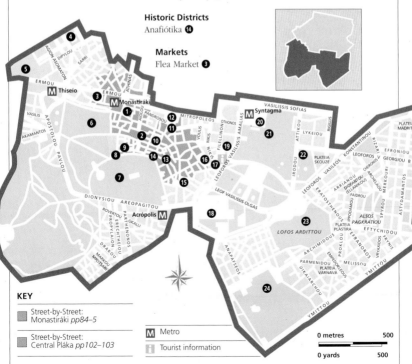

KEY

Street-by-Street: Monastiráki *pp84–5*

Street-by-Street: Central Pláka *p102–103*

Ⓜ Metro

🛈 Tourist information

0 metres 500
0 yards 500

◁ **The remaining columns of the ancient Temple of Olympian Zeus**

Street-by-Street: Monastiráki

This old area of the city takes its name from the little sunken monastery in Plateía Monastirakíou. The former heart of Ottoman Athens, Monastiráki is still home to the bazaar and market stalls selling everything from junk to jewellery. The Fethiye Mosque and the Tzistarákis Mosque, home of the Kyriazópoulos Museum, stand as reminders of the area's Ottoman past. Roman influences are also strong in Monastiráki. The area borders the Roman Agora and includes the remains of Emperor Hadrian's library and the unique Tower of the Winds, a Hellenistic water clock. Monastiráki mixes the atmospheric surroundings of ancient ruins with the excitement of bargaining in the bazaar.

Flea Market
Plateía Avissynías is the heart of the flea market, which extends through the surrounding streets. It is particularly popular on Sundays ❸

KEY

– – – Suggested route

STAR SIGHTS

★ Tower of the Winds

Ifaístou is named after Hephaistos, the god of fire and metal craftsmanship. Areos is named after Ares, the war god.

Monastiráki metro station

0 metres   50

0 yards   50

The Fethiye Mosque is situated in the corner of the Roman Agora. It was built by the Turks in the late 15th century to mark Mehmet the Conqueror's visit to Athens.

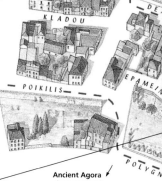

Ancient Agora (see pp90–91)

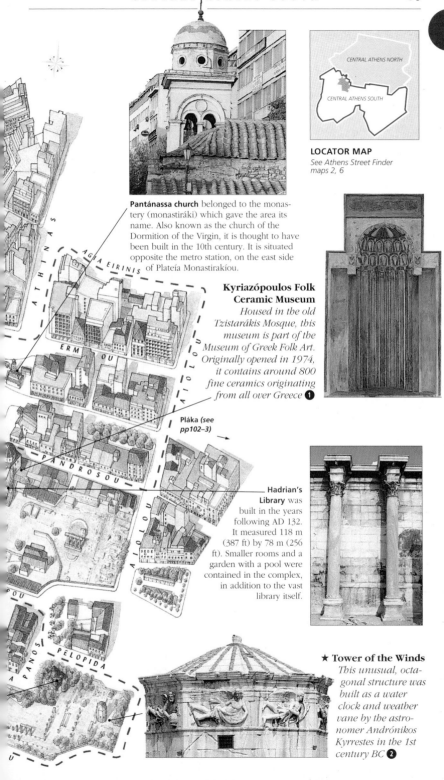

LOCATOR MAP
*See Athens Street Finder
maps 2, 6*

Pantánassa church belonged to the monastery (monastiráki) which gave the area its name. Also known as the church of the Dormition of the Virgin, it is thought to have been built in the 10th century. It is situated opposite the metro station, on the east side of Plateía Monastirakíou.

Kyriazópoulos Folk Ceramic Museum
Housed in the old Tzistarákis Mosque, this museum is part of the Museum of Greek Folk Art. Originally opened in 1974, it contains around 800 fine ceramics originating from all over Greece ❶

Pláka *(see pp102–3)*

Hadrian's Library was built in the years following AD 132. It measured 118 m (387 ft) by 78 m (256 ft). Smaller rooms and a garden with a pool were contained in the complex, in addition to the vast library itself.

★ **Tower of the Winds**
This unusual, octagonal structure was built as a water clock and weather vane by the astronomer Andrónikos Kyrrestes in the 1st century BC ❷

Kyriazópoulos Folk Ceramic Museum ❶

Μουσείο Ελληνικής Λαϊκής Τέχνης, Συλλογή Κεραμικών Β. Κυριαζοπούλου

Tzistarákis Mosque, Areos 1, Monastiráki. **Map** 6 D1. **Tel** *210 324 2066.* Ⓜ *Monastiráki.* ◷ *9am– 2:30pm Mon & Wed–Sun.* ◖ *main public hols.* ▨

This colourful collection of ceramics was donated to the Greek Folk Art Museum in 1974 by Professor Vasíleios Kyriazópoulos. Now an annexe of the Folk Art Museum, the Kyriazópoulos Folk Ceramic Museum is housed in the imposing Tzistarákis Mosque (or the Mosque of the Lower Fountain). Of the hundreds of pieces on display, many are of the type still used today in a traditional Greek kitchen, such as terracotta water jugs from Aígina, earthenware oven dishes from Sífnos and storage jars from Thessaly and Chíos. There are also some ceramic figures and plates, based on mythological and folk stories, crafted by Minás Avramídis and Dimítrios Mygdalinós who came from Asia Minor in the 1920s.

The mosque itself is of as much interest as its contents. It was built in 1759 by the newly appoint-ed Turkish *voivode* Tzistarákis. The *voivode* was the civil

Ceramic of a young girl from Asia Minor

governor who possessed complete powers over the law courts and the police. He collected taxes for his own account, but also had to pay for the sultan's harem and the treasury. His workmen dynamited the 17th column of the Temple of Olympian Zeus *(see p111)* in order to make lime to be used for the stucco work on the mosque. Destruction of ancient monuments was forbidden by Turkish law and this act of vandalism was the downfall of Tzistarákis. He was exiled the same year. The mosque has now been well restored after earthquake damage in 1981.

Tower of the Winds ❷

Αέρηδμς

Within Roman Agora ruins, Pláka. **Map** 6 D1. **Tel** *210 324 5220.* Ⓜ *Monastiráki.* ◷ *Apr–Oct: 8am– 7pm daily; Nov–Mar: 8:30am–3pm daily.* ◖ *main public hols.* ▨ ▨ ♿

The remarkable Tower of the Winds is set within the ruins of the Roman Agora. Constructed from marble in the 2nd century BC by the Syrian astronomer Andrónikos Kyrrestes, it was built as a combined weather vane and water clock. The name comes from the external friezes, personifying the eight winds. Sundials are etched into the walls beneath each relief.

The tower is well preserved, standing today at over 12 m (40 ft) high with a diameter of 8 m (26 ft). Still simply called Aérides ("the winds") by Greeks today, in the Middle Ages it was thought to be either the school or prison of Socrates, or even the tomb of Philip II of Macedon *(see p242)*. It was at last correctly identified as the Horologion (water clock) of Andronikos in the 17th century. All that remains today of its elaborate water clock are the origins of a complex system of water pipes and a circular channel cut into the floor which can be seen inside the tower.

The west and southwest faces of the Tower of the Winds

The west- and north-facing sides each contain a hole which lets light into the otherwise dark interior of the tower.

Northwest entrance

Reservoir

This interior floorplan of the tower shows the compass direction of the building's eight sides. External friezes personify each of the eight winds.

NORTH

Boreas blows the cold north wind through a large conch shell.

NORTHWEST

Skiron scatters glowing ashes from a bronze vessel.

WEST

Zephyros is a semi-naked youth scattering flowers.

Flea Market **❸**
Παζάρι

From Plateía Monastirakíou to Plateía Avyssinías, Pláka. **Map** 5 C1. **M** Thiseío. 8am–2pm Sun.

A banner welcomes visitorsto Athens' famous flea market, past the ubiquitous tourist trinket shops of Adrianoú and Pandrósou streets. For the locals, the true heart of the market lies just west of Plateía Monastirakíou, in Plateía Avyssinías and its warren of surrounding streets.

On Sunday mornings when the shops are closed, the market itself bursts into action. Traders set out their bric-a-brac on stalls and the pavement and many bargains

Shoppers browsing in Athens' lively flea market

can be found, especially the colourful handwoven woollen cloths and the many bangles and beads sold by hippies. More expensive items are also on sale, including brassware, leatherware and silverware.

During the week the shops in the surrounding area are

open and filled with much the same as the Sunday stalls. Individual shops each have their own specialities, so hunt around before making a purchase. You can buy almost anything, from antiques and old books to taverna chairs and army surplus gear.

The southwest wind, Lips, heralds a swift voyage. The reliefs show that each wind was given a personality according to its characteristics, and each promises different conditions. Gentle Zephyros and chilly Boreas, mentioned in Western literature and represented in art and sculpture, are the best known of these.

Whirling dervishes used the tower as a monastery in the mid-18th century. The dervishes were a Muslim order of ascetics. The tower's occupants became a popular attraction for Grand Tour visitors who came to witness the weekly ritual of a frenzied dance, which is known as the sema.

Relief carving of mythological figure

Metal rod casting shadow

Lines of sundial carved into wall of tower

SOUTHWEST	SOUTH	SOUTHEAST	EAST	NORTHEAST

Lips holds the *aphlaston* (or stern ornament) of a ship as he steers.	**Notos** is the bearer of rain, emptying a pitcher of water.	**Euros** is a bearded old man, warmly wrapped in a cloak.	**Apeliotes** is a young man bringing fruits and corn.	**Kaïkias** empties a shield full of icy hailstones on those below.

Miss T K, by Giánnis Mitarákis,
in the Municipal Art Gallery

Municipal Art Gallery ❹
Πινακοθήκη του Δήμου
Αθηναίων

Pireos 51, Plateía Koumoundoúrou,
Omónoia. **Map** 1 C4. **Tel** 210 324
3022. M Omónoia. ⬭ 9am–1pm &
5–9pm Mon–Fri, 9am–1pm Sat &
Sun. ⬭ 3 Oct, main public hols. ◨

This little-visited museum
has one of the finest archive
collections of modern
Greek art. Designed by architect Panagiótis Kálkos in
1872, the home of the
museum is the old Neo-
Classical Foundling Hospital.
It was built to cope with the
city's population explosion
towards the end of the 19th
century; unwanted babies
were left outside the main
entrance to be cared for
by hospital staff.
   The Municipality
of Athens has been
amassing the col-
lection since 1923. It
now offers a fine
introduction to the
diverse styles of
modern Greek artists.
Many paintings are passionate
reflections on the Greek
landscape, such as Dímos
Mpraésas's (1878–1967) landscapes of the Cyclades, or
Konstantínos Parthénis's
(1882–1964) paintings of olive
and cypress trees.
   There are also portraits by
Giánnis Mitarákis and still lifes
by Theófrastos Triantafyllídis.
Paintings such as Nikólaos
Kartsonákis's *Street Market*
(1939) also reveal the folk
roots that are at the heart of
much modern Greek art.

Kerameikós ❺
Κεραμεικός

This ancient cemetery has been a burial ground since
the 12th century BC. The Sacred Way led from Eleusis
(see pp156–7) to Kerameikós and the Panathenaic Way
set out from the Dípylon Gate here to the Acropolis *(see
pp94–7)*. Most of the graves remaining today are along
the Street of the Tombs. The sculptures excavated in the
early 1900s are in the National Archaeological Museum
(see pp68–71) and the Oberlander Museum; however,
plaster copies of the originals can be seen *in situ*.

Grave Stele of Hegeso
*This is from the family burial
plot belonging to Koroibos
of Melite. It shows his wife,
Hegeso, admiring her jewels
with a servant and dates
from the late 5th century BC.*

**Precinct of
Aristion**

**The Precinct of
Lysimachides**
contains a marble dog,
originally one of a pair.

The Sanctuary of Hekate was
sacred to the ancient goddess
of the underworld. It contained
an altar and votive offerings.

STREET OF THE TOMBS

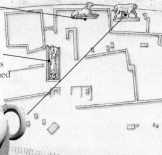

**Oberlander
Museum**

**South
terrace**

**★ Tomb of Dionysios
of Kollytos**
*This fine tomb belongs to a
rich treasurer. A bull often
represents the god Dionysos.*

STAR MONUMENTS

★ Tomb of Dionysios of
Kollytos

★ Stele of Demetria and
Pamphile

STREET OF
THE TOMBS
Most of the monuments in
the Street of the Tombs
date from the 4th century
BC. The different styles,
from the lavish *stelae*
(relief sculptures) to the
simple *kioniskoi* (small
columns), all reveal the
dignity that is typical of
Greek funerary art.

LOCATOR MAP

Stele of Dexileos
Dexileos was a young man killed in 394 BC during the Corinthian War. The son of Lysanias, he is seen on the relief slaying an enemy.

VISITORS' CHECKLIST

Ermoú 148, Thiseío. **Map** 1 B5.
Tel 210 346 3552. M *Thiseío.*
☐ Apr–Oct: 8am–7pm daily;
Nov–Mar: 8am–3pm Tue–Sun,
11am–3pm Mon. 🦽 📷

Oberlander Museum
This museum is named after Gustav Oberlander (1867–1936), a German-American industrialist whose donations helped fund its construction in the 1930s. In Gallery 1, some large fragments from grave *stelae* found incorporated into the Dipylon and Sacred Gates are exhibited. These include a marble sphinx (c.550 BC) that once crowned a

Winged sphinx from grave stele

grave *stele*. Galleries 2 and 3 offer an array of huge Protogeometric and Geometric amphorae and black-figure *lekythoi* (funerary vases). The most moving exhibits come from children's graves and include pottery toy horses and terracotta dolls. There are also examples of some of the 7,000 *ostraka* (voting tablets) *(see pp90–91)* found in the bed of the river Eridanos. Among the superb painted pottery, there is a red-figure *hydria* (water vase) of Helen of Troy and a *lekythos* of Dionysos with satyrs.

This tumulus was the burial place of an old Attic family dating from the 6th century BC.

Tomb of Hipparete

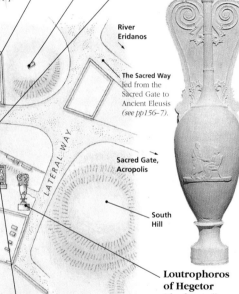

River Eridanos

The Sacred Way led from the Sacred Gate to Ancient Eleusis *(see pp156–7).*

Sacred Gate, Acropolis

South Hill

LATERAL WAY

Loutrophoros of Hegetor
The farewell scene depicted on this two-handled vase is typical of the less ornate style of commemorative funerary art.

★ **Stele of Demetria and Pamphile**
This moving sculpture shows the seated Pamphile with her sister Demetria behind her. This was one of the last ornate stelae to be made in the late 4th century BC.

Geometric funerary amphora from the Oberlander Museum

Ancient Agora 6

Αρχαία Αγορά

Voting lot

The Agora, or market-place, formed the political heart of ancient Athens from 600 BC. Democracy was practised in the *Bouleuterion* (Council) and the law courts, and in open meetings. Socrates was indicted and executed in the state prison here in 399 BC. The theatres, schools and stoas filled with shops also made this the centre of social and commercial life. Even the city mint that produced Athens' silver coins was here. The American School of Classical Studies began excavations of the Ancient Agora in the 1930s, and since then the vast remains of a complex array of public buildings have been revealed.

View across the Agora from the south showing the reconstructed Stoa of Attalos on the right

The Panathenaic Way was named after the Great Panathenaia festival which took place every four years.

Library of Pantainos

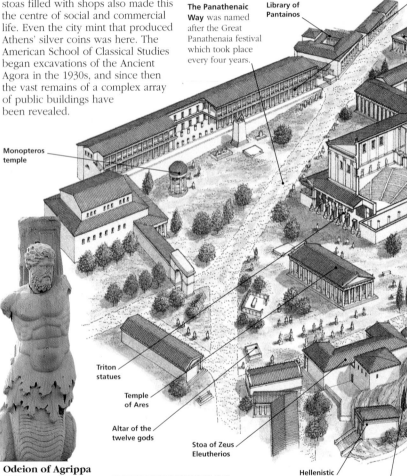

Monopteros temple

Triton statues

Temple of Ares

Altar of the twelve gods

Stoa of Zeus Eleutherios

Hellenistic temple

Temple of Apollo Patroös

Odeion of Agrippa
This statue of a triton (half-god, half-fish) once adorned the façade of the Odeion of Agrippa. It dates from AD 150 and is now in the Agora museum.

RECONSTRUCTION OF THE ANCIENT AGORA

This shows the Agora as it was in c.AD 200, viewed from the northwest. The main entrance to the Agora at this time was via the Panathenaic Way, which ran across the site from the Acropolis in the southeast to the Kerameikós in the northwest.

0 metres		50
0 yards		50

Stoa of Attalos
This colonnaded building was reconstructed in the mid-20th century as a museum to house finds from the Ancient Agora site.

Statue of Hadrian
Hadrian was Emperor of Rome from AD 117–38. Athens was under his authority. The statue dates from the 2nd century AD.

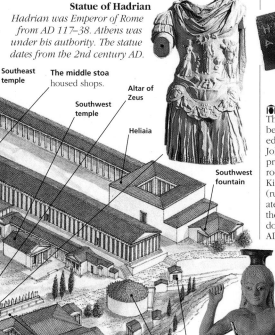

Southeast temple

The middle stoa housed shops.

Altar of Zeus

Southwest temple

Heliaia

Southwest fountain

Latrines

The Tholos was the Council headquarters.

Bouleuterion or Council chamber

Monument of the Eponymous Heroes

Oil flask in the Archaic style

Metroön

Arsenal

Hephaisteion
This temple, also known as the Theseion, is the best-preserved building on the site. It was built c.449–440 BC.

Ostrakon condemning a man named Hippokrates to exile

🏛 **Stoa of Attalos**

This fine building was rebuilt between 1953 and 1956, helped by a huge donation from John D Rockefeller, Jr. An impressive two-storey stoa, or roofed arcade, founded by King Attalos of Pergamon (ruled 159–138 BC), it dominated the eastern quarter of the Agora until it was burnt down by the Heruli tribe in AD 267. Reconstructed using the original foundations and ancient materials, it now contains a museum whose exhibits reveal the great diversity and sophistication of ancient life. Artifacts include rules from the 2nd-century AD Library of Pantainos, the text of a law against tyranny from 337 BC, bronze and stone lots used for voting and a *klepsýdra* (water clock) used for timing speeches. *Ostraka* (voting tablets on which names were inscribed) bear such famous names as Themistokles and Aristeides the Just, the latter banished, or "ostracized", in 482 BC. More everyday items, such as terracotta toys and portable ovens, and hobnails and sandals found in a shoemaker's shop, are equally fascinating. Also on display are some beautiful black-figure vases and an unusual oil flask moulded into the shape of a kneeling boy.

Acropolis **❼**
Ακρόπολη

In the mid-5th century BC, Perikles persuaded
the Athenians to begin a grand programme of
new building work in Athens that has come to
represent the political and cultural achievements
of Greece. The work transformed the Acropolis
with three contrasting temples and a monumental
gateway. The Theatre of Dionysos on the south
slope was developed further in the 4th century
BC, and the Theatre of Herodes Atticus was
added in the 2nd century AD.

LOCATOR MAP

★ Porch of the Caryatids
*These statues of
women were used
in place of columns
on the south porch
of the Erechtheion.
The originals, four
of which can be
seen in the Acropolis
Museum, have been
replaced by casts.*

An olive tree now
grows where Athena
first planted her tree
in a competition
against Poseidon.

The Propylaia was built
in 437–432 BC to form a
new entrance to the
Acropolis *(see p96)*.

★ Temple of Athena Nike
*This temple to Athena of
Victory is on the west side of
the Propylaia. It was built in
426–421 BC (see p96).*

The Beulé Gate
was the first
entrance to
the Acropolis
(see p96).

**Pathway to
Acropolis
from ticket
office**

STAR SIGHTS

★ Parthenon

★ Porch of the
  Caryatids

★ Temple of
  Athena Nike

Theatre of Herodes Atticus
*Also known as the Odeion of
Herodes Atticus, this superb
theatre was originally built
in AD 161. It was restored in
1955 and is used today for
outdoor concerts (see p100).*

◁ The Porch of the Caryatids on the Erechtheion

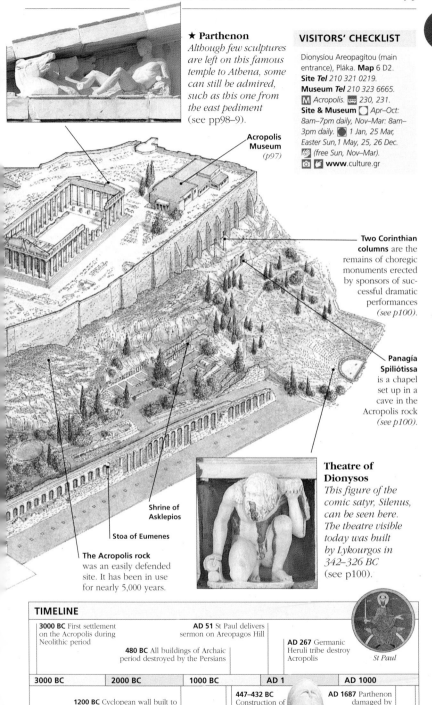

★ Parthenon
Although few sculptures are left on this famous temple to Athena, some can still be admired, such as this one from the east pediment (see pp98–9).

Acropolis Museum *(p97)*

VISITORS' CHECKLIST

Dionysíou Areopagítou (main entrance), Pláka. **Map** 6 D2.
Site *Tel* 210 321 0219.
Museum *Tel* 210 323 6665.
Ⓜ *Acropolis.* ▦ *230, 231.*
Site & Museum ◯ *Apr–Oct: 8am–7pm daily, Nov–Mar: 8am–3pm daily.* ● *1 Jan, 25 Mar, Easter Sun,1 May, 25, 26 Dec.* ◪ *(free Sun, Nov–Mar).*
◙ ▧ *www.culture.gr*

Two Corinthian columns are the remains of choregic monuments erected by sponsors of successful dramatic performances *(see p100).*

Panagía Spiliótissa is a chapel set up in a cave in the Acropolis rock *(see p100).*

Theatre of Dionysos
This figure of the comic satyr, Silenus, can be seen here. The theatre visible today was built by Lykourgos in 342–326 BC (see p100).

Shrine of Asklepios

Stoa of Eumenes

The Acropolis rock was an easily defended site. It has been in use for nearly 5,000 years.

TIMELINE

3000 BC First settlement on the Acropolis during Neolithic period

AD 51 St Paul delivers sermon on Areopagos Hill

480 BC All buildings of Archaic period destroyed by the Persians

AD 267 Germanic Heruli tribe destroy Acropolis

St Paul

3000 BC	2000 BC	1000 BC	AD 1	AD 1000

1200 BC Cyclopean wall built to replace original ramparts

510 BC Delphic Oracle declares Acropolis a holy place of the gods, banning habitation by mortals

447–432 BC Construction of the Parthenon under Perikles

Perikles (495–429 BC)

AD 1687 Parthenon damaged by Venetians

AD 1987 Restoration of the Erechtheion completed

Exploring the Acropolis

Relief of Mourning Athena

Once through the first entrance, the Beulé Gate, straight ahead is the Propylaia, the grand entrance to the temple complex. Before going through here, it is worth exploring the Temple of Athena Nike, on the right. Beyond the Propylaia are the Erechtheion and the Parthenon (*see pp98–9*) which dominate the top of the rock. There are also stunning views of Athens itself from the Acropolis. Since 1975, access to all the temple precincts has been banned to prevent further damage. Buildings located at the foot of the Acropolis and the hills immediately to the west are covered on pages 100–101.

View of the Acropolis from the southwest

⋔ Beulé Gate

The gate is named after the French archaeologist Ernest Beulé who discovered it in 1852. It was built in AD 267 after the raid of the Heruli, a Germanic people, as part of the Roman Acropolis fortifications. It incorporates stones from the *choregic* monument (*see p109*) of Nikias that was situated near the Stoa of Eumenes. Parts of the original monument's dedication are still visible over the architrave. There is also an inscription identifying a Roman, Flavius Septimius Marcellinus, as

donor of the gateway. In 1686, when the Turks destroyed the Temple of Athena Nike, they used the marble to build a bastion for artillery over the gate.

⋔ Temple of Athena Nike

This small temple was built in 426–421 BC to commemorate the Athenians' victories over the Persians. The temple frieze has representative scenes from the Battle of Plataiaí (479 BC). Designed by Kallikrates, the temple stands on a 9.5-m (31-ft) bastion. It has been used as both observation post and an ancient shrine to the goddess of Victory, Athena Nike, of whom there is a remarkable sculpture situated on the balustrade. Legend records the temple site as the place from which King Aegeus threw himself into the sea, believing that his son Theseus had been killed in Crete by the Minotaur. Built

of Pentelic marble, the temple has four Ionic columns 4 m (13 ft) high at each portico end. It was reconstructed in 1834–8, after being destroyed in 1686 by the Turks. On the point of collapse in 1935, it was again dismantled and reconstructed according to information resulting from more recent research.

⋔ Propylaia

Work began on this enormous entrance to the Acropolis in 437 BC. Although the outbreak of the Peloponnesian War in 432 BC curtailed its completion, its architect Mnesikles created a building admired throughout the ancient world. The Propylaia comprises a rectangular central building divided by a wall into two porticoes. These were punctuated by five entrance doors, rows of Ionic and Doric columns and a vestibule with a blue-coffered ceiling decorated with gold stars. Two wings flank the main building. The north wing was home to the *pinakothíki*, an art gallery.

During its chequered history – later as archbishop's residence, Frankish palace, and Turkish fortress and armoury – parts of the building have been accidentally destroyed; it even suffered the misfortune of being struck by lightning in 1645, and later the explosion of the Turkish gunpowder store (*see p98*).

⋔ Erechtheion

Built between 421 and 406 BC, the Erechtheion is situated on the most sacred site of the Acropolis. It is said to be where Poseidon left his trident marks in a rock, and Athena's olive tree sprouted, in their battle for possession of the city. Named after Erechtheus, one of the mythical kings of Athens, the temple was a sanctuary to both Athena Polias, and Erechtheus-Poseidon.

Famed for its elegant and extremely ornate Ionic architecture and caryatid columns in the shape of women, this extraordinary monument is built on different levels. The large rectangular cella was divided into three

The eastern end of the Erechtheion

rooms. One contained the holy olive wood statue of Athena Polias. The cella was bounded by north, east and south porticoes. The south is the Porch of the Caryatids, the maiden statues which are now in the Acropolis Museum.

The Erechtheion complex has been used for a range of purposes, including a harem for the wives of the Turkish *disdar* (commander) in 1463. It was almost completely destroyed by a Turkish shell in 1827 during the War of Independence *(see pp40–41)*. Recent restoration has caused heated disputes: holes have been filled with new marble, and copies have been made to replace original features that have been removed to the safety of the museum.

A youth leading a cow to sacrifice, from the Parthenon's north frieze

♩ Acropolis Museum

Built below the level of the Parthenon, this museum is located in the southeast corner of the site. Opened in 1878, it was reconstructed after World War II to accommodate a collection devoted

to finds from the Acropolis. Treasures include fine statues from the 5th century BC and well-preserved segments of the Parthenon frieze.

The collection begins chronologically in **Rooms I, II** and **III** with 6th-century BC works. Fragments of painted pedimental statues include mythological scenes of Herakles grappling with various monsters, ferocious lions devouring calves, and the more peaceful votive statue of the *Moschophoros*, or Calf-Bearer, portraying a young man carrying a calf on his shoulders (c.570 BC).

Room V houses a pediment from the old Temple of Athena showing part of a battle where the figures of Athena and Zeus against the giants represent the Greek triumph over primitive forces. **Room IV** has recently restored sculptures dating from c.550 BC and **Rooms IV** and **VI** also contain a unique collection of *korai* from c.550–500 BC. These were votive statues of maidens offered to Athena. They represent the development of ancient Greek art – moving from the formal bearing of the *Peplos Kore* to the more natural body movement of the *Kore of Euthydikos* and *Almond-Eyed Kore*. Other representative statues of this later period are the *Mourning Athena*, head of the *Blond Boy* and the *Kritios Boy*.

Rooms VII and **VIII** contain, among other exhibits, a well-preserved *metope* from the south side of the Parthenon

The *Moschophoros* (Calf-Bearer), a sculpture from the Archaic period

showing the battle between the Lapiths and centaurs. The remaining parts of the Parthenon frieze depict the Panathenaic procession, including the chariot and *apobates* (slaves riding the chariot horses), the *thallophoroi* (bearers of olive branches), and a sacrificial cow being led by youths.

Room IX ends the collection with four caryatids from the Erechtheion south porch. They are the only ones on display in Athens and are carefully kept in a temperature-controlled environment.

THE ELGIN MARBLES

These famous sculptures, also called the Parthenon Marbles, are held in the British Museum in London. They were acquired by Lord Elgin in 1801–3 from the occupying Turkish authorities. He sold them to the British nation for £35,000 in 1816. There is great controversy surrounding the Marbles. While some argue that they are more carefully preserved in the British Museum, the Greek government does not accept the legality of the sale and many believe they belong in Athens. A famous supporter of this cause was the Greek actress and politician, Melína Merkoúri, who died in 1994.

The newly arrived Elgin Marbles at the British Museum, in a painting by A Archer

The Parthenon
Ο Παρθενώνας

One of the world's most famous buildings, this temple was begun in 447 BC. It was designed by the architects Kallikrates and Iktinos, primarily to house the 12 m (40 ft) high statue of Athena Parthenos (Maiden), sculpted by Pheidias. Taking nine years to complete, the temple was dedicated to the goddess in 438 BC. Over the centuries, it has been used as a church, a mosque and an arsenal, and has suffered severe damage. Built as an expression of the glory of ancient Athens, it remains the city's emblem to this day.

View of the Parthenon today, from the west

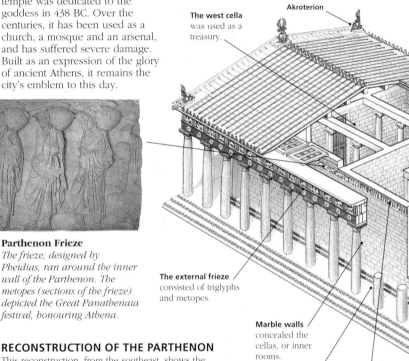

The west cella was used as a treasury.

Akroterion

The external frieze consisted of triglyphs and metopes.

Marble walls concealed the cellas, or inner rooms.

Parthenon Frieze
The frieze, designed by Pheidias, ran around the inner wall of the Parthenon. The metopes (sections of the frieze) depicted the Great Panathenaia festival, honouring Athena.

RECONSTRUCTION OF THE PARTHENON

This reconstruction, from the southeast, shows the Parthenon as it was in the 5th century BC. It was 70 m (230 ft) long and 30 m (100 ft) wide. The entablature of this peripteral temple (with a single row of columns around the edge) was painted in blue, red and gold.

Each column was constructed from fluted drums of marble. The fluting was added once the columns were in place.

The Elgin Marbles *(see p97)* were taken largely from the internal frieze.

Explosion of 1687
During the Venetian siege of the Acropolis, General Francesco Morosini bombarded the Parthenon with cannon-fire. The Turks were using the temple as an arsenal at the time and the ensuing explosion demolished much of it, including the roof, the inner structure and 14 of the outer columns.

Statue of Athena
The huge chryselephantine (ivory and gold) statue of Athena, patron goddess of Athens, was the focus of the Parthenon. No trace of it remains today, but this smaller Roman copy can be seen in the National Archaeological Museum (see pp68–71).

THE ILLUSION OF PERFECTION

Every aspect of the Parthenon was built on a 9:4 ratio to make the temple completely symmetrical. The sculptors also used visual trickery to counteract the laws of perspective. The illustration below is exaggerated to show the techniques they employed.

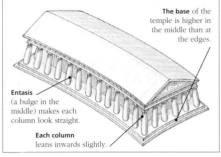

The base of the temple is higher in the middle than at the edges.

Entasis (a bulge in the middle) makes each column look straight.

Each column leans inwards slightly.

The internal columns were in two rows and Doric in style.

The roof was made from Pentelic marble tiles supported on wooden rafters.

Northeast Corner
This corner shows the remains of the pediment sculptures and the vertical carvings of the triglyphs alternating with the faded metope carvings.

The steps curved upwards slightly at the centre to make them appear level from a distance.

Entrance

View of the East Cella
The cella was the inner room of the temple. In the case of the Parthenon, there were two – east and west. The east cella contained the enormous cult statue of Athena and the offerings bestowed upon it. The west cella was the back room, reserved for the priestess.

Around the Acropolis

Throne from the Theatre of Dionysos

The area around the Acropolis was the centre of public life in Athens. In addition to the Agora in the north *(see pp90–91)*, there were the two theatres on the south slope, used for drama festivals in honour of the god Dionysos. Political life was largely centred on the Pnyx and the Areopagos, the hills lying to the west of the Acropolis: the Assembly met on the former and murder trials were heard by a council of ex-magistrates on the latter. Other ancient remains and the Acropolis Study Centre provide a fascinating insight into daily life in ancient Athens.

The remains of the Theatre of Dionysos

⋔ Theatre of He rodes Atticus

This small Roman theatre seats 5,000 spectators and is still in use today *(see p119)*. Built by the Roman consul Herodes Atticus between AD 161 and 174, in memory of his wife, the shape was hollowed out of the rocks on the southern slope of the Acropolis. The semicircular orchestra in front of the stage was repaved with alternating blue and white marble slabs in the 1950s. Behind the stage, its distinctive colonnade once contained statues of the nine Muses. The whole theatre was originally enclosed by a cedarwood roof that gave better acoustics and allowed for all-weather performances.

⋔ Theatre of Dionysos

D. Areopagitou, Makrygiánni. **Tel** 210 322 4625. ☐ Apr–Oct: 8am–7pm; Nov–Mar: 8:30am–2:30pm daily

Cut into the southern cliff face of the Acropolis, the Theatre of Dionysos is the birthplace of Greek tragedy, and was the first theatre built of stone. Aeschylus, Sophocles,

Euripides and Aristophanes all had their plays performed here, during the dramatic contests of the annual City Dionysia festival, when it was little more than a humble wood-and-earth affair. The theatre was rebuilt in stone by the Athenian statesman Lykourgos between 342–326 BC, but the ruins that can be seen today are in part those of a much bigger structure, built by the Romans, which could seat 17,000. They used it as a gladiatorial arena, and

added a marble balustrade with metal railings to protect spectators. In the 1st century AD, during Emperor Nero's reign, the orchestra was given its marble flooring, and in the 2nd century AD the front of the stage was decorated with reliefs showing Dionysos's life. Above the theatre there is a cave sacred to the goddess Artemis. This was converted into a chapel in the Byzantine era, dedicated to **Panagía i Spiliótissa** (Our Lady of the Cave), and was the place where mothers brought their sick children. Two large Corinthian columns nearby are the remains of choregic monuments erected to celebrate the benefactor's team winning a drama festival. The Sanctuary of Asklepios to the west, founded in 420 BC, was dedicated to the god of healing. Worshippers seeking a cure had to take part in purification rites before they could enter the temple precincts.

🗔 Acropolis Study Centre

Makrygiánni 2–4, Makrygiánni. **Tel** 210 923 9381. ☐ 10am–6pm daily.

This handsome Neo-Classical building functions as a research centre and storehouse of historical information on the Acropolis. The ground floor is dedicated to an exhibition introducing the New Acropolis Museum, a stunning glass structure designed by Swiss architect Bernard Tschumi. The new museum is under construction at the southern base of the Acropolis and is scheduled to be completed in 2007, though no opening date has been announced.

Interior of the Panagía Spiliótissa chapel, above the Theatre of Dionysos

Areopagos Hill

There is little left to see on this low hill today, apart from the rough-hewn, slippery steps and what are thought to be seats on its summit. The Areopagos was used by the Persians and Turks during their attacks on the Acropolis citadel, and played an important role as the home of the Supreme Judicial Court in the Classical period. It takes its name, meaning the "Hill of Ares", from a mythological trial that took place here when the god Ares was acquitted of murdering the son of Poseidon. The nearby **Cave of the Furies** inspired the playwright Aeschylus *(see p57)* to set Orestes trial here in his play *Eumenides* (The Furies). The hill also achieved renown in AD 51, when St Paul delivered his sermon "On an unknown God" and gained his first convert, Dionysios the Areopagite, who subsequently became the patron saint of Athens.

Cross from Agios Dimítrios church

Pnyx Hill

If Athens is the cradle of democracy, Pnyx Hill is its exact birthplace. During the 4th- and 5th-century BC the *Ekklesia* (citizens' assembly) met here to discuss and vote upon all but the most important matters of state, until it lost its powers during Roman rule. In its heyday, 6,000 Athenians gathered 40 times a year to listen to speeches and take vital political decisions. Themistokles, Perikles and Demosthenes all spoke from the *bema* (speaker's platform) that is still visible today. Carved out of the rock face, it formed the top step of a platform that doubled as a primitive altar to the god Zeus. There are also the remains of the huge retaining wall which was built

to support the semicircular terraces that placed citizens on a level with the speakers. It completely surrounded the auditorium which was 110 m (358 ft) high.

Agios Dimítrios

Dionysiou Areopagitou, south slope of Acropolis. ○ daily. 🛇 except Sun.

This Byzantine church is often called Agios Dimítrios Loumpardiáris, after an incident in 1656. The Turkish *disdar* (commander) at the time, Yusuf Aga, laid plans to fire a huge cannon called Loumpárda, situated by the Propylaia *(see p96)*, at worshippers in the church as they celebrated the feast day of Agios Dimítrios. However, the night before the feast, lightning struck the Propylaia, miraculously killing the commander and his family.

Filopáppos Hill

The highest summit in the south of Athens, at 147 m (482 ft), offers spectacular views of the Acropolis. It has always played a decisive defensive role in Athens' history – the general Demetrios Poliorketes built an important fort here overlooking the strategic Piraeus road in 294 BC, and Francesco Morosini bombarded the Acropolis from here in 1687. Popularly called Filopáppos

The Asteroskopeíon on the Hill of the Nymphs

Hill after a monument still on its summit, it was also known to the ancient Greeks as the Hill of Muses or the Mouseion, because the tomb of Musaeus, a disciple of Orpheus, was traditionally held to be located here.

Built between AD 114–16, the Monument of Philopappus was raised by the Athenians in honour of Caius Julius Antiochus Philopappus, a Roman consul and philhellene. Its unusual concave marble façade, 12 m (40 ft) high, contains niches with statues of Philopappus and his grandfather, Antiochus IV. A frieze around the monument depicts the arrival of Philopappus by chariot for his inauguration as Roman consul in AD 100.

Hill of the Nymphs

This 103-m (340-ft) high tree-clad hill takes its name from dedications found carved on rocks in today's Observatory Garden. The Asteroskopeíon (Observatory), built in 1842 by the Danish architect Theophil Hansen, with funds from philanthropist Baron Sína, occupies the site of a sanctuary to nymphs associated with childbirth. The modern church of Agía Marína nearby has similar associations of childbirth; pregnant women used to slide effortlessly down a smooth rock near the church, in the hope of an equally easy labour.

The Monument of Philopappus AD 114–116

Street-by-Street: Central Pláka

Plaka is the historic heart of Athens. Even though only a few houses date back further than the Ottoman period, it remains the oldest continuously inhabited area of the city. One explanation of its name comes from the word *pliaka* (old), which was used to describe the area by Albanian soldiers in the service of the Turks who settled here in the 16th century. Despite the crowds of tourists and the many Athenians, who come to eat in the tavernas or browse in antique shops, it still retains the feel of a residential neighbourhood.

Mitrópoli
Athens' cathedral was built in the second half of the 19th century 🔟

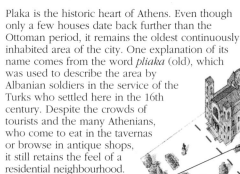

Thoukydídou is named after the historian Thucydides (c.460–400 BC).

★ Panagía Gorgoepíkoös
This tiny 12th-century church, also known as the Little Cathedral, has some beautiful carvings ⓫

Museum of Greek Popular Musical Instruments
A range of folk instruments is displayed in this museum which was opened in 1991 ❿

Monastiráki
(see pp84–5)

Acropolis
(see pp94–101)

University of Athens Museum
Occupying the university's original home, this museum has memorabilia from the university's early days, including these old medical artifacts ❾

Ancient Agora
(see pp90–1)

Kanellópoulos Museum
Privately owned, this museum has exquisite works of art from all areas of the Hellenic world ❽

Plateía Syntágmatos
(see p112)

Greek Folk Art Museum
Offering the best of Greek folk art, this has everything from shadow puppets to terracotta ornaments 16

LOCATOR MAP
See Street Finder maps 5–6

0 metres 50
0 yards 50

NIKODIMOU

YPEREIDOU

AACHOU

THOUKYDIDOU

KEKROPS

CHATZIMICHALI

SOTIROS

KYDATHINAION

ADRIANOU

ADRIANOU

TRIPODON

THESPIDOS

Agios Nikólaos Ragavás
This 11th-century, Byzantine chapel is a popular location for weddings 13

Plateía Lysikrátous
Named after the monument in its centre, this square was a favourite haunt of the poet Byron 15

KEY
– – – Suggested route

STAR SIGHT
★ Panagía Gorgoepíkoös

Anafiótika
The whitewashed houses and winding streets resembling a Cycladic village were built in the 19th century by settlers from the island of Anáfi 14

Rempétika musicians, Museum of Greek Popular Musical Instruments

Kanellópoulos Museum [8]
Μουσείο Κανελλοπούλου

Corner of Theorías & Pános 12, Pláka. **Map** 6 D2. *Tel* 210 321 2313. M *Monastiráki.* ☐ 8:30am–3pm Tue–Sun, noon–3pm Good Fri. ◑ 1 Jan, 25 Mar, Easter Sun, 25, 26 Dec. ⚑ �◎

In an immaculately restored Neo-Classical town house, this museum contains what was the private collection of wealthy collectors Pávlos and Alexándra Kanellópoulos. A varied collection of artifacts from all over the Hellenistic world, the three floors of exhibits include a selection of coins, 6th-century BC helmets, 5th-century BC gold Persian jewellery and Attic vases. There are also Cycladic figurines, some unusual terracotta figures

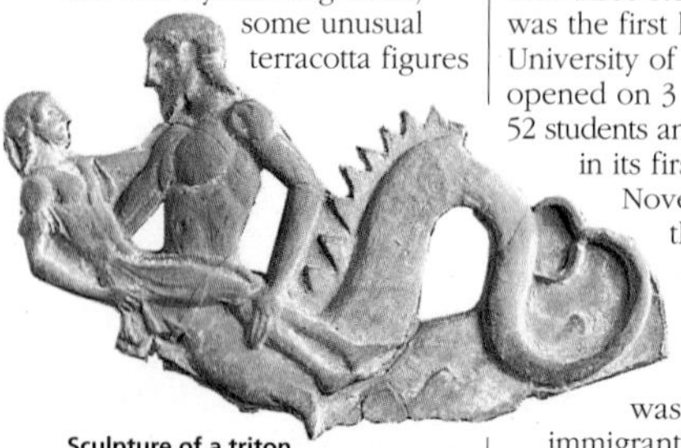

Sculpture of a triton from the Kanellópoulos Museum

of actors in their theatrical masks and a fine 2nd-century AD El Faiyûm portrait of a woman.

A huge block of stone that fell from the walls of the Acropolis, so heavy that the museum was built around it, can still be seen as an exhibit on the ground floor.

University of Athens Museum [9]
Μουσείο Ιστορίας του Πανεπιστημίου Αθηνών

Thólou 5, Pláka. **Map** 6 E2. *Tel* 210 368 9500. M *Monastiráki.* ☐ Apr–Oct: 5–9pm Mon & Wed, 9:30am–2:30pm Tue, Thu & Fri; Nov–Mar: 9:30am–2:30pm Mon–Fri. ◑ main public hols.

This three-storey house was the first home of the University of Athens. It opened on 3 May 1837 with 52 students and 33 professors in its first year. In November 1841 the University moved to its new quarters and from 1922 the building was home to many immigrant families. While they were there, a taverna

known as the "Old University" was opened on the ground floor.

In 1963 the building was declared a National Monument. Later reacquired by the university, the old building was opened as a museum in 1974. Today, the "Old University", as it is still known, has an eclectic collection of memorabilia such as corporeal body maps, anatomical models, scientific instruments and medicine jars. There is also a display about the university's past professors and students.

Museum of Greek Popular Musical Instruments [10]
Μουσείο Ελληνικών Λαϊκών Μουσικών Οργάνων

Diogénous 1–3, Aérides Square. **Map** 6 D1. *Tel* 210 325 0198. M *Monastiráki.* ☐ 10am–2pm Tue–Sun, noon–6pm Wed. ◑ 17 Nov, main public hols.

Cretan musicologist Phoebus Anogianákis donated over 1,200 musical instruments from his impressive collection to the Greek State in 1978. In 1991 this study centre and museum was opened, devoted to the history of popular Greek music, including Anogianákis's collection. The museum traces the development of different styles of island music and the arrival of *rempétika* (Greek "blues") from Smyrna in 1922.

Instruments from all over Greece are displayed on the three floors, with recordings and headphones available at every exhibit. The basement contains a selection of church and livestock bells, as well as water whistles, wooden clappers and flutes, which are sold during pre-Lenten carnival celebrations. The ground floor has wind instruments on display including *tsampoúna*, bagpipes made from goatskin. On the first floor, there is a selection of string instruments, such as the bouzouki, the *santoúri* and the Cretan *lýra*. There is also a beautiful 19th-century ivory and tortoiseshell lute.

Panagía Gorgoepíkoös ⓫
Παναγία η Γοργοεπήκοöς

VISITORS' CHECKLIST

Plateia Mitropóleos, Pláka.
Map 6 E1. Ⓜ *Monastiráki.*
◯ *7am–7pm daily.* ✚

Bas-relief from south façade

This domed cruciform church is built entirely from Pentelic marble, now weathered to a rich corn-coloured hue. Dating from the 12th century, it measures only 7.5 m (25 ft) long by 12 m (40 ft) wide. The size of the church is in scale with Athens when it was just a village in the 12th century. Adorned with friezes and bas-reliefs taken from earlier buildings, the exterior mixes the Classical and Byzantine styles. Although dedicated to Panagía Gorgoepíkoös (the Madonna who Swiftly Hears) and Agios EleQthérios (the saint who protects women in childbirth), it is often affectionately known as the Mikrí Mitrópoli (Little Cathedral).

The south façade of the church, dwarfed by the giant Mitrópoli

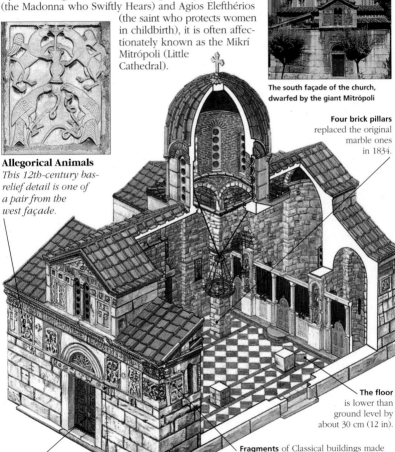

Allegorical Animals
This 12th-century bas-relief detail is one of a pair from the west façade.

Four brick pillars replaced the original marble ones in 1834.

The floor is lower than ground level by about 30 cm (12 in).

Main entrance

Fragments of Classical buildings made from Pentelic marble were combined with new Byzantine sections in the style of a Classical frieze.

Lintel Frieze
This relief depicting the months of the year dates from the 4th century BC. The central cross was added in the 12th century.

Modern mosaics above the main entrance to Athens' cathedral, Mitrópoli

Mitrópoli
Μητρόπολη

Plateía Mitropóleos, Pláka. **Map** 6 E1.
Tel 210 322 1308. M *Monastiráki.*
⬚ *7am–7pm daily.*

Work began in 1840 on this huge cathedral, using marble from 72 demolished churches for its walls. The cornerstone was laid in a ceremony by King Otto and Queen Amalía on Christmas Day 1842. It took another 20 years to finish the building, using three different architects (François Boulanger, Theophil Hansen and Dimítrios Zézos) which may account for its slightly ungainly appearance. On 21 May 1862, it was formally dedicated to Evangelismós Theotókou (the Annunciation of the Virgin) by the king and queen. At 40 m (130 ft) long, 20 m (65 ft) wide and 24 m (80 ft) high, it is the largest church in Athens.

The cathedral is the official seat of the Bishop of Athens, and remains a popular city landmark that has been used for ceremonial events from the coronations of kings to the weddings and funerals of the rich and famous.

Inside, there are the tombs of two saints murdered by the Ottoman Turks: Agía Filothéi and Gregory V. The bones of Agía Filothéi, who died in 1589, are still visible in a silver reliquary. Her charitable works included the ransoming of Greek women enslaved in Turkish harems. Gregory V, Patriarch of Constantinople, was hanged and thrown into the Bosphorus in 1821. His body was rescued by Greek sailors and taken to Odessa. It was eventually returned to Athens by Black Sea (Pontic) Greeks 50 years later.

Agios Nikólaos Ragavás
γγιος Νικόλαος ο Ραγυαβάς

Corner of Prytaneíou & Epichármou, Pláka. **Map** 6 E2. *Tel* 210 322 8193.
M *Monastiráki.* ⬚ *1, 2, 4, 5, 9, 10, 11, 12, 15, 18.* ⬚ *8am–noon, 5–8pm daily.* ♿ *limited.*

This typical 11th-century Byzantine church, rebuilt in the 18th century and restored to some of its former glory in the late 1970s, incorporates marble columns and other remains of ancient buildings in its external walls. It is one of the favourite parish churches of Pláka, frequently used for colourful Greek weddings which spill out on to the street at weekends. It was the first church in Athens to have a bell after the War of Independence (1821), and the first to ring out after the city's liberation from the Germans on 12 October 1944.

Anafiótika
Αναφιώτικα

Map 6 D2. M *Monastiráki.*

Nestling beneath the northern slopes of the Acropolis, this area is one of the oldest settlements in Athens. Today, its white-washed houses, cramped streets, lazy cats and pots of

Looking down on Agios Nikólaos Ragavás church from Anafiótika

◁ **View from Anafiótika towards the Ancient Agora**

basil on windowsills still give it the atmosphere of a typical Cycladic village. Its first residents were refugees from the Peloponnesian War *(see p30)*. By 1841, it had been colonized by workmen from Anáfi, in the Cyclades, who eventually gave the area its name. Part of the influx of island craftsmen, who helped to construct the new city following Independence, ignored an 1834 decree declaring the area an archaeological zone, and completed their houses overnight, installing their families by morning. By Ottoman law, this meant the authorities were powerless to knock the new houses down.

The area is bounded by two 17th-century churches: Agios Geórgios tou Vráchou to the east, which has a tiny courtyard filled with flowers, and Agios Symeón to the west, which contains a copy of a miraculous icon, originally brought from Anáfi.

Akrokérama, or terracotta sphinxes, on a roof in Anafiótika

Plateía Lysikrátous ⓯
Πλατεία Λύσικράτους

Lysikrátous, Sélley & Epimenídou, Pláka. **Map** 6 E2. 🚊 *1, 5, 9, 18.*

Situated in the east of the Pláka district, this square is named after the monument of Lysikrates that dominates it. Despite Lord Elgin's attempts to remove it to England, the elegant structure is the city's only intact choregic monument. These monuments were built to commemorate the victors at the annual choral and dramatic festival at the Theatre of Dionysos *(see p100)*. They take their name from the rich sponsor *(choregos)* who produced the winning team. Built in 334 BC, this is the earliest known example where Corinthian

capitals are used externally. Six columns rise in a circle to a marble dome, decorated with an elegant finial of acanthus leaves which supported the winner's bronze trophy. It bears the inscription "Lysikrates of Kikynna, son of Lysitheides, was choregos; the tribe of Akamantis won the victory with a chorus of boys; Theon played the flute; Lysiades, an Athenian, trained the chorus; Evainetos was archon". The Athenians elected nine magistrates known as archons each year, and referred to the year by the name of one of them, the "eponymous archon." A frieze above this inscription, probably the theme of the winners' performance, depicts a battle between Dionysos, the god of theatre, and Tyrrhenian pirates. Surrounded by satyrs, the god transforms them into dolphins and their ship's mast into a sea serpent.

Capuchin friars converted the monument into a library. Grand tour travellers, such as Chateaubriand (1768–1848) and Byron *(see p149)*, stayed at their convent, which was founded on the site in 1669.

The monument of Lysikrates, named after the *choregos* of the winning team of actors

Byron was inspired while staying there and wrote some of his poem, *Childe Harold*, sitting in the monument during his final visit to Athens in 1810.

Not far from the monument is the beautifully restored 11th–century Byzantine church of Agía Aikateríni (St Catherine). In 1767 it was given to the monastery of St Catherine of Mount Sinai. It was renovated but in 1882 the monastery was forced to exchange it for land elsewhere and it became a local parish church.

ICON PAINTERS IN PLAKA

Pláka is littered with small artists' studios where icons are still painted using traditional methods. The best are situated just south of Plateía Mitropóleos, among the ecclesiastical shops selling vestments and liturgical objects, on Agías

Filothéis and Apóllonos streets. In some workshops, painters still use the Byzantine method of painting in egg-based tempera on specially treated wood. Customers of all religions can order the saint of their choice in a variety of different sizes. A medium-sized icon depicting a single saint, 25 cm by 15 cm (10 in by 6 in) and copied from a photograph, takes about one day to complete.

Ornate embroidery from Ioánnina, Epirus, on display in the Greek Folk Art Museum

Greek Folk Art Museum 🔟
Μουσείο Ελληνικής Λαϊκής Τέχνης

Kydathinaíon 17, Pláka. **Map** 6 E2.
Tel 210 321 3018. 🚍 2, 4, 9, 10, 11, 12, 15. 🚊 1, 5. ⏱ 10am–2pm Tue–Sun. ⬤ main public hols. 📷 ♿ limited. 📷

Greek folk art, including some unrivalled regional embroidery and costumes from the mainland and Aegean islands, fills five floors in this fascinating museum. The collection also covers the renaissance of decorative crafts in the 18th and 19th centuries, to reveal a rich heritage of traditional techniques in skills such as weaving, woodcarving and metalwork.

The ground floor has an extensive collection of fine embroidery work, showing a wide range of techniques.

Displays on the mezzanine floor include ceramics, metalwork and woodcarving. The ceramics range from architectural works, such as chimneys, to decorative or practical pieces such as household pots. Made from terracotta

Decorative plate
from Rhodes

and faïence, they include both glazed and unglazed pieces. The metalwork on view includes examples made from copper, bronze, iron, steel and pewter. Many are covered with intricate decoration. The woodcarving products are equally impressive in their decoration, often being inlaid with mother-of-pearl, ivory or silver. The wood used varies widely, from walnut to fragrant cedar and wild olive. Also on the mezzanine are disguise costumes. Their origin is thought to be in the ancient Greek drama festivals in honour of Dionysos which made use of overtly expressive masks. The puppets from the Karagkiózis theatre *(see p151)* amused the audience by satirizing topical political and social life.

The first floor houses popular paintings, including works by Theófilos Chatzimichaïl *(see p218)*. There is an excellent collection of silverware on the second floor of the museum, with displays of various ecclesiastical items such as chalices and crosses, as well as secular pieces, such as ornate weaponry and delicate jewellery. Examples of traditional weaving and stone-carving can be found on the third floor. The range of materials used for weaving includes lamb's wool, goat's hair, silk and plant fibres. Traditional costumes are also on show on this floor. The decorations and design, which are frequently elaborate, vary according to the geographical region. Costumes from many different areas are on display.

Jewish Museum of Greece 🔟
Εβραϊκό Μουσείο της Ελλάδας

Níkis 39, S'yntagma. **Map** 6 F2.
Tel 210 322 5582. Ⓜ Sýntagma. 🚍 1, 2, 4, 5, 9, 10, 11, 12, 15, 18. ⏱ 9am–2:30pm Mon–Fri, 10am–2pm Sun. ⬤ Main public hols & Jewish festivals. ♿ 📷 📷

This small museum traces the history of Greece's Jewish communities which date back to the 3rd century BC. The exhibits present a revealing portrait of the Sephardic Jews, who fled Spain and Portugal in the 15th century, to settle throughout Greece in the religiously tolerant years of the Ottoman Empire.

Among the examples of traditional costumes and religious ceremonial instruments, one item of particular interest is the reconstruction of the *ehal*. This is the ark containing the Torah from the Pátra synagogue, which dates from the 1920s. It was rescued by Nikólaos Stavroulákis, founder of the museum, who has also written several books about the Greek Jews, on sale in the museum bookshop.

Moving displays of documentation record the German occupation of Greece during World War II when 87 per cent of the Jewish population here was wiped out. Over 45,000 Greeks from Thessaloníki alone were sent to Auschwitz and other concentration camps during a period of five months in 1943.

Reconstruction of the ark from Pátra

Hadrian's Arch, next to the Temple of Olympian Zeus

Temple of Olympian Zeus 🔞
Ναός του Ολυμπίου Διός

Corner of Amalías & Vasilíssis Olgas,
Pláka. **Map** 6 F3. *Tel 210 922 6330.*
🚃 2, 4, 11. ⏰ Apr–Oct: 8:30am–
7pm daily; Nov–Mar: 8:30am–3pm
daily. 🔵 main public hols. 🎟 (free
Sun, Nov–Mar) 📷 ♿ limited.

The temple of Olympian Zeus
is the largest in Greece,
exceeding even the Parthenon
in size. Work began on this
vast edifice in the 6th century
BC, in the reign of the tyrant
Peisistratos, who allegedly
initiated the building work to
gain public favour. Although
there were several attempts
over many years to finish the
temple, it was not completed
until 650 years later.

The Roman Emperor
Hadrian dedicated the temple
to Zeus Olympios during the
Panhellenic festival of AD
132, on his second visit to
Athens. He also set up a gold
and ivory inlaid statue of the
god inside the temple, a copy
of the original by Pheidias at
Olympia *(see pp170–72)*.
Next to it he placed a huge
statue of himself. Both these
statues have since been lost.

Only 15 of the original 104
Corinthian columns remain,
each 17 m (56 ft) high – but
enough to give a sense of the
enormous size of this temple,
which would have been
approximately 96 m (315 ft)
long and 40 m (130 ft)
wide.

Corinthian capitals were added
to the simple Doric columns by
a Roman architect in 174 BC.

The temple is situated next
to Hadrian's Arch, built in AD
131. It was positioned deliber-
ately to mark the boundary
between the ancient city and
the new Athens of Hadrian.

**The Russian Church of
the Holy Trinity**

Russian Church of the Holy Trinity 🔞
Ρωσική εκκλησία
Αγίας Τριάδας

Filellínon 21, Pláka. **Map** 6 F2.
Tel 210 323 1090. 🚃 1, 2, 4, 5, 9,
10, 11, 12, 15, 18. ⏰ 7:30–10am
Mon–Fri, 7–11am Sat & Sun.
🔵 main public hols. ♿ limited.

Still in use by the Russian
community, this was once
the largest church in the
city. Built in 1031 by
the Lykodímou family (also
called Nikodímou), it was
ruined by an earthquake in
1701. In 1780 the Turkish
voivode (governor), Hadji Ali
Haseki, partly demolished
the church to use its materials
for the defensive wall that
he built around the city.
During the siege of the city
in 1827, it received more
damage from Greek shells
fired from the Acropolis.

The church remained
derelict until the Russian
government restored it 20
years later. It was then reconsecrated as the Church
of the Holy Trinity.

A large cruciform building,
its most unusual feature is a
wide dome, 10 m (33 ft) in
diameter. Its interior was
decorated by the Bavarian
painter Ludwig Thiersch.
The separate belltower
also dates from the 19th
century, its bell a gift
from Tsar Alexander II.

The remaining Corinthian columns of the Temple of Olympian Zeus

The Tomb of the Unknown Soldier in Plateía Syntágmatos

Plateía Syntágmatos ❷⓪
Πλατεία Σύνταγματος

S'yntagma. **Map** 6 F1. 🚍 *1, 5, 9, 10, 12, 15, 18.* Ⓜ *Sýntagma.*

This square (also known as Sýntagma Square) is home to the Greek parliament, in the Voulí building, and the Tomb of the Unknown Soldier, decorated with an evocative relief depicting a dying Greek hoplite warrior. Unveiled on 25 March 1932 (National Independence Day), the tomb is flanked by texts from Perikles's famous funeral oration. The other walls that enclose the square are covered in bronze shields celebrating military victories since 1821.

The National Guard (*évzones*) are on continuous patrol in front of the tomb, dressed in their famous uniform of kilt and pom-pom clogs. They are best seen at the changing of the guard, every Sunday at 11am.

National Gardens ❷①
Εθνικός Κήπος

Borders Vasilíssis Sofías, Iródou Attikoú, Vasilíssis Olgas & Vasilíssis Amalías, Sýntagma. **Map** 7 A1. Ⓜ *Sýntagma.* 🚍 *1, 3, 5, 7, 8, 10, 13, 18.* ◌ *dawn–dusk.* **Botanical Museum, zoo, cafés** ◌ *7:30am–3pm daily.*

Behind the Vouli parliament-building, this 16-ha (40-acre) park, cherished by all Athenians and formerly known as the "Royal Gardens", was renamed the National Gardens by decree in 1923. Queen Amalía ordered the creation of the park in the 1840s; she even used the fledgling Greek Navy to bring 15,000 seedlings from around the world. The gardens were landscaped by the Prussian horticulturalist Friedrich Schmidt, who travelled the world in search of rare plants.

Although the gardens have lost much of their original grandeur, they remain one of the most peaceful spots in the city. Shady paths meander past small squares, park benches and ponds filled with goldfish. A huge feral cat population is also resident in the park. Remains of Roman mosaics excavated in the park and an old aqueduct add atmosphere. Modern sculptures of writers, such as Dionýsios Solomós, Aristotélis Valaorítis and Jean Moreas, can be found throughout the park. There is also a small **Botanical Museum** to visit, a ramshackle zoo, and cafés. South of the park lies the **Záppeion**

exhibition hall, an impressive building in use today as a conference centre. It was donated by Evángelos and Konstantínos Záppas, cousins who made their fortunes in Romania. Built by Theophil Hansen, architect of the Athens Academy (*see p81*), between 1874 and 1888, it also has its own gardens. The elegant café next door to the Záppeion is a pleasant place to relax and refresh after a walk around these charming, peaceful gardens.

The tranquil National Gardens

Presidential Palace ❷②
Προεδρικό Μέγαρο

Iródou Attikoú, Sýntagma. **Map** 7 A2. Ⓜ *Sýntagma.* 🚍 *3, 7, 8, 13.* ◐ *to the public.*

This former royal palace was designed and built by Ernst Ziller (*see p81*) in c.1878. It was occupied by the Greek Royal Family from 1890 until the hasty departure of King Constantine in 1967. It is still guarded by the *évzones* whose barracks are at the top of the street. After the abolition of the monarchy, it became the official residence of the President of Greece and he still uses it today when hosting dignitaries. Its well-maintained gardens can just be seen through the iron railings.

Vouli parliament building in Plateía Sýntagmatos, guarded by *évzones*

For hotels and restaurants in this region see pp264–7 and pp284–8

Kallimármaro Stadium ㉓

Καλλιμάρμαρο Στάδιο

Archimídous 16, Pagkráti. **Map** 7 B3.
Tel *210 752 6386.* 🚎 *3, 4, 11.*
🕐 *8am–sunset daily.* ♿

This huge marble structure set in a small valley by Ardittós Hill occupies the exact site of the original Panathenaic Stadium built by Lykourgos in 330–329 BC. It was first reconstructed for gladiatorial contests during Hadrian's reign (AD 117–138), then rebuilt in white marble by the wealthy Roman bene-factor Herodes Atticus for the Panathenaic Games in AD 144. Neglected for many years, its marble was gradually quarried for use in new buildings or burnt down to make lime.

In 1895 Geórgios Avérof gave four million drachmas in gold for the restoration of the stadium in time for the start of the first modern Olympic Games on 5 April 1896. Desi-gned by Anastásios Metaxás, the present structure is a faith-ful replica of Herodes Atticus's

Some of the ornate tombs in the First Cemetery of Athens

stadium, as described in the *Guide to Greece* by Pausanias *(see p56).* Built in white Pen-telic marble, it is 204 m (669 ft) long and 83 m (272 ft) wide and seats up to 60,000. Be-tween 1869 and 1879 architect Ernst Ziller excavated the site. His finds included a double-headed statue of Apollo and Dionysos, one of many used to divide the stadium's running track down its length. The sta-tue is on show in the National Archaeological Museum *(see pp68–71).* During the 2004 Olympics, Kallimármaro hosted the Marathon finish.

First Cemetery of Athens ㉔

Πρώτο Νεκροταφείο Αθηνών

Entrance in Anapáfseos, Méts.
Map 7 A4. **Tel** *210 923 6118.* 🚎 *2, 4.* 🕐 *7am–sunset daily.* ♿ *limited.*

Athens' municipal cemetery, which is not to be confused with the Kerameikós, the ancient cemetery *(see p88–9),* is a peaceful place, filled with pine and olive trees and the scent of incense burn-ing at the well-kept tombs.

Fine examples of 19th-century funerary art range from the flamboyance of some of the marble mauso-leums to the simplicity of the *belle époque Kimoméni* or *Sleeping Girl (see p42).* Created by Giannoúlis Chalepás, this beautiful tomb is found to the right of the main cemetery avenue where many of Greece's foremost families are buried.

Among the notable 19th– and 20th-century figures with tombs here are Theódoros Kolokotrónis *(see p80),* British philhellene historian George Finlay (1799–1875), German archaeologist Heinrich Schliemann *(see p180),* the Nobel prize-winning poet Giórgos Seféris (1900–71) and the actress and politician Melína Merkoúri (1922–94).

In addition to the large number of tombs for famous people that are buried here, the cemetery contains a moving, single memorial to the 40,000 Athenians who perished through starvation during World War II.

A lone athlete exercising in the vast Kallimármaro Stadium

SHOPPING IN ATHENS

Shopping in Athens offers many delights. There are open-air street markets, quiet arcades, traditional arts and crafts shops, and designer fashion boutiques to rival Paris and New York. Most Athenians go to the triangle which is formed by Omónoia, Sýntagma and Monastiráki squares to buy everyday household items, clothes and shoes. For leather goods, bargain hunters should head for Mitropóleos, Ermoú, Aiólou and nearby streets. Along the smarter Stadíou and Panepistimíou, there are world-class jewellers and large clothing stores. The maze of arcades in the centre also houses smart leather-goods shops, booksellers, cafés and *ouzerís*.

The most stylish shopping is to be found in Kolonáki where some of the city's most expensive art galleries and antique shops are clustered among the foreign and Greek designer outlets selling the latest fashions. Around Athinás, Monastiráki and Pláka there is an eclectic mix of aromatic herb and spice stores, religious retailers selling icons and church candlesticks, second-hand bookshops with rare posters and prints, and catering stores packed with household goods such as pots and pans.

Colourful shadow puppet

OPENING HOURS

Shops generally open from 8am–2pm or 9am–3pm, Monday to Saturday. On Tuesdays, Thursdays and Fridays there is late shopping from 5:30–9pm. The exceptions are department stores, tourist shops, supermarkets, florists and *zacharoplasteía* (cake shops) which often open for longer. Many shops also close every year throughout August, the time when many Greeks take their holidays.

DEPARTMENT STORES AND SUPERMARKETS

The main stores are **Attica** and **Notos Galleries**. They stock a wide range of beauty

Shoppers in Adrianoú at the centre of Monastiráki flea market

Lambrópoulous, one of the largest department stores in Athens

products, clothes, gifts, and household goods. Attica is not as big as Notos Galleries but it is more exclusive, with departments for clothes, cosmetics and gifts. **Carrefour** is a supermarket chain as are **AB Vassilópoulos** and **Champion–Marinópoulos**, both located in the city centre.

MARKETS

Athens is famous for its flea-markets. **Monastiráki** market starts early in the morning every Sunday, when dealers set out their wares along Adrianoú and neighbouring streets. Hawkers of *salépi* (a drink made from sesame seeds) and gypsy clarinet players weave through the crowds.

The commercial tourist and antique shops of Pandrósou and Ifaístou, which collectively refer to themselves as "Monastiráki Flea Market", are open every day. Friday, Saturday and Sunday mornings are the best times to visit Plateía Avissynías, when dealers arrive with piles of bric-a-brac.

For food, the **Central Market** is excellent, as are the popular *laïkés agorés* (street markets) selling fruit and vegetables, which occur daily in different areas. Centrally located *laïkés agorés* include one on **Xenokrátous** in Kolonáki which takes place each Friday.

Greeks buy in bulk and stallholders will find it strange if you try to buy very small quantities of things. It is not really acceptable to buy less than half a kilo (1lb) of a fruit or vegetable. In most cases, you will be given a bag to serve yourself – do not be afraid to touch, smell and even taste.

ART AND ANTIQUES

As authentic Greek antiques become increasingly hard to find, many shops are forced to import furniture, glassware and porcelain from around the globe. Fortunately, however, there are still reasonable buys in old Greek jewellery, brass and copperware, carpets and embroidery, engravings and prints. Some can be found at **Antiqua**, just off Plateía Syntágmatos. Kolonáki is a prime area for small, exclusive stores around Sólonos, Skoufá and their side streets. Try the **Athens Design Centre** for bowls, platters and vases painted in bright colours, and **Serafetinídis** for excellent antique kilims and carpets. Kolonáki is also the art centre with well-established galleries selling paintings and prints. The **Zoumpouláki Galleries** specialize in art and antiques.

Monastiráki also has many antique shops. Look out for **Giórgos Goútis** – these are two stores selling 19th-century jewellery and costumes. Try **Iákovos Serapian** for popular art and glassware and **Nikólaos Pashalidis** for copperware. **Martínos** has some beautiful, ornate icons and silverware.

Antique jewellery and ornaments in Giórgos Goútis

TRADITIONAL FOLK ART AND CRAFTS

Affordable popular folk art, crafts and souvenirs are plentiful in Monastiráki and Pláka. There are innumerable stores filled with ecclesiastical ephemera and cramped icon painters' studios. Many shops stock elegant wood carvings, rustic painted wooden trays and richly coloured *flokáti* rugs *(see p209)*. **Amorgós** is packed with fine wood

The famous shoemaker and poet Stávros Melissinós

carvings and puppets as seen in the Karagkiózis theatre in Maroúsi *(see p151)*. Among the more unusual shops offering unique services is **Stávros Melissinós** in Psyrrí. This self-styled poet sandal-maker makes a wide variety of sturdy sandals and leather goods and is famous for handing out translations of his work as a parting gift.

The **National Welfare Organization** offers an excellent selection of different goods including tapestries, rugs and needlepoint cushions. Beautiful carved shepherds' crooks from Epirus as well as a large variety of finely crafted ceramics can be found at the fascinating **Centre of Hellenic Tradition**.

JEWELLERY

Athens is justly famed for its jewellery stores. There is no shortage in Monastiráki and Pláka, which is full of small shops selling gold and silver. But the best known are to be found in Voukourestíou, which is packed with such exclusive jewellers as **Anagnostópoulos**. Window displays also dazzle at the designer of world class fame, **Zolótas**, whose own pieces copy museum treasures. Another famous name is that of the designer Ilías Lalaoúnis, whose collections, inspired by Classical and other archaeological

sources, such as the gold of Mycenae, are eagerly sought by the rich and famous. At the **Ilías Lalaoúnis Jewellery Museum** over 3,000 of his designs are exhibited, and there is also a workshop where you can watch the craftsmen demon-strate the skills of the goldsmith and buy some of the jewellery.

MUSEUM COPIES

Museum shops provide some of the better buys in the city. Well-crafted, mostly tasteful copies draw on the wide range of ancient and Byzantine Greek art. They come in all shapes and sizes, from a life-size Classical statue to a simple Cycladic marble bowl. Many fine reproductions of the exhibits in the **Benáki Museum** *(see pp78–9)* can be bought from a collection of silverware, ceramics, embroidery and jewellery in the museum shop.

The **Museum of Cycladic Art** *(see pp74–5)* has some fine Tanagran and Cycladic figurines, bowls and vases for sale. There is a large selection of reproduction statues and pottery at the **National Archaeological Museum** *(see pp68–71)* souvenir shop. Apart from the museums, the Plaka shop **Orféas** offers good quality marble and pottery copies of Classical Greek works as well as glittering Byzantine icons.

Display of red- and black-figure reproduction vases for sale

Periptero in Kolonáki selling English and Greek newspapers

BOOKS, NEWSPAPERS AND MAGAZINES

All the *periptera* (kiosks) in the city centre sell foreign newspapers and magazines. English publications include the weekly *Athens News* and the monthly magazine *Odyssey*. Athens' wealth of bookshops includes many selling foreign language publications. **Raÿmóndos**, situated on Voukourestíou, offers the widest selection of foreign magazines, but for foreign books, go to the huge branch of **Eleftheroudákis** on Panepistimíou, with seven floors of English and Greek books, and a café. Try **Androméda Books** for Classical and archaeological subjects and **Ekdotikí Athinón** for history and guide books.

One of the many designer stores to be found in Kolonáki

CLOTHES & ACCESSORIES

Although there are some famous Greek designers, such as **Aslánis** who produces colourful party dresses, and **Parthénis** whose hallmark is black and white minimalism, most fashion stores concentrate on imported clothes. However, there are plenty of high-quality clothes: every designer label can be found in the city's main fashion centre, Kolonáki. There are branches of such famous names as **Gucci**, **Ralph Lauren** and **Max Mara**. Such upmarket stores as **Sótris**, **Bettina** and **Mohnblumchen** typify the area's urban chic. For good-quality high-street fashion there is the Spanish chain, **Zara**.

KITCHENWARE

Cavernous catering stores in the side streets around the Central Market specialize in classic Greek kitchen- and tableware. There are tiny white cups and copper saucepans used to make Greek coffee, long rolling pins for making filo pastry, and metal olive oil pourers. **Kotsóvolos** in Athínas has a huge range of cheap and cheerful equipment, including traditional *kantária* (wine-measuring jugs), used to serve retsina in restaurants, round *tapsiá* (metal roasting dishes), and *saganákia* (two-handled pans) used for frying cheese. More stylish products can be found at **Méli Interiors** in Kolonáki. A good selection of tinware is on display, as well as traditional Greek pottery and miniature taverna chairs.

FOOD AND DRINK

There are myriad gourmet treats in Athens, including unusual *avgotáracho* (smoked cod roe preserved in beeswax), herbs and spices, cheeses and wines. The bakeries and *zacharoplasteía* (patisseries) are irresistible, brimming with delicious breads and biscuits, home-made ice cream and yoghurt. **Aristokratikón**, off Plateía Syntágmatos, sells luxurious chocolates and marzipan. One of Athens' best patisseries, **Asimakópoulos**, is crammed with decadent *mpaklavás* and crystallized fruits. **Loumidis**, near Omónoia, is the best place to buy freshly-ground coffee.

The Central Market on Athinás is one of the most enticing places for food shopping. It is surrounded by stores packed with cheeses, olives, pistachio nuts, dried fruits and pulses such as *fáva* (yellow split peas) and *gígantes* (butter beans). You will find a range of herbs and spices at **Bahar**, in particular dried savory and sage, lemon verbena and saffron. A new delight is **Green Farm**, part of a chain of organic supermarkets.

Two enterprising *câves* (wine merchants), **Oino-Pnévmata** in Irakleítou and **Cellier** in Kriezótou, offer a broad range of wines and spirits from the new generation of small Greek wineries. **Vrettós** in Pláka has an attractive and varied display of own-label spirits and liqueurs.

A crammed Athenian kitchenware store

DIRECTORY

DEPARTMENT STORES AND SUPERMARKETS

AB Vassilópoulos
Stadíou 19, S'yntagma.
Map 2 F5.
Tel 210 322 2405.
One of several branches.

Attica
Panepistimiou 9,
Sýntagma. **Map** 2 F5.
Tel 211 180 2600.

Carrefour
Palaistínis 1, Alimos.
Tel 210 989 3100.

**Champion-
Marinópoulos**
Kanári 9, Kolonáki. **Map** 3
A5. *Tel 210 362 4907.*
One of several branches.

Notos Galleries
Aiólou 99 and Lykoúrgou
26, Omónoia. **Map** 2 E4.
Tel 210 324 5811.

MARKETS

Central Market
Athinás, Omónoia.
Map 2 D4.

Monastiráki
Adrianoú & Pandrósou,
Pláka. **Map** 6 E1.

Xenokrátous
Xenokrátous, Kolonáki.
Map 3 C5.

ART AND ANTIQUES

Anita Patrikiadou
Pandrósou 58,
Monastiráki. **Map** 6 D1.
Tel 210 325 0539.

Antiqua
Amaliás 2, Sýntagma.
Map 4 F2.
Tel 210 323 2220.

**Athens Design
Centre**
Valaritou 4, Kolonáki.
Map 2 F5.
Tel 210 361 0194.

Giórgos Goútis
Dimokritou 10,
Kolonáki. **Map** 3 A5.
Tel 210 361 3557.

Iákovos Serapian
Ifaistou 6, Monastiráki.
Map 5 C1.
Tel 210 321 0169.

**Katerina
Avdelopoulou-Vonta**
Lykavittoú 8, Kolonáki.
Map 3 A5.
Tel 210 361 6386.

Martínos
Pandrósou 50, Pláka.
Map 6 D1.
Tel 210 321 3110.

Nikólaos Pashalidis
Ifaistou 11, Monastiráki.
Map 5 C1.
Tel 210 324 0405.

Serafetinídis
Pat. Ioakim 21, Kolonáki.
Map 3 B5.
Tel 210 721 4186.

**Zoumpouláki
Galleries**
Kriezótou 7, Kolonáki.
Map 2 F5.
Tel 210 363 4454.
One of three branches.

TRADITIONAL FOLK ART AND CRAFTS

Amorgós
Kódrou 3, Plaka. **Map** 6 E1.
Tel 210 324 3836.

**Centre of Hellenic
Tradition**
Mitropóleos 59 (Arcade) –
Pandrósou 36, Monastiráki.
Map 6 D1.
Tel 210 321 3023.

**National Welfare
Organization**
Filellinon 14, Sýntagma.
Map 6 F1.
Tel 210 321 8272.

Stávros Melissinós
Ag. Theklas 2, Psyrrí.
Map 2 D5.
Tel 210 321 9247.

JEWELLERY

Anagnostópoulos
Voukourestíou 8, Kolonáki.
Map 2 F5.
Tel 210 360 4426.

**Ilías Lalaoúnis
Jewellery Museum**
Karyatidon & P. Kallisperi
12, Pláka. **Map** 6 D3.
Tel 210 922 1044.

Zolótas
Stadiou 9 & Kolokotroni,
Kolonáki. **Map** 2 F5.
Tel 210 322 1222.

MUSEUM COPIES

Orféas
Pandrósou 28B, Pláka.
Map 6 D1.
Tel 210 324 5034.

BOOKS, NEWSPAPERS AND MAGAZINES

Androméda Books
Mavromicháli 46,
Exárcheia. **Map** 2 F3.
Tel 210 360 0825.

Ekdotikí Athinón
Akadímias 34, Kolonáki.
Map 2 F5.
Tel 210 360 8911.

Eleftheroudákis
Panepistimíou 17,
Kolonáki. **Map** 2 F5.
Tel 210 331 4180.

Raÿmóndos
Voukourestíou 18,
Kolonáki. **Map** 2 F5.
Tel 210 364 8189.

CLOTHES & ACCESSORIES

Aslánis
Anagnostopoúlou 16,
Kolonáki. **Map** 3 A4.
Tel 210 360 0049.

Bettina
Pindarou 40, Kolonáki.
Map 3 A5.
Tel 210 339 2094.

Gucci
Tsakálof 27, Kolonáki.
Map 3 A5.
Tel 210 360 2519.

Max Mara
Akadímias 14, Kolonáki.
Map 3 A5.
Tel 210 360 2142.

Mohnblumchen
Plateía Dexamenís 7,
Dexaméni. **Map** 3 B5.
Tel 210 723 6960.

Parthénis
Dimokrítou 20, Kolonáki.
Map 3 A5.
Tel 210 363 3158.

Ralph Lauren
Voukourestíou 9, Kolonáki.
Map 3 A5.
Tel 210 361 7122.

Sótris
Anagnostopoúlou 30,
Kolonáki.
Map 3 A4.
Tel 210 363 9281.
One of two branches.

Zara
Skoufa 22, Kolonáki.
Map 3 A5.
Tel 210 324 3101.
One of several branches.

KITCHENWARE

Kotsóvolos
Athínas 52, Omónoia.
Map 2 D4.
Tel 210 289 1000.

Méli Interiors
Voukourestiou 41,
Kolonáki.
Map 3 A5.
Tel 210 360 9324.

FOOD & DRINK

Aristokratikón
Karagiórgi Servías 9,
Sýntagma.
Map 2 E5.
Tel 210 322 0546.

Asimakópoulos
Chariláou Trikoúpi 82,
Exárcheia.
Map 3 A3.
Tel 210 361 0092.

Bahar
Evripídou 31, Omónoia.
Map 2 D4.
Tel 210 321 7225.

Cellier
Kriezótou 1, Kolonáki.
Map 3 A5.
Tel 210 361 0040.

Green Farm
Dimokrítou 13, Kolonáki.
Map 3 A5.
Tel 210 361 4001.

Loumidis
Aiolou 106, Omónoia.
Map 2 E4.
Tel 210 321 1461.

Oino-Pnévmata
Irakleítou 9A, Kolonáki.
Map 3 A5.
Tel 210 360 2932.

Vrettós
Kydathinaíon 41, Pláka.
Map 6 E2.
Tel 210 323 2110.

ENTERTAINMENT IN ATHENS

Athens excels in the sheer variety of its open-air summer entertainment. Visitors can go to outdoor showings of the latest film releases, spend lazy evenings in garden bars with the heady aroma of jasmine, or attend a concert in the atmospheric setting of the Herodes Atticus Theatre, which sits beneath the Acropolis.

Athens listings magazine

The Mousikís Mégaron Concert Hall has given the city a first-class classical concert venue and draws some of the best names in the music world. For most Athenians, however, entertainment means late-night dining in tavernas, followed by bar– and club-hopping until the early hours. There is also an enormous number of large discotheques, music halls and intimate *rempétika* clubs, playing traditional Greek music, throughout Athens. Whatever your musical taste, there is something for everyone in this lively city. Sports and outdoor facilities are also widely available, in particular watersports, which are within easy reach of Athens along the Attic coast.

LISTINGS MAGAZINES

The most comprehensive Greek weekly listings magazine is *Athinorama*, which is published on Thursdays. It lists events and concerts, and the latest bars and clubs. The English language publications such as the weekly *Athens News* and the bimonthly *Odyssey* also have listings sections. All publications are generally available at kiosks.

BOOKING TICKETS

Although it is necessary to book tickets in advance for the summer Athens Festival *(see p46)* and for concerts at the Mégaron Concert Hall, most theatres and music clubs sell tickets at the door on the day of the performance. However, there is also a central ticket

office, open daily from 10am to 4pm, located near Plateía Syntágmatos, where tickets can be purchased for concerts at both the Mégaron Concert Hall and for the various events of the summer Athens Festival *(see p46)*.

THEATRE AND DANCE

There are many fine theatres scattered around the city centre, often hidden in converted Neo-Classical mansion houses or arcades. Numerous popular revues that combine an entertaining mixture of contemporary political satire and comedy are regularly performed in theatres such as the **Lampéti**.

Some excellent productions of 19th-century Greek and European plays are staged at the **National Theatre**. Playhouses such as the

Ibsen at the Evros Theatre, Psyrrí

Evros, **Athinón**, **Alfa** and **Vrettánia** also mount Greek-language productions of works by well-known 19th– and 20th-century playwrights such as Ibsen.

The major classical venues, including the National Theatre, put on contemporary dance and ballet as well as plays and operas. The **Dóra Strátou Dance Theatre** on Filopáppos Hill performs traditional regional Greek dancing nightly between May and September.

The Dóra Strátou Dance Theatre performing traditional Greek dancing outdoors

The doorway to the outdoor Refresh Dexamení cinema

CINEMA

Athenians love going to the cinema, especially from late May to September when the warm weather means that local open-air cinemas are open. All foreign-language films are subtitled, with the exception of children's films which are usually dubbed. The last showing is always at 11pm, which makes it possible to dine before seeing a movie.

The city centre has several excellent, large-screen cinemas showing the latest international releases. **Ideál**, **Elly** and **Astor Nescafé** are large, comfortable, indoor cinemas equipped with with Dolby Stereo sound systems. The **Alphaville-Bar-Cinema** and **Aavóra** tend to show a comprehensive range of art-house and cult movies.

Athenians like to hang out at the bars and tavernas next to open-air cinemas, such as **Refresh Dexamení** in Kolonáki or the **Riviéra** in Exarcheía, before catching the last performance. The acoustics are not always perfect but the relaxed atmosphere, in the evening warmth, with street noises, typically cats and cars, permeating the soundtrack, is an unforgettable experience. These cinemas seem more like clubs, with tables beside the seats for drinks and snacks. The outdoor

Thiseíon cinema comes with the added attraction of a stunning view of the Acropolis.

CLASSICAL MUSIC

The annual Athens Festival, held throughout the summer, attracts the major international ballet and opera companies, orchestras and theatrical troupes to the open-air **Herodes Atticus Theatre**, which seats 5,000 people, and to other venues around the city. This has always been the premier event of the classical music calendar. In 1991, the **Mousikís Mégaron Concert Hall** was inaugurated, providing a year-round venue for opera, ballet and classical music performances. This majestic marble building contains two recital halls with superlative acoustics, an exhibition space, a shop and

a restaurant. The Olympia Theatre is home to the **Lyrikí Skiní** (National Opera), and stages excellent ballet productions as well as opera.

Details of concerts held at cultural centres such as the **French Institute** can be found in listings magazines and newspapers.

TRADITIONAL GREEK MUSIC

The lively Greek music scene thrives in a variety of venues throughout central Athens. The large music halls of Syngróu advertise on omni-present billboards around the city. **Diogénis Studio**, **Fever** and **Rex** attract the top stars and their loyal fans. The more old-fashioned venues in Pláka, such as **Zoom** and **Mnisikléous**, offer more intimate surroundings for the haunting sounds of *rempétika* music, which draws its inspiration and defiant stance from the lives of the urban poor.

Rempétiki Istoría and **Taksími** are two of the places at which you can hear genuine bouzouki (Greek mandolin) music. Both bars have well-known bouzouki players, and reasonable prices.

Mpoémissa attracts a much younger crowd, more concerned with dancing the night away than with the authenticity of the music.

Accordionist in Plateía Kolonakíou

A classical concert at the Herodes Atticus Theatre

ROCK AND JAZZ MUSIC

International acts usually perform at large stadiums or the open-air **Lykavittós Theatre** as part of the annual Athens Festival. The **Gagarin**, a successfully converted cinema, also attracts the very cream of foreign and Greek rock bands. Greek bands can be enjoyed at the **An Club**, which offers patrons the intriguing prospect of Greek rock-and-roll dinner dancing.

The city's premier jazz venue is the **Half Note Jazz Club**. The club is housed in a former stonemason's workshop and is located opposite the First Cemetery. The Half Note is a cosy and popular venue, presenting the best of foreign contemporary jazz.

Alternatively, to hear Afro-Latin music, head for **Cubanita Havana Club** which features Cuban bands whose performances are often as lively as their music.

Marathon runner in Athens retracing the path of his ancestors

SPORT

Most taxi drivers will reel off their favourite football team to passengers before they have had a chance to mention their destination. Such is the Athenian passion for football that the two main rival teams, Panathenaïkós and Olympiakós, are always the subject of fervent debate. Each team is backed by a consortium of private companies, each of which also owns a basketball team of the same name. Football matches are played every Wednesday and Sunday during the September to May season. The basketball teams play weekly, in what is the latest popular national sport.

Lack of adequate parkland within the city means that joggers are a rare sight, despite the annual **Athens Open Marathon** every October. The athletes run from Marathon to the Kallimármaro Stadium in the centre of Athens *(see p113)*. The **Olympiakó Stadium** in Maroúsi seats 80,000 and was built in 1982. Its glass roof was designed by Spanish architect Santiago Calatrava for the 2004 Olympic games. The Panathenaïkós football team are based here. It has excellent facilities for all sports and includes an indoor sports hall, swimming pools and tennis courts in its 100 ha (250 acres) of grounds. The new **Karaïskáki Stadium** in Néo Fáliro is the home of the Olympiakós football team. There are also facilities there for many other sports including volleyball and basketball. Another famous event is the **Acropolis Rally**, a celebration of vintage cars, held around the Acropolis every spring. It attracts some 50 to 100 cars.

Outside the city centre, there are more facilities on offer, including bowling at the **Bowling Centre of Piraeus** and golf at the fine 18-hole **Glyfáda Golf Course**, which is located close to the airport. Tennis courts are available for hire at various places, including the **Pefki Tennis Club**.

Proximity to the Attic coast means that a large variety of watersports is on offer. Windsurfing and water-skiing are widely available on most beaches. Contact the **Hellenic Water-Ski Federation** for details of water-skiing schools offering tuition. There are several scuba-diving clubs, such as the **Aegean Dive Centre**, offering lessons for all levels.

Live music in one of the city's popular rock clubs

NIGHTCLUBS

Athens is a hive of bars and nightclubs that come and go at an alarming rate. The new up-and-coming areas of town are Gazi and Psyrrí, where a number of trend-setting bar-restaurants have opened: the best, such as **Home** and **Soul**, also have dance floors. Large clubs such as **Club 22** and **Privilege** offer special DJ nights and are based in Athens in the winter and move to surprise locations on the Attica coast in summer.

Basketball, an increasingly popular national sport among the Greeks

DIRECTORY

THEATRE AND DANCE

Alfa
Patisíon 37 & Stournári, Exárcheia.
Map 2 E2.
Tel 210 523 8742.

Athinón
Voukourestíou 10, Kolonáki.
Map 2 E5.
Tel 210 331 2343.

Dóra Strátou Dance Theatre
Filopáppou Hill, Filopáppou.
Map 5 B4.
Tel 210 921 4650.

Lampéti
Leof Alexándras 106, Avérof. Map 4 D2.
Tel 210 646 3685.

National Theatre
Agíou Konstantínou 22, Omónoia.
Map 1 D3.
Tel 210 522 3242.

Vrettánia
Panepistimíou 7, Sýntagma. Map 2 E4.
Tel 210 322 1579.

CINEMA

Aavóra
Ippokrátous 180, Neápolis.
Map 2 E4.
Tel 210 646 2253.

Alphaville-Bar-Cinema
Mavromicháli 168, Neápolis.
Map 2 F4.
Tel 210 646 0521.

Astor Nescafé
Stadiou 28, Kolonáki.
Map 2 E5.
Tel 210 323 1297.

Attikon Cinemax Class
Stadiou 19, Kolonáki.
Map 2 E5.
Tel 210 322 8821.

Elly
Akadimias 64, Omónia.
Map 2 E3.
Tel 210 363 2789.

Ideál
Panepistimíou 46, Omónoia.
Map 2 E4.
Tel 210 382 6720.

Refresh Dexamení
Plateía Dexamenís, Dexamení.
Map 3 B5.
Tel 210 362 3942.

Riviéra
Valtetsioú 46, Exárcheia. Map 2 F3.
Tel 210 384 4827.

Thiseíon
Apostólou Pávlou 7, Thiseío. Map 5 B2.
Tel 210 347 0980.

CLASSICAL MUSIC

French Institute
Sína 29–31, Kolonáki.
Map 3 A4.
Tel 210 339 8601.

Herodes Atticus Theatre
Dionysíou Areopagítou, Acropolis. Map 6 C2.
Tel 210 323 9132.

Lyrikí Skiní, Olympia Theatre
Akadimías 59, Omónoia. Map 2 F4.
Tel 210 361 2461.

Mousikís Mégaron Concert Hall
V Sofías & Kókkali, Stégi Patrídos. Map 4 E4.
Tel 210 728 2333.

TRADITIONAL GREEK MUSIC

Diogénis Studio
Leof A Syngroú 259, N. Smyrni.
Tel 210 942 5754.

Fever
Leof. A Syngrou & Lagousitsi 25, Kallithéa.
Tel 210 921 7333.

Mnisikléous
Mnisikleous 22, Pláka. Map 6 D1.
Tel 210 322 5558.

Mpoémissa
Solomoú 19, Exárcheia. Map 2 D2.
Tel 210 384 3836.

Rempétiki Istoría
Ippokrátous 181, Neápoli.
Map 3 C2.
Tel 210 642 4937.

Rex
Panepistimíou 48, Sýntagma.
Map 2 E4.
Tel 210 381 4591.

Taksími
C Trikoúpi & Isávron 29, Neápoli.
Map 3 A2.
Tel 210 363 9919.

Zoom
Kydathinaíon 39, Pláka. Map 6 E2.
Tel 210 322 5920.

ROCK, JAZZ AND ETHNIC MUSIC

An Club
Solomoú 13–15, Exárcheia.
Map 2 E2.
Tel 210 330 5056.

Cubanita Havana Club
Karaiskáki 28, Psyrri.
Map 1 C5.
Tel 210 331 4605.

Gagarin
Liosíon 205, Attiki.
Map 1 C1.
Tel 210 654 7600.

Half Note Jazz Club
Trivonianoú 17, Stádio.
Map 6 F4.
Tel 210 921 3310.

Lykavittós Theatre
Lykavittós Hill.
Map 3 B4.
Tel 210 722 7209.

NIGHTCLUBS

Akrotiri
Vas. Georgiou 11, Agios Kosmas.
Tel 210 985 9147.

Club 22
Vouliagménis 22.
Map 6 F5.
Tel 210 924 9814.

Home
Voutadon 34, Gazi.
Map 1 A5.
Tel 210 346 0347.

Island
Limanakia Vouliagmenis, Várkiza.
Tel 210 965 3563.

Privilege
Deligianni 50 & Georganta, Kifisiá.
Tel 210 801 8340.

Soul
Evripidou 65, Psyrrí.
Map 2 D4.
Tel 210 331 0907.

SPORT

Aegean Dive Centre
Zamanou 53 & Pandhoras, Glyfáda.
Tel 210 894 5409.
www.adc.gr

Bowling Centre of Piraeus
Profítis Ilías, Kastélla.
Tel 210 412 7077.

Glyfáda Golf Course
Panopis 15 & Kypros, Glyfáda.
Tel 210 894 6820.

Hellenic Water-Ski Federation
Leof Possidónos, 16777 Athens.
Tel 210 994 4334.

Karaïskáki Stadium
Néo Fáliro.
Tel 210 481 2902.

Olympiakó Stadium
Leof Kifisías 37, Maroúsi.
Tel 210 683 4000.

Pefki Tennis Club
Peloponnissou 3, Ano Pefki
Tel 210 806 6162.

ATHENS STREET FINDER

Map references given for sights in Athens refer to the maps on the following pages. References are also given for Athens hotels *(see pp264–7)*, Athens restaurants *(see pp284–8)* and for useful addresses in the *Survival Guide* section *(see pp302–27)*. The first figure in the reference tells you which Street Finder map to turn to, and the letter and number refer to the grid reference. The map below shows the area of Athens covered by the eight Street Finder maps (the map numbers are shown in black). The symbols used for sights and features are listed in the key below.

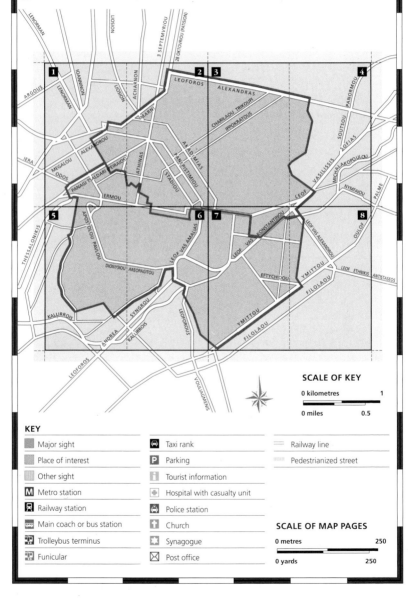

SCALE OF KEY

0 kilometres   1

0 miles   0.5

KEY

■ Major sight	🚕 Taxi rank	═ Railway line
■ Place of interest	**P** Parking	Pedestrianized street
▥ Other sight	ⓘ Tourist information	
M Metro station	✛ Hospital with casualty unit	
🚉 Railway station	🚓 Police station	
🚌 Main coach or bus station	✝ Church	
🚎 Trolleybus terminus	✡ Synagogue	**SCALE OF MAP PAGES**
🚟 Funicular	⊠ Post office	0 metres 250
		0 yards 250

Street Finder Index

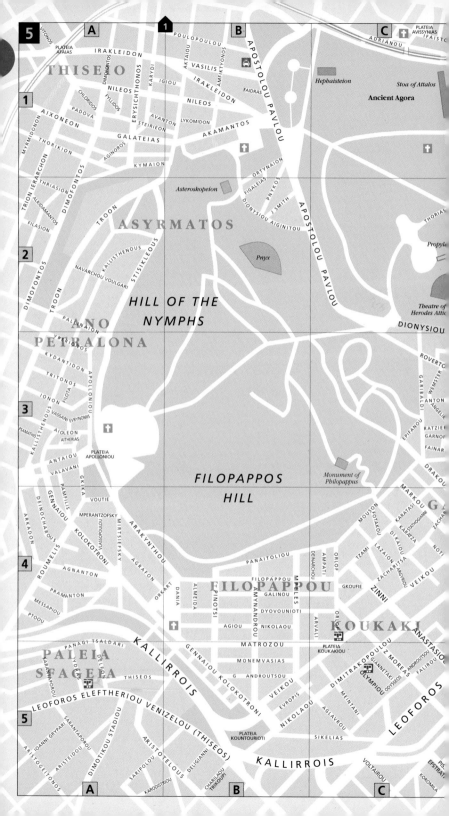

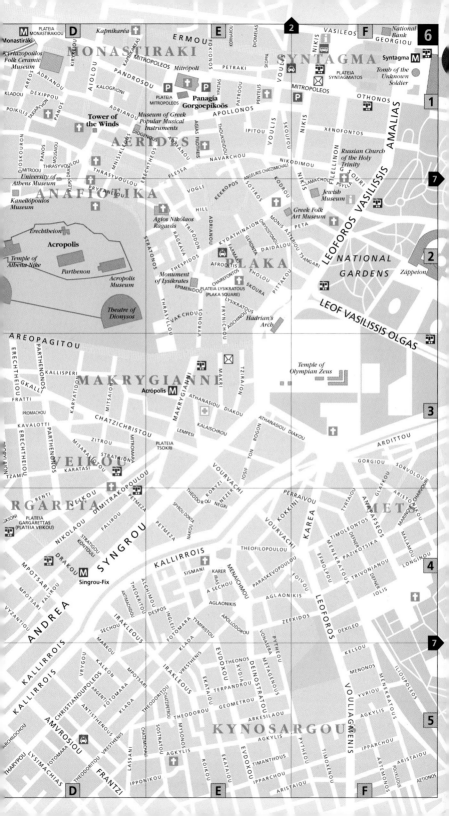

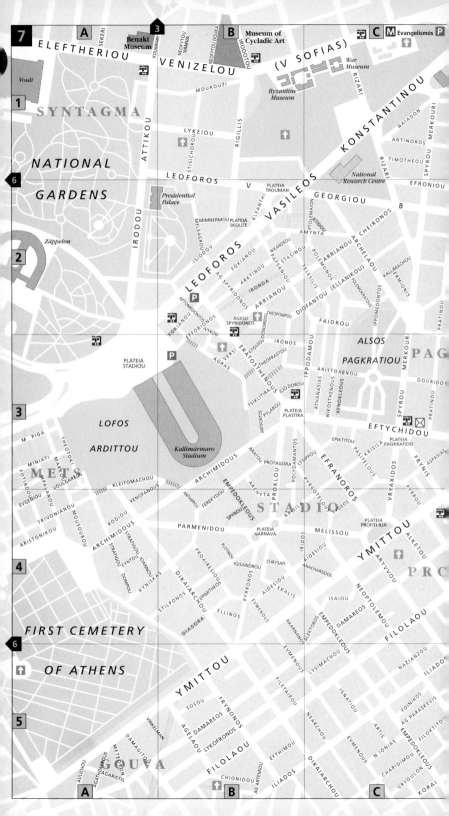

MAINLAND GREECE

Mainland Greece at a Glance

The unique attraction of the mainland lies in the wealth of ancient remains, set in landscapes of great natural beauty. Classical sites are most notable in the south, around Athens, and the coasts of Attica and the Peloponnese, while Macedonian remains can be seen in the temperate northeast. Byzantine monasteries and churches are found all over the country, particularly on the holy peninsula of Mount Athos which is governed by its 20 monasteries.

The Metéora area (see pp216–17) *combines extraordinary sandstone pinnacles with some of the first medieval monasteries in Greece, perched on the rocky peaks.*

Delphi *(see pp228–31) is home to the evocative ruins of an ancient religious complex and theatre situated on Mount Parnassus.*

NORTHERN GREECE *(see pp232–57)*

CENTRAL AND WESTERN GREECE *(see pp202–31)*

Ancient Olympia (see pp170–73) *was, from the 8th century BC to the 4th century AD, the site of the Panhellenic Games, forerunner of today's Olympics. One of the best-preserved buildings is the Temple of Hera* (left), *dating from around the 6th century BC.*

THE PELOPONNESE *(see pp158–201)*

Mystrás *(see pp192–3) is one of the best-preserved Byzantine complexes in Greece, exemplified in this church of Agía Sofía. It is a medieval city, and held out against the Ottomans until 1460.*

The Máni peninsula *(see pp194–9) is dotted with tower houses.*

0 kilometres   50

0 miles   25

Thessaloníki's *Archaeological Museum (see pp246–7) has spectacular gold finds from the tombs of the Macedonian kings, and this bronze head from around AD 235 of Alexander Severus.*

Osios Loúkas *monastery (see pp222–3) is beautifully set in a flowering orchard. The octagonal design of the 11th-century dome was widely copied. Its plain exterior conceals the gold-ground mosaics inside.*

Mount Athos has, since 1060, been entirely occupied by monks *(see pp252–4).*

Ancient Corinth (see pp162–6), *capital of the Roman province of Achaia, was renowned for its luxury and elegance, exemplified by this ornate capital.*

AROUND ATHENS *(see pp140–57)*

The Monastery of Dafní (see pp152–3) *is a famous work of Byzantine architecture with outstanding medieval mosaics decorating the interior of the church.*

Athens

Mycenae (see pp178–80), *one of Greece's oldest sites, dates back to 1550 BC; the Lion Gate was the entrance to the citadel. Mycenae was possibly ruled by Agamemnon.*

Epidaurus *(see pp184–5)* has one of the best-preserved theatres in Greece.

Monemvasía (see pp186–8) *means "one way in", a reference to the strategic advantage of this heavily fortified Byzantine seaport. Its former role as the main port of Byzantine Greece is reflected in the buildings of the old town.*

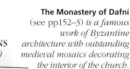

AROUND ATHENS

ATTICA

*T*he area around Athens, known as Attica, is the spiritual heart-
land of ancient and modern Greece. Its archaeological sites
have attracted generations of scholars and plunderers alike,
and its mountains and coastline have provided important refuge in
times of strife. Today the golden beaches along the eastern coast
attract those simply wishing to escape the bustle of modern Athens.

The land of Attica was the basis of Athenian wealth. The fine marble from the quarries on Mount Ymittós and Mount Pentéli was used for the temples and sculptures of ancient Athens. The silver from Lávrio financed their construction, and the produce from the local agricultural areas fed the population.

Waiting for a ferry in Piraeus

Attica has witnessed many significant historical events. The plain of Marathon was the site of one of the greatest battles in Greek history. Piraeus, now Greece's largest and busiest port, was also the port of ancient Athens. The Classical temples at lesser-known archaeological sites around the countryside, such as Eleusis, Ramnoús and Brauron, offer a rural retreat from the overcrowding and pollution of the city. At Soúnio, the majestic, well-preserved Temple of Poseidon on the cape has been a beacon for mariners for centuries.

The Byzantine era also left a great legacy of fine architecture to the region. Two of the best examples of this are the imposing monasteries of Dafní and Kaisarianí, with their ornate mosaics and elegant stonework.

South of Athens, the summer heat of the Attic plain is ideal for growing crops. Grapes are a speciality in the Mesógeia (Midland) region, which produces some of the finest retsina in the country. North of Athens, the pine-forested Mount Párnitha provides interesting walks and offers superb views over the city from the summit.

The peaceful ruins of the Parthenon of the Bear Maidens at Ancient Brauron

◁ **The Christ Pantokrátor figure in the dome of the *katholikón* of the Monastery of Dafní**

Around Athens

Beyond the endless urban sprawl of Athens, the region around the city, known as Attica, offers the diversity of wild mountains, Byzantine monasteries and churches, evocative archaeological sites and sandy beaches. Not surprisingly, such easy accessibility to the coast and countryside has led to overcrowding in Athens' suburbs, and pollution around Piraeus and Ancient Eleusis. The hills of Mount Párnitha and Ymittós are rich in wildlife, with deserted trails, caves and icy spring water. In the summer months, Athenians move out to the Attic Coast, where the well-kept beaches have every kind of watersport facility, and there are bars and clubs. Towards the cape at Soúnio there are countless fish tavernas by the sea and quiet rocky coves ideal for snorkelling.

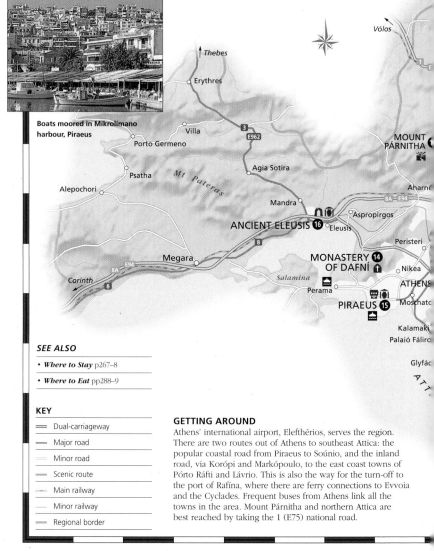

Boats moored in Mikrolímano harbour, Piraeus

Vólos

Thebes

Erythres

Villa

Porto Germeno

Psatha

Alepochori

Mt Pateras

Agia Sotira

MOUNT PÁRNITHA

Aharné

Mandra

Aspropirgos

ANCIENT ELEUSIS **16**   Eleusis

Peristeri

Megara

MONASTERY **14** OF DAFNÍ

Nikea

ATHENS

Corinth

Salamina

Perama

PIRAEUS **15**   Moschato

Kalamaki

Palaió Fáliro

Glyfác

SEE ALSO

KEY

═══	Dual-carriageway
───	Major road
───	Minor road
─ ─	Scenic route
─·─	Main railway
───	Minor railway
═══	Regional border

GETTING AROUND

Athens' international airport, Elefthérios, serves the region. There are two routes out of Athens to southeast Attica: the popular coastal road from Piraeus to Soúnio, and the inland road, via Korópi and Markópoulo, to the east coast towns of Pórto Ráfti and Lávrio. This is also the way for the turn-off to the port of Rafína, where there are ferry connections to Evvoia and the Cyclades. Frequent buses from Athens link all the towns in the area. Mount Párnitha and northern Attica are best reached by taking the 1 (E75) national road.

The Temple of Poseidon on the cape at Soúnio

LOCATOR MAP

SIGHTS AT A GLANCE

0 kilometres   10

0 miles   5

ATTICA

Skala Oropou
Aghii Apostoli
ANCIENT OROPÓS ①
Kalamos
Kapandriti
Lake Marathónas
Ag. Marina
② **RAMNOÚS**
③ **MARATHÓNAS**
Schinias
Ekali
⑫ **KIFISIÁ**
Amarousi
Nea Makri
Zoumberi
Máti
Pendeli
Pallini
④ **RAFÍNA**
MONI KAÏSARIANÍS
⑪
Spata
Loutsa
mittos
⑩ **PAIANÍA**
Mt Ymittos
ANCIENT BRAURON ⑤
Vravrona
giroupolis
Koropi
⑥ **PÓRTO RÁFTI**
Markópoulo
oula
Vári
Kaliva Thorikou
Kaki Thalassa
Vouliagméni
Agia Marina
Varkiza
Keratea
⑨ **COAST**
Lagonissi
Anávysos
Makrónisos
LÁVRIO ⑦
Palia Fokea
⑧ **SOÚNIO**

The *katholikón* of Moní Kaïsarianís

View of the Enkoimitírion at Oropós

Ancient Oropós ❶
Ωρωπός

Kálamos, Attica. **Road map** D4.
Tel 22960 22426. ▣ Kálamos.
◯ daily. ● main public hols. ▨

The peaceful sanctuary of
Oropós nestles on the left
bank of the Cheímarros, a
small river surrounded by
pine trees and wild thyme
bushes. It is dedicated to
Amphiáraos, a hero credited
with healing powers whom,
according to mythology,
Zeus rescued when he was
wounded in battle. It is said
that the earth swallowed up
Amphiáraos while he was
riding his chariot, and that he
then miraculously reappeared
through the sacred spring at
this site. In ancient times visitors would throw coins into
the spring in the hope of
being granted good health.

The Amphiaraion
sanctuary came to
prominence as a
healing centre in
the 4th century BC,
when its Doric
temple and sacri-
ficial altar were
built, attracting the
sick from all over
Greece. Houses
erected during the
Roman period,
when the area
became a popular
spa centre, are still
visible on the right
bank of the river.
The Enkoimitírion
was the site's most
interesting building.
It was a long stoa, the remains of which are still
visible today, where the
patients underwent treat-
ment by *enkoimisis*. This
gruesome ritual en-
tailed the sacrifice of a
goat in whose bloody
hide the patient would
then spend the night.
The next morning,
priests would pre-
scribe medicines
based on their inter-
pretations of the
dreams of the patient.

**Marble throne from
the theatre at Oropós**

Above the Enkoimitírion are
the remains of an impressive
theatre, which has a well-
preserved *proskenion* (stage)
and five sculpted marble
thrones, once reserved for the
use of priests and guests of
honour. On the right bank of
the valley, opposite the altar,
is a water clock dating from
the 4th century BC.

Ramnoús ❷
Ραμνούς

Attica. **Road map** D4. **Tel** 22940
63477. ▣ ◯ daily (Sanctuary of
Nemesis only). ● main public hols.
▨ ♿

Ramnoús is a remote but
beautiful site, overlooking
the gulf of Evvoia. It is home
to the only Greek sanctuary
dedicated to the goddess of
vengeance, Nemesis. The
sanctuary was demolished
when the Byzantine Emperor
Arcadius decreed in AD 399
that all temples left standing
should be destroyed. Thus
only the remains of this
sanctuary can be seen today.

Within its compound, two
temples are preserved side
by side. The smaller and
older Temple of Themis
dates from the 6th
century BC. Used as
a treasury and
storehouse in
ancient times, its
impressive poly-
gonal walls are all
that now survive.
Within the cella,
some important
statues of the
goddess and her priestess,
Aristonoë, were uncovered.
They can now be seen in the
National Archaeological
Museum (see pp68–71).

The larger Temple of Nemesis
dates from the mid-5th century
BC. It is very similar in design
to the Hephaisteion in Athens'
Agora (see pp90–91) and the
Temple of Poseidon at Soúnio
(see p148). Built in the Doric

The remains of the Temple of Nemesis at Ramnoús

style, the temple contained a statue of Nemesis by Agorakritos, a disciple of Pheidias *(see p98)*. The statue has been partially reconstructed from fragments, and the head is now in the British Museum.

Marathónas ❸
Μαραθώνας

Attica. **Road map** D4. **Tel** *22940 55155.* ▦ **Site & Museum** ☐ *Tue–Sun.* ● *main public hols.* ▨

The Marathon Plain is the site of the great Battle of Marathon, where the Athenians defeated the Persians. The burial mound of the Athenians lies 4 km (2 miles) from the modern town of Marathónas. This tumulus is 180 m (590 ft) in circumference and 10 m (32 ft) high. It contains the ashes of the 192 Athenian warriors who died in the battle. The spot was marked by a simple *stele* of a fallen warrior, Aristion, by the sculptor Aristocles. The original is now in the National Archaeological Museum *(see pp68–71)* in Athens. There is a copy at the site, inscribed with an epigram by the ancient poet Simonides: "The Athenians fought at the front of the Greeks at Marathon, defeating the gold-bearing Persians and stealing their power."

In 1970 the burial mound of the Plataians and royal Mycenaean tombs were found nearby in the village of Vraná. The Plataians were the only other Greeks who sent warriors in time to assist the Athenians already at the battle. The **Marathon Museum** displays archaeological finds from these local sites. There are also some beautiful

Plate discovered in the tomb of Plataians

Egyptian-style statues from the 2nd century AD, found on the estate of Herodes Atticus, on the Marathon Plain. This wealthy benefactor was born and bred in this area. He is known for erecting many public buildings in Athens, including the famous theatre located on the southern slope of the Acropolis *(see p100)* that was named in his honour.

Environs

Just 8 km (5 miles) west of Marathónas is **Lake Marathónas**, which is crossed by a narrow causeway. This vast expanse of water is man-made. The impressive dam, made from white Pentelic marble, was built in 1926. It created an artificial lake that was Athens' sole source of water up until 1956. The lake is fed by the continuous streams of the Charádras and Varnávas which flow down from Mount Párnitha *(see p151)* and makes a good setting for a picnic.

The quayside at the port of Rafína

Rafína ❹
Ραφήνα

Attica. **Road map** D4. ▦ *8,600* ▦ ▦

The charm of Rafína is its lively fishing port, packed with caïques and ferries. After Piraeus it is the main port in Attica. Frequent buses from Athens bring passengers for the regular hydrofoil and ferry connections to the Cyclades and other Aegean islands.

One of the administrative *demes* (regions) of ancient Athens, Rafína is a long-established settlement. Although there is little of historical or archaeological interest, the town offers a selection of excellent fish restaurants and tavernas. Choose one by the waterside to sit and watch the hustle and bustle of this busy port.

Environs

North of Rafína, a winding road leads to the more picturesque resort of **Máti**. Once a quiet hamlet, it is packed today with trendy cafés and bars, apartment blocks and summer houses owned by Athenians.

THE BATTLE OF MARATHON

When Darius of Persia arrived at the Bay of Marathon with his warships in 490 BC, it seemed impossible that the Greeks could defeat him. Heavily outnumbered, the 10,000 Greek hoplites had to engage 25,000 Persian warriors. Victory was due to the tactics of the commander Miltiades, who altered the usual battle phalanx by strengthening the wings with more men. The Persians were enclosed on all sides and driven back to the sea. Around 6,000 Persians died and only 192 Athenians. The origins of the marathon run also date from this battle. News of the victory was relayed by a runner who covered the 41 km (26 miles) back to Athens in full armour before dying of exhaustion.

Vase showing Greek hoplites fighting a Persian on horseback

Ancient Brauron ⑤
Βραυρώνα

Situated near modern Vravrona, Brauron
is one of the most evocative sites near
Athens. Although little remains of its former
architectural glory, finds in the museum
reveal its importance as the centre of
worship of Artemis, goddess of childbirth and
protectress of animals *(see p53)*. Legend
relates that it was founded by Orestes and
Iphigéneia, the children of Agamemnon,
who introduced the cult of Artemis into Greece.
Evidence of Neolithic and Mycenaean remains
have been found on the hill above the site, but
the tyrant Peisistratos brought Brauron its fame in
the 6th century BC when he made the worship
of Artemis Athens' official state religion.

| 0 metres | 30 |
| 0 yards | 30 |

KEY TO THE SANCTUARY OF ARTEMIS

① Temple of Artemis
② Chapel of Agios Geórgios
② Sacred House
④ Tomb of Iphigéneia
⑤ Parthenon of the Bear Maidens
⑥ Dormitories
⑦ Stoa
⑧ Stone Bridge

The Parthenon of the Bear Maidens at Brauron

Exploring Ancient Brauron

The centre of this compact site
lies just north of the prehistoric acropolis. The 5th-century
BC Doric **Temple of Artemis**,
of which only the foundations
remain, formed the focal point
of the sanctuary to the goddess. Beside the temple stands
a late Byzantine chapel, dedicated to **Agios Geórgios**.
From here a path leads southeast to the oldest cult site in
the sanctuary. This is said to
be the **Tomb of Iphigéneia**,

the high priestess of Artemis.
Next to it are the foundations
of the **Sacred House**, which
was used as a home by the
cult's priestesses. The most
extensive remains at the site
are to the northeast, at the
**Parthenon of the Bear
Maidens**. This courtyard may
have been the place where
young girls performed the

bear dance. Surrounded by a
late 5th-century BC **stoa**, the
courtyard had rooms behind
that were used as dining
areas and **dormitories**. Only
the foundations remain, but
the stone sleeping couches
and bases of statues can still
be seen. There is also a
5th-century BC **stone bridge**
to the west.

The small Byzantine chapel
of Agios Geórgios

BRAURONIA CEREMONY

Held every four years in the spring, the Brauronia festival
was celebrated in atonement for the killing of one of
Artemis's sacred pet bears. Although little is known about
the mysterious rites today, Aristophanes mentions the
"bear dance" that
initiates had to
perform in his
play *Lysistrata*.
Disguised as bears
and adorned with
saffron-coloured
robes, young girls,
aged between 5
and 10, performed
a dance honouring
this sacred animal.

Relief showing pilgrims approaching the
altar of Artemis at the Brauronia ceremony

**Mycenaean vase from the
Brauron Museum, 1200–1100 BC**

📷 Brauron Museum

This fascinating museum
has a wealth of finds
from the site. In
Room 1, there are
cases filled with
assorted votive
offerings such as
miniature vases and
jewellery. In Room 2
are the serene statues
of árktoi ("bear
maidens"). Room 3
has a fine votive
relief of the gods
Zeus, Leto, Apollo
and Artemis, and
the remains of an
altar. Rooms 4
and 5 offer a variety of prehistoric and Mycenaean finds,
including some ornate
Geometric vases.

**Statue of a
bear maiden**

RETSINA

Although many Greeks prefer drinking whisky to wine these
days, retsina is still favoured by millions of tourists. Around
16 million bottles were drunk in 1994, and 50 per cent of
them were exported around the world. The
unique, distinctive flavour comes from the
Aleppo pine resin which is added in small
quantities to the grape juice during fermen-
tation. This method has been used since
antiquity to preserve and flavour wine in
Greece. Since entry into the EEC (now
called the EU) in 1981, traditional
production areas have had their own
appellations. Aficionados agree that some
of the best retsina comes from the
Mesógeia appellation in Attica, where the
Savatiano grape is cultivated. Kourtákis,
the largest producers of retsina, have
their vineyards in Markópoulo and Koropí.

**Collection of
pine resin**

Pórto Ráfti ❻
Πόρτο Ράφτη

Attica. **Road map** D4. 🏛 *3,300.* 🚌

Porto Rafti takes its name from
Ráfti island which is visible just
off the headland. On the island
is a colossal marble statue of
a seated female, made in the
Roman period, known as "the
tailor" *(ráftis)*. It was most likely
built to be used as a beacon for
shipping and would have lit up
the harbour. Pórto Ráfti has one
of the best natural harbours in
Greece, although the town
itself has never developed
into an important seafaring
port. In April 1941, during
World War II, 6,000 New
Zealand troops were
successfully evacuated from
the beach. Today it is primarily
a pleasant holiday resort, with
tavernas and bars. The area is
rich in archaeological history.

Many Mycenaean tombs have
been found south of the bay
of Pórto Ráfti, at Peratí, a port
that flourished in the 7th and
6th centuries BC.

Environs

The remains of a fortress that
was built during the
Chremonidean War (268–261
BC) between Egypt and
Macedon can be seen on the
southern **Koróni** headland.
The northern coastline of
Peratí is pockmarked with
unexplored caves, and attracts
many people who come to
swim in the clear water and
fish off the craggy rocks.

Markópoulo, a thriving
market town and viticultural
centre 8 km (5 miles) inland,
is famous for its tavernas.
Spicy sausages are for sale
in the butchers' shops and
the bakeries are fragrant with
the smell of fresh bread.

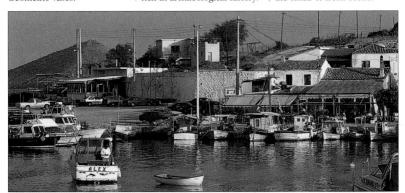

Pórto Ráfti harbour with Ráfti island in the background

One of the many 19th-century Neo-Classical buildings in Lávrio

Lávrio ❼
Λαύριο

Attica. **Road map** D4. 🚗 *8,800.*
🚌 🚇 🚶 *Thu.*

Lavrio was famous for its silver mines in ancient times. They were used as a source of revenue for the Athenian state and financed Perikles's programme of grand public buildings in Athens in the 5th century BC *(see p30).* They also enabled the general Themistokles to construct a fleet capable of beating the Persians at the Battle of Salamis in 480 BC. It was this excellent naval fleet which established Athens as a naval power. Before their final closure in the 20th century, the mines were also exploited by French and Greek companies for other minerals such as manganese and cadmium.

Originally worked by slaves, over 2,000 mine shafts have been discovered in the surrounding hills, and some are now open to visitors as the **Mineralogical Museum**. It is the only such museum in Greece. Traces of ore and minerals in the rock face can be seen on tours of the old mines. Since their closure the area has suffered high unemployment. The old Neo-Classical houses and empty harbourfront warehouses indicate the former prosperity of the town. Makrónisos, the narrow island opposite the port, was used as a prison for political detainees during the Civil War *(see p42).*

🏛 **Mineralogical Museum**
Leof Andréa Kordelá. *Tel* 22920 26270. ⏱ *10am–noon Wed, Sat & Sun.* 📷 ♿

Soúnio ❽
Σούνιο

9 km (5.5 miles) of Lávrio, Attica.
Road map D4. *Tel* 22920 39363. 🚌 *to Lávrio.* ⏱ *9am–sunset daily.* 📷 🏛

The temple of Poseidon, built on a site set back from sheer cliffs tumbling into the Aegean Sea at Soúnio (Cape Sounion), was ideally located for worship of the powerful god of the sea. Its brilliant white marble columns have been a landmark for ancient and modern mariners alike.

The present temple, built in 444 BC, stands on the site of older ruins. An Ionic frieze, made from 13 slabs of Parian marble, is located on the east side of the temple's main approach path. It is very eroded but is known to have depicted scenes from the mythological battle of the Lapiths and centaurs, and also the adventures of the hero Theseus, who was thought to be the son of Poseidon, according to some legends.

The Doric columns of the Temple of Poseidon

Local marble, taken from quarries at nearby Agriléza, was used for the temple's 34 slender Doric columns, of which 15 survive today. The temple also possesses a

The ruins of the Temple of Poseidon on Soúnio

unique design feature which helps combat the effects of sea-spray erosion: the columns were cut with only 16 flutings instead of the usual 20, thus reducing the surface area exposed to the elements.

When Byron carved his name on one of the columns in 1810, he set a dangerous precedent of vandalism at the temple, which is now covered with scrawled signatures.

A waterside restaurant at Várkiza, along the Attic coast

Attic Coast
Παραλία Αττικύς

Attica. **Road map** D4.

The coastal strip from Piraeus to Soúnio is often called the "Apollo Coast" after a small Temple of Apollo discovered at Vouliagméni. It is covered with beaches and resort towns that are always very busy at weekends, and particularly so in the summer holiday season.

One of the first places along the coast from Piraeus is the tiny seaside resort of **Palaió Fáliro** which is home to the Phaleron War Cemetery. In this quiet spot is the Athens Memorial, erected in May 1961 to 2,800 British soldiers who died in World War II.

Noisy suburbs near Athens airport, like **Glyfáda** and **Alimos** (famous as the birthplace of the ancient historian Thucydides), are very commercialized with a large number of marinas, hotels and shopping malls.

At chic **Vouliagméni**, with its large yacht marina, luxury

BYRON IN GREECE

The British Romantic poet Lord Byron (1788–1824) first arrived in Greece in 1809 at the tender age of 21, and travelled around Epirus and Attica with his friend John Cam Hobhouse. In Athens he wrote *The Maid of Athens*, inspired by his love for his landlady's daughter, and parts of *Childe Harold*. These publications made him an over-night sensation and, when back in London in 1812, he proclaimed: "If I am a poet it is the air of Greece which has made me one." He was received as a hero on his return to Greece in 1823, because of his desire to help fight the Turks in the War of Independence *(see pp40–41)*. However, on Easter Sunday 1824 in Mesolóngi, he died of a fever without seeing Greece liberated. Proving in his case that the pen is mightier than the sword, Byron is still venerated in Greece, where streets and babies are named after him.

Lord Byron, in traditional Greek costume, by T Phillips (1813)

---

hotels line the promontory. A short walk northwards away from the coast, beside the main road, is the enchanting Vouliagméni Lake. This unusual freshwater lake lies beneath low, limestone cliffs. The stunning stretch of warm, sulphurous water has been used for years to bring relief to sufferers of rheumatism. There are changing rooms and a café close by.

At **Várkiza**, the wide bay is filled with windsurfers. By the main road there is a luxury club-restaurant, *Island*. Open throughout the summer season, it serves cocktails and Mediterranean cuisine and attracts a glamorous crowd. From Várkiza, a road snakes inland to **Vári**, renowned for

its restaurants serving meat dishes. The Vári cave is located about 2 km (1 mile) north of the village. Inside is a freshwater spring and some fine stalactites have developed. Some minor Classical ruins remain in the caves, although many have been removed. There is unrestricted access and no admission charge.

From Várkiza to Soúnio, the coastal road is lined with quiet bathing coves, fish tavernas and luxury villas. **Anávysos** is a thriving market town surrounded by vineyards and fields. In its harbour, caïques sell locally caught fish every day, and there is a small street market every Saturday, with stalls piled high with seasonal fruit and vegetables.

Colourful stall of local produce in Anávyssos

Sculpture in the gardens of the Vorrés Museum

Paianía ❿
Παιανία

Attica. **Road map** D4. 🏘 *9,700.* 🚌
🚊 *Tue.*

Just east of Athens, Paianía
is a town of sleepy streets
and cafés. In the main square,
the church of **Zoödóchou
Pigís** has some fine modern
frescoes by the 20th-century
artist Fótis Kóntoglou. The
birthplace of the orator
Demosthenes (384–322 BC),
Paianía is more famous today
for the **Vorrés Museum**. Set
in beautiful gardens, this
features private collector
Ion Vorrés' eclectic array of
ancient and modern art. The
museum is divided into two
sections, encompassing 3,000
years of Greek history and
heritage. The first is housed

in what was the
collector's private
home: two tradi-
tional village
houses filled with
ancient sculptures,
folk artifacts, ce-
ramics, Byzantine
icons, seascapes
and furniture. The
second section,
housed in a spe-
cially built modern
building, offers a
unique overview
of contemporary
Greek art since
the 1940s, with
many excellent
works by more
than 300 differ-
ent painters and
sculptors, encom-
passing every
major art movement from
Photo-Realism to Pop Art.

🏛 **Vorrés Museum**
Diadóchou Konstantínou 1. **Tel** *210
664 4771.* ⏱ *10am–2pm Sat & Sun.*
🚫 *Aug & main public hols.* 🚫 ♿

Environs
Above Paianía, the **Koutoúki
Cave** is hidden in the foothills
of Mount Ymittós. It was found
in 1926 by a shepherd looking
for a goat which had fallen into
the 12,200 sq m (130,000 sq
ft) cave. There are tours every
half hour, with son et lumière
effects lighting up the stalagmites and stalactites. The tem-
perature inside is 17°C (62°F).

🕳 **Koutoúki Cave**
4 km (2.5 miles) W of Paianía.
Tel *210 664 2108.* ⏱ *9am–4:30pm
daily.* 🚫

Moní Kaïsarianís ⓫
Μονή Καισαριανής

5 km (3 miles) E of Athens, Attica.
Road map D4. **Tel** *210 723 6619.*
🚌 *to Kaisarianís.* ⏱ *8:30am–3pm
Tue–Sun.* ⚫ *main public hols.* 🚫

Located in a wooded valley
of Mount Ymittós, Moní
Kaïsarianís was founded in
the 11th century. In 1458,
when Sultan Mehmet II
conquered Athens, the
monastery was exempted
from taxes in recognition of
the abbot's gift to the sultan
of the keys of the city. This
led to great prosperity until
1792, when it lost these
privileges and went into
decline. The complex was
used briefly as a convent after
the War of Inde-
pendence, until
1855. Its build-
ings were even-
tually restored
in 1956.
    The small
katholikón is
dedicated to the
Presentation of
the Virgin. All
the frescoes
date from the
16th and 17th
centuries. The

**Decorative
stonework on
Moní Kaïsarianís**

finest are those in the narthex,
painted by the Peloponnesian
artist Ioánnis Ýpatos in 1682.
    The large, peaceful gardens
in the monastery are owned
by the Athens Friends of the
Tree Society, who planted
them after all the trees were
cut down during World War II.
Just above the monastery, the
source of the River Ilissós has

Moní Kaïsarianís, hidden in the hills around Mount Ymittós

been visited since antiquity for its sacred Kylloú Péra spring whose water is reputed to cure sterility; water still gushes from an ancient marble ram's-head fountain on the eastern side of the monastery. Before the Marathon dam was built (see p145), the spring was Athens' main source of water.

Kifisiá ⓬
Κηφισιά

12 km (7.5 miles) NE of Athens, Attica.
Road map D4. 🚗 40,000. 🚇
Ⓜ Kifisiá.

The tiny chapel of Agía Triáda on the hillside of Mount Párnitha

Kifisia has been a favourite summer retreat for many Athenians since Roman times. Once the exclusive domain of rich Greeks, it is congested today with apartment blocks and shopping malls. Traces of its former tranquillity can still be seen by taking a ride in a horse-drawn carriage. These wait by the metro station offering drives down shady streets lined with mansions and villas, built in a bizarre variety of hybrid styles such as Alpine chalet and Gothic Neo-Classicism.

The **Goulándris Natural History Museum**, which opened in 1974, is housed in one of these villas. Its large collection covers all aspects of Greece's varied wildlife and minerals. There are 200,000 varieties of plants in the herbarium, and over 1,300 examples of taxidermy; the stuffed creatures are carefully displayed in their natural habitats.

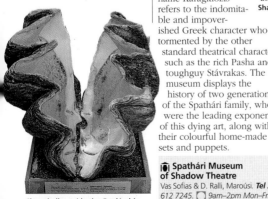

Clam shell outside the Goulándris Natural History Museum, Kifisiá

🏛 Goulándris Natural History Museum
Levídou 13. **Tel** 210 801 5870.
🕐 9am–2:30pm Sat–Thu, 10am–2:30pm Sun. 🔵 main public hols. 🅿

Environs
In Maroúsi, a suburb of Kifisiá, is the small **Spathári Museum of Shadow Theatre**, which is devoted to the fascinating history of the Karagkiózis puppet theatre. Shadow theatre came to Greece from the Far East, via players who used to travel throughout the Ottoman Empire performing for the aristocracy in the 18th century. It was soon transformed into a popular folk art by entertainers who would travel around Greece with their makeshift theatres. The name Karagkiózis refers to the indomitable and impoverished Greek character who is tormented by the other standard theatrical characters such as the rich Pasha and toughguy Stávrakas. The museum displays the history of two generations of the Spathári family, who were the leading exponents of this dying art, along with their colourful home-made sets and puppets.

Puppet from the Museum of Shadow Theatre

🏛 Spathári Museum of Shadow Theatre
Vas Sofias & D. Ralli, Maroúsi. **Tel** 210 612 7245. 🕐 9am–2pm Mon–Fri & 6–8pm Wed. 🔵 main public hols.

Mount Párnitha ⓭
Ορος Πάρνηθα

Attica. **Road map** D4. 🚌 to Acharnés, Thrakomakedónes & Agía Triáda.

In ancient times, Mount Párnitha sheltered wild animals. Today, this rugged range, which extends nearly 25 km (16 miles) from east to west, is rich in less dangerous fauna. Tortoises can be seen in the undergrowth and birds of prey circle the summit of Karampóla at 1,413 m (4,635 ft). Wild flowers are abundant, particularly in autumn and spring when cyclamen and crocus carpet the mountain. There are spectacular views of alpine scenery, all within an hour's drive of the city. At the small town of **Acharnés**, a cable car ascends to a casino perched at over 900 m (3,000 ft).

Still little used by hikers, the mountain has plenty of demanding trails. The most popular walk leads from Thrakomakedónes, in the foothills of the mountain, to the Báfi refuge. This uphill march takes about two hours, and offers superb views of the surrounding mountain scenery. Starting with thorny scrub typical of the Mediterranean *maquis*, it follows well-trodden paths to end among alpine firs and clear mountain air. Once at the Báfi refuge, it is worth walking on to the Flampoúri refuge which has some dramatic views.

Monastery of Dafní ⓮
Μονή Δαφνίου

Fresco detail

The monastery of Dafni was founded in the 5th century AD. Named after the laurels (*dáfnes*) that used to grow here, it was built with the remains of an ancient sanctuary of Apollo, which had occupied this site until it was destroyed in AD 395. In the early 13th century, Otto de la Roche, the first Frankish Duke of Athens, bequeathed it to Cistercian monks in Burgundy. Greek Orthodox monks took the site in the 16th century, erecting the elegant cloisters just south of the church. An earthquake in 2000 means that the beautiful gold-leaf Byzantine mosaics in the *katholikón* (main church) cannot be seen until restoration is completed.

Aerial view of the monastery complex

The Gothic exonarthex was built almost 30 years after the main church.

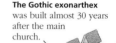

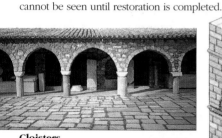

Cloisters
This arcade was built in the 16th century. On the other side of the courtyard, above a similar arcade, are the monks' cells.

The symmetry of the design makes Dafní one of the most attractive examples of Byzantine architecture in Attica.

Esonarthex

Exonarthex

Entrance

Entrance

KEY TO MOSAICS IN THE KATHOLIKON

WALLS
1 Resurrection
2 Adoration of the Magi
4 Archangel Gabriel
5 Archangel Michael
6 Nativity of the Virgin
8 St John the Baptist
9 Entry into Jerusalem
12 Dormition of the Virgin
13 Last Supper
14 Washing of the Feet
15 Betrayal by Judas
16 Prayer of Sts Anne and Joachim
17 Blessing of the Priests
18 Presentation of the Virgin
20 St Thomas

CEILING AND DOME
3 Nativity
7 Annunciation
10 Christ Pantokrátor
11 Transfiguration
19 Baptism

★ Christ Pantokrátor

The Pantokrátor ("Almighty") gazes sternly down from the dome of the katholikón. *Around the central figure are images of the 16 prophets.*

VISITORS' CHECKLIST

10 km (6 miles) NW of Athens, Attica. **Road map** D4. **Tel** 210 581 1558. ▓ ⚫ for restoration (phone for details).

The dome is 8 m (26 ft) in diameter and 16 m (52 ft) high at the centre.

Nave

The Transfiguration

This is in the northwest corner under the dome. Elijah and Moses are on either side of Christ and the apostles Peter, James and John are below.

The Windows

Elaborate three-tiered brickwork surrounds each of the windows.

Ticket office and museum

STAR MOSAICS

★ Christ Pantokrátor

★ Esonarthex Mosaics

★ Esonarthex Mosaics

These mosaics include depictions of the Last Supper *and the* Washing of the Feet. *The finest is the* Betrayal by Judas. *Christ stands unmoved as Judas kisses Him.*

Piraeus ⑮
Πειραιάς

One of the biggest Mediterranean ports, Piraeus is also one of the largest cities in Greece. It has been the port of Athens since ancient times. The Long Walls between Piraeus and Athens were started in 480 BC by Themistokles. However, Sulla destroyed the walls in 86 BC and by the Middle Ages Piraeus was little more than a fishing village. When Athens became the Greek capital in 1834, Piraeus was once again revitalized, with Neo-Classical buildings and modern factories. In 1923, 100,000 refugees came here from Asia Minor, bringing their culture and contributing to the cosmopolitan feel of this port city.

Waiting for a ferry

Small boats moored in peaceful Mikrolímano harbour

Harbour) houses many colourful fishing caïques. It is popular for its waterside fish restaurants and has a more relaxing ambience than the larger harbours.

On the coastal road between Pasalimáni and Mikrolímano, smart bars and clubs inhabit the renovated Neo-Classical mansions in the gentrified **Kastélla** neighbourhood. Even traditionally working-class areas, such as Drapetsóna (the most important manufacturing centre of the country) are now popular for their late-night restaurants.

🏛 Municipal Theatre
Agíou Konstantínou 2. **Tel** 210 412 0333. ☐ Tue–Sun.
The Neo-Classical façade of this imposing building is one of the delights of Piraeus. Designed by Ioánnis Lazarímos (1849–1913), who based his plans on the Opéra Comique in Paris, it has seating for 800, making it one of the largest modern theatres in Greece. It took nearly ten years to complete and was finally

View across Kentrikó Limáni with ferries in the foreground

Exploring Piraeus
After the Junta (see p43) razed many irreplaceable public buildings in the town centre in the early 1970s, civic pride re-emerged with a vengeance. Beside the Municipal Theatre, there are elegant open-air restaurants and fountains in the shade of Neo-Classical façades. On the streets behind the main banks and ticket offices that rim the **Kentrikó Limáni** (the main ferry port), there are smart restaurants and shops, as well as some fine examples of Neo–Classical architecture, such as the **Town Hall**. For information on ferry departures from Kentrikó Limáni, see page 323.

South of the railway station around Navarínou lies the lively market area, including fishmongers', fruit and vegetable stalls, ships' chandlers and hardware stores. On Sunday mornings there is also a bustling flea market, which is centred on the antique shops around Plateía Ippodameías, and also on Alipédou and Skylítsi streets.

There are two harbours in Piraeus, situated east of Kentrikó Limáni. **Pasalimáni** (Pasha's Port, also known as Limáni Zéas) was once used to harbour the Ottoman fleet. Today it is filled with luxurious yachts. Once known simply as Zéa, Pasalimáni used to be one of Themistokles's major naval ports, with dry docks for 196 triremes. Marína Zéas, the mouth of Pasalimáni, is a jetty used as a dock for hydrofoils to the Argo-Saronic islands. The second harbour, **Mikrolímano** (Little

Façade of the Municipal Theatre

inaugurated on 9 April 1895. Today, it is the home of both the **Municipal Art Gallery** and also the **Pános Aravantinoú Museum of Stage Decor**. The Museum of Stage Decor has displays of set designs by the stage designer Pános Aravantinoú (who worked with the Berlin opera in the 1920s), as well as general ephemera from the Greek opera.

🏛 Archaeological Museum

Charilaóu Trikoúpi 31. **Tel** 210 452 1598. ◻ 8:30am–3pm Tue–Sun. ⬤ main public hols. 🔲 ♿

This museum is home to some stunning bronzes. Found by workmen in 1959, these large statues of Artemis with her quiver, Athena with her helmet decorated with owls, and Apollo reveal the great expressiveness of Greek sculpture. The Piraeus *koúros* of Apollo, dating from 520 BC, is the earliest full-size bronze

to be discovered. There is also a seated cult statue of the earth goddess Cybele and a fine collection of Greek and Roman statues and grave stelae. Near the museum are the remains of the 2nd-century BC **Theatre of Zéa**; the remains include a well-preserved orchestra.

Statue of Athena in the Archaeological Museum

🏛 Hellenic Maritime Museum

Aktí Themistokléous, Freatýda. **Tel** 210 451 6264. ◻ 9am–2pm Tue–Fri (to 2:30pm Sat). ⬤ main public hols, Aug. 🔲

On the quayside of Marína Zéas, an old submarine marks the entrance to this fascinating museum. Its first room is built around an original section of Themistokles's Long Walls. More than 2,000 exhibits, such as models of triremes, ephemera from naval battleships and paintings of Greek *trechantíri* (fishing caïques), explore the world of Greek seafaring. From early

voyages around the Black Sea by trireme, to 20th-century emigration to the New World by transatlantic liner, the museum unravels the complexities of Greek maritime history. Exhibits include models of ships, maps, flags, uniforms and pictures. The War of Independence is well documented with information and memorabilia about the generals who served in it. The old naval ship *Averof*, which was the flagship of the Greek fleet up until 1951, has been fully restored and is berthed nearby. As part of the museum, the ship is also open to visitors.

VISITORS' CHECKLIST

10 km (6 miles) SW of Athens, Attica. **Road map** D4. 🚕 200,000. ⚓ Kentrikó Limáni. 🚌 Kékropos (for Peloponnese), Kanári (for Northern Greece). Ⓜ Piraeus. 🚆 Plateía Koraï (for Athens), Plateía Karaïskáki (other destinations). 🛈 EOT Athens (210 331 0392). 🕙 Sun (flea market). 🎭 theatre & music festival: May–Jul.

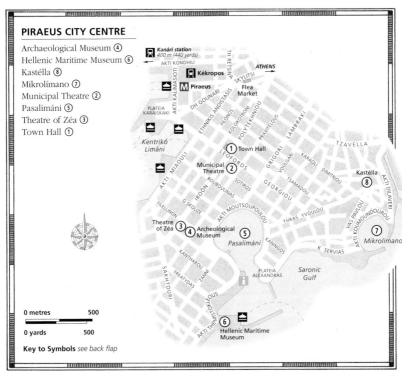

PIRAEUS CITY CENTRE

Archaeological Museum ④
Hellenic Maritime Museum ⑥
Kastélla ⑧
Mikrolímano ⑦
Municipal Theatre ②
Pasalimáni ⑤
Theatre of Zéa ③
Town Hall ①

Kanári station 400 m (440 yards)

AKTI KONDHILI
🚆 Kékropos
Ⓜ Piraeus
Flea Market
ATHENS
AKTI KALIMASIOTI
TH. RETSINA
SKYLITSI
PLATEIA KARAISKAKI
DH. GOUNARI
ETHNIKIS ANDISTASIS
FILONOS
KOLOKOTRONI
POLYTEKHNIOU
PRAXITELOUS
Kentrikó Limáni
AKTI MIAOULI
LEOFOROS
Town Hall ①
Municipal Theatre ②
BOUBOULINAS
SOTIROS
GEORGIOU
GRIGORI LAMBRAKI
VOULGARI
KARAOLI
TSAMADOU
TZAVELLA
DIMITRIOU
Kastélla ⑧
AKTI DILAVERI
Theatre of Zéa ③
④ Archeological Museum
⑤ Pasalimáni
IROON
G. SKOUZE
FILELLINON
AKTI MOUTSOUPOULOU
THRAS YVOULOU
KANINGOS
K. SERVIAS
VAS PAVLOU
AKTI KOUMOUNDOUROU
⑦ Mikrolímano
KANTHAROU
FREATYDAS
ZANNI
SAKHTOURI
PLATEIA ALEXANDRAS
Saronic Gulf

0 metres 500
0 yards 500

⑥ Hellenic Maritime Museum
AKTI THEMISTOKLEOUS

Key to Symbols *see back flap*

Ancient Eleusis ⑯
Αρχαία Ελευσίνα

Eleusis was an ancient centre of religious devotion that culminated in the annual Eleusinian Mysteries. These attracted thousands of people from around the Greek-speaking world, for whom the only initial requirement for becoming a *mystes* (or initiate) was to be neither a murderer nor a barbarian. Both men and women were freely admitted. Existing from Mycenaean times, the sanctuary was closed by the Roman Emperor Theodosius in AD 392, and was finally abandoned when Alaric, king of the Goths, invaded Greece in AD 396, bringing Christianity in his wake.

Anaktoron
This small rectangular stone edifice had a single entrance. It was considered the holiest part of the site. Meaning "palace", it existed long before the Telesterion, which was built around it.

Telesterion
Designed by Iktinos, this temple was built in the 5th century BC. It was constructed to hold several thousand people at a time.

4th-century BC shops and bouleuterion (council chamber)

Temple of Kore hewn out of rock

Roman houses

THE ELEUSINIAN MYSTERIES

Perhaps established by 1500 BC and continuing for almost 2,000 years, these rites centred on the myth of the grieving goddess Demeter, who lost her daughter Persephone (or Kore) to Hades, god of the Underworld, for nine months each year (*see p52*). Participants were sworn to secrecy, but some evidence of the details of the ceremony does exist. Sacrifices were made before the procession from the Kerameikós (*see pp88–9*) to Eleusis. Here the priestesses would reveal the vision of the holy night, thought to have been a fire symbolizing life after death for the initiates.

A priestess with a *kiste mystika* (basket)

ANCIENT ELEUSIS

This reconstruction is of Eleusis as it was in Roman times (c.AD 150) when the Mysteries were still flourishing. The view is from the east. Although there is little left today, it is still possible to sense the awe and mystery that the rites of Eleusis inspired.

Ploutonion
This cave is said to be where Persephone was returned to earth. It was a sanctuary to Hades, god of the Underworld and the abductor of Persephone.

VISITORS' CHECKLIST

Gioka 2, Eleusis, 22 km (14 miles) NW of Athens, Attica.
Road map D2. **Site & Museum**
Tel 210 554 6019.
8:30am–3pm Tue–Sun.
main public holidays.

Relief from the Telesterion, now in the museum

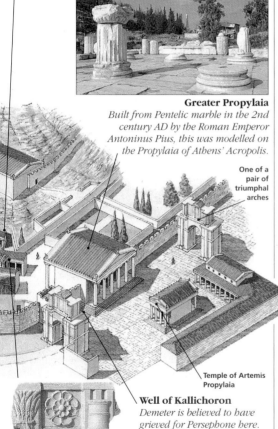

Greater Propylaia
Built from Pentelic marble in the 2nd century AD by the Roman Emperor Antoninus Pius, this was modelled on the Propylaia of Athens' Acropolis.

One of a pair of triumphal arches

Temple of Artemis Propylaia

Well of Kallichoron
Demeter is believed to have grieved for Persephone here.

Lesser Propylaia
This fragment shows sheaves of grain and poppies, which were used to make kykeon, the drink of the initiates.

Eleusis Museum
This small museum, south of the Telesterion, has five rooms. The entrance hall contains a copy of the famous relief from the Telesterion showing Triptólemos receiving grain from Demeter. Also in this room are a large 7th-century BC amphora and a copy of the Ninnion votive painting, one of the few remaining representations of the Eleusinian Mysteries. The other rooms are arranged on the left of the hall. In the first of these there is an elegant 6th-century BC *koúros* and a 2nd-century BC Roman statue of Dionysos. In the second room there are two models of the site. The third room has a Classical period terracotta sarcophagus and a large caryatid from the Lesser Propylaia carrying a *kiste mystika* basket on her head. The last room has a variety of pottery fragments, including examples of unusual terracotta containers that were used to carry foodstuffs in the annual *kernoforía* procession.

Fleeing maiden

THE PELOPONNESE

PELOPONNESE

*O*ne of the primary strongholds and battlefields of the 1821–31 Revolution, the Peloponnese is the kernel from which the modern Greek state grew. This enormous peninsula, which falls short of being an island by the mere 6-km (4-mile) width of the Corinth isthmus, also has some of the most spectacularly varied scenery and monuments on the mainland.

The name "Peloponnese" means "island of Pelops", who in legend was fed to the gods by Tantalos, his father. Resurrecte d, he went on to sire the Atreid line of kings, whose semi-mythical misadventures and brooding citadels were given substance by the discovery of remains at Mycenae. Today the ancient and medieval sites of the Argolid region, to the south of Corinth, contrast with the elegantly Neo-Classical town of Náfplio.

Leonidas statue, Spárti town

In the west lies Ancient Olympia, the athletic and religious nexus of the ancient world and inspiration for the games' revival in modern times. The lush coastal plain of Ileía, heart of an early medieval Crusader principality, spawned Frankish-Byzantine architecture, most famously at Chlemoútsi.

More purely Byzantine art adorns the churches of Mystrás, Geráki and the remote Máni region, whose warlike medieval inhabitants claimed to be descended from the warriors of ancient Sparta. Imposing Venetian fortifications at the beach-fringed capes of Methóni, Koróni and Monemvasía allowed the Venetians to play a role here after most of their other Aegean possessions were lost to the Ottomans.

In Arcadia, at the centre of the Peloponnese, lushly cultivated valleys rise to conifer-draped mountains and deep gorges such as the Loúsios; cliff-side monasteries and sombre hill-towns, like Stemnítsa, are a world apart from the popular Mediterranean image of Greece.

Restaurant terrace overlooking the sea, Monemvasía

◁ **Náfplio, seen from the stairs leading to the town's Venetian citadel, Palamídi**

Exploring the Peloponnese

Ancient and medieval ruins are abundant on the Peloponnese, and provide the main focus of sightseeing. Though there are few highly developed resorts away from the Argolid and Ileía, such areas as the Loúsios Gorge and Kalógria attract thousands of trekkers and naturalists. A rural economy is still paramount inland, with Pátra being the only large city. The landscape is dominated by forested mountains and the west coast, between Pátra and Methóni, boasts some of the finest beaches in the Mediterranean.

Karýtaina village, Loúsios Gorge

GETTING AROUND

Major roads link Athens and Pátra via Corinth, and also connect Corinth to Trípoli. Secondary roads are more interesting, and mostly paved, if dangerously narrow. Public transport consists of the bus service between major towns, and a rather creaky rail system. One line runs slowly around the north and west coasts, the other cuts diagonally through the middle via Trípoli, both lines converging at Kalámata. Ferries and hydrofoils (*see p323*) serve various points on the east coast, such as Monemvasía and Neápoli. There is also an airport at Kalámata.

SIGHTS AT A GLANCE

Ancient Corinth pp162–6 ❶
Ancient Messene ❸⓪
Ancient Neméa ❹
Ancient Olympia pp170–73 ❿
Ancient Tegéa ⓭
Ancient Tiryns ⓰
Ancient Troezen ⓳
Andrítsaina ⓬
Argos ⓮
Chlemoútsi Castle ❾
Corinth Canal ❷
Kalávryta–Diakoftó Railway ❻
Epidaurus pp184–5 ⓲
Geráki ㉑
Heraion of Perachóra ❸
Inner Máni pp198–9 ㉕
Kalógria ❽
Koróni ㉖
Loúsios Gorge pp174–5 ⓫
Methóni ㉗
Monemvasía pp186–8 ⓴
Mount Chelmós ❺
Mycenae pp178–80 ⓯
Mystrás pp192–3 ㉓
Náfplio pp182–3 ⓱
Nestor's Palace ㉙
Outer Máni pp194–5 ㉔
Pátra ❼
Pýlos ㉘
Spárti ㉒

Gýtheio harbour, Inner Máni

Río

Aígio

PÁTRA ❼

Diakoftó

KALÓGRIA ❽

Káto Achaΐa

KALÁVRYTA–DIAKOFTÓ RAILWAY ❻

Lápas

Káto Vlasiá

Kalávryta

Kyllíni

Lechainá

Erýmanthos 2224m

MOUNT CHELMÓS ❺

CHLEMOÚTSI CASTLE ❾

Gastoúni

Lámpeia

Amaliáda

Ladon

ANCIENT OLYMPIA ❿

Lagkádia

Pyrgos

Dimitsána

Krésten

LOÚSIOS GORGE ⓫

Stemnítsa

ANDRÍTSAINA ⓬

Zacháro

Karýtaina

Megalópoli

P E L O

Nédas

Kyparissía

Meligalás

Filiatrá

Messinía

❸⓪ **ANCIENT MESSE**

Chóra

Messíni

NESTOR'S PALACE ㉙

Kalámata

Sfaktiría

㉘ **PÝLOS**

Messiniakós Kólpos

METHÓNI ㉗

Kardamý

Sapiéntza

KORÓNI ㉖

Schíza

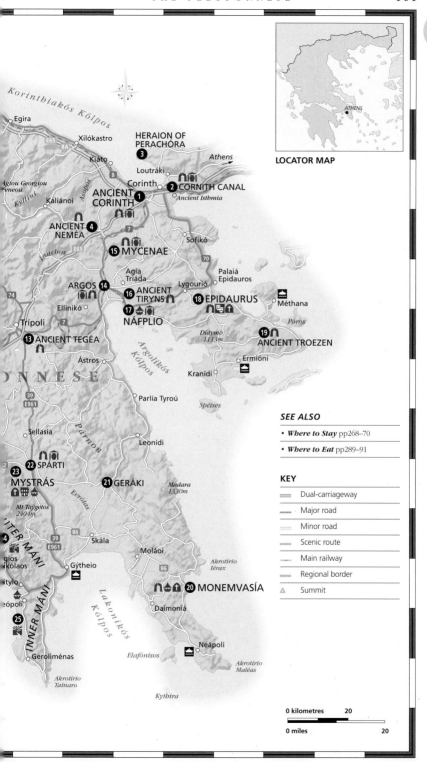

LOCATOR MAP

Korinthiakós Kólpos

Egira

Xilókastro

Kiáto

HERAION OF
PERACHÓRA
3

Loutráki

Athens

Corinth

2 CORNITH CANAL

Agíou Georgiou Feneoú

Kaliánoi

ANCIENT
CORINTH **1**

Ancient Isthmia

Kyllíni

ANCIENT
NEMÉA **4**

Sofikó

Inachos

15 MYCENAE

Agía
Triáda

Palaiá
Epidauros

Lygourió

ARGOS **14**

16 ANCIENT
TIRYNS

18 EPIDAURUS

Méthana

Ellinikó

17
NÁFPLIO

Póros

Trípoli

*Dídymo
1113m*

19
ANCIENT TROEZEN

13 ANCIENT TEGÉA

Argolikós Kólpos

Ástros

Ermióni

Kranídi

ONNESE

Parlía Tyroú

Spétses

Sellásia

Párnon

Leonídi

22 SPÁRTI

23
MYSTRÁS

21 GERÁKI

*Madara
1330m*

Evrótas

Mt Taÿgetos
2404m

ITER MÁNI

Skála

*gios
ikólaos*

Moláoi

*Akrotírio
Iérax*

ítylo

Gýtheio

eópoli

25

INNER MÁNI

*Lakonikós
Kólpos*

20 MONEMVASÍA

Daïmoniá

Geroliménas

Elafónisos

Neápoli

*Akrotírio
Maléas*

*Akrotírio
Taínaro*

Kythira

SEE ALSO

• *Where to Stay* pp268–70
• *Where to Eat* pp289–91

KEY

	Dual-carriageway
	Major road
	Minor road
	Scenic route
	Main railway
	Regional border
△	Summit

0 kilometres 20

0 miles 20

Ancient Corinth ●
Αρχαία Λόρινθος

Ancient Corinth derived its prosperity from its position on a narow isthmus between the Saronic and Corinthian gulfs. Transporting goods across this isthmus, even before the canal *(see p167)* was built, provided the shortest route from the eastern Mediterranean to the Adriatic and Italy. Founded in Neolithic times, the town was razed in 146 BC by the Romans, who rebuilt it a century later. Attaining a population of 750,000 under the patronage of the emperors, the town gained a reputation for licentious living which St Paul attacked when he came here in AD 52. Excavations have revealed the vast extent of the city, destroyed by earthquakes in Byzantine times. The ruins constitute the largest Roman township in Greece.

LOCATOR MAP

The bema (platform), was where St Paul was accused of sacrilege by the Jews of Corinth.

Bouleuterion

The agora was the hub of Roman civic life.

South stoa

★ Lechaion Way
This marble-paved road linked the port of Lechaion with the city, ending at a still-surviving stairway and an imposing propylaion (entrance).

The Peirene fountain's springs still supply the local modern village.

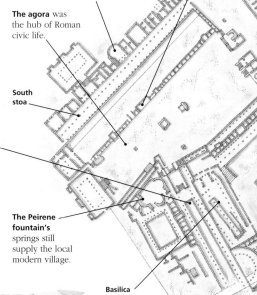

Basilica

RECONSTRUCTION OF ANCIENT CORINTH (C.AD 100)

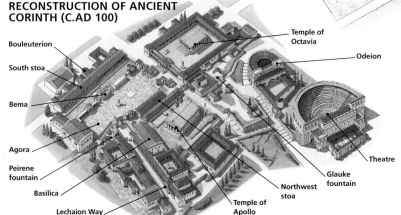

Bouleuterion

South stoa

Bema

Agora

Peirene fountain

Basilica

Lechaion Way

Temple of Apollo

Northwest stoa

Glauke fountain

Theatre

Odeion

Temple of Octavia

Temple of Octavia

These three ornate Corinthian columns, topped by a restored architrave, are all that remain of a temple, standing on a platform, dedicated to the sister of the Emperor Augustus.

Acrocorinth
(see p166)

The museum contains artifacts from the site *(see p166).*

Odeion

This was one of several buildings endowed by Herodes Atticus, the wealthy Athenian and good friend of the Emperor Hadrian.

The theatre was modified in the 3rd century AD so water could be piped in and mock sea battles staged.

The Glauke fountain's four cisterns were hewn from a cubic monolith and filled by an aqueduct from the hills.

The northwest stoa had two series of columns, the outer being Doric and the inner Ionic.

★ Temple of Apollo

The most striking structure of the lower city, this temple was one of the few buildings preserved by the Romans when they rebuilt the site in 46 BC. At the southeast corner an ingenious stepped ramp leads to the temple terrace.

The surviving Doric columns of the Temple of Apollo, Ancient Corinth ▷

Exploring Acrocorinth and the Museum

Excavations of recent years have yielded numerous artifacts now on view in the museum, and have revealed the vast extent of the ancient city which included the summit of Acrocorinth. Altogether, the ruins constitute the largest Roman township in Greece, since few earlier structures were restored after the Romans destroyed the town in 146 BC. Acrocorinth became one of medieval Greece's most important fortresses and can now be reached by a road which climbs the western face of the hill from the lower town.

Acrocorinth

Acrocorinth, 4 km (2 miles) above the main city, has been held and refortified by every occupying power in Greece since Roman times. Entry is on the west, where the peak's natural defences are weakest, through three successive gateways from different eras. The lowest is mostly Turkish; the middle, Frankish; and the third and highest, Byzantine, though it and two adjacent towers incorporate abundant ancient masonry. Beyond sprawls a 24-ha (60-acre) terraced wilderness of minaret stumps, Muslim tombs, and lonely mosques or chapels – all that remains of the town abandoned almost two hundred years ago, when its last defenders, the Turks, were defeated.

The lower elevation at the southwest corner of the 5-km (3-mile) circuit of walls sports a Venetian tower, while the true, northeast summit bears the scant foundations of an Aphrodite temple, attended in antiquity by 1,000 sacred

Mosaic of Bacchus (Dionysos), 2nd century AD, in the museum

prostitutes. It was against such practices that St Paul wrote his two "letters to the Corinthians". Today its attraction is one of the most sweeping views in the whole of Greece, up to 60 km (37 miles) in all directions from the Geráneia range in the northeast, to the peaks of Zíria in the southwest. Towards Zíria, a prominent nearby hill, Penteskoúfi, was fortified by the Franks during the 13th century.

Acrocorinth could withstand lengthy sieges owing to the presence of the upper Peirene spring, on the southeast side of the ramparts. A stairway descends to a vaulted, subterranean chamber pool; in dry seasons the water recedes to expose a column supporting an ornate Hellenistic pediment.

Museum

The site museum, just south of the odeion, ranks among Greece's best provincial collections. All periods of the ancient town's history are represented, though the Roman gallery in the west wing is particularly rich. Here pride of place goes to 2nd-century AD mosaics lifted from the floors of nearby villas: a head of Bacchus (Dionysos) set in a circular geometric pattern, a nude shepherd playing his flute to three cows, and a goat napping under a tree. The north doorway is flanked by two columns in the shape of Phrygian prisoners, shown with their arms crossed, their tunics and long hair seeming to prefigure medieval art. Also housed in the west wing are some of the 274 objects stolen from the museum in 1990 and recovered nine years later in Miami. The east gallery features older artifacts. Attic ware from the 5th century BC (see pp60–61), including the famous "Owl" vase, is rarer than the 7th- and 6th-century BC pottery, some painted with fantastic beasts, for which Corinth was noted.

At the shrine of Asklepios, just within the northern boundary of the ancient city walls, votive offerings in the shape of afflicted body parts were found and are on display in a back room, the precursors of the *támmata* or metal *ex votos* left in modern Orthodox churches. Other oddities include a 6th-century marble sphinx and Hellenistic pediments with lion-head spouts.

Stone reliefs in the central courtyard include depictions of the Labours of Herakles (see p53), one of which was performed nearby at the sanctuary of Neméa.

The entrance to Acrocorinth, with its three gateways

Ships passing through the Corinth Canal with the road bridge overhead

Corinth Canal ❷
Διώρυγα της Κορίνθου

Peloponnese. **Road map** C4.
🚌 Loutráki.

Stormy cape Matapan, or Taínaro (see p199), the southernmost point of the Peloponnese, was one of the dreaded capes of antiquity; rather than risk sailing around it, boats would be unloaded on one shore of this isthmus, dragged the 6 km (4 miles) across on the díolkos (paved slipway), and then refloated.

The traffic enriched Corinth and inspired plans for a canal. Emperor Nero began construction, but the project was only completed between 1882 and 1893. The 23-m (75-ft) wide canal is obsolete in an age of giant container ships which easily weather the cape, but small freighters squeezing through are regularly seen from the road bridge above.

Environs
Near the southern end of the canal is the site of **Ancient Isthmia**, once the major local religious centre (devoted to Poseidon) and location of the biennial Isthmian Games. Today only foundations of Poseidon's temple (7th century BC) and the remains of a starting gate for track events in the adjacent, vanished stadium are traceable.

The site museum stresses finds from Kechriés, Corinth's eastern port; unique exhibits include panels of painted glass or stone embedded in a resin matrix. They were intended to decorate an Isis temple but were never used owing to an earthquake in AD 375.

ⵌ Ancient Isthmia
Southern end of Corinth Canal. **Site & Museum** *Tel* 27410 37244. ⬜ 8:30 am–3pm daily (site only). ⬤ main public hols; Museum closed for renovation in 2006. Call for details. 📷 ♿

Heraion of Perachóra ❸
Ηραίον της Περαχώρας

13 km (8 miles) W of Loutráki, Peloponnese. **Road map** C4. 🚌

Probably founded during the 8th century BC, the Heraion of Perachóra (a nearby village) was primarily a religious centre. Only foundations and column stumps remain of the Archaic temple of Hera Limeneia, plus an altar and a Classical stoa, but the site has an incomparable setting, above a tiny cove on the south shore of Cape Melangávi, close to a 19th-century lighthouse.

Scenic Vouliagméni Lake, 3 km (2 miles) east, is fringed by Aleppo pines, with the best swimming and a selection of tavernas at its west end.

View of the Sanctuary of Hera at Perachóra, Cape Melangávi

Ancient Neméa ❹
Αρχαία Νεμέα

5 km (3 miles) NE of Neméa, Peloponnese. **Road map** C4. *Tel* 27460 22739. 🚌 Site ⬜ May–Oct: 8:30am–7pm daily; Nov–Apr: 8:30am–3pm daily. **Museum** ⬜ 8:30am–3pm Tue–Sun. ⬤ main public hols. 📷 ♿

Evocatively occupying an isolated rural valley, the site of Ancient Neméa is a local landmark with the Doric columns of its 4th-century Zeus temple plainly visible from afar. Below them lie the broken remains of column drums toppled by vandals between the 4th and 13th centuries AD. At the west end of the temple's complete floor, the deep *adyton* (underground crypt) has been exposed.

A short walk to the southwest, under a giant modern shelter, a Hellenistic bathhouse is being excavated; so far only the plunge-pool and feed system have been revealed. Recent digs have uncovered the Byzantine village which took root here in the 4th century, including graves, kilns, a basilica built above the ancient pilgrims' inn and a baptistry.

The **museum** has interesting reconstructions and old engravings. The Hellenistic stadium, 400 m (1,300ft) to the southeast, has the earliest known vaulted entrance tunnel.

Three Doric columns of the Temple of Zeus, Ancient Neméa

The peaks of Mount Chelmós, seen from the southeast at dawn

Mount Chelmós ❺

Όρος Χελμός

Peloponnese. **Road map** C4.
🚂 to Kalávryta.

Rising to 2,355 m (7,729 ft), Mount Chelmós is the third highest point of the Peloponnese, its foothills cloaked in extensive forests and divided by deep gorges. The most famous of these is Mavronéri, where the waterfall cascading from the remote north face of the summit is claimed to be the source of the mythical river Styx.

Overlooking the wooded Feneoú valley, on the southeastern slopes, stands the remote monastery of **Agíou Georgíou Feneoú**, originally founded in 1693, though mostly dating to the mid-18th century. The *katholikón*, with its high dome and transept, offers unusual frescoes. A stairway leads to a "secret" school, which functioned during the Ottoman years.

Moní Agías Lávras, 6 km (4 miles) from Kalávryta, played a pivotal role in the Greek Revolution. The Archbishop of Pátra raised the standard of revolt here on 25 March 1821, the banner now being the centrepiece of a nationalist shrine in the upstairs treasury *(see pp40–41)*.

Founded in 961, the monastery has been rebuilt after its destruction by the Germans in 1943. On the day before their arrival, the Germans had set fire to the town of Kalávryta, where they perpetrated one of their worst occupation atrocities, massacring 1,436 men and boys in reprisal for local resistance. The cathedral clock is permanently stopped at the time the killing began.

The **Cave of the Lakes**, near Kastriá, was known in ancient times but was lost until its rediscovery in 1964. It is arranged on three levels, and groups can visit the first 350 m (1,150 ft) of the cave, down to the second of 15 lakes. The massive stalactite-hung caverns were formed by an underground river, which still flows during the winter.

🦇 Cave of the Lakes
16 km (10 miles) S of Kalávryta. **Tel** 26920 31633. ⬚ 9am–4pm daily. 🎫

Old steam locomotive at Diakoftó

Kalávryta-Diakoftó Railway ❻

Οδοντωτός Σιδηρόδρομος Καλαβρύτων–Διακοφτού

Peloponnese. **Road map** C4.
Tel 26910 43206. 🚂 several daily Kalávryta–Diakoftó.

The most enjoyable narrow-gauge railway in Greece was engineered between 1889 and 1896 by an Italian company to bring ore down from the Kalávryta area. Over 22 km (14 miles) of track were laid, over 6 km (4 miles) of which relies on a third rail (a "rack and pinion" system), engaged where grades are up to one in seven. Two of the original steam locomotives, replaced in 1959, are displayed at Diakoftó. For a good view of the mechanism, travel by the driver.

En route there are 14 tunnels and many bridges over the Vouraïkós Gorge. The single station of Méga Spílaio, with two modest hotels, is roughly halfway. The station is the start of a 45-minute trail up to **Moní Méga Spílaio**. Though its age is uncertain, this is believed to be the oldest monastery in Greece.

Pátra ❼
Πάτρα

Peloponnese. **Road map** C4. 🏛
231,000. 🚤 🚌 🚍 🛈 Othónos
Amalías 6 (2610 461740). ◻
8am–10pm daily.

Greece's third largest city and
second port is no beauty.
Tower blocks dominate the
few elegantly arcaded streets
of this planned Neo-Classical
town. Where Pátra excels is in
its celebration of carnival –
the best in Greece – for which
the city's large gay
community and student body
both turn out in force.

On the ancient acropolis
the originally Byzantine
kástro bears marks of every
subsequent era. The vast
bailey, filled with gardens and
orchards, often hosts public
events, as does the nearby
brick Roman odeion.

At the southwest edge of
town, the mock-Byzantine
basilica of **Agios Andréas**
stands where St Andrew was
supposedly martyred, and
houses his skull and a
fragment of his cross.

Environs
Founded in 1861, the **Achaïa
Klauss Winery** was Greece's
first commercial winery and is
now one of the largest
vintners in Greece. It
produces 30 million litres (7
million gallons) a year, with
grapes gathered from across
the country. Tours include a
visit to the Imperial Cellar,
where Mavrodaphne, a fortified
dessert wine, can be tasted.

🍷 Achaïa Klauss Winery
6 km (4 miles) SE of Pátra. **Tel** 2610
368100. ◻ 11am–7pm daily (to 5pm
in winter). ⬛ main public hols. ♿ 📷

Kalógria ❽
Καλόγρια

Peloponnese. **Road map** B4.
🚍 to Lápas. 🛈 Lápas town hall
(26930 31234).

The entire lagoon-speckled
coast, from the Araxos river
mouth to the Kotýchi lagoon,
ranks as one of the largest wetlands in Europe. Incorporating
the Strofiliá marsh and a 2,000-
ha (5,000-acre) umbrella pine

Sandy beaches of Kalógria

dune-forest, the area enjoys
limited protection as a reserve.
Development is confined to a
zone between the Prokópos
lagoon and the excellent, 7-km
(4-mile) beach of Kalogriá. The
dunes also support Aleppo
pines and valonea oaks, while
bass, eels and water snakes
swim in the marsh channels.

Migratory populations of
ducks, including pintails and
coots, live at Kotýchi, while
marsh harriers, owls, kestrels
and falcons can be seen all
year round. A new **Visitor
Centre** at Lápas runs nature
trails through the dunes nearby.

🛈 Visitor Centre
Kotýchion Strofiliás, **Tel** 26930
31651. ◻ 8:30am–2:30pm Mon–
Fri. ⬛ main public hols. ♿ 📷

Chlemoútsi Castle ❾
Χλεμούτσι

Kástro, Peloponnese. **Road map** B4.
◻ daily.

The most famous Frankish
castle in Greece, known also
as "Castel Tornesi" after the
gold *tournois* coin minted
here in medieval times, was
erected between 1219 and 1223
to defend thriving Glaréntza
port (Kyllíni) and the principality capital of Andreville
(Andravída). To bolster the
weak natural defences, exceptionally thick walls and a
massive gate were built; much
of the rampart catwalk can
still be followed. The magnificent hexagonal keep has
echoing, vaulted halls; a plaque
by the entry commemorates
the 1428–32 residence of
Konstantínos Palaiológos, the
last Byzantine emperor, while
he was governor of Ileía.

Steps lead to a roof for views
over the Ionian islands and
the coastal plain. Chlemoútsi
is now being reconstructed,
with the enormous fan-shaped
courtyard already used for
summer concerts.

The modern Byzantine-style basilica of Agios Andréas, Pátra

Ancient Olympia ⑩
Ολυμπία

At the confluence of the rivers Alfeiós and
Kládeos, the Sanctuary of Olympia enjoyed
over 1,000 years of esteem as a religious and
athletics centre. Though the sanctuary
flourished in Mycenaean times *(see pp26–7)*,
its historic importance dates to the coming
of the Dorians and their worship of Zeus,
after whose abode on Mount Olympos the
site was named. More elaborate temples and
secular buildings were erected as the sanctuary
acquired a more Hellenic character, a process
completed by 300 BC. By the end of the reign
of Roman Emperor
Hadrian (AD 117–38),
the sanctuary had begun
to have less religious
and political significance.

Aerial view south over the Olympia site today

The Temple of Hera, begun
in the 7th century BC, is one
of the oldest temples in Greece.

The Philippeion,
commissioned by Philip II,
honours the dynasty of
Macedonian kings.

Olympia Museum
(see p172)

Main entrance

**Pheidias's
Workshop**
*A huge statue of
Zeus (see p241) was
made here. The ruins
include those of
a 5th-century
AD basilica.*

The Heroön
housed an altar dedicated
to an unknown hero.

0 metres	50
0 yards	50

Palaestra
*This was a training centre
for wrestlers, boxers and long-
jumpers. Much of the colonnade
which surrounded the central
court has been reconstructed.*

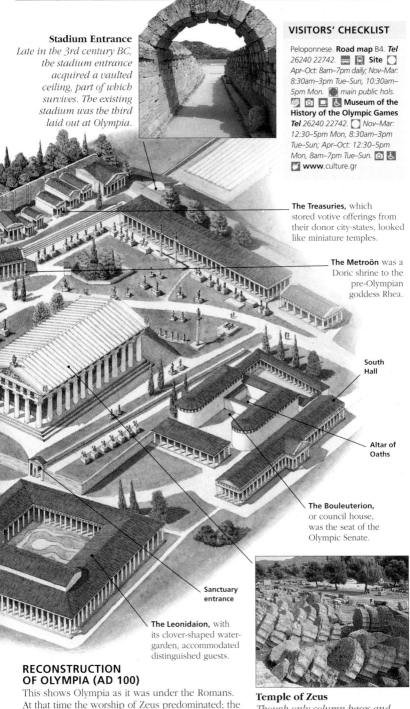

Stadium Entrance
Late in the 3rd century BC, the stadium entrance acquired a vaulted ceiling, part of which survives. The existing stadium was the third laid out at Olympia.

VISITORS' CHECKLIST

Peloponnese. **Road map** B4. **Tel** 26240 22742. 🚌 🚉 **Site** ◯ *Apr–Oct: 8am–7pm daily; Nov–Mar: 8:30am–3pm Tue–Sun, 10:30am–5pm Mon.* ⬤ *main public hols.* 🎫 📷 💺 ♿ **Museum of the History of the Olympic Games Tel** 26240 22742. ◯ *Nov–Mar: 12:30–5pm Mon, 8:30am–3pm Tue–Sun; Apr–Oct: 12:30–5pm Mon, 8am–7pm Tue–Sun.* 📷 ♿ 🖥 www.culture.gr

The Treasuries, which stored votive offerings from their donor city-states, looked like miniature temples.

The Metroön was a Doric shrine to the pre-Olympian goddess Rhea.

South Hall

Altar of Oaths

The Bouleuterion, or council house, was the seat of the Olympic Senate.

Sanctuary entrance

The Leonidaion, with its clover-shaped water-garden, accommodated distinguished guests.

RECONSTRUCTION OF OLYMPIA (AD 100)

This shows Olympia as it was under the Romans. At that time the worship of Zeus predominated; the games were dedicated to him, and his temple (containing a huge statue of the god) was at the heart of the Olympian enclosure.

Temple of Zeus
Though only column bases and tumbled sections remain, they clearly indicate the grandeur of this 5th-century BC Doric temple.

Exploring the Olympia Archaeological Museum

Archaic clay head of Hera

The Olympia Archaeological Museum, built opposite the excavation site to display its many treasures, officially opened in 1982 and is one of the richest museums in Greece. Except for the central hall, devoted solely to the pediment and metope sculptures from the Zeus temple, and the corner room dedicated to the games, the exhibits are arranged chronologically over 12 rooms, proceeding clockwise from the entrance hall from prehistory, through the Classical period, to the Romans.

Prehistoric, Geometric and Archaic Galleries

To the left of the entrance hall, room 1 contains finds from the Prehistoric period including pottery and 7th century BC bronze reliefs. There is also a model of the early Helladic Pelopian Tumulus. Exhibits in room 2 include a bronze tripod cauldron, elongated male figures upholding cauldron handles and griffin-headed cauldron ornaments, popular in the 7th century BC. There are also bronze votive animals from the Geometric period, found in the area surrounding the altar of Zeus. Room 3 has lavishly painted terracotta architectural members from various buildings in the sanctuary.

Classical Galleries

Weapons, especially helmets, were a favourite offering to Zeus made by pilgrims and athletes at Olympia. Two famous ones used in the Persian Wars *(see p29)* are shown in room 4: an Assyrian helmet, and that of Miltiades, victor at the Battle of Marathon *(see p145)*. This room also contains a 5th-century BC Corinthian terracotta of *Zeus and Ganymede*, the most humanized of the portrayals of Zeus.

The central hall houses surviving relief statuary from the Temple of Zeus. Unusually, both pediments survive, their compositions carefully balanced though not precisely symmetrical. The more static east pediment tells of the chariot race between local king Oinomaos and Pelops, suitor for the hand of the king's daughter Hippodameia. Zeus stands between the two contestants; a soothsayer on his left foresees Oinomaos's defeat, and the two local rivers are personified in the corners. The western pediment, a metaphor of the tension between barbarism and civilization, portrays the mythological *Battle of the Lapiths and the Centaurs*. The centaurs, invited to the wedding of Lapith king Peirithous, attempt, while

Zeus and Ganymede, in terracotta

drunk, to abduct the Lapith women. Apollo, god of reason, is central, laying a reassuring hand on Peirithous's shoulder as the latter rescues his bride from the clutches of the centaur chief. Theseus is seen to the left of Apollo preparing to dispatch another centaur, while other women watch from the safety of the corners. The interior metopes, far less intact, depict the *Twelve Labours of Herakles*, a hero mythically associated with the sanctuary.

In its own niche, the fragmentary 5th-century BC *Nike* (room 6), by the sculptor Paionios, was a thanks-offering from Messene and Náfpaktos, following their victory over Sparta during the Peloponnesian War *(see p30)*. A plaster reconstruction allows visualization of the winged goddess on the back of an eagle as she descends from heaven to proclaim victory.

The more complete *Hermes*, by Praxiteles, also has a room to itself (room 8), and shows the nude god carrying the infant Dionysos to safety, away from jealous Hera. The arm holding the newborn deity rests on a tree-trunk hung with Hermes' cape; Dionysos reaches for a bunch of grapes in the elder god's now-vanished right hand. Room 7 is devoted to Pheidias's workshop and the tools and materials used to create his gold and ivory statue of Zeus.

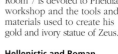

Statue of *Hermes* by Praxiteles

Hellenistic and Roman Galleries

Room 9 contains late Classical and Hellenistic finds including the terracotta sima of the Leonidaion. Rooms 10 and 11 are devoted to a series of statues of Roman emperors and generals and a marble bull dedicated by Regilla, wife of Herodes Atticus. Displays in room 12 include glass from the Late Roman cemetary at Frangonisi, Miraka, in which athletes and sanctuary officials were buried.

The Origins of the Olympic Games

The establishment of the Olympic Games in 776 BC is traditionally treated as the first certain event in Greek history. Originally, men's sprinting was the only event and competitors were local; the first recorded victor was Koroivos, a cook from nearby Elis. During the 8th and 7th centuries BC, wrestling, boxing, equestrian events and boys' competitions were added. The elite of

Title page of 1896 Games brochure

many cities came to compete and provided victory trophies although, until the Romans took charge in 146 BC, entry was restricted to Greeks. Local cities disputed control of the games, but a sacred truce guaranteed safe conduct to spectators and competitors. Part of a pagan festival, the Christians did not approve of the games and they were banned by Theodosius I in AD 393.

The ancient pentathlon *consisted of sprinting, wrestling, javelin- and discus-throwing, and the long jump (assisted by swinging weights). From 720 BC, athletes competed naked and women were excluded from spectating.*

Wrestling and boxing *are depicted on this 6th-century BC amphora. The boxers are shown wearing* himantes, *an early type of boxing glove made of leather straps wrapped around the hands and wrists.*

The Olympic revival *came in 1896, when the first modern games were held in Athens (see p113). They were organized by the Frenchman Baron Pierre de Coubertin.*

TIMELINE

Discus-thrower	**470–456 BC** Temple of Zeus constructed; Olympia at its zenith	**AD 393** Games forbidden by Emperor Theodosius I	**1896** Modern games revived **1875** Systematic German excavations begin, continuing to the present

3000 BC	**2000 BC**	**1000 BC**	**AD 1**	**AD 1000**

3rd millennium BC Site of Olympia first inhabited	**776 BC** First recorded games **AD 67** Nero competes, unfairly rescheduling the games, and "wins" most prizes		**AD 600** Alfeiós River begins to bury the site in silt **AD 551** Earthquake destroys much of site

Loúsios Gorge ⓫
Φαράγγι του Λούσιου

Walkers in the gorge

Although merely a tributary of the Alfeiós River, the Loúsios stream in its upper reaches boasts one of the most impressive canyons in Greece. Scarcely 5 km (3 miles) long, the Loúsios Gorge is nearly 300 m (985 ft) deep at the narrowest, most spectacular portion. Because of its remote mountain setting near the very centre of the Peloponnese, the Loúsios region was one of the strongholds of the revolutionaries during the Greek War of Independence *(see pp40–41)*. Medieval monasteries and churches cling to the steep cliffs of the gorge, and hiking trails have recently been marked, connecting some of the area's highlights. The picturesque villages *(see p176)* of the canyon's east bank make suitable touring bases.

Dimitsána is the best place to join the path.

TRIPOLI

ZATUNA

Palaiochóri

LOÚSIOS GORGE

Loúsios

Néa Moní Filosófou
Situated on the west bank amid the narrows, this 17th-century monastery was recently renovated and restaffed by a caretaker monk. Frescoes in the church date from 1693 and illustrate many seldom-depicted biblical episodes, such as the Gadarene Swine.

★ Ancient Gortys
The Asklepieion, or therapeutic centre, of Ancient Gortys occupies a sunken excavation on the west bank. It includes the foundations of a 4th-century BC temple to Asklepios, the god of healing.

Agios Andréas, an 11th-century chapel, stands just below the Loúsios narrows.

Kókkoras Bridge
This restored medieval bridge once carried the age-old road linking the regions of Arcadia and Ileía. Anglers fish for trout here in the icy river water.

STAR SIGHTS

★ Moní Aimyalón

★ Ancient Gortys

★ Moní Agíou Ioánnou Prodrómou

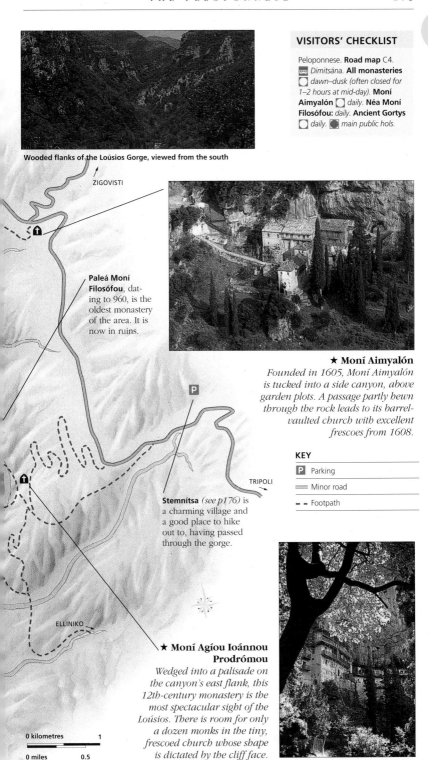

Wooded flanks of the Loúsios Gorge, viewed from the south

VISITORS' CHECKLIST

Peloponnese. **Road map** C4.
🚌 *Dimitsána.* **All monasteries**
🕐 *dawn–dusk (often closed for
1–2 hours at mid-day).* **Moní
Aimyalón** 🕐 *daily.* **Néa Moní
Filosófou:** *daily.* **Ancient Gortys**
🕐 *daily.* 🌑 *main public hols.*

ZIGOVISTI

**Paleá Moní
Filosófou**, dat-
ing to 960, is the
oldest monastery
of the area. It is
now in ruins.

★ **Moní Aimyalón**
*Founded in 1605, Moní Aimyalón
is tucked into a side canyon, above
garden plots. A passage partly hewn
through the rock leads to its barrel-
vaulted church with excellent
frescoes from 1608.*

KEY

P   Parking

═══   Minor road

– –   Footpath

TRIPOLI

Stemnítsa *(see p176)* is
a charming village and
a good place to hike
out to, having passed
through the gorge.

ELLINIKO

★ **Moní Agíou Ioánnou
Prodrómou**
*Wedged into a palisade on
the canyon's east flank, this
12th-century monastery is the
most spectacular sight of the
Loúsios. There is room for only
a dozen monks in the tiny,
frescoed church whose shape
is dictated by the cliff face.*

0 kilometres   1

0 miles   0.5

Exploring Around the Loúsios Gorge

Overlooking the gorge are some of the most beautiful hill-towns in the Arcadia region, making good bases for exploring the area. The best-marked trail is between Nea Moni Filosófou and Moni Prodrómou (take water and food). Dimitsána has two bus services daily to Trípoli, one via Stemnítsa, while two weekday buses between Andrítsaina and Trípoli can be picked up below Karýtaina. Getting around by car is best, though taxis are available. Winters can be chilly and wet, with snow chains required.

Bridge over the Alfeiós river, below Karýtaina, complete with chapel

The narrow streets of Dimitsána

Dimitsána

Spread along an airy ridge with the River Loúsios on three sides and glorious views down the valley, Dimitsána stands on the Classical site of Ancient Teuthis. The town boasts four belfries; that of **Agía Kyriakí** is illuminated at night, while the three-level **Pyrsogiannítiko** bell tower was erected by skilled Epirot masons in 1888.

Two clerics involved in the 1821 Revolution against Turkish rule *(see pp40–41)* were born here. The birthplace of Archbishop Germanós of Pátra, who helped instigate the Revolution, is marked by a plaque near the summit of westerly Kástro hill. A plaque dedicated to Patriarch Gregory V stands in the market; he was hanged in Istanbul when news of the revolt reached the Sultan.

Dimitsána's mansions date from its heyday as a trade centre in the 18th century. There were 14 powder factories here during the War of Independence – the town's **Water Mill Museum** has exhibits on powdermaking.

🏛 **Water Mill Museum**
Dimitsána. *Tel* 27950 31630. 🕐 Wed–Mon. 🔴 *main public hols.*

Stemnítsa

Situated in a large hollow, the village of Stemnítsa forms a naturally hidden fortress. In medieval times, Stemnítsa was one of Greece's main metalworking centres. Today, the village boasts a well respected school for gold and silver smiths. A **Folk Museum** recreates workshops of indigenous craftsmen and local house interiors, and hosts a top-floor gallery of weaponry, textiles and ceramics belonging to the Savvopoúlou family.

Among a number of magnificent medieval churches, those of **Treís Ierárches**, near the Folk Museum, and 10th-century **Profítis Ilías**, up on Kástro hill, have frescoes in excellent condition. Also at Kástro, the 12th-century **Panagía Mpaféro**, has an unusual portico, while the **Moní Zoödóchou Pigís**, on the northerly hillside, was where the revolutionary chieftains held their first convention during the War of Independence; it is for this reason that Stemnítsa was called the first capital of Greece.

🏛 **Folk Museum**
Stemnítsa. *Tel* 27950 81252. 🕐 Wed–Mon. 🔴 *main public hols.*

Karýtaina

In a strategic position on a bend of the Alfeiós, Karýtaina is now a virtual ghost town of less than 200 inhabitants. It has a 13th-century **Kástro**, dating to the time when the town was the seat of a Frankish barony. The castle was the hideout of Theódoros Kolokotrónis, who survived a long Turkish siege here in 1826. Nearby, the **Panagía tou Kástrou** boasts restored 11th-century column capitals with intricate reliefs.

Environs

East of Karýtaina, a bridge over the Alfeiós dates to 1439; four of six original arches survive, with a tiny chapel built into one pier.

The town of Dimitsána, seen from the east

Andrítsaina ⑫
Ανδρίτσαινα

Peloponnese. **Road map** C4.
900.

Despite its current role as the gateway to the Temple of Bassae, the sleepy town of Andrítsaina is hardly touched by tourism. Tavernas and shops around its central square, home to a lively morning produce market, make few concessions to modernity in either their cuisine or their vivid displays. These are echoes of the 18th century, when this was a major market centre. Downhill from the 18th-century fountain of Traní, a **Folk Museum** features local rag-rugs, traditional dress and metalware.

🏛 Folk Museum
Andrítsaina. ◻ *daily.* ● *main public hols.*

Environs
The 5th-century BC **Temple of Bassae** graces a commanding knoll, occupying the most remote site of any major ancient sanctuary. Today it hides under an enormous tent, until 50 million euros (£33 million) can be raised to re-install the architraves. Without them, winter frost damages the temple's colonnades, now reinforced by scaffolding.

Below Bassae lies the modern village of Figaleía, named after the ancient town to the west. The citizens of Ancient Figaleía built the temple in thanks to Apollo Epikourios for stopping a plague. A path descends to the gorge of the Néda river.

⛩ Temple of Bassae
14 km (9 miles) S of Andrítsaina.
Tel *26260 22275.* ◻ *8am–sunset daily.*

Ancient Tegéa ⑬
Τεγέα

Peloponnese. **Road map** C4.
Tel *27150 56540.* **Site** ◻ *daily.*
Museum ◻ *8:30am–3pm Tue–Sun.*
● *main public hols.*

South of modern Trípoli, the remains of the ancient city of Tegéa lie near the village of Aléa. The most impressive ruin is the 4th-century BC Doric temple of Athena Aléa, with its massive column drums, the second largest temple in the Peloponnese after Olympia's Temple of Zeus (*see p171*). The site **museum** has sculpture from the city, including a number of fragments of the temple pediment.

Argos ⑭
Αργος

Peloponnese. **Road map** C4.
20,000.

Although one of the oldest settlements in Greece, modern Argos is a busy, rather shabby market town, with its open-air fairground next to a restored Neo-Classical market-place. To the east of the central square, the **Archaeological Museum** exhibits local finds from all eras. Highlights include a bronze helmet and breastplate, and an Archaic pottery fragment showing Odysseus blinding Polyphimos, as well as a *krater* (bowl) from the 7th century BC.

The most visible traces of Ancient Argos lie on the way to Trípoli, where Roman baths and an amphitheatre are dwarfed by the size of one of the largest and most steeply raked theatres in the Greek world. From here a path climbs Lárisa hill, one of Argos's two ancient acropoleis.

🏛 Archaeological Museum
E of Plateía Agíou Pétrou. ***Tel*** *27510 68819.* ◻ *8:30am–3pm Tue–Sun.*
● *main public hols.*

Environs
Heading south of Ancient Argos, past the theatre, a minor road leads to the village of **Ellinikó** on the outskirts of which stands an intact pyramidal building. Dating from the 4th century BC, the structure is thought to have been a fort guarding the road to Arcadia.

Lérna, further south, is a 2200-BC palace dubbed the "House of the Tiles" for its original terracotta roofing. It now shelters under a modern protective canopy. Adjacent Neolithic house foundations and two Mycenaean graves, inside the palace foundations, suggest two millennia of habitation. Settlers were attracted by springs which powered watermills and still feed a deep seaside pond. This was the home of the legendary nine-headed serpent Hydra, which Herakles killed as one of his Labours (*see p53*).

Typical street-café scene at the traditional town of Andrítsaina

Seating in the ancient theatre of Argos, seen from the stage

Mycenae ⑮
Μυκήναι

The fortified palace complex of Mycenae, uncovered by the archaeologist Heinrich Schliemann (*see p180*) in 1874, is one of the earliest examples of sophisticated citadel architecture. The term "Mycenaean", more properly late Bronze Age, applies to an entire culture spanning the years 1700–1100 BC. Only the ruling class inhabited this hilltop palace, with artisans and merchants living just outside the city walls. It was abandoned in 1100 BC after a period of great disruption in the region.

Secret Stairway
A flight of 99 steps drops to a cistern deep beneath the citadel. Connected by pipes to a spring outside, the cistern was added to protect the water supply in times of siege.

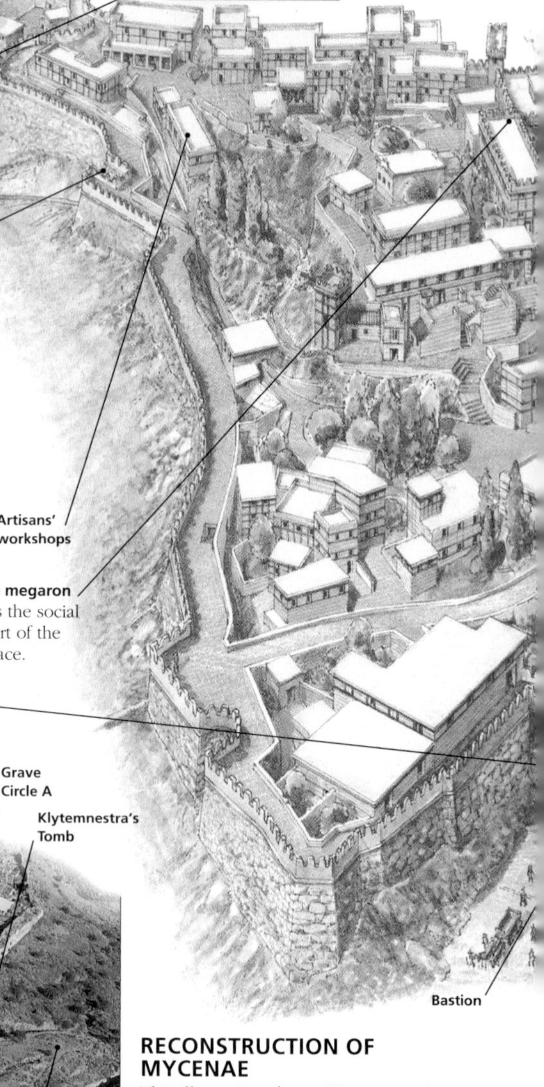

Northeast gate

Lion Gate
The Lion Gate was erected in the 13th century BC, when the walls were realigned to enclose Grave Circle A. It takes its name from the lions carved above the lintel.

Artisans' workshops

The megaron was the social heart of the palace.

MYCENAE TODAY

Secret Stairway
Royal Palace
Grave Circle A
Klytemnestra's Tomb
Bastion
Lion Gate
Path to the Treasury of Atreus
Grave Circle B

RECONSTRUCTION OF MYCENAE

This illustration shows Mycenae as it was in the time of the House of Atreus and the 1250 BC Trojan War (*see pp54–5*). Most tombs lie outside the walls (*see p180*).

Royal Palace

Situated at the acropolis summit, only the floors remain of this central structure. Burn-marks dating to its destruction in 1200 BC are still visible on the stone.

The "Cyclopean" walls, up to 14 m (46 ft) wide, were unbreachable. Later Greeks imagined that they had been built by giants.

The houses of Mycenae yielded a number of tablets inscribed with an archaic script, known as Linear B, deciphered by Michaïl Ventrís in 1952.

The House of Tsoúntas, named after its discoverer, was a minor palace.

Great ramp

Grave Circle A

This contained six royal family shaft-graves containing 19 bodies. The 14 kg (31 lb) of gold funerary goods are on display in Athens (see p70).

Klytemnestra, after murdering her husband, Agamemnon

THE CURSE OF THE HOUSE OF ATREUS

King Atreus slaughtered his brother Thyestes's children and fed them to him; for this outrage the gods laid a curse on Atreus and his descendants *(see p180)*. Thyestes's surviving daughter, Pelopia, bore her own father a son, Aigisthos, who murdered Atreus and restored Thyestes to the throne of Mycenae. But Atreus also had an heir, the energetic Agamemnon, who seized power.

Agamemnon raised a fleet to punish the Trojan Paris, who had stolen his brother's wife, Helen. He sacrificed his daughter to obtain a favourable wind. When he returned he was murdered by his wife, Klytemnestra, and her lover – none other than Aigisthos. The murderous pair were in turn disposed of by Agamemnon's children, Orestes and Elektra.

Exploring the Tombs of Mycenae

Mycenae's nobles were entombed in shaft graves, such as Grave Circle A *(see p179)* or, later, in *tholos* ("beehive") tombs. The *tholos* tombs, found outside the palace walls, were built using successive circles of masonry, each level nudged steadily inward to narrow the diameter until the top could be closed with a single stone. The entire structure was then buried, save for an entrance approached by a *dromos* or open-air corridor.

The entrance to the Treasury of Atreus, with a gap over its lintel

Treasury of Atreus

The Treasury of Atreus *(see p179)* is the most outstanding of the *tholos* tombs. Situated at the southern end of the site, the tomb dates from the 14th century BC and is one of only two double-chambered tombs in Greece. It has a 36-m (120-ft) *dromos* flanked by dressed stone and a small ossuary (the second chamber) which held the bones from previous burials. A 9-m (30-ft) long lintel stone stands over the entrance; weighing almost 120 tonnes (264,550 lb), it is still not known how it was hoisted into place, and is a tribute to Mycenaean building skills.

The treasury is also known as the Tomb of Agamemnon. However, the legendary king and commander of the Trojan expedition *(see pp54–5)* could not have been buried here, as the construction of the tomb predates the estimated period of the Trojan War by more than 100 years.

Tomb of Klytemnestra

Of the other *tholos* tombs only the so-called Tomb of Klytemnestra, which is situated just west of the Lion Gate, is as well preserved as that of Atreus. It is a small, single-chambered sepulchre with narrower and more steeply inclined walls, but the finely masoned *dromos* and similar triangular air hole over the entrance (which also relieved pressure on the lintel) date it to the same period.

HEINRICH SCHLIEMANN

Born in Mecklenburg, Germany, Heinrich Schliemann (1822–90) was self-educated and by the age of 47 had become a millionaire, expressly to fund his archaeological digs. Having discovered Troy and demonstrated the factual basis of Homer's epics, he came to Mycenae in 1874 and commenced digging in Grave Circle A. On discovering a gold death mask which had preserved the skin of a royal skull, he proclaimed: "I have gazed upon the face of Agamemnon!" Although archaeologists have since dated the mask to 300 years earlier than any historical Trojan warrior, the discovery corroborated Homer's description of "well-built Mycenae, rich in gold".

TREASURY OF ATREUS

Unlike their Greek contemporaries who would cremate their dead, the Mycenaeans buried their deceased in tombs. In the Treasury of Atreus, a Mycenaean king was buried with his weapons and enough food and drink for his journey through the Underworld.

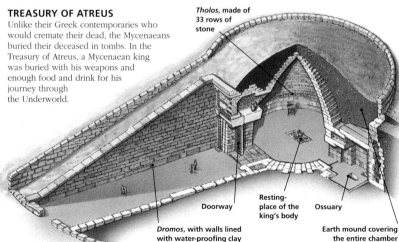

Tholos, made of 33 rows of stone

Doorway

Resting-place of the king's body

Ossuary

Dromos, with walls lined with water-proofing clay

Earth mound covering the entire chamber

Ancient Tiryns ⑯
Τίρυνθα

4 km (2 miles) NW of Náfplio, Peloponnese. **Road map** C4.
Tel 27520 22657. 🚌 ☐ *8:30am–3pm daily.* 📷

The 13th-century BC citadel of Tiryns confirms Homer's epithet "mighty-walled". A 700-m (2,300-ft) circuit of Cyclopean walls (named after the giants who could be imagined manoeuvering the huge blocks into place) attains a thickness of 8 m (26 ft). The fortifications, over double their present height, were necessarily stronger than those of Mycenae since Tiryns was not on a naturally strong site.

Excavated ruins of the Cyclopean walls, Tiryns

The bluff on which it stood was only 18 m (59 ft) higher than the surrounding plain which, in ancient times, was a salt marsh.

An inclined ramp to the east, designed with sharp turns to expose attackers' unshielded sides, leads to the massive middle gate, the lintel of which has long been missing. At the southern end of the complex, beyond and beneath the vanished inner gate, a gallery with a pointed corbel ceiling has had its walls polished by the fleeces of sheep which have sheltered here for centuries. On the west side, a stone stairway between inner and outer walls, leading to a postern gate, has been completely preserved. The lower, northern acropolis was the last to be enclosed and was used to protect commoners, animals and (as at Mycenae) a water supply.

Environs
The early 13th-century Byzantine church of the Panagías rears up startlingly in the cemetery at **Agía Triáda**, a village which is 5 km (3 miles) north of Tiryns. The walls are constructed of ancient masonry to shoulder height; above that, at the southeast corner of the building, the builders have inserted an entire Classical grave *stele*.

Further north, the **Argive Heraion** was the Archaic and Classical religious centre of the Argolid. The most impressive remains are those of a late 5th-century BC temple. Home to the priestesses of Hera, and a huge ivory-and-gold cult statue of the goddess, the temple was flanked by stoas, identifiable by remaining column stumps. Above the temple is the ledge where the Achaian leaders swore loyalty to Agamemnon before sailing for Troy. To the west, complete with drain-gutter, stands the "Peristyle Building" where *symposia* were hosted.

> 🏛 **Argive Heraion**
> 10 km (6 miles) N of Tiryns.
> ☐ *8:30am–3pm daily.*

Náfplio ⑰

See pp182–3.

Epidaurus ⑱

See pp184–5.

Tower of Theseus, Ancient Troezen

Ancient Troezen ⑲
Τροιζήνα

60 km (37 miles) E of Náfplio, Peloponnese. **Road map** D4.
☐ *unrestricted access.*

Near the modern village of Troizína are the sparse ruins of ancient Troezen, the legendary birthplace of the hero Theseus and the setting for Euripides' incestuous tragedy *Hippolytus*. Remains from many eras are scattered over a wide area; most conspicuous are three Byzantine chapels known as *Episkopí*, from the time when this was the seat of the Bishops of Damála.

The town was built on a high bluff isolated by two ravines; the westerly Damála Gorge is sheer, and half an hour's walk up it a natural rock arch called the "Devil's Bridge" spans the canyon. Near the lower end of the gorge stands the "Tower of Theseus", Hellenistic at its base, medieval higher up.

Foundations of the Argive Heraion, seen at dawn

Náfplio ❶

Ναύπλιο

With its marble pavements, looming castles and remarkably homogenous architecture, Náfplio is the most elegant town in mainland Greece. It emerged from obscurity in the 13th century and endured many sieges during the struggles between Venice and Turkey for the ports of the Peloponnese. The medieval quarter, to the west, is mostly a product of the second Venetian occupation (1686–1715). From 1829 until 1834, the town was the first capital of liberated Greece.

View over Náfplio from the stairway to the Palamídi fortress

Exploring Náfplio

Defended to the south by the Akronafplía and Palamídi fortresses and to the north by Boúrtzi castle, Náfplio occupies the northern side of a peninsula at the head of the Argolic Gulf. Since the Venetian period, **Plateía Syntágmatos** has been the hub of public life, and still looks much as it did three centuries ago when a couple of mosques were erected by the victorious Ottomans. One stands at the east end of the square and now houses a cinema;

President Kapodístrias

Vouleftikó Mosque, to the south, was where the Greek parliament (voulí) first met. West of the bus station, **Agios Geórgios** cathedral was built as a mosque during the first Ottoman occupation (1540–1686). Also converted is the **Catholic church**, another early mosque near the top of Potamiánou, which contains a

monument honouring fallen philhellenes, including George Washington's nephew. Four Turkish fountains survive from the second Turkish occupation (1715–1822). The most famous are the scroll-arched one behind the "Cinema" Mosque and another opposite **Agios Spyrídon** on Kapodistríou; this is near where President Kapodístrias was assassinated on 9 October 1831. There are less elaborate Ottoman fountains up the steps at number 9 Tertsétou, and at the corner of Potamiánou and Kapodistríou.

🏛 Archaeological Museum

Plateía Syntágmatos. **Tel** 27520 27502. ⬜ 8:30am–3pm Tue–Sun. ⬤ main public hols.

Exhibits, housed in a Venetian warehouse, largely centre on Mycenaean artifacts from various local sites, including Tiryns (see p181). Noteworthy are a Neolithic *thylastro* (baby-bottle), a late Helladic octopus vase, a full set of bronze Mycenaean armour and a complete Mycenaean boar's tusk helmet. There is also a large selection of Prehistoric, Archaic and Classical pottery.

🏛 Folk Art Museum

Vas. Alexandrou 1. **Tel** 27520 28379. ⬜ 9am–3pm Wed–Mon. 🖼

This award-winning museum, established in a former mansion by the Peloponnesian Folklore Foundation, is devoted, in the main, to textiles. Regional costumes are exhibited across two floors with Queen Olga's stunning blue and white wedding gown taking pride of place on the first floor. Also on the first floor are paintings by major Greek artists Giánnis Tsaroúchis and Theófilos Chatzimichaïl (see p218). On the second floor are guns and an impressive grandfather clock decorated with revolutionary scenes.

⚓ Boúrtzi

NW of harbour.

This island fortress acquired its appearance during the second Venetian occupation, and until 1930 had the dubious distinction of being the local executioner's residence. It defended the only navigable passage in the

The fortified isle of Boúrtzi, north of Náfplio harbour

bay; the channel could be closed off by a chain extending from the fortress to the town.

♙ Akronafplía

W of Palamídi. ☐ unrestricted access.

Akronafplía, also known as Its Kale ("Inner Castle" in Turkish), was the site of the Byzantine and early medieval town, and contains four Venetian castles built in sequence from west to east.

Palamídi fortress seen from the isle of Boúrtzi

The most interesting relic is the Venetian Lion of St Mark relief over the 15th-century gate just above the Catholic church. The westernmost "Castle of the Greeks" was Náfplio's ancient acropolis, now home to the clocktower, a major landmark.

♙ Palamídi

Polyzoïdou. **Tel** 27520 28036. ☐ Apr–Oct: 8am–6:45pm daily; Nov–Mar: 8am–2:45pm daily. ⬤ main public hols. ☒

Palamídi, named after the Homeric hero Palamedes, the son of Náfplios and Kliméni, is a huge Venetian citadel built between 1711 and 1714. It was designed to withstand all contemporary artillery, though it fell to the Ottomans in 1715 after a mere one-week siege, and to the Greek rebels lead by Stáïkos Staïkópoulos on 30 November 1822, after an 18-month campaign.

The largest such complex in Greece, Palamídi consists of a single curtain wall enclosing seven self-suffcient forts, now named after Greek heroes; the gun slits are aimed at each other as well as outward, in case an enemy managed to penetrate the

VISITORS' CHECKLIST

Peloponnese. **Road map** C4. ☒ 12,000. ☐ corner of Polyzoïdou. ☐ Syngroú. ☐ Ikostispémptis Martíou 24 (27520 24444). ☐ 9am–1pm & 4–8pm daily. ☒ Náfplio Cultural Festival: Jul.

defences. Fort Andréas was the Venetian headquarters, with a Lion of St Mark in relief over its entrance. The Piazza d'Armi, from where Náfplio assumes toy-town dimensions below you, offers arguably the best views in the country. At the summit, an eighth fort, built by the Ottomans, looks south towards Karathóna beach.

Detail above fountain, Agía Moní

Environs The 12th-century convent of **Agía Moní** nestles 4 km (2 miles) outside Náfplio; the octagonal dome-drum rests on four columns with Corinthian capitals. Just outside the walls, in an orchard, the Kánathos fountain still springs from a niche decorated with animal reliefs; this was ancient Amymone, where the goddess Hera bathed each year to renew her virginity.

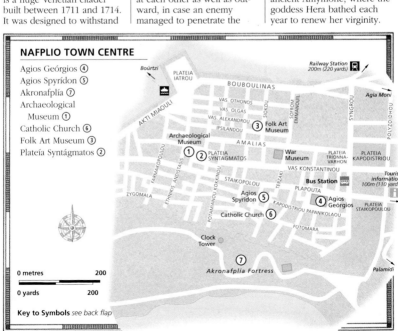

NAFPLIO TOWN CENTRE

Agios Geórgios ④
Agios Spyrídon ⑤
Akronafplía ⑦
Archaeological Museum ①
Catholic Church ⑥
Folk Art Museum ③
Plateía Syntágmatos ②

Boúrtzi
PLATEIA IATROU
BOUBOULINAS
Railway Station *200m (220 yards)*
Agia Moni
AKTI MIAOULI
VAS. OTHONOS
VAS. OLGAS
VAS. ALEXANDROU
IPSILANDOU
SIOKOU
SOFRONI EMMANOUIL
SYNGROU
POLYZOIDOU
Archaeological Museum
AMALIAS
Folk Art Museum ③
FARMAKOPOULOU
ETHNIKIS ANDISTASIS
PLATEIA SYNTAGMATOS
① ②
War Museum
PLATEIA TRIONNA-VARHON
PLATEIA KAPODISTRIOU
STAIKOPOULOU
POTAMIANOU-KOKKINOU
VAS. KONSTANTINOU
ZYGOMALA
Agios Spyrídon ⑤
TERZAKI
Bus Station
PLAPOUTA
Tourist information 100m (110 yards)
KAPODISTRIOU PAPANIKOLAOU
Agios Geórgios ④
PLATEIA STAIKOPOULOU
Catholic Church ⑥
FOTOMARA
Clock Tower
⑦
Akronáflia Fortress
Palamídi

0 metres   200
0 yards   200

Key to Symbols see back flap

Epidaurus ⑱
Επίδαυρος

Though most renowned for its magnificent theatre, the Sanctuary of Epidaurus was an extensive therapeutic and religious centre, dedicated to the healing god Asklepios. A mortal physician deified by Zeus after his death for retrieving a patient from the underworld, Asklepios was depicted in his temple here clutching a staff and flanked by a dog and a serpent – common symbols of natural wisdom. This sanctuary was active from the 6th century BC until at least the 2nd century AD, when the traveller-historian Pausanias recorded a visit.

Dusk over Epidaurus during a modern production at the theatre

The Theatre

Designed by Polykleitos the Younger late in the 4th century BC, the theatre is well known for its near-perfect acoustics which are endlessly demonstrated by tour group leaders. Owing to the sanctuary's relative remoteness, its masonry was never pilfered, remaining unrestored until only recently. It has the only circular *orchestra* (stage) to have survived from antiquity, though the altar that once stood in the centre has now gone. Two side corridors, or *paradoi*, gave the actors access to the stage; each had a monumental gateway whose pillars have

now been re-erected. Behind the *orchestra* and facing the auditorium stand the remains of the *skene*, the main reception

Foundations of the *tholos* building in the Asklepieion

hall, and the *proskenion* which was used by performers as an extension of the stage. Today, the theatre is still the venue for a popular summer festival of ancient drama.

The Asklepieion

Most of the Asklepieion, or Sanctuary of Asklepios, is being re-excavated and many of its monuments are off-limits. One of the accessible sites is the *propylaia*, or monumental gateway, at the north edge of the sanctuary, its original entrance. Also preserved are a ramp and some buckled pavement from the Sacred Way which led north from the gateway to the coastal town of ancient Epidaurus. At the

RECONSTRUCTION OF THE THEATRE

Surrounding the central *orchestra*, the north-facing *cavea* (cavity) of the theatre is 114 m (374 ft) across and is divided into blocks by 36 staircases.

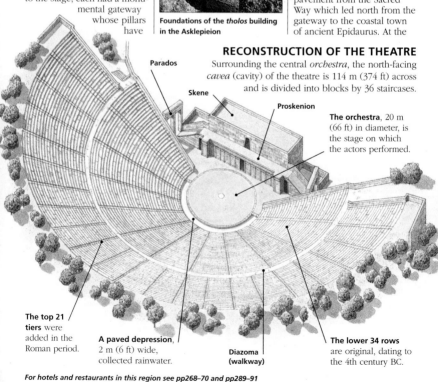

Parados

Skene

Proskenion

The orchestra, 20 m (66 ft) in diameter, is the stage on which the actors performed.

The top 21 tiers were added in the Roman period.

A paved depression, 2 m (6 ft) wide, collected rainwater.

Diazoma (walkway)

The lower 34 rows are original, dating to the 4th century BC.

Overview of today's site showing the stadium at the bottom (west)

northwestern end of the sanctuary stand the remains of the *tholos* (a circular building of uncertain function, also designed by Polykleitos) whose concentric passages are thought to have been used either as a pit for sacred serpents, or possibly as the locale for rites by the cult's priests. Patients slept in the *enkoimitírion* – a hall north of the *tholos* where they would await a diagnostic dream or a

visit from the harmless serpents. Therapeutic mineral springs, which are still on tap beside the museum, also played a part in the curing of patients who were brought here. Only the foundations of Asklepios's temple have survived, lying to the east of the *tholos*.

Another undisturbed point is the late Classical stadium south of the *tholos*. With intact rows of stone benches and a

starting line still visible, this was used during the quadrennial festival in honour of Asklepios. The Romans built an odeion inside the Hellenistic gymnasium, to host the festival's musical contests.

Environs
The adjacent village of Lygourió reflects the importance of the region during Byzantine times. There are three Byzantine churches, the most distinguished being the 14th-century **Koímisis tis Theotókou**, which has superb early medieval frescoes.

THE ORIGINS OF GREEK DRAMA

Greek drama developed from ritual role-play at festivals of Dionysos *(see p52)*. First came group dancing –6th-century BC Athenian vases show groups elaborately costumed, often as animals. In the late 6th century BC, the first Greek theatres appeared: rectangular (later round) spaces with seats on three sides. Singing and dancing choruses were joined by individual actors, whose masks made visible at a distance the various character roles, all played by just three male actors. The depiction of animal choruses on vases suggests humorous presentation, but the earliest plays in Athens were tragedies, staged in sets of three by a single writer *(see p57)*, in which episodes from epic poems and mythology were acted out. Historical events were rarely dramatized as they were politically sensitive.

Masks *were worn by actors to express the personality of the characters they played.*

Comedy became part of the dramatic festival at Athens only in the 480s BC.

Theatre was mass entertainment and had to cater for large numbers – during the Roman period, the theatre at Epidaurus could hold 13,000 people – but it is uncertain whether women were permitted to attend the performances.

Souvenir statuettes, *such as this terracotta figurine of a sinister character from one of the later comedies, could be bought as mementos after performances.*

The chorus, *though chiefly an impersonal commentator, often spoke directly to the characters, questioning them on the wisdom of their actions.*

Monemvasía ⑳
Μονεμβασία

Mural above the main entrance to Agía Sofía

A fortified town built on two levels on a rock rearing 350 m (1,150 ft) above the sea, Monemvasía well deserves its nickname, "the Gibraltar of Greece". A town of 50,000 in its 15th-century prime, Monemvasía enjoyed centuries of existence as a semi-autonomous city-state, living off the commercial acumen (and occasional piracy) of its fleets and its strategic position astride the sea lanes from Italy to the Black Sea. Exceptionally well defended, it was never taken by force but fell only through protracted siege *(see p188)*. Though the upper town is in ruins, most of the lower town is restored.

Pathway to Upper Town
A paved stair-street zigzags up the cliff face from the lower town to the tower gate of the upper town (see p188).

★ Agía Sofía ——————
Standing at the summit of Monemvasía, this beautiful 13th-century church is the only intact remnant of the upper town (see p188).

Giánnis Rítsos's House
Immediately next to the gate, the birthplace of prominent poet and communist Giánnis Rítsos (1909–90) is marked by a plaque and a bust at the front.

Western gate

The mosque has been refurbished as a museum to display local finds, including some fine marble works.

Panagía Myrtidiótissa
The façade of this 18th-century church sports a Byzantine inscription and a double-headed eagle from an earlier Byzantine church.

STAR SIGHTS

★ Agía Sofía

★ Walls

VISITORS' CHECKLIST

Peloponnese. **Road map** C5. 🚌
800. 🚏 Main square. ⛴ Géfira.
ℹ️ 27320 61210 (number for the
tourist police, available during
summer). **Mosque Museum:**
Tel 27320 61403. 🕐 8:30am–
3pm Tue–Sun. ⬤ Mon & main
public hols.

"The Gibraltar of Greece"
*Monemvasía was severed from the mainland by an
earthquake in AD 375, remaining an island until the
causeway was built in the 6th century.*

Agios Nikólaos, begun in 1703,
resembles Myrtidiótissa
in its masonry, cruciform plan
and cement-covered dome.

★ Walls
*The 16th-century walls are
900 m (2,953 ft) long and up
to 30 m (98 ft) high. Much of
the parapet can be walked.*

The east gate opens
on to a former burial
ground known
as Lípsoma.

Panagía Chrysafítissa
has its bell hanging
from a cypress tree.

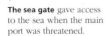

The sea gate gave access
to the sea when the main
port was threatened.

Christós Elkómenos
*Restored in 1697, this 13th-
century cathedral with its Venetian belfry is stark inside; the only
decoration is the plaque of two
peacocks above the door.*

The cliff-top church of Agía Sofía, at dawn, Monemvasía upper town

THE SIEGE OF MONEMVASIA

The siege of Monemvasía by the Greeks, early in the War of Independence (see pp40–41), began on 28 March 1821. Due to a Greek ruse, the town's Turkish garrison was badly supplied with food, and reinforcements failed to arrive. By late June, both Christians and Muslims were forced to eat weeds, cats and mice, some even resorting to cannibalism. Turkish civilians in the lower town urged surrender, but the garrison of the upper town refused. The besiegers also seemed set to give up, but one night, the Greek commander inside the town convinced three messengers to swim from the Portello Gate to the revolutionary forces on the mainland, giving them word to persevere. They did, and on 1 August the Turks surrendered, handing over the keys of the city to the Greek Prince Kantakouzinós.

The taking of Monemvasía by Prince Kantakouzinós

Exploring the Upper Town

First fortified in the 6th century as a refuge from raiding Avars, the upper town is the oldest part of Monemvasía. Largely in ruins, the area is now under the protection of the Greek archaeological service. Though in medieval times it was the most densely populated part of the peninsula,

Ruins of Monemvasía's 13th-century fortress

the upper town is deserted today, the last resident having departed in 1911.

A path climbs the cliff face above the town's north-western corner, leading to an entrance gate which still has its iron slats. Directly ahead a track leads to the summit's best-preserved building, the church of **Agía Sofía**. It was founded by Emperor Andronikos II (1282–1328) in emulation of Dafní monastery (see pp152–3) near Athens. With its 16-sided dome, the church perches on the brink of the northerly cliff and is visible from a considerable distance inland. The west portico is Venetian, while the niche on the south wall dates from its use as a mosque. A few frescoes surviving from the early 14th century are badly faded, but the *Ancient of Days* can be discerned in the sanctuary's vault, as can the *Birth of John the Baptist* in the north vault. Carved ornamentation has fared better, such as the

marble capitals flanking the south windows, depicting mythical monsters and a richly dressed woman.

To the west are the remains of a 13th-century **fortress**, amid the debris of former barracks, guardrooms and a gunpowder magazine from the Venetian period. A vast **cistern** recalls the times of siege when great quantities of water had to be stored. Food supplies, entirely imported, were more of a problem, as was demonstrated by the siege of 1821.

Agía Paraskeví, viewed from Byzantine Geráki

aisle and narthex added after 1262; a carved marble screen and varied frescoes decorate its interior.

Below the west gate, 13th-century **Zoödóchou Pigís** sports a complete Gothic door and south window, while inside later frescoes include *Christ on the Road to Calvary.*

At the base of the hill, the domeless, 14th-century church of **Agía Paraskeví** has a fine *Nativity* in its cross vault, plus a painting of the donor family on the west wall.

Geráki ㉑
Γεράκι

Peloponnese. **Road map** C5.
2,000.

Occupying a spur of Mount Párnonas, Geráki is like a miniature Mystrás with its kástro overlooking the frescoed Byzantine churches on the slopes below. The polygonal **kástro** was built in 1254–5 by the Frank, Jean de Nivelet, though it was ceded in 1262 to the Byzantines, together with Monemvasía and Mystrás. Inside, 13th-century **Agios Geórgios** is a hybrid Franko-Byzantine church, the third

Environs
Four more churches stand a short drive to the west in **Geráki** village. Both 12th-century Agios Athanásios and 13th-century Agios Sózon share a cross-in-square plan, with a high dome on four piers. Market edicts of the Roman Emperor Diocletian, inscribed on stone, flank the doorway of barrel-vaulted, 14th-century Agios Ioánnis Chrysóstomos, covered inside with scenes from the life of Christ and the Virgin. Tiny Evangelístria has a Pantokrátor fresco in its dome.

7th-century BC clay head of a woman, from Spárti acropolis

Spárti ㉒
Σπάρτη

Peloponnese. **Road map** C5.
20,000. Town Hall, Plateía Kentrikí (27310 26771)
8am–3pm Mon–Fri.

Though one of the most powerful of the Greek city-states, Ancient Sparta was unfortified and has few ruins dating to its heyday. The acropolis lies 700 m (2,300 ft) northwest of the modern town centre. On the western side of the acropolis is the cavity of the Roman theatre, its masonry largely pilfered to build Mystrás, while directly east stands the long, arcaded stoa which once held shops. Of the Artemis Orthia sanctuary just east of town, where Spartan youths were flogged to prove their manhood, only some Roman seating remains. The most interesting finds are on display in the museum.

The highlight of the rich **Archaeological Museum** is the fine collection of Roman mosaics, including two lions rampant over a vase, Arion riding his dolphin, Achilles disguised as a woman on Skýros, and a portrait of Alkibiades. A Classical marble head of a warrior, possibly Leonidas I (*see p224*), was found on the acropolis, while bas-reliefs of Underworld serpent-deities hail from a sanctuary of Apollo at Amyklés, 8 km (5 miles) south of Spárti. Bizarre ceramic masks are smaller replicas of those used in dances at the Artemis Orthia sanctuary.

Archaeological Museum
Agíou Níkonos 71. **Tel** 27310 28575.
8:30am–3pm Tue–Sun.
main public hols.

LIFE IN ANCIENT SPARTA

Rising to prominence around 700 BC, Sparta became one of the most powerful city-states of ancient Greece. Its power was based on rigid social and military discipline, as well as hatred of foreigners, which eventually led to its downfall as it had no allies. The "city" was made up of five villages, where the male citizens lived communally in constant readiness for war. Warriors were selected at the age of seven and subjected to rigorous training – whipping contests, with young boys as the victims, were held in the sanctuary of Artemis Orthia. Sparta was able to support its citizens as professional soldiers because it had conquered neighbouring Messenia, and the enslaved population provided all the food required. Sparta led the Greek forces against the Persians, but ceased to be a major power after defeat by Thebes in 371 BC.

5th-century BC bronze figurine of a Spartan warrior

Mystrás ㉓
Μυστράς

Double-eagle marble plaque, Mitrópolis

Majestic Mystras occupies a panoramic site on a spur of the severe Taÿgetos range. Founded by the Franks in 1249 to replace medieval Spárti, it soon passed to the Byzantines, under whom it became a town of 20,000 and, after 1348, the seat of the Despots of Morea. The despotate acted semi-independently and had become the last major Byzantine cultural centre by the 15th century, attracting scholars and artists from Italy and Serbia as well as Constantinople. One result was the uniquely cosmopolitan decoration of the Mystrás churches – their pastel-coloured frescoes, crowded with detail, reflect Italian Renaissance influence.

PLAN OF MYSTRAS

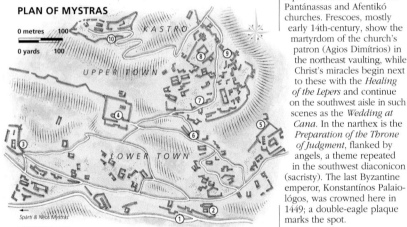

0 metres 100

0 yards 100

KASTRO

UPPER TOWN

LOWER TOWN

Spárti & Néos Mystrás

KEY TO PLAN

① Lower town entrance
② Mitrópolis
③ Moní Perivléptou
④ Moní Pantánassas
⑤ Vrontóchion
⑥ Monemvasía Gate
⑦ Despots' Palace
⑧ Agia Sofía
⑨ Upper town entrance
⑩ Kástro

Exploring Mystrás

Now in ruins, Mystrás consists of a lower and upper town, linked by the Monemvasía Gate. The site can be entered from the castle at the top of the upper town or from the base of the lower town. Allow half a day for exploring the monasteries, churches, palaces and houses which line the narrow, winding streets. An unusual northwest-to-southeast alignment of the churches is dictated by the site's steep topography.

◁ *Healing of the Paralytic* fresco, Moní Pantánassas, Mystrás

VISITORS' CHECKLIST

5 km (3 miles) W of Spárti, Peloponnese. **Road map** C5. *Tel* 27310 83377. to Néos Mystrás. ☐ May–Sep: 8:00am–7pm daily; Oct–Apr: 8:30am–3pm daily. ☐ 1 Jan, 25 Mar, Good Fri, Easter Sun, 1 May, 25, 26 Dec.

courtyard. Like many Balkan cathedrals, it began life in 1291 as a barrel-vaulted nave flanked by two aisles. The domes were added early in the 1400s in a clumsy attempt to equal the architecture of the Pantánassas and Afentikó churches. Frescoes, mostly early 14th-century, show the martyrdom of the church's patron (Agios Dimítrios) in the northeast vaulting, while Christ's miracles begin next to these with the *Healing of the Lepers* and continue on the southwest aisle in such scenes as the *Wedding at Cana*. In the narthex is the *Preparation of the Throne of Judgment*, flanked by angels, a theme repeated in the southwest diaconicon (sacristy). The last Byzantine emperor, Konstantínos Palaiológos, was crowned here in 1449; a double-eagle plaque marks the spot.

⛪ Mitrópoli

The Mitrópoli, situated by the lower town entrance, is the oldest church in Mystrás. It is approached through a double

The 14th-century fresco of the *Nativity* in the south vault of Moní Perivléptou

⛪ Moní Perivléptou

Squeezed against the rock face, the 14th-century monastery of Perivléptou has a compact, three-aisled church. Its small dome retains a fresco of the Pantokrátor, flanked by the Virgin and prophets, arranged in diminishing order of importance. The 14th-century frescoes, the most refined in Mystrás, focus on the 12 major church feasts. They include a vivid *Nativity* and *Baptism* in the south vault, the *Transfiguration* and *Entry into Jerusalem*, complete with playing children, in the west aisle, and *Doubting Thomas* and the *Pentecost* in the north vault, decorating the wall over the entrance.

The hillside with remains of Byzantine Mystrás, seen from the south

🔒 Moní Pantánassas

Dating to 1428, Pantánassas was the last church built at Mystrás. With its decorated apses and the brickwork of its arcaded belfry it imitates Afentikó in the Vrontóchion as an eclectic architectural experiment. The highest frescoes, from 1430, are of most merit, particularly a vivid *Raising of Lazarus* in the northeast vault. Both the *Nativity* and the *Annunciation* in the southwest vault feature animals. The southeast aisle displays the *Descent into Hell*, in which Christ raises Adam and Eve from their coffins, opposite a lively *Entry into Jerusalem*.

🔒 Vrontóchion

A 13th-century monastic complex built by Abbot Pachómios, the Vrontóchion was the cultural centre of medieval Mystrás – in the 15th century, the Neo-Platonist philosopher Geórgios Gemistós, or Plethon, (1355–1452) taught here. It has

two churches; the earliest, Agioi Theódoroi, dates from 1295 and has the largest dome at Mystrás, supported on eight arches. Few frescoes survive. The early 14th-century Afentikó (or Panagía Odigítria) is richly frescoed, with six domes. The galleries and two north-side chapels are shut, but in the west gallery dome a *Virgin Orans* (praying) and *Prophets* are visible; in the south vault, a crowded *Baptism* includes water monsters. Above the altar, apostles gesticulate towards the aura of the rising Christ in the *Ascension*. The best-preserved frescoes can be found in the north bay of the narthex.

🏛 Despots' Palace

The Despots' Palace consists of two wings which are now being reconstructed. The northeast wing was begun by the Franks; the northwest hall, erected after 1348 and a rare example of Byzantine civic

architecture, has the throne room of the rulers of the Cantacuzene and Palaiológos dynasties. The square was a venue for public events under the despots and a marketplace under the Ottomans.

The ruins of the Despots' Palace, viewed from the south

♣ Kástro

Flanked by sheer ravines to the south and west, and crowning the summit of the upper town, the kástro is reached by a path leading from the upper entrance which stands above the church of Agía Sofía. Built by Guillaume de Villehardouin in 1249, the kástro retains its original Frankish design, though it was greatly altered by the Byzantines and Turks. A double circuit of curtain walls encloses two baileys and a walkway can be taken around most of the structure, affording panoramic views over the lower town.

It was here that the German writer Goethe, in Part Two of *Faust*, set the meeting of Faust and Helen of Troy, revived after 3,000 years.

Afentikó church, part of the Vrontóchion complex

For hotels and restaurants in this region see pp268–70 and pp289–91

Outer Máni ❷⁴
Έξω Μάνη

A harsh, remote region, bounded by mountains to the north, the rocky Máni was the last part of Greece to embrace Christianity, doing so in the 9th century with an enthusiasm borne out by dozens of surviving Byzantine chapels. Though well defended against invaders, the area has a history of internal feuding which led to the building of its many tower houses. A ravine at Oítylo divides Inner Máni, to the south *(see pp198–9)*, from the more fertile Outer, or Messenian, Máni which boasts some of the finest country in the Mediterranean.

LOCATOR MAP

ANAVRYTÍ & PALAIOPANAGÍA
Exochóri
Kardamý li
PIGADIA & KALAMÁTA • Stoúpa
MOUNT TAYGETOS
OUTER MÁNI
Agios Nikólaos
Langáda
GERAKI & MONEMVASÍA
Gýtheio
Oítylo • Néo Oítylo

Oítylo

Though administratively within the region of Lakonía, by tradition the village of Oítylo (pronounced "Itilo") belongs to the Outer Máni. It affords superb panoramic views over Limeníou Bay and across a flanking ravine, traditionally the border betwen the Inner and Outer Máni, to Kelefá Castle *(see p198)*. Its relatively good water supply fosters a lush setting around and below the village, with cypresses and a variety of orchard trees. Unlike most Mániot villages, Oítylo is not in economic decline. Its many fine houses include graceful 19th-century mansions. The village was capital of the Máni between the 16th and 18th centuries, and was the area's most infamous slave-trading centre; both Venetians and Turks were sold to each other here. A plaque in the square, written in French and Greek, commemorates the flight, in 1675, of 730 Oítylots to Corsica – 430 of whom were from the Stefanópoulos clan. Seeking refuge from the Turks, the Oítylots were granted passage by the Genoese and, once in Corsica, founded the villages of Paomia and Cargèse. These towns account for the stories of Napoleon's part-Mániot origins.

Environs

From the southwestern corner of Oítylo, a broad path descends west to **Moní Dekoúlou**, nestled in its own little oasis. The 18th-century church features an ornate *témblon* (wooden altar screen) and vivid original frescoes; though they have been preserved by the darkness, a torch is required to see them now. The monastery is only open in the evenings or by prior arrangement with the resident caretakers.

The village of **Néo Oítylo** stands 4 km (2 miles) south of the monastery. Quietly secluded, the village has a pebble beach with fine views.

THE MANIOT FEUDS

By the 15th century, a number of refugee Byzantine families had settled in the Máni, the most powerful forming a local aristocracy known as the Nyklians. Feuding between clans over the inadequate land was rife, though only Nyklians had the right to construct stone towers, which attained four or five storeys and came to dominate nearly every Mániot village.

Pétros Mavromichális

Once commenced, blood feuds could last months, even years, with periodic truces to tend to the crops. Clansmen fired at each other from facing towers, raising them in order to be able to catapult rocks on to opponents' roofs. The hostilities ended only with the total destruction or submission of the losing clan. Historically, the most important clans were those of Mavromichális at Areópoli, Grigorákis at Gýtheio and Troupákis at Kardamýli, whose members boasted of never having been completely subjugated by any foreign power. The Ottomans wisely refrained from ruling the Máni directly, but instead quietly encouraged the clans to feud in order to weaken potential rebellions, and appointed a Nyklian chieftain as *bey* (regional lord) to represent the sultan locally. Under the final *bey*, Pétros Mavromichális, the clans finally united, instigating the Greek Independence uprising on 17 March 1821 *(see pp40–41)*.

Oítylo viewed from the northwest, looking towards Kelefá Castle

Agios Spyrídon south window, framed with marble reliefs

Kardamýli

Kardamýli was the lair of the Troupákis family, important rivals of the Mavromichális clan. Nicknamed Moúrtzinos or "Bulldogs" for their tenacity in battle, they claimed to be descended from the Byzantine dynasty of Palaiológi. Olive oil *(see p283)* used to be the chief source of income for Kardamýli, but this has now been superseded by tourism.

Inland rises the ancient and medieval acropolis, heralded by twin Mycenaean chamber tombs. In Old Kardamýli (sign posted) are Troupákis-built towers which stand alongside the 18th-century church of **Agios Spyrídon**. This building is made of Hellenistic masonry

and graced by a pointed, four-storey belfry; the south window and doorway are framed by intricate marble reliefs.

Environs

Two paths lead from Kardamýli, one upstream along the **Vyrós Gorge** where two monasteries shelter beneath the cliffs; the other to the villages of Gourniés and Exochóri. A short drive to the south, **Stoúpa** is popular for its two sandy bays; novelist Níkos Kazantzákis (1883–1957) lived here briefly and partly based his *Zorba the Greek* character on a foreman who worked nearby. The village of **Agios Nikólaos**, a short walk to the south, curls around Outer Máni's most photogenic harbour. It has four tavernas and the closest beach is at Agios Dimítrios, 3 km (2 miles) further south.

Mount Taÿgetos

The distinctive pyramidal summit and knife-edged ridge of Mount Taÿgetos, standing at 2,404 m (7,885 ft), divides the regions of Messinía and Lakonía. Formed of limestone and densely clad in black pine and fir, the range is the

Taÿgetos, seen through the Vyrós Gorge

watershed of the region and offers several days of wilderness trekking to experienced, well-equipped mountaineers.

Anavrytí and Palaiopanagiá, on the east, and Pigádia and Kardamýli on the west, are the usual trailhead villages. Various traverses can be made by using the Vyrós and Ríntomo gorges which drain west from the main ridge; an unstaffed alpine refuge at Varvára-Deréki, above Palaiopanagiá, is the best starting point for those wanting to head straight for the summit.

The ridge of Mount Taÿgetos with an olive grove in the foreground

Inner Máni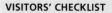
Μέσα Μάνη

Inner, or Lakonian, Máni is divided into two regions – the "Shadowed", western flank and the "Sunward", eastern shore. The former is famous for its numerous caves and churches, the latter for its villages which perch dramatically on crags overlooking the sea. With its era of martial glory over *(see p194)*, Inner Máni is severely depopulated, its only future being as a holiday venue. Retired Athenians of Mániot descent have restored the famous towers as hunting lodges for the brief autumn shoot of quail and turtle dove.

VISITORS' CHECKLIST

Peloponnese. **Road map** C5.
Gýtheio. Areópoli. Vasiléos
Georgiou 20, Gýtheio (27330
24484). **Museum of the Máni**
Marathonísi Islet. **Tel** 27330
22676. 9am–3pm daily.
Pýrgos Diroú Caves 12 km (7
miles) S of Areópoli. **Tel** 27330
52223. Oct–May: 8am–3pm;
Jun–Sep: 8:30am–5:30pm daily.

LOCATOR MAP

Gýtheio
Oítylo
Kelefá
Pássavá
INNER MÁNI
Areópoli
Pýrgos Diroú
Charoúda
Vámvaka
Stavrí
Káto Gardenítsa
Ano Mpoulárioi
Gerolimínas
Váthela
CAPE TAÍNARO

Gýtheio
The lively town of Gýtheio is the gateway to the Máni peninsula and one of the most attractive coastal towns in the southern Peloponnese. It was once the naval base of Ancient Sparta *(see p189)*, though the main ancient relic is a Roman theatre to the north. The town was wealthy in Roman times when it exported the purple molluscs used for colouring imperial togas. Until World War II, Gýtheio exported acorns used in leather-tanning, gathered by women and children from nearby valleys.

The town's heart is Plateía Mavromicháli, with the quay extending to either side lined by tiled, 19th-century houses. The east-facing town enjoys sunrises over Cape Maléas and the Lakonian Gulf while snowy Mount Taÿgetos looms beyond a low ridge to the north.

In the bay, and linked to the waterfront by a causeway, lies the islet of Marathonísi, thought to be Homer's Kranaï islet. It was here that Paris of Troy and Helen spent their first night together *(see p52)*. It is dominated by the Tzanetbey Grigorákis tower, a crenellated 18th-century fortress which now houses the **Museum of the Máni**. The subject of the exploration of the Máni in medieval times is covered on the ground floor, while the exhibits of the upper storey place the tower houses in their social context.

Environs
Standing 12 km (7 miles) to the southwest, the **Castle of Passavá** was built in 1254 by the Frankish de Neuilly clan to guard a defile between Kelefá and Oítylo. Its name stems from *passe-avant*, the clan's motto, though the present building is an 18th-century Turkish construction. The Turks left the castle in 1780 after Tzanetbey Grigorákis avenged the murder of his uncle by massacring 1,000 Muslim villagers inside. Today's overgrown ruins are best approached from the southwest.

Areópoli
The Mavromichális *(see p194)* stronghold of Tsímova was renamed Areópoli, "the city of Ares" (god of war), for its role in the War of Independence *(see p40)*; it was here that the Mániot uprising against the Turks was proclaimed by Pétros Mavromichális. Now the main town of the Máni, its central old quarter features two 18th-century churches: **Taxiarchón** boasts the highest belltower in the Máni, as well as zodiacal apse reliefs, while **Agios Ioánnis**, adorned with naive frescoes, was the chapel of the Mavromichális.

Environs
Ottoman **Kelefá Castle**, standing 10 km (6 miles) north of Areópoli, is the second castle guarding the Máni. It was built in 1670 to command the bays of Oítylo and Liméni and counter the impending Venetian invasion *(see p38)*.

19th-century houses lining the harbour of Gýtheio

◁ **Semi-ruined tower houses of Vátheia village, the architectural jewel of the Máni**

The bastions of the pentagonal curtain walls are preserved. The castle can be reached from the Areópoli– Gýtheio road (sign posted) and from a footpath from Oítylo.

Pýrgos Diroú Caves
This cave system is one of the largest and most colourful in Greece. During summer, crowds take a 30-minute punt ride along the underground stream which passes through Glyfáda cavern, reflecting the overhanging stalactites. A 15-minute walk then leads to the exit. A nearby chamber, called Alepótrypa cave, is drier and, though currently shut, is just as spectacular with waterfalls and a lake. Until an earthquake closed the entrance, the cave was home to Neolithic people, and a separate **museum** reveals their life and death.

The Shadowed Coast
Between Pýrgos Diroú and Geroliménas lies the 17-km (11-mile) shore of the Shadowed Coast. Once one of the most densely populated regions of the Máni, it is famous for its numerous Byzantine churches built between the 10th and 14th centuries. The ruins of many Mániot tower houses can also be found.

Among the finest churches is 11th-century **Taxiarchón**, at Charoúda, with its interior covered by vivid 18th-century frescoes. Heading south, the road continues to **Agios Theódoros**, at Vámvaka, where the dome is supported by

Corner turret of Ottoman Kelefá Castle, near Areópoli

carved beams; birds bearing grapes adorn its marble lintel.

Káto Gardenítsa boasts the 12th-century **Agía Soteíra**, with its frescoed iconostasis and domed narthex, while 12th-century **Episkopí**, near Stavrí, has a complete cycle of 18th-century frescoes.

Near Ano Mpoulárioi village, doorless **Agios Panteleímon** offers 10th-century frescoes (the earliest and the most primitive in the Máni), while in the village, the 11th-century **Agios Stratigós** bears a set of 12th- and 13th-century frescoes – the *Acts of Christ* is the most distinguished.

Vátheia, 10 km (6 miles) east of Geroliménas, is one of the most dramatically located of the villages; overlooking the sea and Cape Taínaro, its bristling tower houses constitute a showpiece of local architectural history.

Tower houses of Vátheia village, viewed from the southeast

For hotels and restaurants in this region see pp268–70 and pp289–91

Koróni 26
Λορώνη

Peloponnese. **Road map** C5.
⚐ 1,400. ⛴

One of the "eyes of Venice" (along with Methóni), Koróni surveys the shipping lanes between the Adriatic and Crete. It stands at the foot of a Venetian castle, begun in 1206, whose walls now shelter the huge **Timíou Prodrómou** convent. A Byzantine chapel and foundations of an Artemis temple stand by the gate of the convent whose cells and chapels command fine views.

The town, lying beneath the castle and divided by stepped streets, dates to 1830. It has changed little recently and many houses retain elaborate wrought-iron balconies, horizontal-slat shutters and tile "beaks" on the undulating roofs. A lively seafront is the sole concession to tourism.

Methóni 27
Νεθώνη

Peloponnese. **Road map** B5.
⚐ 1,300. ⛴

Methoni, a key Venetian port, controlled the lucrative pilgrim trade to Palestine after 1209. With the sea on three sides, its rambling **castle** is defended on its landward side by a Venetian moat, bridged by the French in 1828. The structure combines Venetian, Ottoman and even French military architecture. The remains within the walls include two ruined *hamams*

(baths), a Venetian church, minaret bases and the main street. Boúrtzi, an islet fortified by the Turks, stands beyond the Venetian sea-gate.

♦ Castle
🕐 9am–7pm daily (9am–3pm winter).

Pýlos 28
Πύλος

Peloponnese. **Road map** C5.
⚐ 2,500. ⛴

The town of Pylos, originally known as Avaríno, (later Navaríno) after the Avar tribes which invaded the area in the

BATTLE OF NAVARINO

An unexpected naval engagement which decided the War of Independence (see pp40–41), the Battle of Navaríno took place on 20 October 1827. Victory here by the French, Russian and English allies over the Ottoman fleet broke the Greek-Ottoman deadlock and resolved the problem of the Sultan's refusal of an armistice. The allied fleet of 27 ships, commanded by admirals Codrington, de Rigny and Heyden, entered Navaríno Bay where Ibrahim Pasha's armada of 89 lay anchored. The outnumbered allies merely intended to intimidate Ibrahim into leaving the bay, but were fired upon, and a full-scale battle ensued. By nightfall three-quarters of the Ottoman fleet was sunk, with negligible allied casualties; Greek independence was now inevitable. The admirals are honoured by an obelisk in their namesake square in Pýlos.

Scene from the dramatic *Battle of Navarino*, painted by Louis Ambroise Garneray (1783–1857)

6th century, is French in design, like Methóni. Life is confined to Plateía Trión Navárchon and the seafront on either side.

To the west, the castle of **Niókastro**, Ottoman and Venetian in origin, was extensively repaired by the French after 1828; their barracks are now a gallery of antiquarian engravings by the artist René Puaux (1878–1938). An institute of underwater archaeology is situated in the former dungeons of the hexagonal keep. The roof gives views over the outer bailey, immense Navaríno Bay and Sfaktiría island, site of a memorable Athenian victory over the Spartans.

The fortified islet of Boúrtzi, off the coast at Methóni, with its 16th-century octagonal tower

For hotels and restaurants in this region see pp268–70 and pp289–91

The arcaded former mosque, now Sotíros church, Pýlos

The perimeter walls are dilapidated, but it is possible to walk along the parapet, starting from the imposing west bastion overlooking the mouth of the bay, and finishing above the east gate. The domed and arcaded church of **Sotíras**, once a mosque, is the only medieval survival in the outer bailey.

♟ Niókastro
Town centre. *Tel* 27230 22010.
☐ 8:30am–3pm Tue–Sun. ● main public hols. 🖼 ♿ limited.

Environs
Boat tours visit a number of memorials on and around **Sfaktiría**, which commemorate those sailors lost in the Battle of Navaríno, foreign philhellenes and revolutionary heroes.

The north end of Navaríno Bay, 11 km (7 miles) north of Pýlos, has excellent beaches, especially **Voïdokoiliá** lagoon, where Telemachos, Odysseus's son, disembarked to seek news of his father from King Nestor. You can walk up the dunes to **Spiliá tou Néstora**, an impressively large cave, which may have been the inspiration for Homer's cave in which Nestor and Neleus kept their cows. A more strenuous path continues to Palaiókastro, the ancient acropolis and FrankoVenetian castle, built on Mycenaean foundations.

Nestor's Palace 🏛
Ανάκτορο του Νέστορα

16 km (10 miles) NE of Pýlos, Peloponnese. **Road map** B5. 🚌 **Site** *Tel* 27630 31437. ☐ 8:30am–3pm daily. Museum *Tel* 27630 31358. ☐ 8:30am–3pm Tue–Sun. ● main public hols. 🖼 ♿ limited.

Discovered in 1939, the 13th-century BC Palace of Mycenaean King Nestor was excavated by Carl Blegen from 1952. Hundreds of tablets in the ancient Linear B script were found, as well as a bathtub and olive oil jugs (the contents of which fuelled the devastating fire of 1200 BC). Today, only waist-high walls and column bases suggest the typical Mycenaean plan of a two-storey complex around a central hall. The **museum**, 3 km (2 miles) away in Chóra, has frescoes from the palace.

13th-century BC bathtub excavated from Nestor's Palace

Ancient Messene 🏛
Αρχαία Νεσσήνη

34 km (21 miles) NW of Kalamáta, Peloponnese. **Road map** C5. *Tel* 27240 51201. 🚌 **Site** ☐ 8:30am– sunset daily. **Museum** ☐ 8am–2:30pm Tue–Sun. 🖼 ● main public hols.

Ancient Messene is now confusingly known as Ithómi – named after the mountain that sits overhead. It is an underrated, intriguing site, still undergoing excavation. The city walls are 9 km (6 miles) long and date from the 4th century BC. They enclose a vast area that incorporates the foundations of a Zeus temple, and the acropolis on Mount Ithómi to the northeast. The massive, double Arcadia Gate situated on the north side is flanked by square towers.

The archaeological zone includes the picturesque village of Mavrommáti, whose water is still supplied by the ancient Klepsýdra fountain at the heart of the site. Below the village you will find an odeion (amphitheatre), a *bouleuterion* (council hall), stoas and a monumental stairway, all of which surround the foundations of an Asklepios temple. Just a little way further down the hill from here lies a well-preserved stadium.

Remains of the Arcadia Gate, with its fallen lintel, Ancient Messene

CENTRAL AND WESTERN GREECE

EPIRUS · THESSALY · STEREA ELLADA

*C*entral and Western Greece encompasses many of the lesser-known regions of mainland Greece and is, therefore, little touched by tourism. Though Epirus has produced a distinctive and largely autonomous culture, Stereá Elláda has always been of strategic importance, with the pass at Thermopylae and the Vale of Tempe providing invasion routes into the very heart of Greece.

This region of Greece is dominated by the central plain of Thessaly (the former bed of an inland sea) and the sights of interest lie largely on the periphery. Isolated by the Píndos mountains, the Epirus region, to the west, has the strongest of regional identities, having played a minor role in ancient Greece and maintained a large degree of autonomy under the Turks. The regional capital, Ioánnina, is thus a fascinating mixture of Turkish architecture and the local traditions of silversmithing and wood carving.

To the east, the grand Katára Pass, guarded in Ottoman times by the town of Métsovo, cuts through the mountains, providing access to the Byzantine

Woman from Métsovo, northern Píndos

Metéora monasteries which soar on the summits of the area's steeply eroded peaks.

In Stereá Elláda, one of the country's most important ancient sights, the ruins of the Delphic Oracle, stands only a short drive away from the Monastery of Osios Loúkas, perhaps the finest of late Byzantine buildings, decorated with some of the period's greatest mosaics.

While the Gulf of Corinth has many popular resorts, the towns of Lamía, Arta, Tríkala, and Mesolóngi (where the British poet Lord Byron died) make few concessions to tourism and so offer a more accurate picture of life in Greece today: its markets, tavernas, church-going and the evening *vólta*.

Megálo Pápigko, one of the many remote, once-isolated villages of Zagória in the Epirus region

◁ **The Byzantine Monastery of Osios Loúkas, with the belltower in the foreground**

Exploring Central and Western Greece

Stretching from Attica in the south to Macedonia in the
north, the vast expanse of Central and Western Greece
has a little of everything, from excellent beaches to the
venerable towns of Ioánnina and Métsovo with their
craftsmen's guilds and Ottoman heritage. The Pílio
offers the best combination of scenery and coastal
resorts, while no one should miss the two prime
attractions of Ancient Delphi, site of the oracle
of Apollo, and the Byzantine splendour of the
monasteries of Metéora. Walkers should
head north where, in addition to the
Víkos Gorge, the Píndos Mountains
have several of Greece's highest
peaks. The flora and fauna are
both splendid here, especially
in spring, but wildlife
enthusiasts should not miss
the wonderful wetlands
around Mesolóngi
and the beautiful
Amvrakikós Gulf,
near Arta.

KEY

═══	Dual-carriageway
───	Major road
───	Minor road
= =	Road under construction
───	Scenic route
───	Main railway
▬▬	National border
▬▬	Regional border
△	Summit

Agíou Nikoláou, one of Metéora's
soaring monasteries

SIGHTS AT A GLANCE

Map labels

Kónitsa
Aóos
VÍKOS GORGE **3**
Kalpáki
ZAGÓRIA **2**
PÍNDOS MOUNTAINS
E90
Vovoúsa
Píndos National Park
Kozáni
MÉTSOVO **4**
METÉORA
E92
E90
Pérama
Kalampáka
Thýamis
Filiátes
IOÁNNINA **5**
DODÓNI **6**
Athamánon
Ágios Nikolaos
Igoumenitsa
Tómaros 1974m
Pramanda
Avgó 2148m
Kakarditsa 2429m
Paramythiá
E55
EPIRUS
Mouzá
PÁRGA **7**
Kleisoúra
Glyki
Karáva 2184m
Necromanteíon of Efýra
Lourós
Aracthos
Filippiáda
Pyramíva 1782m
KASSÓPI **8**
ÁRTA **10**
Píeri 2128m
Nikópoli
Menidí
PRÉVEZA **9**
Amvrakikós Kólpos
Aktio
Makrynóros
Tríki
Techniti Límni Kremastón
Lefkáda
E952
Vónitsa
Amfilochía
Katoúna
Lefkáda
STEREA
Meganísi
Kálamos
Límni Ozeróś
E55
Agrínio
Acheloos
Límni Trichonía
Astakós
Matarágka
Neochóri
Aitolikó
21
MESOLÓNGI
Patraïkós Kólpos

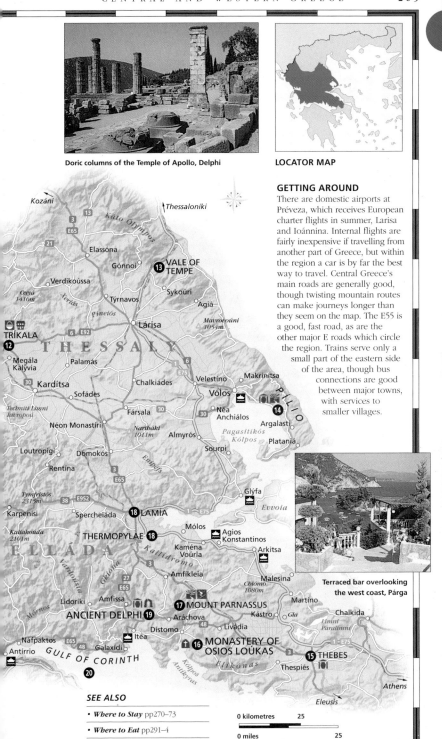

Doric columns of the Temple of Apollo, Delphi

LOCATOR MAP

GETTING AROUND

There are domestic airports at Préveza, which receives European charter flights in summer, Larisa and Ioánnina. Internal flights are fairly inexpensive if travelling from another part of Greece, but within the region a car is by far the best way to travel. Central Greece's main roads are generally good, though twisting mountain routes can make journeys longer than they seem on the map. The E55 is a good, fast road, as are the other major E roads which circle the region. Trains serve only a small part of the eastern side of the area, though bus connections are good between major towns, with services to smaller villages.

Terraced bar overlooking the west coast, Párga

SEE ALSO

- *Where to Stay* pp270–73
- *Where to Eat* pp291–4

0 kilometres   25

0 miles   25

Lake Drakolímni, behind the sheer cliffs of Astráka

Píndos Mountains ❶
Οροσειρά Πίνδου

Epirus. **Road map** B2. ✈ 🚌 *Ioán-nina.* 🛈 *Dodónis 39, Ioánnina (26510 41868).* ⬜ *Mon–Sat.*

The Píndos is a vast range stretching from the Greek border with Albania south beyond Métsovo. It extends east into Macedonia, and west towards the Ionian Sea, incorporating two national parks, Greece's second longest

gorge and its second highest mountain, Oros Smólikas, standing at 2,640 m (8,660 ft). The Píndos National Park lies just inside western Macedonia, between Métsovo and Vovoúsa, while the Víkos–Aóos National Park is a boot-shaped area encompassing the Víkos Gorge *(see p208)* and the Aóos River.

The peaks are snow-covered from October until May, when the melting snows water the ground, producing swathes of lilac crocus, gentians,

grass-of-Parnassus and many species of orchid *(see p23)*. The protection offered by the parks provides the visitor with an increased chance of seeing roe deer, wild boar and the European wild cat, all of which exist in small numbers.

Smólikas is accessible during summertime for those who are well equipped and prepared for camping or staying in mountain huts. Slightly easier to reach from the fascinating Zagorian villages by the Víkos Gorge are Gamíla 2,500 m (8,200 ft) and Astráka 2,440 m (8,000 ft), while the two mountain lakes both called Drakolímni are each worth the effort it takes to get to them. One is below Gamíla, near a sheer drop to the Aóos River, while the other stands beneath Smólikas.

Although there are good walking guides and maps of the area, with mountain huts to stay in and accommodation in some of the larger villages, visitors should not venture into the mountains unless they are prepared for the terrain and are experienced walkers. The weather can change quickly, and in many places you will be a long way from any kind of settlement – though this is one of the main attractions of the Píndos Mountains. They show the rugged side of Greece, offering remote valleys and routes where few visitors venture.

WILDLIFE OF THE PINDOS MOUNTAINS

Visitors to the coastal lowlands are often sceptical when told that wolves and bears still survive in Greece. However, despite the severe erosion of their natural habitat over the last 20 years, both European wolves and European brown bears can be found. The Píndos mountains, and particularly the northern regions towards Albania, continue to harbour the greatest numbers of these endangered and now protected creatures. They are extremely wary of man, having been persecuted by farmers and goatherds down the centuries. Therefore, visitors should consider themselves very fortunate if they see a bear. Wolves are just as hard to see but more evident, as they can often be heard howling at dawn and dusk, and will even respond to imitations of their howls. They pose no real threat to visitors.

The silver European wolf, a rare native of the region

One of the 80 European brown bears of the northern Píndos

Zagória 2

Ζαγόρια

Epirus. **Road map** B2.

Some of Europe's most spectacular scenery can be found only 25 km (15 miles) north of Ioánnina *(see p210)*, in the area known as Zagória. Though the soil is largely un-cultivable, on the forested hillsides some 45 traditional Epirot villages still survive; many of them boast imposing *archontiká* (mansions) dating to prosperous 18th– and 19th-century Ottoman times when Zagória was granted autonomy.

Vlach and Sarakatsan shepherds *(see p209)* make up most of the settled population. Over the winter months, the shepherds used to turn to crafts, forming into guilds of itinerant masons and wood-carvers, who would travel the Balkans selling their trades. This hard and ancient way of life is under threat, as the villagers, and especially the younger generation, prefer to earn their living from tourism.

A series of arched packhorse bridges are among the most memorable monuments to the skills of the local people and are unique features of the region. Two especially fine examples can be seen at either end of the village of **Kípoi**.

Vítsa village, by the Víkos Gorge

Southwestern Zagória is the busiest area, with a bus from Ioánnina to Monodéndri bringing in walkers and climbers. Some of the villages in the east of the region, such as **Vrysochóri**, were refuges for guerrillas during World War II and therefore burnt by the Germans; they have recovered only slowly.

Near the almost-deserted village of **Vradéto**, a 15th-century muletrack zigzags its way up a steep rockface beyond which the path leads to a stunning view of

the spectacular Víkos Gorge *(see p208)*. **Monodéndri**, opposite Vradéto, is the usual startingpoint for the gorge trail, though another path can be taken from **Vítsa**. Nearby are the two villages of **Megálo Pápigko** and **Mikró Pápigko**. They are 4 km (2 miles) apart and their names reflect their sizes, but even "big" Pápigko is no more than a scattering of houses around cobbled streets, with a choice of restau-rants, and rooms available in renovated mansions.

Further south, though still surrounded by mountains, is the relatively thriving village of **Tsepélovo**. It has a bus service to Ioánnina and a restored mansion which pro-vides accommodation, as well as a number of *pensions* and tavernas. Its cobbled streets and slate-roofed houses pro-vide a perfect portrait of a Zagorian village.

Packhorse bridge near the village of Kípoi

ZAGORIAN VILLAGES

Scattered across the lime-stone wilderness of the north Píndos, the villages of Zagória lie to the southwest of the Aóos River between Ioánnina and Kónitsa.

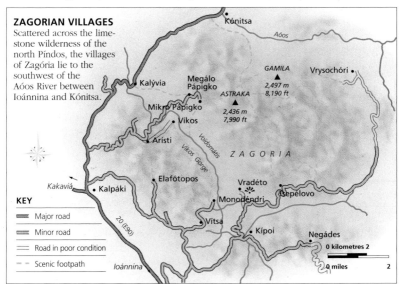

Kónitsa

Aóos

GAMILA ▲ 2,497 m 8,190 ft

Vrysochóri

Kalývia

Megálo Pápigko

ASTRAKA ▲ 2,436 m 7,990 ft

Mikró Pápigko

Víkos

Arísti

Víkos Gorge   *Voïdomátis*

Z A G O R I A

Kakaviá   Kalpáki

Elafótopos

Vradéto

Monodéndri

Tsepélovo

Vítsa

Kípoi

Negádes

KEY

▬▬ Major road

▭▭ Minor road

═══ Road in poor condition

- - Scenic footpath

20 (E90)

Ioánnina

0 kilometres 2

0 miles   2

Víkos Gorge Walk ❸

To trek the length of the Víkos Gorge is to undertake what is arguably the greatest walk in Greece. Carved by the Voïdomátis River, the sheer, deeply eroded limestone walls rise to 915 m (3,000 ft). The gorge cuts through the Víkos-Aóos National Park, established in 1975. Cairns and waymarks define the route which snakes through the boulder-strewn ravine bed and continues up through stands

Greek tortoise

of beech, chestnut and maple to the higher ground. Several birds of prey, including the Egyptian vulture, are commonly seen circling in the thermals, and lizards and tortoises abound. Though the main route through the gorge begins at Monodéndri, a shorter 4-km (2-mile) walk can be made between the northern villages of Mikró Pápigko and Víkos.

Megálo Pápigko ⑤
One of the area's protected traditional villages, stone-built Megálo Pápigko stands at 950 m (3,117 ft), beneath the cliffs of Pýrgi.

Rock pinnacle ④
For the Pápigko villages, cross the Víkos here beneath a landmark pinnacle of rock. The path branches to the west for Vítsiko.

Agía Triáda ③
After three hours you pass the white shrine of Agía Triáda, standing opposite a well.

Oxiá Viewpoint ②
From Monodéndri, a road can be taken to the Oxiá site, one of the area's finest viewpoints, along with Mpelóï opposite.

Monodéndri ①
With its magnificent views over the gorge, this village is the most popular start for the walk. The path is signposted from the church in the lower square.

0 kilometres   5

0 miles   2

KEY

– – Walk route	🏛 Monastery
═══ Minor road	🔆 Viewpoint
═══ Road in poor condition	🅿 Parking

TIPS FOR WALKERS

Starting point: Monodéndri.
Getting there: 40 km (25 miles) NW of Ioánnina, by car or bus.
Length: 14 km (8 miles) to Megálo Pápigko.
Difficulty: Straightforward, though hiking boots required.
Walking time: 6–7 hours.

Métsovo **4**
Μέτσοβο

Epirus. **Road map** B2. 🏔 *3,500.* 🚌
ℹ️ *26560 41233.*

Situated close by the Katára
Pass (the route crossing the
Píndos Mountains), Métsovo
has a vitality unique among
Greek mountain towns. It was
originally a small village
inhabited by Vlach shepherds,
though it became one of the
region's most important commercial centres after being
granted tax privileges in
return for guarding the pass
during Ottoman times *(see
pp38–9)*. Local merchant
families invested their new
wealth in the town and
continue to do so today by
providing endowments and
grants to encourage industry
among the local craftspeople.

One such family was the
Tosítsas, and some idea of the
size of their wealth can be
gained by touring the
rebuilt 18th-century
Archontikó Tosítsa,
which has been pre-
served as a museum.
Rising to three floors,
the mansion contains
an armoury and
washroom on the
ground floor, with
huge wood-panelled
reception rooms and

Shepherds' crooks, rugs and silverware in a souvenir shop in Métsovo

bedrooms upstairs, carpeted
with beautiful, locally woven
kilim rugs. Intricate gold- and
silverware are on display, as
well as collections of Epirot
costumes and embroidery.
Would-be visitors must wait
outside for the half-hourly
guided tour.

Another of Métsovo's bene-
factors was the writer and
politician Evángelos Avérof
(1910–90) who founded the
Avérof Gallery. The core of

Interior of the Archontikó Tosítsa, Métsovo

the gallery is Avérof's own
collection of some 200 paintings and sculptures he
acquired over the years,
always with the ambition of
opening a museum of
modern Greek art in his
home town. His collection
has been expanded to show
the work of several dozen
Greek artists from the 19th
and 20th centuries.

Ancient traditions have
survived in the area, from the
simple craft of carving
shepherds' crooks (from the
town's sheep farming days) to
embroidery and wine- and
cheese-making. Some of the
older men (and a few women)
still wear traditional costumes;
you can see them, dressed in
black, sitting in the shelters and
cafés around the town square.
The shelters are needed during
winter when the town, at 1,156
m (3,793 ft) becomes a
popular ski resort. The rugs on
sale in the souvenir shops also
reflect this alpine character.

🏛 **Archontikó Tosítsa**
Off main thoroughfare. **Tel** *26560
41084.* ◻ *9am–1:30pm & 3–5pm
daily.* 📷

🏛 **Avérof Gallery**
Off central square. **Tel** *26560
41210.* ◻ *Oct–Jun: 10am–4pm
daily; Jul–Sep: 10am–7pm daily.* 📷

Environs
Fifteen minutes' walk south,
signposted from the centre of
town, stands the small and
charming 14th-century **Moní
Agíou Nikoláou**. Now it is
inhabited only by caretakers
who are more than happy to
show visitors the church's
vivid post-Byzantine frescoes,
the monks' living quarters and
their own supplies of flowers,
fruit and vegetables.

VLACH SHEPHERDS

Of unknown origin, the nomadic Vlach shepherds are
today centred in the Píndos Mountains, particularly in and
around Métsovo. Their language, which has no written
form, is a dialect of Latin origin, and it is thought that they
might be descended from Roman settlers who
moved through Illyria into the northern
Balkans. Traditionally, their way of life has
been transhumant – spending summers in
the mountains before moving down to the
plains of Thessaly with their sheep for
six months to avoid the worst of the
winter snows. It is a hard way of life
which is gradually disappearing,
and the shepherds who remain
can be found in such villages as
Métsovo and Vovoúsa in Epirus,
or Avdélla, Samarína and Smíxi
in western Macedonia – their
traditional summer settlements.
Their winter homes lie mainly
around Kastoriá *(see p240).*

Zagorian Vlach shepherd

Ioánnina ⑤

Ιωάννινα

Chalice made of Ioánninan silver

The capital of the Epirus region, Ioánnina prospered during Ottoman times (see pp38–9) when its famous craftsmen's guilds, including the silversmiths', were formed. The Turkish influence is most visible in the fortress area which extends on a small headland into Lake Pamvótis (it was once moated on its landward side). Though dating to the 13th century, the area was rebuilt in 1815 by Ali Pasha, the Turkish tyrant most closely associated with it. Inside the fortress precinct a village-like peace reigns, though the bustle of the bazaar and the modern area is a reminder that this is still the region's busiest city.

Aslan Pasha Mosque, housing the Popular Art Museum

Ioánnina and the isle of Nisí, seen from the north

👁 Municipal Museum

Aslan Pasha Mosque. **Tel** 26510 26356. ⏲ Jun–Aug: 9am–4pm daily; Sep–May: 8am–3 pm. 🔲 main public hols. 🖾
Situated in the northern corner of the fortress, this small museum is housed within the Aslan Pasha Mosque, built by Aslan Pasha in 1618. While the interior of the mosque itself, which retains the original decoration on its dome, makes a visit worthwhile, the weapons and costumes on display tell something of Ioánnina's recent past. Turkish furniture inlaid with mother-of-pearl can also be found, alongside Jewish rugs and tapestries.

👁 Byzantine Museum

Inner Fortress. **Tel** 26510 25989. ⏲ Jun–Sep: 8am–7pm Tue–Sun; Nov–May: 8am–5pm. 🔲 main public hols. 🖾
This modern museum, situated in the inner fortress, contains a few items from local archaeological excavations, but the core is an imaginative display of icons from the 16th to the 19th centuries. Silverware, for which the town is renowned, is displayed in a separate annexe, once the treasury, with a reconstruction of a typical silversmith's workshop.

👁 Archaeological Museum

Plateía 25 Martíou 6. **Tel** 26510 33357. ⏲ undergoing renovations; call to check opening hours. 🖾
Set in a small park, the excellent Archaeological Museum displays a small collection of artifacts, including items from the site of Dodóni. These include a bronze eagle from the 5th century BC, statuettes of young children and lead tablets inscribed with questions for the oracle.

👁 Popular Art Museum

Michaíl Angélou 42. **Tel** 26510 20515. ⏲ 9am–2pm Tue, Thu, Fri, 3–5pm Wed, Sat. 🔲 main public hols. 🖾
At the far end of a side street, almost opposite the Archaeological Museum is the mansion containing a collection of local crafts. As well as silver-work and traditional costumes, there are woven textiles made by the nomadic, tent-dwelling Sarakatsans who number less than the Vlach tribe (see p209).

ALI PASHA

Ali Pasha was born in Albania in 1741 and, in 1788, was installed at Ioánnina by the Turks as Pasha of Epirus. Though a murderer, he was a great administrator who made the town one of the wealthiest in Greece. His aim was to gain independence from his overlords and by 1820 he had an empire stretching from Albania to the Peloponnese. When news spread of his intention to create a Greco-Albanian state, Sultan Mahmud II of Turkey dispatched troops to put him to death. After a long siege within the fortress at Ioánnina, Ali Pasha agreed to meet the Turkish commander on the island of Nisí where, on 24 January 1822, he was hunted down, trapped and killed.

Tapestry of Ali Pasha (centre), Moní Agíou Panteleímonos, Nisí

🏞 Nisí

15 minutes by boat NE from fortress.
Though its first inhabitants
were the monks who came
here in the early years of the
13th century, the single village
on the isle of Nisí owes its
existence to 17th-century refugees from Mániot feuds (see
p194). Its main building is
Moní Agíou Panteleímonos,
where the reconstructed room
in which Ali Pasha was shot
can be visited, the bullet holes
still visible in the floor. Other
rooms contain a few of his
possessions, some costumes
and period prints.

Stalactites in the Pérama Caves

Environs

Greece's largest cave network,
the **Pérama Caves**, are near
the village of Pérama, 4 km
(2 miles) north of Ioánnina.
They were discovered in 1940
by a shepherd hiding from the
Germans, but only fully explored years later. Now there
are regular guided tours taking visitors along the 1,700 m
(5,600 ft) of passages, where
multicoloured lights pick out
the stalactites and stalagmites.

🏞 Pérama Caves

Pérama. **Tel** 26510 81521. ⬤ 8am–
7pm daily (to 6pm Oct–Mar). 🔲

The theatre of Dodóna, one of the largest in Greece

Dodóna ❻
Δωδώνη

Epirus. **Road map** B3. **Tel** 26510
82287. 🚌 ⬤ 8am–7pm daily (to 5pm
Oct–May). ⬤ main public hols. 🔲 ♿

Dating to at least 1000 BC,
the Oracle of Zeus at Dodóna
is the oldest in Greece and
was second in status
only to the one at Delphi (see
pp228–9). The site is located
22 km (14 miles) southwest
of Ioánnina in a placid green
valley on the eastern slopes
of Mount Tómaros.

The oracle focused on a
sacred oak tree ringed with
tripods which held a number
of bronze cauldrons placed so
that they touched each other.
Prophecies were divined from
the sound these made, in
harmony with the rustling
of the oak leaves, when one
of the cauldrons was struck.
Petitioners would inscribe
their questions on lead tablets
for the priestess to read
to Zeus; some of
these have been
found on the
site and can
be seen in the
Archaeological
Museum in
Ioánnina. The
reputed power
of the oak tree
was such that
Jason, on his
quest for the
Golden Fleece (see

**Justinian, the last Roman
Emperor to visit Dodóna**

p220), travelled across from
the Pílio to acquire one of its
branches to attach to his ship,
the Argo. By the 3rd century
BC a colonnaded courtyard
was built around the tree for

protection; it contained a small
temple of which only foundations remain. The tree was
uprooted in AD 393 on the
orders of the Roman Emperor
Theodosios (ruled 379–395)
in accordance with his policy
of stamping out pagan practices. He also believed that
buried treasure might be
found beneath the site.

The main feature of Dodóna
today is the theatre which,
with its capacity for 17,000
spectators, is one of the
largest in Greece. Its huge
walls rise to 21 m (69 ft) and
are supported by solid towers
where kestrels now nest. Used
by the ancient Greeks for
dramatic performances, the
Romans later converted it to
an arena for animal fights;
bulls and big cats would have
been kept in the two triangular
pens on either side of the
stage. The whole structure of
the theatre was restored in
the early 1960s and is now
used for performances
during the summer.
Dodóna also in-
cludes the ruins
of a stadium,
acropolis and
Byzantine
basilica – all
reminders of
the time when
this empty
valley was the
location of a
flourishing
market town.

Dodóna fell into ruin in the
6th century AD when the
Roman Emperor Justinian
decided to found the new
and more easily defendable
city of Ioánnina.

The tiered, amphitheatre-shaped town of Párga, seen across Párga Bay

Párga 🅐
Πάργα

Epirus. **Road map** B3. 🅰 2,000. 🚌
🛈 Alexandrou Pága 18 (26840
31222). 🕮 daily in summer. 🛍 Tue.

Parga, the main beach resort
of Epirus, is a busy holiday
town whose charms are often
overwhelmed by the number of
summer visitors. The Venetian
fortress dominating the west
side of the harbour was built
in the late 16th century on the
site of a building destroyed in
1537 during a brief period of
Turkish rule. The Ottomans
later returned under the command of Ali Pasha (see p210),
who bought the town from the
British in 1819. After this, many
of Párga's inhabitants left for
Corfu, though it was regained
by the Greeks in 1913.

There are two
small beaches
within walking
distance of the
town centre and
two larger ones
about 2 km
(1 mile) away:
Váltos, the
biggest, is to
the north and
Lychnos to the
southwest. Fish
restaurants line
Párga's waterfront,
affording fine
views across the
harbour to a group
of small islands.

Environs
37 km (23 miles) south of
Párga is the **Necromanteion of
Efyra** (Oracle of the Dead), the
mythological gateway to Hades.
Steps descend to the vaults
where, in the 4th century BC,
drugs and mechanisms may
have heightened the sensation
of entering the Underworld
for visitors who sought advice
from the dead.

🔷 **Necromanteion of Efyra**
🕮 8am–3pm daily. 🅰

Kassópi 🅑
Κασσώπη

Zálongo, Epirus. **Road map** B3.
🚌 🕮 daily.

The Kassopians were a tribe
which lived in this region
in the 4th century BC. The
remains of their capital city
stand on a hillside plateau
overlooking the
Ionian Sea, from
where the island of
Paxoí is plainly
visible. Kassópi
is reached by a
pleasant walk
through pine
groves from
the village of
Kamarína. A
site plan

**Greek
Orthodox
priests in
Párga**

illustrates the layout of the
once-great city, now the
home of birds and lizards.

Just above it is **Moní
Zalóngou**, with its monument
commemorating the women
of Soúli who threw them-
selves from the cliffs in 1806
rather than be captured by
Turkish-Albanian troops.

The remains of the city of Kassópi

Préveza 🅒
Πρέβεζα

Epirus. **Road map** B3. 🅰 13,000.
✈ 🚢 🚌 🛈 Eleftheriou Venizélou
(26820 21078). 🛍 daily (fish).

Often seen as a transit point,
the charming town of
Préveza repays a longer visit,
particularly for the lively atmosphere among its waterfront
cafés and tavernas. It is
picturesquely situated on the
northern shore of the narrow
"Channel of Cleopatra", at the
mouth of the Amvrakikós Gulf.
It was here that the naval
Battle of Actium was fought
in 31 BC (see p34).

Two ruined forts, on either side of the straits, recall the town's Venetian occupation in 1499, though in 1798 it passed, via the French, into the hands of Ali Pasha *(see p210)*.

Environs
Seven km (4 miles) north of Préveza stand the ruins of **Nikópoli** ("Victory City"), built by the Roman Emperor Octavian to celebrate his victory at Actium. The city was founded on the site where the emperor's army was camped. Later sacked by the Goths, it was finally destroyed by the Bulgars in 1034. The remains are dominated by the city walls and the theatre. A museum displays artifacts from the site which is quite overgrown.

Nikópoli
Tel 26820 41336. ☐ 8:30am–3pm daily. ⊙ main public hols. (museum only).

Arta ⑩
`Άρτα

Epirus. **Road map** B3. 33,000. ✉ ℹ️ *Plateía Krystálli (26810 78557).* ⊙ 8am–2:30pm Mon–Fri. ✦ Mon–Sat (veg).

Though it is the second largest town in Epirus, after Ioánnina, Arta remains largely untouched by tourism and offers a chance to see a traditional Greek market town. It has a lively, bazaar-like market area, established by the Turks who occupied Arta from 1449 to 1881. The **fortress** dates from the 13th century when the city was the capital of the despotate of Epirus. Stretching from Thessaloníki to Corfu, this was an independent Byzantine state set up after the fall of Constantinople in 1204 *(see p37)*. It lasted until the start of

Timber-framed houses in the Old Quarter of Tríkala

the Turkish occupation. Some of the town's many 13th- and 14th-century Byzantine churches can be found in the streets near the fortress. The most striking is the **Panagía Parigorítissa**. Built between 1283 and 1296, it is a three-tier building topped with towers and domes. **Agía Theódora**, on Pýrrou, contains the marble tomb of the saintly wife of 13th-century Epirot ruler Michael II.

Approaching from the west, the main road into town crosses the river Arachthos by a 17th-century stone **bridge**. According to local folklore, the builder of the bridge, frustrated by each day's work being ruined by the river at night, was advised by a bird that the problem could be solved by putting his wife in the bridge's foundations. This he did, burying her alive, after which the bridge was successfully completed.

Metéora ⑪

See pp216–17.

Tríkala ⑫
Τρίκαλα

Thessaly. **Road map** C2. 68,000. ☐ ✉ ⊙ Mon–Sat.

Trikala was the home of Asklepios, the god of healing, and today is the market centre for the very fertile plain of Thessaly. As such it is a thriving town with a number of remains from its Turkish past. One is the **market** near the main square, another the **Koursoúm Tzamí**, a graceful mosque built in 1550 on the south side of the River Lithaíos. Surrounding the **fortress** is the Old Quarter of Varósi, with a number of Byzantine churches *(see pp20–21)*. The fortress is built on the site of the ancient acropolis, which was built in the 4th century BC. It is situated in beautiful grounds overlooking the river.

Vale of Tempe ⑬
Κοιλάδα των Τεμπών

Thessaly. **Road map** C2. ✉

As the E75 approaches Macedonia, it follows the river Pineíos through the Vale of Tempe – the fertile valley where Apollo was said to have purified himself after slaying the serpent Python. Close to the **Wolf's Jaws** or **Lykostómio** (the narrowest point of the gorge) is the **Spring of Daphne**, where a bridge leads to the chapel of **Agía Paraskeví**, carved out of the rock. The **Kástro Gónnon** at the northern end of the Vale was built by Perséas, leader of the Macedonians during the war with Rome *(see pp32–33)*, to control what has long been a vital route between Central and Northern Greece.

The arched packhorse bridge of Arta, leading into town from the west

Metéora ⑪
Μετέωρα

Icon of Our Lord, Varlaám

Monastic cells

The natural sandstone towers of Metéora (or "suspended rocks") were first used as a religious retreat when, in AD 985, a hermit named Barnabas occupied a cave here. In the mid-14th century Neílos, the Prior of Stagai convent, built a small church. Then in 1382 the monk Athanásios, from Mount Athos, founded the huge monastery of Megálo Metéoro on one of the many pinnacles. Twenty-three monasteries followed, though most had fallen into ruin by the 19th century. In the 1920s stairs were cut to make the remaining six monasteries more accessible, and today a religious revival has seen the return of monks and nuns.

MEGALO METEORO
VARLAAM
AGIOS NIKOLAOS
ROUSANOU
Kalampáka
AGIA TRIADA
Kalampáka
AGIOS STEFANOS

Outer walls

LOCATION OF MONASTERIES OF METEORA

Rousánou
Moní Rousánou, perched precariously on the very tip of a narrow spire of rock, is the most spectacularly located of all the monasteries. Its church of the Metamórfosis (1545) is renowned for its harrowing frescoes, painted in 1560 by the iconographers of the Cretan school.

VARLAAM
Founded in 1518, the monastery of Varlaám is named after the first hermit to live on this rock in 1350. The *katholikón* was built in 1542 and contains some frescoes by the Theban iconographer Frágkos Katelános.

Megálo Metéoro
Also known as the Great Meteoron, this was the first and, at 623 m (2,045 ft), highest monastery to be founded. By the entrance is a cave in which Athanásios first lived. His body is buried in the main church.

◁ Moní Rousánou on the left in the foreground, with Moní Varlaám towering behind

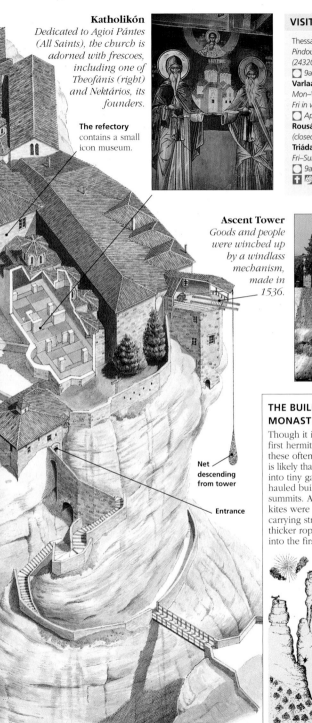

Katholikón
Dedicated to Agioi Pántes (All Saints), the church is adorned with frescoes, including one of Theofánis (right) and Nektários, its founders.

The refectory contains a small icon museum.

VISITORS' CHECKLIST

Thessaly. **Road map** B2. 🚌 🏛
Pindou & Ioannina sts, Kalampáka (24320 76100). **Megálo Metéoro** ⬤ *9am–5pm Mon, Thu–Sun.* **Varlaám** ⬤ *9am–2pm, 3–5pm Mon–Wed, Fri–Sun (also closed Fri in winter).* **Agíou Nikoláou** ⬤ *Apr–Oct: 9am–3:30pm daily.* **Rousánou** ⬤ *9am–6pm daily (closed Wed in winter).* **Agías Triádas** ⬤ *9am–6pm Mon–Wed, Fri–Sun.* 🏛 **Agíou Stefánou** ⬤ *9am–noon, 3–5pm Tue–Sun.* 🏛 📷 *all monasteries.*

Ascent Tower
Goods and people were winched up by a windlass mechanism, made in 1536.

Net descending from tower

Entrance

THE BUILDING OF THE MONASTERIES

Though it is unknown how the first hermits reached the tops of these often vertical rock faces, it is likely that they hammered pegs into tiny gaps in the rock and hauled building materials to the summits. Another theory is that kites were flown over the tops, carrying strings attached to thicker ropes which were made into the first rope ladders.

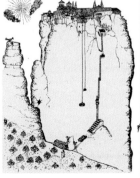

Pílio ❶
Πήλιο

Taxiárchis church fresco, Miliés

The mythological home of the forest-loving centaurs, the Pílio peninsula, with its woods of chestnut, oak and beech, is one of the most beautiful regions of the mainland. The mountain air is sweet with the scent of herbs which, in ancient times, were renowned for their healing powers. The area became populated in the 13th century by Greeks retreating from the Ottomans (see pp38–9), under whose rule they were taxed onerously. Most villages were built close to mountain monasteries, though the thick stone walls and narrow windows of a typical Pílio house indicate how uncertain their freedom really was. After centuries of protecting their culture, this is now one of the few areas of Greece to have a strong local cuisine.

Makrinítsa
Cars are banned from the steep cobbled streets of this traditional village (see p220).

Anakasiá, now little more than a suburb of Vólos, has a museum to the Greek painter Theófilos Chatzimicháïl.

Vólos is the capital of the region, straddling the only route into the peninsula. It has an excellent Archaeological Museum (see p220).

Agía Kyriakí
Overlooked by the isolated hilltop village of Tríkeri, this small fishing port lacks a beach and hotels but has a working boatyard and good, simple fish tavernas for those very few visitors who take the trouble to travel here.

THEOFILOS CHATZIMICHAIL

Born on Lésvos in 1873, Theófilos came to the Pílio in 1894 after reportedly killing a Turk in Smyrna. His favoured medium was the mural, though he also painted ceramics and the sides of fishing boats, *kafeneío* counters or horse carts when the mood struck him. He executed numerous mural commissions in the Pílio, notably at the Kontós mansion in Anakasiá. Though unhappily isolated, and mocked by the locals for his strange habits (he dressed in the costumes of his heroes, including Alexander the Great), he had a passion for all things Greek. After Lésvos's unification with Greece in 1912, he returned home destitute and ill. His fortunes changed after meeting his future patron Stratís Eleftheriádis who provided for the painter's needs until Theófilos's death in 1934.

Konstantinos Palaiológos mural (1899) by Theófilos

KEY

▬	Major road
═	Minor road
═	Non-asphalt road
- - -	Ferry route
ℹ	Tourist information
✳	Viewpoint

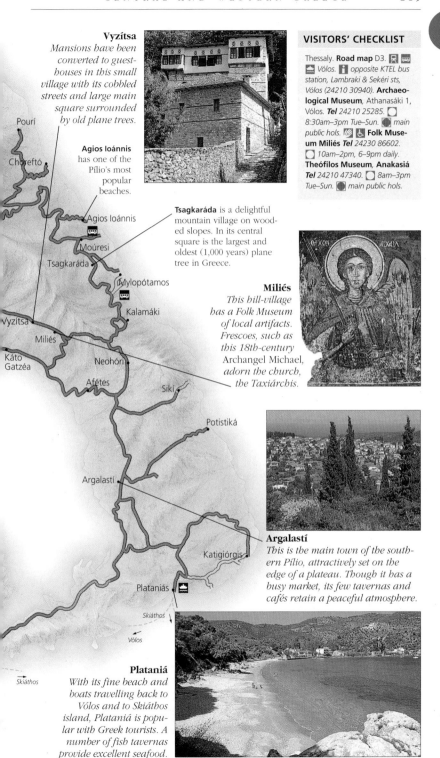

Vyzítsa
Mansions have been converted to guesthouses in this small village with its cobbled streets and large main square surrounded by old plane trees.

Agios Ioánnis
has one of the Pílio's most popular beaches.

Tsagkaráda is a delightful mountain village on wooded slopes. In its central square is the largest and oldest (1,000 years) plane tree in Greece.

Miliés
This hill-village has a Folk Museum of local artifacts. Frescoes, such as this 18th-century Archangel Michael, adorn the church, the Taxiárchis.

VISITORS' CHECKLIST

Thessaly. **Road map** D3.
Vólos. opposite KTEL bus station, Lambraki & Sekéri sts, Vólos (24210 30940). **Archaeological Museum**, Athanasáki 1, Vólos. **Tel** 24210 25285.
8:30am–3pm Tue–Sun. main public hols. **Folk Museum Miliés Tel** 24230 86602.
10am–2pm, 6–9pm daily. **Theófilos Museum, Anakasiá Tel** 24210 47340. 8am–3pm Tue–Sun. main public hols.

Pourí

Choreftó

Agios Ioánnis

Moúresi

Tsagkaráda

Mylopótamos

Kalamáki

Vyzítsa

Miliés

Káto Gatzéa

Neohóri

Afétes

Sikí

Potistiká

Argalastí

Katigiórgis

Plataniás

Skiáthos

Vólos

Skiáthos

Argalastí
This is the main town of the southern Pílio, attractively set on the edge of a plateau. Though it has a busy market, its few tavernas and cafés retain a peaceful atmosphere.

Plataniá
With its fine beach and boats travelling back to Vólos and to Skiáthos island, Plataniá is popular with Greek tourists. A number of fish tavernas provide excellent seafood.

Exploring the Pílio

Travelling by car, a circular tour of the northern villages can be made in a day following the road southeast from Vólos to Afétes, via Tsagkaráda. The hills in this region rise to 1,650 m (5,415 ft) at the summit of Mount Pílio, and in addition to dense woodlands, the area produces a large number of apples, pears, peaches and olives. While less dramatic, the southern Pílio is still hilly enough to ensure that many villages are at the end of single "dead end" roads, making travel here time consuming.

Restored traditional mansions on the hillside of Makrinítsa

through the "Vólos Riviera", providing a circular route of the mountainous northern Pílio. On weekends during summer, a traditional Pílion train runs from Káto Lechónia to Miliés. From the popular inland resorts of **Miliés** and **Vyzítsa** (the latter preserved as a "traditional settlement" by the government), the road turns north past Tsagkaráda to **Agios Ioánnis**. This is the main resort of the east coast, the beaches of Papá Neró and Pláka are particularly fine and are both within easy walking distance. Some of the Pílio's best restaurants can be found in nearby **Moúresi**.

Returning towards Vólos, take the turning to **Makrinítsa** – a traditional mountain village, regarded as the most important destination for any traveller of the area. Founded in the 13th century by refugees from the first sacking of Constantinople (*see p37*), the village has beautiful churches, the most impressive being Agios Ioánnis, and the Moní Theotókou. Several traditional mansions also survive, some functioning as guest houses. Close to Agios Ioánnis, there is a café with an interior decorated with frescoes painted by the artist Theófilos (*see p218*).

Anakasiá is the last village before Vólos and home to the delightful Theófilos Museum.

Vólos

Vólos is one of Greece's fastest-growing industrial centres and, since it was devastated by earthquakes in the 1950s, it is difficult to imagine its mythological past. Once the site of ancient Iolkós, the home of Jason, who went in search of the Golden Fleece, Vólos's history is illustrated by what can be found in the excellent **Archaeological Museum**. The museum contains an extensive collection of painted funerary stelae from the 3rd century BC, found at Dimitriás

on the far side of the Gulf of Vólos. Collections of Neolithic pottery from the nearby sites of Sésklo and Dimíni can also be found and there is a room dedicated to the Ancient games held in Thessaly, many of which involved horses.

Northern Villages

From Vólos the road leads southeast, past Ano Lechónia,

Fisherman with his nets at the waterfront, Vólos

JASON AND THE ARGONAUTS

According to legend, the Golden Fleece came from a winged ram sent by Hermes, the gods' messenger, to protect two children, Helle and Phrixus, from their evil stepmother. Though Helle drowned, Phrixus was reared in Kolchis, in present-day Georgia, where the ram was sacrificed and its fleece given to the king, Aeëtes. Years later, Jason, Phrixus's cousin, set sail from the kingdom of Iolkós (now Vólos) after his half-brother usurped the throne. Jason was in search of the Fleece, which made its wearer invincible. With a crew of 50, Jason came to Kolchis where King Aeëtes set several tasks before relinquishing the Fleece. After falling in love with the king's daughter, Medea, Jason achieved his tasks and the Argonauts carried the Fleece back to Iolkós in triumph.

Detail from *The Golden Fleece* (c.1905) by Herbert Draper (1864–1920)

For hotels and restaurants in this region see pp270–73 and pp291–4

Sarcophagus detail outside the Thebes Archaeological Museum

Thebes ⑮
Θήβα

Stereá Elláda. **Road map** D4.
👥 20,000. 🚉 🚌

Although it was briefly the most powerful city of Greece, in the 4th century BC, the Thebes of today is little more than a quiet provincial town. It played an important role in the power struggles of Classical Greece, until defeated by Philip II of Macedon. Thebes' original acropolis has been built over through the years, but excavations have unearthed Mycenaean walls as well as jewellery, pottery and important tablets of Linear B script which are now in the **Archaeological Museum**. One of the highlights of the museum is the collection of Mycenaean sarcophagi, similar to those found on Crete. The museum's courtyard and well-tended garden stand alongside a 13th-century Frankish tower, all that remains of a castle ruined in 1311 by the Catalans.

A bridge over the river bed, a short walk eastwards from the museum, marks the traditional site of the Fountain of Oedipus, where the legendary King Oedipus is said to have

THE LEGEND OF OEDIPUS

According to legend, Oedipus was the ill-fated son of Laius and Jocasta, the king and queen of Thebes. Even before his birth, the Delphic Oracle *(see p228)* had foretold that he would kill his father and become his mother's husband. To defy the prophecy, Laius abandoned Oedipus, though the child was rescued and reared by the king and queen of Corinth whom Oedipus believed to be his real parents. Years later, when he heard of the prophecy, Oedipus fled to Thebes, killing a man on his way, unaware that he was King Laius. On reaching Thebes, he found the city gates barred by the Sphinx which vanquished by solving one of its riddles. The Thebans made him their king and he married the widowed Jocasta. When the truth about his past was revealed, Oedipus blinded himself and spent his final days as an outcast.

Oedipus and the Sphinx, from a 5th-century BC cup

washed blood from his hands after unwittingly killing his father on his way to the city.

🏛 **Archaeological Museum**
Plateía Threpsiádou 1. **Tel** 22620 27913. ☐ Apr–Oct: 8am–7pm Tue–Sun; Nov–Mar: 8am–2:30pm Tue–Sun. 🎫 ♿

Environs
Ten km (6 miles) north lie the ruins of **Gla**, once a Mycenaean stronghold *(see pp178–80)*. Its walls are 3 km (2 miles) long and up to 5 m (16 ft) high, surrounding a hill where the ruins of a palace and agora can be found.

Monastery of Osios Loúkas ⑯

See pp222–3.

Mount Parnassus ⑰
Όρος Παρνασσός

Stereá Elláda. **Road map** C3. 🚌 Delfoí. 🚉 Vasiléon Pávlou & Freideríkis 44, Delfoí (22650 82900). ☐ 7:30am–2:30pm daily.

Rising to a height of 2,457 m (8,061 ft), the limestone mass of Mount Parnassus dominates the eastern region of Stereá Elláda. The lower slopes are covered with Cephalonian fir, and beneath them, in summer, the wild-flower meadows burst into colour. Vultures and golden eagles are common, as are wolves which come down from the Píndos Mountains *(see p206)* in winter.

The village of **Aráchova** is the best base for exploring the area and is renowned for its wine, cheese and sheep-skin rugs. There are many mountain trails for summer hikes, though a detailed walking map is recommended. Reaching the top of Liákoura, the highest peak, involves a long hike and camping overnight on the mountain.

From Aráchova, the ski centre at **Fterólaka** is only 26 kms (16 miles) away. Open from December to April, it provides a chair lift to 1,900 m (6,250 ft); from here a ski lift can be taken up to the ski slopes. In summer, Fterólaka functions as an excursion centre.

Fir-covered foothills beneath the ridge of Mount Parnassus

Monastery of Osios Loúkas ⑯
Μονή Οσίου Λουκά

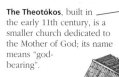

Dedicated to a local hermit and healer, Holy Luke, Osios Loúkas monastery was architecturally one of medieval Greece's most important buildings; built by the Emperor Romanós in c.1011, he extended an earlier church dating from AD 944. The octagonal style of the main church became a hall-mark of late Byzantine church

Madonna mosaic

design (see pp20–21), while the mosaics inside lifted Byzantine art into its final great period. During the time of the Ottoman Empire (see pp38–9), Osios Loúkas witnessed a great deal of fighting, as the cannons in the courtyard testify. Here in 1821, Bishop Isaias declared his support for the Greek freedom fighters.

The Theotókos, built in the early 11th century, is a smaller church dedicated to the Mother of God; its name means "god-bearing".

The north transept contains medallion-shaped mosaics of saints.

The monastic cells are small with arched roofs.

The monastery seen from the west with the slopes of Mount Elikónas in the background

The exterior is a mixture of dressed Póros stone and red brick.

West portal

The narthex is the western entrance hall; it contains a number of mosaics of Christ's Passion.

★ **Washing of the Apostles' Feet**
Based on a style dating to the 6th century, this 11th-century work is the finest of the narthex mosaics. Set on a gold back-ground, it depicts Christ teaching his apostles humility.

STAR FEATURES

★ Washing of the Apostles' Feet

★ Crypt

For hotels and restaurants in this region see pp270–73 and pp291–4

VISITORS' CHECKLIST

8 km (5 miles) E of Dístomo.
Road map C4. **Tel** 22670 22797.
Site & Museum ⬜ May–Sep:
8am–2pm, 4–6pm daily; Oct–Apr:
8am–5pm daily.

Dome
The main dome is decorated with an imposing mural of Christ surrounded by saints and angels, painted in the 16th century to replace fallen mosaics.

The apse has a mosaic of the Virgin and Child predating a devastating earthquake in 1659.

The katholikón, or main church, dates to 1011 and is built in the octagonal style.

★ **Crypt**
This 10th-century shrine, from the original site, contains the sarcophagus of Holy Luke, and such frescoes as this Descent from the Cross.

The southwest chapel has early 11th-century frescoes.

The refectory was used as a workshop as well as for meals; it now contains a museum of Byzantine sculpture.

HOLY LUKE

Born in Aegina in 906, Osios Loúkas ("Holy Luke") is known to have been a spiritual child who, in his early teens, left home to seek isolation in central Greece and developed a reputation as a healer. In around 940 he arrived at this spot on the western slopes of Mount Elikónas, with its glorious view over a peaceful valley of cornfields and groves of almond and olive trees. Here he settled with some disciples, adding the gift of prophecy to his healing powers. He died in 953, by which time the first monastic cells and the site's first small church had been constructed.

The waterfront houses of Galaxídi in the Gulf of Corinth

Lamía and Thermopylae ⑱
Λαμία καί Θερμοπύλαι

Stereá Elláda. **Road map** C3. 🏛
68,000. 🚌 🛈 Leof. Kalivion 14,
Kardeníssi Rd, (22310 32289). 🚆 Sat.

Set in the valley between two wooded hills, Lamía is typical of many medium-sized Greek towns; though it is little known, it has much to offer, with a lively Saturday market. A 14th-century Catalan **kástro**, built on the site of the town's ancient acropolis, provides excellent views over the roofs to the surrounding countryside.

Lamía is chiefly associated with the Lamian War (323–322 BC) when Athens tried to throw off Macedonian rule after the death of Alexander the Great (see pp32–3). This is recalled at the **Lamía Museum**, which also has displays of architectural remains from Delphi (see pp228–31).

A short drive east of Lamía, the Athens road crosses the **Pass of Thermopylae**. It was here, in 480 BC, that an army of some 7,000 soldiers, under the command of Leonidas I of Sparta, met an overwhelming force from Persia whose numbers Herodotus (see p56) cites as 2,641,610. Though Leonidas held the pass for a number of days, the Persians forced a path through and attacked the Greeks from the rear. Only two Greek soldiers survived the ordeal after which all of central Greece, including Athens, fell to the Persians. The Persian land forces were eventually defeated by Athens and her allies at the Battle of Plataiai in 479 BC (see p29).

An impressive bronze statue of King Leonidas, cast in 1955, stands at the roadside opposite the burial mound of the soldiers who died here. Just to the left of the

Statue of King Leonidas at the Pass of Thermopylae

ΜΟΛΩΝ
ΛΑΒΕ

mound are the famous sulphur springs from which Thermopylae was given its name, which means the "Hot Gates".

The present landscape has changed considerably from the narrow gorge of old; the coastline to the north has been extended by the silt brought down by the River Spercheiós, pushing the sea back over 5 km (3 miles).

🛈 **Lamía Museum**
Kástro. **Tel** 22310 29993. ◯
8:30am–3pm Tue–Sun.
◯ main public hols. 🈲 🚻

Ancient Delphi ⑲

See pp228–31.

Gulf of Corinth ⑳
Κορινθιακός Κόλπος

Stereá Elláda. 🚌 to Náfpaktos.

The northern coast of the Gulf of Corinth contains several well-known resorts as well as many tiny coastal villages far removed from the usual tourist route. All are served by major roads which, like the resorts, offer fine views across the gulf to the mountains of the Peloponnese.

From Delphi the main road leads southwards through the largest olive grove in Greece, passing **Itéa**, a busy port. The church of Agios Nikólaos, 17 km (11 miles) west, stands on a hill surrounded by the old stone buildings of **Galaxídi**. The history of the town is told in the Nautical Museum while the 19th-century mansions at the waterfront are reminders of the great wealth brought by the town's shipbuilding industry. Though the industry cleared the region of trees, a reforestation scheme begun early in the 20th century has successfully restored the area to its former shape. The next major town is **Náfpaktos**. Though perhaps less attractive than Galaxídi, it still possesses plenty of charm and character.

A Venetian fortress stands above the town, its ramparts running down as far as the beach, almost enclosing the harbour. The Venetian name for the town was Lepanto. In 1571, the famous naval Battle of Lepanto *(see p38)*, in which the Venetians, Spanish and Genoese defeated the Ottomans, was fought here. A popular story to emerge from the battle purports that the Spanish author Miguel de Cervantes (1547–1616) lost an arm in the conflict, though in fact only his left hand was maimed.

At **Antírrio** the coast comes closest to the Peloponnese, and from here a new suspension bridge and regular car ferry cross the stretch of water known as the "little Dardanelles" to Río, on the southern shore. Beside the harbour stands the originally Frankish and Venetian Kástro Roúmelis. Another castle can be seen across the water on the Peloponnese.

🏛 Nautical Museum
Mouseíou 4, Galaxídi.
Tel 22650 41558. ⬜ 8:30am–4pm Mon–Fri, 10am–4pm Sat & Sun.
⬤ main public hols. 🖼

Mesolóngi ㉑
Μεσολόγγι

Stereá Elláda. **Road map** B3.
🚶 *12,000.* 🚌 🅿 *Tue & Sat.*

Meaning "amid the lagoons", Mesolóngi is a town perfectly located for fishing, though the industry is now in decline. In 1821 the town became a centre of resistance to the Turks during the War of Independence *(see pp40–41)*, when a leader, Aléxandros Mavrokordátos, set up his headquarters here. In January 1824 Lord Byron *(see p149)* came to fight for the liberation of Greece, but died of a fever in April. His heart lies beneath his statue in the Garden of Heroes. Nearby, the Gate of the Exodus is a tribute to those who fought the Turks in 1826. After 12 months, 9,000 battled their way through the blockade; those left behind detonated their explosives just as they were taken by the enemy. This self-sacrifice led to the Turks surrendering Mesolóngi in 1828 without firing a shot. A small museum charts the history of the town.

Statue of Lord Byron at Mesolóngi

SALTPAN BIRDLIFE

With its importance for food preservation, the production of salt is a major enterprise in the Mediterranean, the most extensive areas in Greece being around Mesolóngi and the Amvrakikós Gulf. Seawater is channelled into large artificial lakes, or saltpans, which, with their high concentrations of salt, attract a large amount of wildlife. Brine shrimps thrive, providing food for a wide variety of birds. Two of the most striking waders are the avocet and the great egret, though also common is the black-winged stilt with its long red legs.
The area is also home to Kentish plovers, stone curlews, and the short-toed lark.

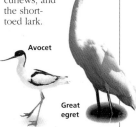

Avocet

Great egret

The fortified harbour of Náfpaktos in the Gulf of Corinth

Ancient Delphi ⓭
Δελφοί

According to legend, when Zeus released two eagles from opposite ends of the world their paths crossed in the sky above Delphi, establishing the site as the centre of the earth. Renowned as a dwelling place of Apollo, from the end of the 8th century BC individuals from all over the ancient world visited Delphi to consult the god on what course of action to take, in both public and private life. With the political rise of Delphi in the 6th century BC and the reorganization of the Pythian Games *(see p230)*, the sanctuary entered a golden age which lasted until the Romans came in 191 BC. The oracle was abolished in AD 393 with the Christianization of the Byzantine Empire under Theodosius.

Siphnian Treasury caryatid

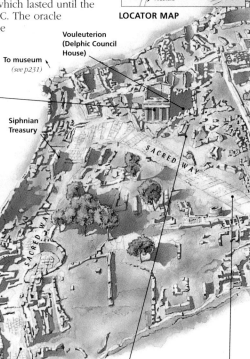

LOCATOR MAP

The Athenian Treasury was built after the Battle of Marathon *(see p145)* and reconstructed in 1906.

Vouleuterion (Delphic Council House)

To museum *(see p231)*

Siphnian Treasury

SACRED WAY

THE ORACLE OF DELPHI

The Delphic Oracle was the means through which worshippers could hear the words of the god Apollo, spoken through a priestess, or *Pythia*, over the age of 50. Questioners paid a levy called a *pelanos* and sacrificed an animal on the altar. The question was then put to the *Pythia* by a male priest. The *Pythia* would answer in a trance, perhaps induced by vapours from a crack in the ground over which she sat on a tripod. Her incantations were interpreted by the priest, though the answers were often ambiguous. King Croesus of Lydia (reigned 560–546 BC) came to ask if he should make war against Cyrus the Great of Persia and was told that if he crossed a river then he would destroy a great empire. In marching on Cyrus his troops crossed the River Halys and he did destroy an empire, though it turned out to be his own.

The main entrance was once a market place (agora) where religious objects could be bought.

The Rock of the Sibyl marks the place where, according to legend, Delphi's first prophetess pronounced her oracles.

★ **Sacred Way**
Leading to the Temple of Apollo, this path was lined with up to 3,000 statues and treasuries, built by city-states to house their people's offerings.

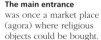

◁ **Dramatic view over the theatre at Delphi**

THE SANCTUARY OF APOLLO

Also known as the Sacred Precinct, this is at the heart of a complex that also included a stadium and a sacred spring *(see pp230–31)*. It is entered through an agora from which the Sacred Way winds through the ruins of memorials and treasuries.

VISITORS' CHECKLIST

Mount Parnassus, Stereá Elláda.
Road map C4. *Tel* 22650 82312.
🚌 **Site** ◻ Apr–Oct: 7:30am–7pm daily (to 6pm Nov–Mar).
Museum ◻ Apr–Oct: 7:30am–6:45pm; Nov–Mar: 8:30am–3pm.
🚫 main public hols. 📷 ♿

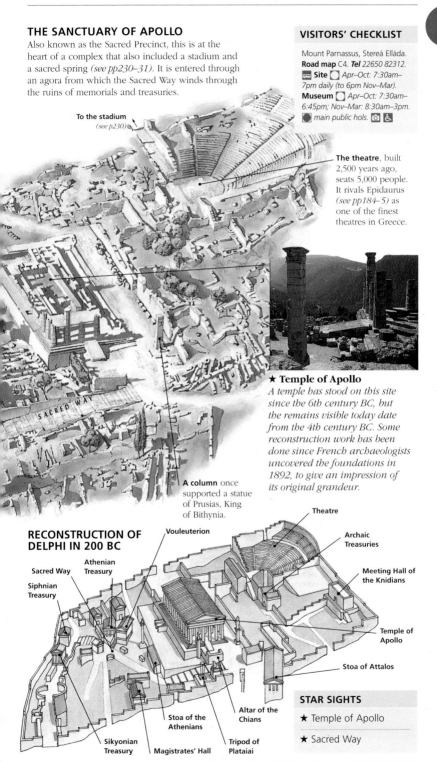

To the stadium
(see p230)

The theatre, built 2,500 years ago, seats 5,000 people. It rivals Epidaurus *(see pp184–5)* as one of the finest theatres in Greece.

★ Temple of Apollo
A temple has stood on this site since the 6th century BC, but the remains visible today date from the 4th century BC. Some reconstruction work has been done since French archaeologists uncovered the foundations in 1892, to give an impression of its original grandeur.

A column once supported a statue of Prusias, King of Bithynia.

SACRED WAY

RECONSTRUCTION OF DELPHI IN 200 BC

Sacred Way
Athenian Treasury
Siphnian Treasury
Sikyonian Treasury
Magistrates' Hall
Stoa of the Athenians
Tripod of Plataiai
Altar of the Chians
Vouleuterion
Theatre
Archaic Treasuries
Meeting Hall of the Knidians
Temple of Apollo
Stoa of Attalos

STAR SIGHTS

★ Temple of Apollo

★ Sacred Way

Exploring Delphi

The first excavations at Delphi began in 1892, uncovering a much larger area than is apparent now. Though it is most famous for the Sanctuary of Apollo, Delphi also had a sanctuary dedicated to the goddess Athena, whose temple, along with a structure known as the *tholos*, can be seen in a second enclosure to the south. North of the theatre is the stadium where the Pythian Games were held. These, after the Olympic Games *(see p173)*, were the most important sporting event in the Greek calendar, providing an opportunity for strengthening the ethnic bond of the Greek nation which was otherwise divided into predominantly rival city-states.

Caryatid from the Siphnian Treasury

The Stadium, viewed from the remains of the entrance archway

⋒ Marmaria Precinct

Southeast of the Temple of Apollo, a path leads to the Marmaria Precinct, or "marble quarry", where the Sanctuary of Athena Pronaia can be found. At the sanctuary's entrance stand the ruins of a 4th-century BC temple dedicated to Athena. At the far end of the sanctuary are the remains of an earlier temple to the goddess, which was built around 510 BC. Between the two temples stands the Marmaria's most remarkable, and most photographed, monument: the circular *tholos*. The purpose of this structure is still unknown. The rotunda dates from the start of the 4th century BC, and was originally surrounded by 20 columns. Three of these columns were re-erected in 1938. They stand to provide some hint of the building's former beauty.

⋒ Stadium

This is one of the very best-preserved stadia in the country. Almost 200 m (655 ft) long and partly hewn out of the rocks above the main sanctuary, it held 7,000 spectators who gathered for the field and track events every four years during the Pythian Games. The games grew out of a musical festival, held in the theatre every eight years, to celebrate Apollo's mythical slaying of the serpent Python. Though poetry and musical recitals remained central to the occasion, from 582 BC athletic events in the stadium were added and the festival became known as the Pythian Games. All prizes in these tournaments were purely honorary; each winner was awarded the traditional laurel wreath and the right to have his statue in the sanctuary.

Made entirely of limestone from Mount Parnassus, the present structure dates from Roman times and most of the seating is still intact. The best-preserved seats are the backed benches on the north side, made for the presidents of the games and honoured guests.

⋒ Castalian Spring

Before entering the Sacred Precinct, it is believed that everyone visiting Delphi for religious purposes, including

The tholos beside the Sanctuary of Athena Pronaia, Marmaria Precinct

athletes, was required to purify themselves in the clear but icy waters of the Castalian Spring – this process principally involved the washing of their hair. The Oracle *Pythia (see p228)* would also wash here before making her pronouncements. The visible remains of the fountain date either from the late Hellenistic or the early Roman period. A number of niches in the surrounding rock once held the votive offerings left for the nymph Castalia, to whom the spring was dedicated.

It is said that the British romantic poet Lord Byron *(see p149)* once plunged into the spring, inspired by the belief that the waters would enhance the poetic spirit.

The niches of the Castalian Spring

🜂 Gymnasium

Water from the Castalian Spring ran down to this area to provide cold baths (until the Romans added hot baths in the 2nd century AD) for athletes training for the Pythian Games. The original cold baths, which can be seen in a square courtyard, are some 9 m (30 ft) in diameter. East of the baths lies the Palaestra, or training area, surrounded by the remains of what once were changing rooms and training quarters. As well as an outdoor running track, a covered track 180 m (590 ft) in length provided a venue for the games in bad weather. The gymnasium was also used for intellectual pursuits – Delphi's poets and philosophers taught here – and built on many levels due to the sloping terrain.

🜛 Delphi Museum

The museum at Delphi contains a collection of sculptures and architectural remains of an importance second only to those of the Athenian Acropolis *(see pp94–101)*.

There are 13 rooms of exhibits, all on the ground floor. In one of the rooms there is a scale model that reconstructs the Sanctuary of Apollo in a triumph of limestone whites, blue marble, gold and terracotta. Surrounded by friezes and statues, the extent of Delphi's size and its former beauty is represented vividly.

Votive chapels, or "treasuries", lined the Sacred Way *(see p228)* and contained offerings of thanks, in the form of money or works of art, from towns grateful for good fortune following a favourable prophecy from the Oracle. The Theban Treasury, for example, was established after the victory of Thebes at the Battle of Leuktra in 371 BC. There are two rooms dedicated to the surviving sculpture from the Siphnian and Athenian treasuries, the wealth of the former illustrated by an outstanding frieze depicting the Greek heroes waging war on the giants. The colossal Naxian Sphinx was presented by the wealthy citizens of Náxos in 560 BC; it stands 2.3 m (7.5 ft) high and once had its place atop a column reaching over 10 m (33 ft) in height.

The most famous of the museum's exhibits is a life-size bronze statue, the *Charioteer*. The statue was commissioned by a Sicilian tyrant named Polyzalos to commemorate a chariot victory in the Pythian Games in 478 BC. Another notable exhibit is the sculpture of *Three Dancing Girls* grouped around a column. The column is believed to have supported a tripod of the kind sat on by the *Pythia* as she went into her oracular trances. The girls are thought to be celebrating the feast of the god Dionysos *(see p52)* who also resided in the sanctuary. His presence was honoured in the winter months when Apollo was resting or away elsewhere. Don't miss the Omphalos, or "navel" stone. This is a Hellenistic or Roman copy of the stone that was believed to have marked the place above which Zeus's eagles met, establishing the sanctuary of Delphi as the centre of the earth *(see p228)*.

The bronze Charioteer

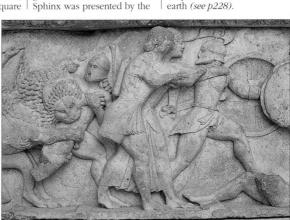

Detail from the frieze of the Siphnian Treasury on display in the museum

NORTHERN GREECE

MACEDONIA · THRACE

Macedonia is Greece's largest prefecture and contains the country's second city, Thessaloníki. It is the homeland of Alexander the Great, and the heart of the ancient Hellenistic empire. In contrast, Thrace has been largely influenced by Turkish culture but, like Macedonia, it is an area of comparatively unexplored natural beauty, with many mountain ranges and rivers.

The name Macedonia derives from the Makednoi, one of the tribes who first inhabited the region in the late 4th century BC. The legacy of the Macedonian Empire is evident in the many ancient sites, including Vergína, the location of Philip's tomb; Pélla, the birthplace of Alexander; and Díon, Philip's city in the foothills of Mount Olympos. During the reign of the Roman Emperor Galerius in the 3rd century AD, many fine monuments were built, including the landmark arch in Thessaloníki. The Byzantine era also left an outstanding legacy of architecture, seen in the many churches that abound throughout Northern Greece. Muslim influences remain strong, particularly

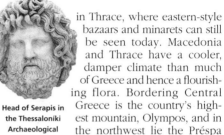

Head of Serapis in the Thessaloníki Archaeological Museum

in Thrace, where eastern-style bazaars and minarets can still be seen today. Macedonia and Thrace have a cooler, damper climate than much of Greece and hence a flourishing flora. Bordering Central Greece is the country's highest mountain, Olympos, and in the northwest lie the Préspa Lakes, part of a wildlife reserve. Local produce includes tobacco from Thrace, and wine from Náousa.

In contrast to the busy beaches on its western side, the Chalkidikí peninsula in Macedonia has the holy Mount Athos to the east. After a purported visit from the Virgin Mary, the Byzantine Emperor Monomáchos banished women and children from the site. This decree is still valid today.

Villagers at a taverna in the Néstos Valley

◁ Moní Grigoríou on the holy peninsula of Mount Athos

Exploring Northern Greece

Northern Greece offers varied pleasures. The bustle of modern Thessaloníki can be combined with a beach holiday in Chalkidikí, or with an exploration of some of the ancient Macedonian sites. Lovers of natural history will appreciate the National Park around the Préspa Lakes on the border with Albania, and the Dadiá Forest and Evros River Delta to the east near Turkey. Walkers will want to explore the paths of Mount Olympos. Kastoriá and Kavála, two relatively little-known Greek towns, both reward a lengthy visit as well as making excellent bases for travelling further afield. Kavála offers access to the fascinating but little-visited region of Thrace. This region's three main towns – Xánthi, Komotiní and Alexandroúpoli – all offer the attractive combination of Greek and Turkish influence. Alexandroúpoli is also ideal as a family holiday resort with its beaches and seafront cafés.

A typical stall at the fruit and vegetable market in Xánthi, selling local produce

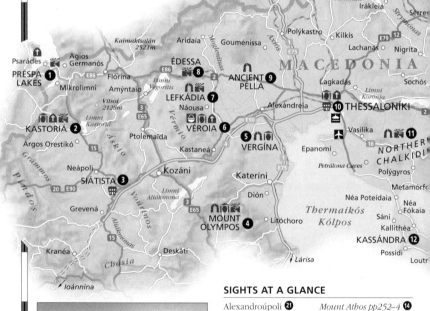

Reedbeds by the Mikrí Préspa lake

SIGHTS AT A GLANCE

GETTING AROUND

Thessaloníki's airport serves both international and domestic routes. Airports at Kastoriá, Kozáni and Alexandroúpoli are for domestic flights only. Ferry connections link Thessaloníki with the Sporades, and Kavála and Alexandroúpoli with the northern Aegean islands. Fast trains travel south from Thessaloníki to Athens, and east into Thrace and beyond to Istanbul. The main E75 highway runs south to Athens while the E90 highway joins Thessaloníki to Thrace. Buses go from Thessaloníki to Alexandroúpoli and Kastoriá.

• ATHENS

LOCATOR MAP

Kastaniés

Orestiáda

Rodópi

Káto
Nevrokópi

Néstos

Dídymóteicho

Falakró

Paranéstio   Echínos   Soufli
                                          E85
NÉSTOS VALLEY 16   Dadiá
tsáni   Dráma   14   Stavroúpoli   T H R A C E   *Sápka*   **DADIÁ FOREST** 22

Alistráti   **XÁNTHI** 17   Íasmos   **KOMOTINÍ** 19
                          Límni Vistonída   Sápes   *Istanbul*
KAVÁLA 15   Xylaganí   Féres
Eleftheroúpoli   **AVDIRA** 18   **MARÓNEIA** 20
Keramoti   21 **ALEXANDROÚPOLI**
Amfípoli   E90   2   *Évros*
Pángaio
                        Thasos

avrós   *Thracian
                                  Sea*

tágeira

Ierissós

Ouranoúpoli

MOUNT ATHOS 14
Vourvouroú
Áthos 2033m
SITHONIÁ 13
Sárti
Pórto Karrás
Pórto   Kalamítsi
oufó

| 0 kilometres | | 50 |
| 0 miles | | 20 |

SEE ALSO

• *Where to Stay* pp273–5
• *Where to Eat* pp294–5

KEY

═══	Dual-carriageway
= =	Major road
───	Minor road
───	Road under construction
───	Scenic route
─·─	Main railway
▬▬▬	International border
───	Regional border
△	Summit

The harbour of Kavála, in eastern Macedonia

Beautiful landscape of the Préspa Lakes

Préspa Lakes ❶
Εθνικός Δρυμός Πρεσπών

Macedonia. **Road map** B1. 🚌 to Flórina. 🏠 Agios Germanós (23850 51452). 🕐 9:30am–2pm daily.

This is the only national park in Greece which is made up largely of water. It is one of the mainland's most beautiful and unspoilt places and was little visited until recently because of its rather inaccessible location. The border with Albania runs through the southwest corner of the Megáli Préspa lake, joining the border of the Former Yugoslav Republic of Macedonia. The Greek area of the lake, together with the smaller Mikrí Préspa lake and surrounding countryside, make up the 255 sq km (100 sq miles) of national park,

established in 1974. The area is so important for wildlife that Mikrí Préspa and the reed beds that fringe it form a park within a park, a core of some 49 sq km (19 sq miles) regarded as a complete protection area. The boundary of the core area is clearly indicated by signs to prevent accidental trespass.

Over 1,300 species of plant can be found here, including the endemic *Centaurea prespana*, which has small daisy-like flowers. There are over 40 species of mammal, such as bears, wolves, otters, roe deer, wild boar and wild cats. The area is also one of the last remaining breeding refuges in Europe for the Dalmatian pelican, whose numbers are down to less than 1,000 pairs worldwide, with about 150 of those nesting in the Préspa Lakes. Other birds more frequently

Wetland Wildlife

In contrast to the dry and stony terrain found in much of Greece, the north has some outstanding wetlands with a range of different habitats. Reed-fringed lake margins hold large colonies of breeding birds and amphibians, while the open water is home to numerous fish and aquatic insects. The marshes are rich in flowers and full of songbirds; the man-made habitats such as saltpans and lagoons offer sanctuary to nesting waders.

Lake Korónia *is easy to view from nearby villages, most of which have their own colonies of white storks. In spring, terrapins and frogs gather in the shallow margins of the lake.*

Kentish plovers nest on the margins of wetlands, such as the Préspa Lakes.

The Préspa Lakes *support colonies of rare Dalmatian pelicans. When nesting they need the peace and quiet this protected area provides.*

The Axiós Delta is home to dragonflies and, on the margins, a wealth of spring flowers and bee orchids.

Whipsnakes are common in northern Greece, particularly around Lake Korónia.

seen include herons, cormorants, egrets, storks, golden eagles and goosanders.

Scattered around the lakes are several small villages. One of these, on the shore of Megáli Préspa, is **Psarádes**, a pretty, traditional village where fishermen provide a boat service on to the lake. From the boat you can see

Psarádes village on the banks of Megáli Préspa

hermitages, icons painted on the rocks by the shore, and two churches: the 15th-century **Panagía Eleoúsa** and the 13th-century **Metamórfosi**. To the east of Mikrí Préspa is **Mikrolímni**.

The village has wet meadows to the north that are rich in birdlife. Southwest of Mikrolímni a path leads to the Ellinikí Etaireía Biological Station, used as a base by research

Fresco from Metamórfosi church

scientists who want to stay in the area while studying.

In summer, the beaches of fine, pale sand that stretch alongside Megáli Préspa can be enjoyed along with a dip in the blue, but rather cold, waters of the lake.

Environs

Northeast of the park lies the village of **Agios Germanós**, which has an 11th-century Byzantine church and a number of pretty, traditional houses, built in the local architectural style. The village is also home to the **Préspa Information Centre** which has a permanent exhibition explaining the ecological importance of the Préspa National Park. Guides are available to show visitors around the park, but this must be arranged in advance.

Just out of the village, a road leads up to the summits of Kaló Neró, at 2,160 m (7,090 ft) and Mázi, at 2,060 m (6,760 ft), which give superb views across the lakes below.

Glossy ibises *have one of their last remaining European strongholds in the wetlands of northern Greece. Seen in good light, their feathers have a metallic sheen.*

Purple herons nest in the reedbeds of the Evros Delta.

Pórto Lágos's lagoons, pools and marshes are a haven for ruddy shelducks.

Xánthi

Kavála

Thrace

Alexandroúpoli

The Néstos Delta *is one of the finest wetlands in Greece. Many species of birds inhabit the extensive reedbanks and clumps of trees, in particular large breeding colonies of herons and egrets.*

The Evros Delta *lies close to the border with Turkey and access to many of the best areas can be difficult. Numerous water birds, including little egrets, nest and feed in easily viewed locations.*

KEY

▨	Préspa Lakes
▨	Axiós Delta
▨	Lake Korónia
▨	Néstos Delta
▢	Pórto Lágos
▨	Evros Delta
--	National boundary

0 kilometres 50

0 miles 50

Fishing on the Préspa Lakes in the early morning ▷

Kastoriá ②
Κaστoριά

Macedonia. **Road map** B2.
17,000. ✈ 10 km (6 miles) S of
Kastoriá. ▦ ℹ Plateía Olympiakí
Flóga (24670 21490). ❋ Wed.

Kastoria is the Greek for
"place of beavers". These
animals used to live in Lake
Kastoriá (also known as Lake
Orestiáda) by which the town
stands, one of the loveliest
settings in Greece. Evidence
of a prehistoric settlement was
unearthed here in 1940. In
200 BC the Romans captured
the town, then known as
Keletron. The beavers first
brought the furriers here in
the 17th century and, despite
the fact that the animals were
extinct in the area by the 19th
century, trading continued.
By then the furriers were
also importing unwanted
fur scraps, including
mink castoffs, and mak-
ing desirable garments
out of them. The fur
trade exists today,
with the crafts-
men still making
the fur coats that
can be bought
in shops here,
in Thessaloníki
and Athens.

The town pros-
pered as a result
of the fur trade, as
its several remain-
ing 17th- and 18th-
century mansions testify.
Most of these are found in the
southeast quarter of the town.
The elegant Skoutári and
Nanzí mansions have interior
courtyards and three floors.
The ground floor in each case
is built of stone; the upper
two are made of wood. They
have fine timbered rooms
fitted with cupboards, hearths
and raised platforms. The
lower stone floor is used
for storage, while the living
quarters are in the wooden
upper floor which juts out
over the street.

The town's **Folk Museum**
is housed in the Aïvazí mansion. Built in the 15th century,
it was lived in until as recently
as 1972. It now has an elo-
quent display of the lifestyle
of the wealthy fur traders.

The Skoutári mansion in Kastoriá,
built in the 18th century

There is typically elaborate
woodwork in the salon on
the upper floor. The kitchens
beneath and the wine cellar
have also been restored.

Another notable feature of
the town are its many Byzantine churches. Fifty-four survive, and most are listed as
ancient monuments, in-
cluding the 11th-century
Panagía Koumbelídiki,
situated towards the
south end of Mitro-
póleos. The church
is named after its
unusually tall
dome (or *kubbe*,
in Turkish). Some
of the churches
are tiny and
hidden away in
Kastoriá's laby-
rinth of streets,
as they were
originally private
chapels. Many
are closed to the
public, with some
of their icons removed, most
of which are now on display in
the **Byzantine Museum**, which
is also confusingly referred to
as the Archaeological Museum.

Apse and cupola of
Panagía Koumbelídiki

The small collection has
exquisite pieces on display,
including some fine icons.

🎨 **Folk Museum**
Kapetán Lázou 10. **Tel** 24670
28603. ⏰ 10am–noon & 3–5pm
daily. ▦ ● main public hols.

🎨 **Byzantine Museum**
Plateía Dexamenís. **Tel** 24670
26781. ⏰ 8:30am–3pm Tue–Sun.
● main public hols.

Siátista ③
Σιάτιστα

Macedonia. **Road map** B2. 5,000.
ℹ Plateía Tsistopoúlou (24650 21280).
Tel 24650 22254 (info on mansions).

Siátista was founded in the
1430s, after the Turkish
conquest of Thessaloníki.
Like Kastoriá, the town
flourished as a result of the
fur trade despite the lack of
local fur. Sable and martin
remnants were brought in,
mainly from Russia, made up
into garments, and then traded
or sold in Western Europe.

The wealth that this created
in the 18th century went into
the building of many fine
mansion houses. The
Ottoman influence in their
decoration is strong. The
Nerantzopoúlou mansion is
one of several in the town
that can be visited. Keys and
directions to the other mansions, including the **Manoúsi**
and **Poulkídou**, can also be
obtained here.

🏛 **Nerantzopoúlou Mansion**
Plateía Chorí. ⏰ Tue–Sun. ● main
public hols.

View across Siátista, in the Mount Askion range, western Macedonia

The impressive peaks of the Mount Olympos range rising above the village of Litóchoro

Mount Olympos ❹
Όλυμπος

17 km (10 miles) W of Litóchoro, Macedonia. **Road map** C2. 🚃 Litóchoro. 🛈 EOS: Evángelou Karavákou 20, Litóchoro (23520 82444).

The name Mount Olympos refers to the whole range of mountains, 20 km (12 miles) across. The highest peak in the range, at 2,917 m (9,571 ft), is Mýtikas. The whole area constitutes the Olympos National Park.

Over 1,700 plant species are found here, many of them endemic to the park. Chamois, boars and roe deer also live in this area.

Roman mosaic from Ancient Díon

The base for walkers is the village of **Litóchoro**, a lively place with several hotels and tavernas. Walking maps are available and a marked trail leads up into the national park. Mýtikas can be reached in a demanding walk of at least six hours. It is imperative to camp out overnight or stay in one of the two mountain refuges, rather than attempt to get up and down in a day.

Environs
About 10 km (6 miles) north of Litóchoro is the village of Díon, which has an excellent museum showing finds from **Ancient Díon**. This site is near the modern village and splendidly set between the coast and the Olympian peaks, its very name deriving from Díos, or "of Zeus". To the Macedonians it was a holy city and in the 4th century BC some 15,000 people lived here. The flat plains were used as a military camp and rallying point by King Philip II of Macedon (see pp32–3). Although Díon was a military camp, rather than a civilian city, there was a temple to Zeus, a theatre and a stadium at the site. Later, the Romans built a city here. The ruins that can be seen today date mainly from that era, and include fine mosaics from the 2nd century AD and well-preserved Roman baths. There is also a theatre and the remnants of a sanctuary dedicated to the Egyptian goddess Isis. She was worshipped by the Romans as a foreign deity, along with many others that were similarly "adopted" into the pantheon. A second temple, dedicated to Zeus, has also been unearthed here.

The bright and modern **Díon Museum** in the village shows films of the excavations, and it is worth seeing before visiting the site. Also on display are toys, kitchen utensils and jewellery, all finds from the sanctuary of Isis. Together they give a vivid picture of life in Ancient Díon.

⚲ Ancient Díon
E of Díon. ☐ 8am–7pm daily (to 5pm in winter). ⬤ main public hols. 🏛

🍴 Díon Museum
Díon. **Tel** 23510 53206. ☐ Apr–Oct: 8am–7pm daily; Nov–Mar: 10:30am–5pm Mon, 8am–5pm Tue–Fri, 8:30am–3pm Sat & Sun. ⬤ main public hols. 🏛

THE HOME OF ZEUS
Zeus, chief and most powerful of the ancient Greek gods, lived on Mount Olympos along with the other immortals and was thought to be responsible for the destinies of men. He was also god of weather and thunderstorms. Many of the myths tell of Zeus's amorous liaisons and his numerous children, some of whom were gods or goddesses and some heroes (see pp52–3). He was worshipped at Olympia and at Dodóni in Epirus, site of the oldest oracle in Greece.

Vergína ❺
Βεργίνα

12 km (7 miles) SE of Véroia, Macedonia. **Road map** C2. ■ **Museum** *Tel 23310 92347.* ◯ *Jun–Oct: noon–7pm Mon, 8:30am–7pm Tue–Sun; Nov–May: 8:30am–3pm Tue–Sat (to 7pm Sun).* ◙ *(tickets also valid for Royal Tombs).*

Outside the village of Vergína, during excavations in 1977, archaeologist Professor Manólis Andrónikos found an entrance to a tomb. The bones inside included a skull with one eye socket damaged, evidence that the tomb belonged to King Philip II of Macedon, who received such a wound in the siege of Methóni. The bones were discovered in a stunning gold funerary box, embellished with the symbol of the Macedonian Sun. The discovery confirmed that this area was the site of Aigai, the first capital of Macedon. The finds from this tomb, as well as finds from several other **Royal Tombs** nearby, are now on display in the museum here and are considered the most important in Greece since Schliemann's discoveries at Mycenae (*see pp178–80*).

A short walk further along the road from Philip's tomb are some earlier discoveries,

Terracotta head of a young man, from the Museum at Véroia

known as the **Macedonian Tombs**. The dark interior hides splendid solid marble doors, as well as a beautiful marble throne.

The **Palace of Palatítsa** stands beyond on a mound. It is thought to have been first occupied in about 1000 BC, though the building itself dates from the 3rd century BC. Today only low foundations remain, along with the ruins of a theatre 100 m (330 ft) below, thought to be the site of Philip II's assassination.

⌂ **Royal Tombs, Macedonian Tombs, Palace of Palatítsa**
Tel 23310 92394. ◯ *8:30am–3pm Tue–Sun.* ⬤ *main public hols.* ◙

THE MACEDONIAN ROYAL FAMILY

The gold burial casket found at Vergína is emblazoned with the Macedonian Sun, the symbol of the king. Philip II was from a long line of Macedonian kings, that began in about 640 BC with Perdiccas I. Philip was the first ruler to unite the whole of Greece as it existed at that time. Also incorrectly known as the Macedonian Star, the Sun is often seen on flags within the region. Much of Greece's pride in the symbol lies in the fact that Alexander the Great used it throughout his empire (*see pp32–3*). He was just 20 when his father was

Burial casket featuring the Macedonian Sun

assassinated at Aigai in 336 BC. He inherited his father's already large empire and also his ambition to conquer the Persians.

In 334 BC Alexander crossed the Dardanelles with 40,000 men and defeated the Persians in three different battles, advancing as far as the Indus Valley before he died at the age of 33. With his death the Macedonian Empire divided.

Véroia ❻
Βέροια

Macedonia. **Road map** C2.
🏠 *48,000.* ■ 🚇 🚍 *Tue.*

The largest town in the region, Véroia is interesting mainly for its 50 or so barnlike churches, which have survived from the 17th and 18th centuries.

The town's **Archaeological Museum** has a selection of interesting exhibits, discovered locally, and the bazaar area bustles on market days, as Véroia is the centre of the local peach-growing industry.

🏛 **Archaeological Museum**
Anoixéos 47. *Tel 23310 24972.*
◯ *8am–3pm Tue–Sun.* ⬤ *main public hols.* ◙

Chília Déndra park at Náousa, near Lefkádia

Lefkádia ❼
Λευκάδια

Macedonia. **Road map** C2.
Tel 23320 41121. ■ ◯ *8:30am–3pm Tue–Sun.* ⬤ *main public hols.*

The four Macedonian Tombs of Lefkádia are set in a quiet agricultural area. The caretaker is usually at one of the two tombs that are sign-posted. The first of these is the **Tomb of the Judges**, or Great Tomb. This, the largest tomb, with a chamber 9 m (30 ft) square and a frescoed façade portraying Aiakos and Rhadamanthys, the Judges of Hades, has been recently restored. Beyond is the **Anthemíon Tomb**, or Tomb

Pebble mosaic of the Lion Hunt from the House of the Lion Hunt at Ancient Pélla

of the Flowers, with well–preserved flower paintings on the roof. The key to the **Tomb of Lyson and Kallikles** is sometimes available from the caretaker. The entrance is through a metal grate in the roof. The fourth tomb, called the **Tomb of Kinch** after its Danish discoverer, or the **Tomb of Niafsta** after its one-time occupant, is closed to visitors.

Environs
Renowned for the large park of Agios Nikólaos, also known as Chília Déndra (1,000 trees), **Náousa** is the home of the Boutari wine-making family. It is situated on the edge of the hills above the plain that extends east to Thessaloníki. Like Edessa, Náousa has waters flowing through it. Riverside tavernas in the park offer fresh trout as well as the good local wine.

Edessa **8**
Έδεσσα

Macedonia. **Road map** C1. 🚹 16,000. 🚌 🚐 🚶 Parko Katarrákton (23810 20300). 🚻 10am–6pm daily. 🍴 Thu.

Edessa is the capital of the modern Pélla region and a popular summer resort. It is renowned for its waterfalls, which plunge down a ravine from the town to the valley floor below. The largest fall is the **Káranos**, at 24 m (79 ft), which has a cave behind it. The surrounding gardens and park are pleasant, with cafés and restaurants.

Ancient Pélla **9**
Πέλλα

38 km (24 miles) NW of Thessaloníki, Macedonia. **Road map** C1. 🚌 **Tel** 23820 31160. **Site** 🕗 8:30am–3pm daily. **Museum** 🕗 8:30am–3pm Tue–Sun. 🚫 main public hols. 🏷 ♿

This small site, which straddles the main road, was once the flourishing capital of Macedon. The court was moved here

Káranos waterfall at Edessa

from Aigai (near modern Vergína) in 410 BC by King Archelaos, who ruled from 413 to 399 BC. It is here that Alexander the Great was born in 356 BC, and later tutored by the philosopher Aristotle. Some sense of the existence of a city can be gained from a plan of the site, which shows where the main street and shops were located. The palace is believed to have been north of the main site, but is still being excavated.

At the site, and in the museum, are some of the best-preserved and most beautiful pebble mosaics in Greece. The stones are uncut and have been carefully picked not only for their size, but also for their warm, subtle colouring. Dating from about 300 BC, the mosaics include vivid hunting scenes. One of the most famous is of Dionysos riding a panther, which is protected from the weather in the now-covered House of the Lion Hunt. This was built at the end of the 4th century BC and originally comprised 12 rooms around three open court-yards, the whole structure being 90 m (295 ft) long by 50 m (165 ft) wide.

Thessaloníki ⑩
Θεσσαλονίκη

Thessaloniki, also known as Salonica, is Greece's second city, founded by King Kassandros in 315 BC. The Romans made it capital of their province of Macedonia Prima in 146 BC, and in AD 395 it became part of the Byzantine Empire. In 1430 it was captured by the Turks who held it until 1912. Today Thessaloníki is a bustling cosmopolitan city. It has a flourishing cultural life and is a major religious centre, with an array of splendid churches (see p248), such as Agía Sofía and Agios Dimítrios, which is the largest church in Greece.

Lion from the Archaeological Museum

Cafés and fountains in the park near Plateía Chánth

Exploring Thessaloníki

Greece's second city is also a very busy port, which adds to the bustle and the wealth of this fascinating metropolis. Situated on the Thermaic Gulf, it has an attractive waterfront promenade, known as the *paralía*, and a pleasant leafy park. It also boasts a large number of beautiful Byzantine churches (see p248). In recent years Thessaloníki has developed its international exhibition facilities and become a major trade fair centre. The city has many museums, including the Archaeological Museum (see pp246–7).

The Great Fire of August in 1917 destroyed nearly half the buildings within the medieval walls, including the entire Jewish quarter. Some, however, survived, and many from the

Furniture shop in the back streets

original Ottoman bazaar have been recently restored. One such building is the **Bezesténi**, once a hall for valuables and now home to plush shops. The **Modiáno**, a covered meat and produce hall, is named after the Jewish family who once owned it. West of Modiano are some of the best *ouzerí* bars, and **Plateía Aristotélous** is home to many posh cafés.

🏛 Arch of Galerius
Egnatía.

The principal architectural legacy of Roman rule is found at the eastern end of the long main street, Egnatía, which was itself a Roman construction, known as Via Egnatia. Here stands the Arch of Galerius, built in AD 303 by Galerius (then Caesar of the East, or deputy emperor) to celebrate his victory over the Persians in AD 297. Its carvings show scenes from the battle.

Section of carving from the Arch of Galerius

There was once a double arch here, with a palace to the south. Some of its remains can be seen in Plateía Navarínou.

🏛 White Tower
On the waterfront. *Tel 2310 267832.*
◯ *8:30am–3pm Tue–Sun.* 🗓

Probably Thessaloníki's most famous sight is the White Tower on the *paralía*. Built in 1430, the Turks added three such towers to the 8-km (5-mile) city walls. Today it houses rotating exhibitions on several floors of small circular rooms. The original stone steps climb up to a roof with lovely views of the *paralía*.

🏛 Rotónda
Filippou.

Standing north of the Arch of Galerius is the Rotónda. It is thought that this impressive building was constructed as a Mausoleum for Galerius, emperor of the eastern Roman Empire AD 305–311. Today it is closed, but it has been used in the past both as a church – it is also known as Agios Geórgios – and as a mosque. The minaret nearby is now the only one in Thessaloníki.

🖼 Museum of Byzantine Culture
Leofórou Stratoú 2. *Tel 2310 868570.*
◯ *10:30am–5pm Mon, 8:30am–3pm Tue–Sun.* 🔵 *main public hols.*
🗓 🅰 www.mbp.gr

Situated behind the Archaeological Museum (see pp246–7), this small, modern museum was opened in 1995. On display are Byzantine icons that date from the 15th to the 19th centuries, and also some fine jewellery. All of the items are beautifully displayed and lit, and there are plans to expand the collection.

White Tower on the seafront

was under Turkish rule. Photographs, newspapers, weapons, documents and personal items tell the story well. Vivid tableaux depict the struggle and its effect on ordinary people. In one, a Turk with a rifle bursts violently into a schoolroom while a Greek freedom fighter hides under the floorboards. This was the celebrated Pávlos Melás, who fought to free Macedonia from the Turks. Also on display in the museum, are his gun and dagger.

🏛 Museum of the Macedonian Struggle

Proxénou Koromilá 23. **Tel** 2310 229778. 🕐 9am–2pm Tue–Fri, 10am–2pm Sat. ⬤ main public hols.
This is situated in a late 19th-century mansion which originally housed the Greek Consulate when Thessaloníki

🏛 Folklife and Ethnological Museum

Vasilíssis Olgas 68. **Tel** 2310 830591.
🕐 9am–3pm Fri–Tue, 10am–10pm Wed. 🈯
This museum is a 20-minute walk from the Archaeological Museum. There are displays

VISITORS' CHECKLIST

Macedonia. **Road map** C2. 🏘 1,000,000. ✈ 25 km (15 miles) SE of Thessaloníki. 🚌 off Koundouriótou. 🚉 Monastiriou. 🚍 78 (local bus), Monastiriou (Intercity buses). 🛈 Airport (2310 471170); Passenger Ferry Terminal (2310 500310). 🎭 Thessaloníki Cultural Festival (cinema): Oct.

of folk costumes, and detailed small models showing rural activities such as breadmaking, ploughing, winnowing, threshing, and children playing. The gruelling life of the nomadic Sarakatsan shepherds is well documented, and a vivid display shows the incredible events at the annual fire-walking ceremony in Lagkadás, a village 20 km (12 miles) northeast of Thessaloníki. The museum also hosts several temporary exhibitions throughout the year and has an extensive archive of fascinating period photography showing the reality of life during the early 20th century.

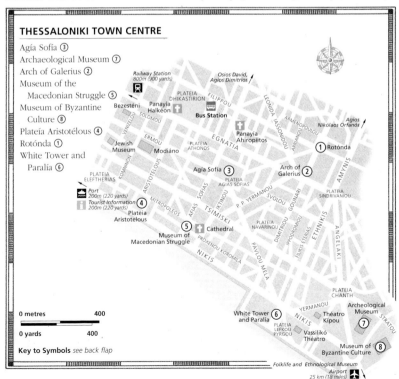

THESSALONIKI TOWN CENTRE

Agía Sofía ③
Archaeological Museum ⑦
Arch of Galerius ②
Museum of the
   Macedonian Struggle ⑤
Museum of Byzantine
   Culture ⑧
Plateía Aristotélous ④
Rotónda ①
White Tower and
   Paralía ⑥

Railway Station
800m (900 yards)

Osios David,
Agios Dimitrios

PLATEIA
DHIKASTIRION
FILIPPOU

Bezesténi
Panayia
Halkéon

Bus Station

LEONIDA IASSONIDOU
ARMENOPOULOU
ARIANDOU

Agios
Nikólaos Orfanós

VENIZELOU
SOLOMOU

ERMOU

Jewish
Museum

Modiáno

PLATEIA
ATHONOS

EGNATIA

Panayia
Ahiropiitos

① Rotónda

AMYNIS

PLATEIA
ELEFTHERIAS

KOMNINON

ARISTOTELOUS

Agía Sofía ③

PLATEIA
AGIAS SOFIAS

Arch of
Galerius ②

GOUNARI

PLATEIA
SINDRIVANIOU

Port
200m (220 yards)
Tourist Information
200m (220 yards) ④

Plateía
Aristotelous

MITRÓPOLEOS

AFAS SOFIAS

TSIMISKI

KTENOU

P. P. YERMANOU

SVOLOU

DIMITRIOU GOUNARI

IPPODROMOU

FILIPOS ETERIAS

EThNIKIS

ANGELAKI

⑤ 🛈 Cathedral

PROXENOU KOROMILA

NIKIS

Museum of
Macedonian Struggle

PLATEIA
NAVARINOU

PAVLOU MELA

PLATEIA
CHANTH

0 metres   400

0 yards   400

White Tower ⑥
and Paralía

YERMANOU
NIKIS

PLATEIA
LEFKOU
FYRGOU

Théatro
Kípou

Vassilikó
Théatro

Archeological
Museum

⑦

STRATOU

Museum of ⑧
Byzantine Culture

Key to Symbols see back flap

Folklife and Ethnological Museum
Airport
25 km (18 miles)

Thessaloníki Archaeological Museum
Αρχαιολογικό Μουσείο Θεσσαλονίκης

This modern museum, opened in 1963, contains a host of treasures. It concentrates on the finds made within the city and at the many sites in Macedonia. The displays progress chronologically through the ages, giving a clear picture of the area's history. The inner rooms surrounding the courtyard house a number of fabulous gold items from ancient Macedon, including the treasures discovered during excavations at Macedonian cemeteries. The annexe basement contains a small exhibition on the prehistory of Thessaloníki.

Glass Vase
During the Roman period, the art of colouring glass came into use, as in this pink vase. Craftsmen experimented with shapes and colours, and a wide variety of glass items have been recovered from Roman tombs in Thessaloníki.

Faïence Vase
Found in a 2nd-century BC grave in Thessaloníki, this ornate vase is from Ptolemaic Egypt and is the only such faïence vase in Greece. Depicted on the bas-relief, among other subjects, is a detail of the goddess Artemis in a forest.

GALLERY GUIDE
An outer circle of rooms surrounds a block of inner rooms housing a collection of Macedonian gold. The outer rooms contain treasures from the first centuries of Thessaloníki and the Kingdom of Macedon. The basement of the annexe holds an exhibition of prehistoric antiquities.

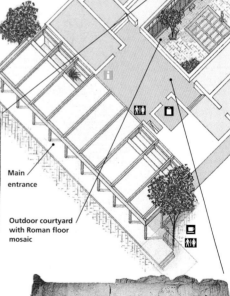

Main entrance

Outdoor courtyard with Roman floor mosaic

★ Floor Mosaics from a Thessaloníki House
These detailed mosaics depicting marine-world mythology are Roman. This mosaic shows a nereid (sea nymph) and a dolphin.

Marble Sarcophagus
This 2nd– or 3rd-century Roman sarcophagus is decorated with a vivid relief depicting an Amazon battle. The Amazons, a mythical warrior tribe of women, were a favourite subject for artists (see p55).

Statue of Harpokrates
The marble statue of Harpokrates, the son of Isis and Osiris, was found in Thessaloníki at the site of a sanctuary devoted to Serapis and other Egyptian gods. It has been dated to the end of the 2nd century.

VISITORS' CHECKLIST

Manóli Andrónikou & Leof Stratoú. **Tel** 2310 830538. ☎ 3. ○ *The museum is undergoing refurbishment, with a couple of rooms open. Phone for opening hours.* ● *main public hols.* 📷 ♿

Head of Serapis
This fine marble head was discovered in the same sanctuary as the statue of Harpokrates and dates from the Roman period. Originally an Egyptian deity, Serapis was adopted by the Romans as a foreign cult.

★ Gold Bracelet from Europos
This gold bracelet is one of the highlights of the collection of Macedonian gold. It dates from the 3rd century BC and is accompanied in the exhibition by other gold finds of the 6th-2nd centuries BC.

KEY TO FLOORPLAN

☐	Prehistoric collection
☐	The Gold of Macedon
☐	The Kingdom of Macedon
☐	Thessaloníki: The First Centuries
☐	Manólis Andrónikos room
☐	Non-exhibition space

STAR EXHIBITS

* ★ Gold Bracelet from Europos

* ★ Floor Mosaics from a Thessaloníki House

* ★ Dervéni Krater

★ Dervéni Krater
Dating from 300 BC, this bronze wine-mixing vase stands 1 m (3 ft) high. The detailed figures of maenads are exquisite; one is shown dancing with a satyr. The volutes at the top are decorated with the head of Herakles.

Exploring Thessaloníki's Churches

Thessaloníki has the richest collection of Byzantine churches in Greece. Of the hundreds of 5th-century basilicas that once stood across the country, only two remain. Both of these, Agios Dimítrios and Acheiropoíïtos, are in Thessaloníki. The 8th-century Agía Sofía is a very significant Byzantine building, both for its mosaics and its role in influencing future architectural development. Three different 14th-century churches – Agios Nikólaos Orfanós, Agioi Apóstoloi and Agía Aikateríni – give an insight into what was a period of architectural innovation.

Agía Sofía church

The mosaic of Ezekiel's vision in Osios David

🔒 Agios Dimítrios

Agíou Dimitríou. ⏰ *6am–9:30pm daily.* ♿ **Crypt** ⏰ *10:30am–8pm Sun, 12:30–7pm Mon, 8am–8pm Tue–Sat.*

This, the largest church in Greece, was entirely rebuilt after the fire of 1917, which destroyed the 7th- and 13th-century fabric of the basilica. The oldest, 3rd-century AD portion is the crypt. Originally a Roman bath, this, according to legend, is the site of the imprisonment, torture and murder in 305 AD of the city's patron saint Dimitrios – a Roman soldier converted to Christianity and martyred on the orders of Emperor Galerius. Six small 5th–7th-century mosaics are found both on the piers flanking the altar and high up on the west side of the church. These mosaics rank among the finest in Greece and include depictions of Dimitrios with young children, or in the company of the church's builders.

🔒 Osios David

Kástro. ⏰ *daily.*

This delightful small chapel was founded some time in the late 5th century. Behind

the altar is an original vivid mosaic of the *Vision of Ezekiel*, rare in that it depicts Christ without a beard. In marvellous condition, it owes its freshness to having been concealed beneath plaster and only discovered in 1921. There are also some frescoes from the 12th century, including a fine *Baptism* and *Nativity*. Although the church is usually locked, there is a caretaker who greets visitors and will unbolt the doors.

🔒 Agía Sofía

Plateía Agías Sofías. ⏰ *8:30am–2pm, 5:30–8pm daily.*

The church of Agía Sofía is dedicated to the Holy Wisdom (Sofiá) of God, just like the mosque of the same name in Istanbul. It was built in the mid-8th century. In 1585 it became a mosque, but was reconsecrated as a church in 1912. It contains many mosaics and frescoes dating back to the 9th and 10th centuries, including a fine *Ascension* scene in the 30-m (100-ft) high dome. The entrance formerly had a portico, which was obliterated during an Italian air raid in 1941. The imposing nature of the building is emphasized by its location in a partially sunken garden.

🔒 Agios Nikólaos Orfanós

Kástro. ⏰ *8am–2:45pm Tue–Sun; key available from warden at Irodhotou 17, opposite the church.* ♿

Situated in a garden plot amongst the lanes of the ancient Kástra district, or upper town, this small, triple-apsed 14th-century church began life as a dependency of the larger Moni Vlatádon, further up the hill. Today, Agios Nikólaos Orfanós retains the richest and best-preserved collection of late Byzantine frescoes in the city. Distributed over the central cella and both aisles, they show rare scenes from the Passion, including Christ mounting the Cross, and Pilate seated in judgement.

Agios Dimítrios, the largest church in Greece

The stretch of sandy beach at Kallithéa on Kassándra

west coast, **Sáni** has excellent beaches and a luxury resort complex. There are quiet bays around the village of **Possídi**, on a promontory halfway down the west coast. On the east coast, **Néa Fókaia** still functions as a fishing village in spite of the steady invasion of tourism, whereas **Kallithéa**, to the south, is the largest resort on Kassándra.

Northern Chalkidikí ❶
Βόρεια Χαλκιδική

Macedonia. **Road map** D2. 🚌 to Polýgyros.

The north of Chalkidikí is a quiet and delightful hilly region, often overlooked by those whose main interests are the beaches to the south. A glimpse of the hidden interior is given when visiting the **Petrálona Caves**, situated on the edge of Mount Katsíka, 55 km (34 miles) southeast of Thessaloníki. It was in these red-rock caverns in 1960, the year after the caves were discovered by local villagers, that a skull was found. It was believed to be that of a young woman, aged about 25 when she died. A complete skeleton was subsequently discovered, and these are the oldest bones yet to be found in Greece, dating back at least 250,000 years, and possibly even 700,000. Amid the stalactites and stalagmites, reconstructions of the cave dwellers have been arranged in the caves, along with the bones, teeth and tools that were also found here.

In the northeast of the area is the small village of **Stágeira**, the birthplace of Aristotle (384–322 BC). On a hilltop, just outside the village, is a huge white marble statue of the philosopher, and there are sweeping views over the surrounding countryside.

Statue of Aristotle, Stágeira

🐾 Petrálona Caves
Mount Katsíka, 55 km (34 miles) SE of Thessaloníki. **Tel** 23730 71671. ⏰ Jun–Sep: 9am–7pm daily (to 5pm Oct–May). 🚫 main public hols. 👁

Kassándra ❶
Κασσάνδρα

Southern Chalkidiki, Macedonia. **Road map** D2. 🚌 to Kassándreia.

Much of this area's population was killed in the War of Independence in 1821, and the numbers never really recovered. Little was left on the promontory of Kassándra other than a few fishing villages. However, over the last 30 years, many resorts have sprung up. **Néa Poteídaia** marks the start of Kassándra proper and straddles the narrow neck of the peninsula, with a good sandy beach, a marina and an attractive town square. On the

Sithonía ❶
Σιθωνία

Southern Chalkidiki, Macedonia. **Road map** D2. 🚌 to Agios Nikólaos.

While the peninsula of Sithonía is only marginally larger than Kassándra, it has fewer resorts and a thickly wooded interior. The peninsula begins at **Metamórfosi** which has a sandy beach shaded by pine trees. **Vourvouroú** is one of the first villages you come to on the north side. A collection of villas spreads along the coast, with a few hotels and a selection of eating places.

To the south of this area is a long undeveloped stretch of coast, with several unspoilt beaches, until you reach the large resort of **Sárti**. At the tip of Sithonía is **Kalamítsi**, little more than a sandy beach and a few bars, while **Pórto Koufó** at the end of the west coast is still a pleasant fishing village set on a bay amid wooded hills. The **Pórto Karrás** resort complex, halfway down the west coast, was set up by the Karrás wine family. It has three hotels, a marina, a shopping centre, watersports, horseriding, a golf course and tennis.

Boats docked at Pórto Koufó on Sithonía

Mount Athos ⑭

`ΑγιονΌρος

Mount Athos monk

To the Greeks, this is the Holy Mountain, which at 2,030 m (6,660 ft) is the highest point of Chalkidikí's most easterly peninsula. Unique in Greece, Athos is an autonomous republic ruled by the 1,700 monks who live in its 20 monasteries. Only adult males may visit the peninsula, but it is possible to see many of the monasteries from a boat trip along the coast. Together, they include some fine examples of Byzantine architecture and provide an insight into monastic life.

Kólpos Agíou Orous

THE MONASTERIES OF ATHOS

— — — Ferry route

Ouranoúpoli
The main town on Athos is where boat trips around the peninsula start.

MOUNT ATHOS FROM THE WEST
This illustration shows the view seen when travelling by boat along the west of Athos. The most northerly monastery is Zográfou and the most southerly is Agíou Pávlou. The eastern monasteries are covered on p254.

Xiropotámou was founded in the 10th century, but the present buildings date from the 18th century.

Zográfou was founded in AD 971, but the present buildings are 18th– and 19th-century.

To Ouranoúpoli ←

Kastamonítou was founded in the 11th century by a hermit from Asia Minor.

Xenofóntos was founded in the late 10th century. A second chapel was built in 1837, using some 14th-century mosaic panels.

0 kilometres   15
0 miles   10

Docheiaríou
This 10th-century monastery houses a fragment of the True Cross and an icon of the Virgin with healing powers.

Agíou Panteleímonos
Also known as Rosikón (of the Russians), this 11th-century monastery's imposing walls hide many colourful onion-domed churches, evidence of the Russian Orthodox influence on Athos.

◁ **The monastery of Agiou Panteleimonos, Mount Athos**

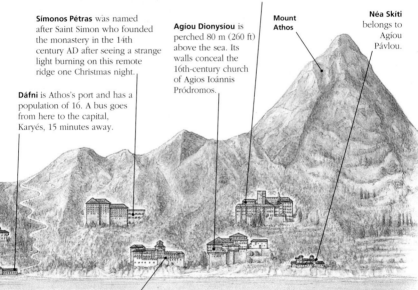

VISITORS' CHECKLIST

Athos Peninsula, Macedonia.
Road map D2 ⛴ *Dáfni (boat
trips from Ouranoúpoli & Thessa-
loníki for the west coast, or from
Ierissós for the east coast).* 🚌 *to
Karyés.* 📷 *donation.*

Agíou Pávlou
*This monastery houses 90
monks, many from Zákynthos
and Kefalloniá, and has
some 13,000 books and
manuscripts in its library.*

Símonos Pétras was named
after Saint Simon who founded
the monastery in the 14th
century AD after seeing a strange
light burning on this remote
ridge one Christmas night.

Agíou Dionysíou is
perched 80 m (260 ft)
above the sea. Its
walls conceal the
16th-century church
of Agios Ioánnis
Pródromos.

**Mount
Athos**

Néa Skíti
belongs to
Agíou
Pávlou.

Dáfni is Athos's port and has a
population of 16. A bus goes
from here to the capital,
Karyés, 15 minutes away.

Grigoríou
*Founded in the 14th centu-
ry, this monastery was totally
rebuilt after a disastrous fire
in 1761 which destroyed all
but a few holy relics. About
40 monks live here today.*

VISITING MOUNT ATHOS
Only 10 non-Orthodox men per
day are allowed to visit Mount
Athos, with a stay of 4 nights. To
apply, send a fax request with
your preferred start date to visit
(and an alternative), together
with a copy of your passport, to
the Thessaloníki Pilgrims' Bureau
at +231 022 2424. Apply well in
advance. Once confirmed, you
must book the monasteries you
wish to visit; the Bureau has the
monastery telephone numbers.
On the day of your visit, be at
the Ouranopolis Pilgrims' Bureau by 8:30am to collect your
Diamenterion (official permit); bring your confirmation and
passport. Boats leave daily at 9:45am for the monasteries. For
more information, contact the Pilgrims Bureau, 109 Egnatia
Street, 54622 Thessaloniki, Greece (tel:+231 025 2578).

Vatopedíou refectory

Exploring Mount Athos

Not all of the 20 monasteries on Athos can be seen from the popular boat trips from Ouranoúpoli, although some boats do go round the whole peninsula. A few are hidden in the mountains and others cling to the eastern coast of the peninsula. In addition to the Greek Orthodox monasteries on Mount Athos, there is one Russian (Agíou Panteleímonos), one Bulgarian (Zográfou) and one Serbian (Chilandaríou). Remote hermitages and monastic villages in the hills of the peninsula are preferred by some monks, as a quieter alternative to the relatively busy monastery life.

The East Coast Monasteries
The first monastery to be founded on Athos was the **Megístis Lávras** (Great Lavra). It is situated at the southeastern end of the peninsula, on a rocky outcrop (*see pp36–7*). It was founded in AD 963 by Athanásios the Athonite, and is the only one of the monasteries never to have suffered from fire. It also has the largest font of all the monasteries, which is outside, shaded by a cypress tree said to have been planted over 1,000 years ago by Athanásios himself.

Painting in Megístis Lávras

Halfway along the eastern coast stand the monasteries of Ivíron and Stavronikíta. **Moní Ivíron** was founded in the late 10th century by a monk from Iberia (modern Georgia), hence its name. Its church was built in the early 11th century and restored in 1513. The monastery's main courtyard contains another 16 chapels, one housing a miraculous icon of the Virgin Mary. **Stavronikíta**, to the north, stands on top of a rocky headland. It was first mentioned in a document dated AD 1012.

Moní Vatopedíou, one of the largest monasteries on Athos, is sited on a small promontory at the northern end of the east coast. It was founded in the latter half of the 10th century, and a notable feature is its *katholikón*, or main church, also built in the 10th century. It contains icons dating from the 14th century, though they have been retouched over the years. A wealthy monastery, it is among the best preserved on Mount Athos.

ORTHODOX LIFE ON MOUNT ATHOS

Monks growing their own fruit and vegetables

Under the Byzantine time system operating on Athos, midnight is at dawn, and morning services begin about an hour before – around 3 or 4am, Greek time. A monk walks around striking a small wooden *símandro* (a carved plank) with a mallet to wake the other monks and call them to prayer. The monks eat two meals a day, consisting mostly of food they grow themselves. There are 159 fasting days in the year when only one meal is allowed which must contain no fish, eggs, cheese, milk or even oil. Meals are eaten after the morning and evening services, and the time in between is spent working, resting and praying.

The Megístis Lávras monastery, with its red *katholikón* in the centre

Kavála **⑮**
Καβάλα

Macedonia. **Road map** D1. ⌂ 56,000. ✈ 35 km (22 miles) SE of Kavála. ⛴ 🚌 ⌂ daily.

Kavála's history goes back to its foundation in the 6th century BC by settlers from Thásos and Erétria. It became part of the Roman Empire in 168 BC, and is where St Paul first set foot on European soil in AD 50 or 51 on his way to Philippi. The biggest impact, however, was the Turkish occupation from 1371 to 1912. It was the Turks who built the 16th-century aqueduct here. Mehmet Ali (1769–1849), the Pasha of Egypt, was born in Kavála. His **birthplace**, a well-preserved house, set in gardens and marked by a bronze statue of Ali on horseback, is open to visitors.

Sculpture by Polýgnotos Vágis

Kavála is a busy city, with an industrial port that also has a ferry service to the northeast Aegean islands. Life centres around the harbour below the castle, which is floodlit at night. At its eastern end there is a busy fish, fruit and vegetable market. To the west is the **Archaeological Museum**, which has finds from Avdíra (see p256), including a dolphin mosaic and a painted sarcophagus. There are also some delicate 3rd-century BC gold laurel wreaths found at Amphipolis, west of Kavála, and clay masks and a 4th-century BC bust of an unknown goddess.

The **Municipal Museum** is housed in a late 19th-century Neo-Classical building to the west of the town hall. It has a collection of costumes and household items, and a good display of work by local artists, in particular Thasiot sculptor Polýgnotos Vágis (1894–1965).

🏛 Mehmet Ali's Birthplace
Theodórou Poulídou 63. **Tel** 2510 220061. 🕐 until 2007.

🏛 Archaeological Museum
Erythroú Stavroú 17. **Tel** 2510 222335. 🕐 8:30am–3pm Tue–Sun. 🕐 main public hols. 🚫 ♿

🏛 Muncipal Museum
Filíppou 4. **Tel** 2510 222706. 🕐 8:30am–2pm Mon–Fri, 9am–1pm Sat. 🕐 main public hols.

Néstos Valley **⑯**
Κοιλάδα του Νέστου

Macedonia/Thrace border. **Road map** D1. 🚌 ✈ Xánthi (liable to be cancelled Nov–Apr).

The Néstos river rises high in the Rodópi mountains in Bulgaria and its meandering course down to the Aegean near the island of Thásos marks the boundary between Macedonia and Thrace. On its way it threads through remote and inaccessible gorges, fed by other rivers and streams, until it passes under the scenic mountain road which links Xánthi in Thrace with the town of Dráma in Macedonia. This road, sometimes closed by snowdrifts in winter, makes for a spectacular scenic drive through the wooded gorge, past the valley's heavy beech forests and scattering of small villages. **Stavroúpoli**, the largest of these villages, has a good café in its village square.

Xánthi **⑰**
Ξάνθη

Thrace. **Road map** E1. ⌂ 25,000. 🚌 🚏 ⌂ Sat.

Founded in the 11th century, it was not until the 1800s that Xánthi flourished with the development of the tobacco industry. Displays on tobacco are included in the **Folk Museum**, housed in two old mansions. The museum's collection includes embroidery, jewellery and costumes. Xánthi's main square has cafés and fountains, and east of the square is the bazaar. This is overflowing on Saturdays when people of all nationalities and religions visit the busiest market in the area.

🏛 Folk Museum
Antiká 7. **Tel** 25410 25421. 🕐 8:30am–2:30pm Wed–Fri, 10:30am–3pm Sat & Sun. 🚫

The town and harbour of Kavála

The lush landscape of the Néstos Valley

The monastery of Agios Nikólaos on the banks of Lake Vistonída

Avdira ⑱
Ἄβδηρα

6 km (4 miles) S of modern Avdira,
Thrace. **Road map** E1. 🚌
Tel 25410 51988. ⬜ 8am–2pm
daily. 🌑 main public hols.

The ancient city of Avdira
was founded in the mid-7th
century BC by refugees from
Klazomenae in Asia Minor. The
site is quite dispersed and
overgrown. Most of what can
be seen today dates from the
Roman period. Some Archaic
and Classical ruins are also
evident, including the acropolis. The remains of its walls
stand on a small headland,
and ancient graves have been
discovered just outside the
walls. Part of the original city
wall can also be seen.

Environs
Along the road from Avdira to
Maróneia is **Lake Vistonída**, a
haven for wildlife. At one end
is Pórto Lágos (see pp236–7),
an old harbour with the white
monastery of Agios Nikólaos.

Komotiní ⑲
Κομοτηνή

Thrace. **Road map** E1.
🏃 38,000. 🚊 🚌 🚤 Tue.

Only 25 km (16 miles) from the
Bulgarian border to the north,
and less than 100 km (62
miles) from Turkey to the east,
Komotiní is a fascinating mix of
Greek and Turkish influence.
First founded in the late 4th
century AD, it was taken by the
Turks in 1363, and remained

part of the Ottoman Empire
until 1920. Over 500 years of
Turkish rule have left their
mark on the town, especially
since the area's Muslims were
excluded from the
population exchange
following the Greek
defeat in Asia Minor
in 1922. There is a
thriving market with
fish, cattle and
tobacco for sale,
along with a good
selection of fresh
produce grown in
fertile land. The
many old wooden
shops sell everything
from bric-a-brac to genuine,
valuable antiques.

A feel of the town's recent
past is given in the well-
cared-for **Museum of Folk
Life and History**. Its few
rooms, in an 18th-century

The domed roof and tall minaret of
a Turkish mosque, Komotiní

mansion, are crammed with
costumes, local copperware
and domestic items. There
is also a particularly good
collection of embroidery,
including examples of a
type known as Tsevrés,
used in Thracian wedding
ceremonies. The town's
Archaeological Museum
displays the best of
the finds from the
sites at ancient
Avdira and Maróneia,
including gold jewel-
lery found in 4th-cen-
tury BC graves at
Avdira. A 4th-century
BC clay mask of
Dionysos is on display, found
at the god's sanctuary at
Maróneia. The museum also
has an extensive coin collection, painted sarcophagi,
votive reliefs and maps.

Finial from a
gravestone,
Archaeological
Museum, Komotiní

🏛 **Museum of Folk Life
and History**
Agiou Georgiou. ⬜ 10am–1pm daily.
🌑 main public hols. 📷 ♿ limited.

🏛 **Archaeological Museum**
Symeonídi 4. **Tel** 25310 22411.
⬜ 9am–2:30pm daily. 🌑 main
public hols.

Maróneia ⑳
Μαρώνεια

5 km (3 miles) SE of modern
Maróneia, Thrace. **Road map** E1. 🚌
to modern Maróneia. ⬜ daily. 🌑
main public hols. 📷 ♿

The road to ancient Maróneia
leads through tobacco and
cotton fields, past woodland
and small rural communities.
A signpost to the harbour of

Agios Charálampos shows the way down a track to the remains of the site that are in a scenic position overlooking the sea. The city flourished from the 8th century BC until AD 1400. Olive groves now cover the area, which sits between Mount Ismaros and the sea, but a small theatre has been discovered and renovated. Further down the track are the remnants of a sanctuary, thought to have been dedicated to Dionysos, whose son, Maron, is credited with founding Maróneia.

Beyond the city of ancient Maróneia is the small but developing harbour of **Agios Charálampos**, surrounded by red cliffs, topped by a large hotel, a taverna and a scattering of houses.

Environs

Medieval **Maróneia** is a tiny but attractive place, mainly a farming community but with some larger mansions that provide evidence of a more prosperous past.

Alexandroúpoli ㉑
Αλεξανδρούπολη

Thrace. **Road map** E1. 🏘 *36,000.*
✈ 🚌 🚆 🚌 🛥 *Tue.*

Alexandroúpoli lacks the cultural mix and history of other large Thracian towns. It was only built up in 1878, under the Turkish name of Dedeagaç (meaning "Tree of the Holy Man"), derived from a group of hermits who first settled here in the 15th

The landmark lighthouse in Alexandroúpoli

century. Prior to that, it was simply an unremarkable fishing village. lexandroúpoli was renamed in 1919 after the Greek king at the time, Aléxandros.

Today the town is a thriving holiday resort with a port, its own domestic airport, and train connections east to Istanbul, north into Bulgaria and west to Thessaloníki.

In the evening the promenade by the long stretch of beach is thronged with people, both visitors and locals. The lighthouse, built in 1800, is situated along the seafront. It is the town's most famous feature and is lit up at night.

Inland from the promenade, is a warren of narrow streets with junk shops, grocers, cobblers, goldsmiths and fish

restaurants. The best eating places are around tiny Plateía Polytechneíou. North from the square, beyond the main road, is the modern cathedral ofAgios Nikólaos, notable for the **Ecclesiastical Art Museum** contained in its grounds. This fine collection of icons and other religious items is unfortunately seldom open, but those with a particular interest in seeing it may ask for access at the cathedral.

🏛 **Ecclesiastical Art Museum**
Palaiológou. ⬜ *variable.* ⬤ *main public hols.*

Dadiá Forest ㉒
Δάσος Δαδιάς

27km (17 miles) N of Féres, Thrace.
Road map F1. 🚌 🚆 *Féres.*
ℹ *1 km (0.5 miles) N of Dadiá village (25540 32209).*

North of the small town of Féres in the Evros valley is the lovely Dadiá pine forest. Covering a series of hills known as the Evros mountains, it is considered to be one of the best places in Europe for observing rare birds. Of special interest is the presence of birds of prey, an indication of the remote location of the forest. There are 39 known species of birds of prey in Europe, 26 of which live and nest in this region.

Rare black vulture

There is an information centre in the heart of the forest, and observation huts have been placed near feeding stations, built to help preserve the rarer species that nest here. This is one of the black vulture's last refuges in eastern Europe. The forest is home to a huge number of protected and endangered species, including imperial eagles, golden eagles, griffon vultures, sparrowhawks and peregrines. Early morning is the best time to watch the different birds as they fly on the first thermals of the day.

Old mansion in modern Maróneia

TRAVELLERS'
NEEDS

WHERE TO STAY 260–275

WHERE TO EAT 276–295

SHOPPING IN GREECE 296–297

SPECIALIST HOLIDAYS AND OUTDOOR
ACTIVITIES 298–301

WHERE TO STAY

Accommodation in Greece is best described as functional in most cases, though a new generation of boutique hotels is slowly emerging. However, it is nearly always abundant in a country so heavily dependent on the tourist industry and, as a consequence, is good value compared with most European destinations. Despite inroads of commercialization in the busier resorts, hospitality off

Doorman at the Grande Bretagne hotel, Athens

the beaten track can still be warm and heartfelt. Various types of accommodation are described over the next four pages. Information is included for the network of campsites and the more limited facilities for hostelling and alpine refuge stays. The listings section *(see pp264–75)* includes over 150 places to stay, ranging from informal *domátia* (rooms) to luxurious hotels and accommodation in restored buildings.

Malvásia Hotel (see p269) at Monemvasía, restored by the EOT during the 1970s

HOTELS

Most Greek hotels are of standard Mediterranean concrete architecture, though in coastal resorts height limits restrict towering structures. Many surviving hotels date from the 1967–74 Junta era, when massive investment in "modern" tourism was encouraged. A very few Neo-Classical, or older, hotels remain, now benefiting from government preservation orders. Hotels built since the 1980s are generally designed with more imagination and sensitivity to the environment. The more expensive hotels will have a correspondingly higher level of service, offered by trained personnel.

CHAIN HOTELS

Greece, with its tradition of family business ownership, has not taken to the idea of chain hotels. However, the largest chain, **Grecotel** comprises 39 smart properties, many of which offer luxurious facilities such as health centres and spas, both in the capital and across the mainland. Other smaller chains, such as **Chandrís** and **Diváni**, offer accommodation in the Athens area, and Diváni also has hotels in central Greece. **Club Mediterranée** and **Stathópoulos Hotels** are two other well-known chains.

RESTORED SETTLEMENTS AND BUILDINGS

During the 1970s, the EOT (Greek Tourist Office) began sponsoring the restoration of derelict buildings in vernacular style. The completed units usually offer value for money and an exceptionally atmospheric environment, though preservation considerations often mean that bathrooms are shared. Such properties are found at Areópoli and Vátheia in the Máni, at Makrinítsa on the Pílio, at Megálo Pápigko in Epirus, and at Monemvasía. Some, such as the complex at

Megálo Pápigko, have recently been privatized, with variable effects on efficiency.

In recent years, private entrepreneurs have seized the initiative in such renovation projects, installing small and medium-sized hotels in centuries-old buildings. Particularly successful ventures can be found at Stemnítsa, Galaxídi, Náfplio, and in several villages of the Zagória region and the Pílio.

DOMATIA

A large proportion of Greek accommodation is in *domátia*, or rented rooms. In the past, these often used to be in the home of the managing family, but nowadays they are far more likely to be within a separate, modern, purpose-built structure. They tend to be good value compared with hotels of a similar standard. Increasingly they have en suite bathrooms, are well appointed with neutral pine furniture, and often have a kitchen for the use of guests. There is usually no communal area, however, and hot water is

Front exterior of the King Othon Hotel, Náfplio (see p269)

◁ Seafront café at Koróni in the Peloponnese

The luxurious spa at Davani Apollon Palace & Spa, Vouliagmeni *(see p268)*

provided either by an electric immersion heater or by a solar heating device.

GRADING

The eot grade Greece's hotels and *domátia*. Hotel categories range from E-class up to A-class, plus deluxe, though there are plans to adopt the international star-grading system for hotels. *Domátia* range from C-class to A-class. There is supposed to be a direct correlation between amenities and the classification, but there are many local deviations – usually the result of a dispute with local authorities.

E-class hotels, with the most basic facilities and narrow profit margins, are almost extinct. D-class still survive, and these should have at least some rooms en suite. In a C-class hotel, all rooms must have en suite baths, and the hotel must have some sort of common area, if only a small combination bar and breakfast area where a basic continental breakfast can be served.

B-class hotels have extra amenities such as a full-service restaurant, a more substantial breakfast, and at least one sports facility, such as a pool or tennis court. A-class hotels are usually at seafront locations, and offer all conceivable diversions, as well as aids for the business traveller, such as conference halls and telecommunications

facilities. Deluxe category hotels are effectively self-contained resort complexes. C-class *domátia*, with baths down the hall and "jail-like" decor, are on the way out, now supplanted by modern B-class blocks that guarantee bathrooms en suite and often have the benefit of a shared kitchen for the use of visitors.

A-class *domátia* are nearly synonymous with apartments. The furnishings are superior and there is generally landscaping outside the building. A well-equipped kitchen is fitted into each unit.

A sign for rooms to rent

PRICES

The price of hotel rooms and *domátia* should correspond to their official category, though this depends on the season and their location. In Athens, for 50 euros or under, it is possible to find a C-class *domátio* for two without en suite bathroom, or an E/D-class hotel; 75 euros should cover a B-class double *domátio,* while A-class *domátia* and C-class hotels charge 100 euros. B-class hotels ask 100 to 150 euros per double room; A-class hotels typically cost 150 to 300 euros. Deluxe resorts are exempt from the EOT

price control scheme and can run in excess of 300 euros per night.

All of these rate approximations are for high season, including VAT and taxes; prices can drop by almost 50 per cent in early spring or late autumn. Hotel rates include breakfast. Stays of less than three nights can carry a surcharge in high season. In mainland skiing resorts there is often a vast difference in weekend and mid-week rates.

OPENING SEASONS

Mainland hotels stay open year-round, except those at seafront resorts, which operate only from May to October. Hotels in skiing areas, conversely, may open only during the winter period.

BOOKING

The most common and cost-effective way of booking accommodation is through a package holiday agency. If you contact a hotel direct, do so by fax so that the transaction is recorded in writing. You may need to provide a credit card number or send travellers' cheques to the value of the first night's stay. It is also possible to book a hotel via the internet. A useful address to try is www.united-hellas.com

Conservatory at Grande Bretagne hotel, Athens *(see p267)*

Monastery on Mount Athos (see p252), Northern Greece

YOUTH HOSTELS

The Greek mainland has three IYHF (International Youth Hostel Federation) – recognized youth hostels (*xenón neótitos*). They are all found in Athens. For more information, contact the **IYHA** (International Youth Hostel Association) in England, or the **YHA** (Youth Hostel Association) in Greece. In addition, there are a handful of unofficial hostels, which can provide a standard of accommodation that is just as good, if not better.

Greek hostels are not nearly as regimented as their northern European equivalents. Even without an IYHF card you can usually stay if a vacancy is available. However, if there are two of you, a less expensive *domátio* is better value.

ALPINE REFUGES

Mountains of the Greek mainland are dotted with over 40 alpine refuges (*katafýgia*). Very few are continuously staffed – two on Mount Olympos (*see p241*) and one on Mount Gamíla, in the Píndos range, being notable exceptions – so you must contact the relevant branch of the **EOS** (Greek Alpine Club) to rent keys. This is expensive and not worthwhile unless you muster a large group. The **EOHO** and **SEO** may also provide information on refuges.

Some of the mountain huts make wonderful base camps, fully equipped with kitchens, bed linen, and well-designed common areas; others are little more than shacks originally built for shepherds or fire-control personnel. Another complication is that, as many were built at a time when approaches to the mountain ranges were quite different, today they are often located well away from the preferred hiking routes.

RURAL TOURISM

Conceived during the 1980s to give women in the Greek provinces a measure of financial independence, rural tourism allows foreigners to stay on a bed-and-breakfast basis in a village house, but also provides the opportunity to participate, if desired, in the daily life of a farming community. Information on agrotourism can be obtained

from visiting www.agrotour.gr or from the Greek National Tourist Organisation website (*see p305*).

MONASTERIES

The less-touristed monasteries and convents in Greece operate *xenónes* or hostels, intended primarily for Greek Orthodox pilgrims on weekend visits. Pilgrims will always have priority, but it is often possible to find a vacancy at short notice.

Accommodation is of the spartan-dormitory variety, with a frugal evening meal and morning coffee also provided; it is customary to leave a donation in the *katholikón* (main church).

The monasteries on Mount Athos are the most accustomed to non-Orthodox visitors, though these are open to men only. Visits – especially in high season – need to be carefully planned, as the procedure for reserving space and obtaining an entry permit to this semi-autonomous monastic republic is suitably Byzantine (*see p253*).

CAMPING

The Greek mainland has nearly 150 campsites that are officially recognized. Most of them are in attractive seafront settings, and usually cater to caravanners as well. The last few still owned by the EOT, or by the local municipality, are being sold off; most are privately run. All but the most primitive sites have hot showers heated by solar power, shady landscaping and a snack bar or café. Power hookups are generally available for an extra fee.

The most luxurious campsites are miniature holiday villages, with swimming pool, tennis courts, laundry rooms, banking and postal facilities, and bungalows for the tentless. Established sites usually have the advantage of mature shady trees. The ground is often

Mountain refuge, Kóziakas mountain, Tríkala

sun-baked and very hard, so short pegs that can be banged in with a mallet are best. For a regularly updated booklet on campsites and their amenities, contact the **Panhellenic Camping Association**.

DISABLED TRAVELLERS

The guide *Holidays and Travel Abroad*, published by **RADAR** (Royal Association for Disability and Rehabilitation) – see page 305 for their address – provides details on wheelchair access to the more established hotels in Greece. Write to the **Holiday Care Service** for an information sheet with hotels and useful

contact numbers in Greece. In the hotel listings of this guide *(see pp264–75)* we have indicated which establishments have suitable facilities, such as lifts and ramps, for the disabled.

Greek information sources for disabled travellers tend to be rudimentary; the EOT only publishes a questionnaire, which can be sent to specific accommodation establishments to assess their suitability.

FURTHER INFORMATION

An invaluable booklet is published yearly by the **Hellenic Chamber of Hotels**. It is called *Guide to Hotels*, and a current copy can be obtained from their office. The booklet covers all officially registered hotels, indicating prices, facilities and their operating season. The guide does not, however, offer information on *domátia* or villas. The EOT also periodically

Camping in one of the valleys of the Píndos mountain range

publishes an informative leaflet entitled *Rural Tourism*. Two other hotel manuals, which are both issued by private organizations, are the *Greek Travel Pages* (GTP) and the *Tourist Guide of Greece*. They are not as complete or authoritative as the EOT guides, but are published more frequently. The GTP is monthly, offering only skeletal information unless the hotel concerned has purchased advertising space; this is also true of the quarterly publication *Tourist Guide of Greece*.

Swimming pool at Karavostasi Beach hotel *(see p271)*

DIRECTORY

CHAIN HOTELS

Chandrís Hotels
Syngroú 385, 17564 Paleó Fáliron, Athens.
Tel 210 947 1000.
www.chandris.gr

Club Mediterranée
Syngroú 123, 17121 Athens. *Tel 801 118 0200.*
www.clubmed.com

Diváni Hotels
Vas. Alexándrou 2, 16121 Athens. *Tel 210 720 7000.*
www.divanis.gr

Grecotel
Ypsilantou 4, 10674 Athens. *Tel 210 728 0433.*
www.grecotel.gr

Stathópoulos Hotels
7 Kapnikareas St & Mitropoleos, 10556 Athens.
Tel 210 322 2706.

HOSTELS

IYHA (UK)
2nd Floor, Gate House, Fretherne Rd, Welwyn Garden City, Hertfordshire AL8 6JH, England.
Tel 01707 324 170.
www.hihostels.com

YHA (Greece)
Student & Traveller's Inn, Kydathinaion 16, Plaka, Athens. *Tel 210 324 4808.*

ALPINE REFUGES

EOHO (Ellinikí Omospondía Chionodromías kai Oreivasías)
(Hellenic Federation of Mountaineering Clubs)
Milióni 5, 10673 Athens.
Tel 210 363 6950.

EOS (Ellinikós Orei-vatikós Sýndesmos)
(Greek Alpine Club)
Filadelfías 126, 13671 Acharnés, Attica.
Tel 210 246 1528.

SEO (Sýllogos Ellínon Oreivatón)
(Association of Greek Climbers) Plateía Aristotélous 5, Thessaloníki.
Tel 2310 224710.

CAMPING

Panhellenic Camping Association
Sólonos 102, 10680 Athens. *Tel 210 362 1560.*

DISABLED TRAVELLERS

Holiday Care Service
Tourism for All,

Hawkins Suite, Enham Place, Enham Alamein, Andover SP11 6JS, England.
Tel 0845 124 9971.
www.holidaycare. org.uk

FURTHER INFORMATION

Greek Travel Pages
Psýlla 6, corner Filellínon, 10557 Athens.
Tel 210 324 7511.
www.gtp.gr

Hellenic Chamber of Hotels
Stadiou 24, Athens.
Tel 210 331 2535.

Tourist Guide of Greece
Patission 137, 11251 Athens.
Tel 210 864 1688.
www.tggr.com

Choosing a Hotel

The hotels in this guide have been selected across a wide price range for their good value, exceptional location, comfort or style. All rooms have private bath unless otherwise indicated. The chart list hotels by region, starting with Athens. For Athens map references, *see pp128–35*; for other map references see inside back cover.

PRICE CATEGORIES
The following price ranges are for a standard double room with tax per night during the high season. Breakfast is not included, unless specified.

€ under 50 euros
€€ 50–90 euros
€€€ 90–130 euros
€€€€ 130–200 euros
€€€€€ over 200 euros

ATHENS

EXARCHEIA Exarchion
€

Themistokléous 55, 106 83 **Tel** *21038 01256* **Fax** *21038 03296* **Rooms** *58*   **Map** *2 F3*

The dated rooms of this 1960s high-rise, with their linoleum floors and dark furniture, are ready for a facelift, but they do have fridges, air conditioning and TVs; given the price and the location in the heart of the district's nightlife scene, you can't complain. The mezzanine breakfast room is cheerful enough. **www.exarchion.gr**

EXARCHEIA Orion-Dryades
€€

Anexartisías 5, corner Emmanouíl Mpenáki, 114 73 **Tel** *21038 27362* **Fax** *21038 05193* **Rooms** *38*   **Map** *3 A2*

These co-managed adjacent hotels, opposite the Lófos Stréfis park, are a mecca for young travellers seeking medium-term accommodation. The cheaper Orion (no en suite rooms) has a rooftop communal lounge with fantastic views; wood-panelled rooms at the Dryades have new baths, while both have self-catering kitchens. **http://orion-dryades.com**

EXARCHEIA Best Western Museum
€€€

Mpoumpoulínas 16, 106 82 **Tel** *21038 05611* **Fax** *21038 00507* **Rooms** *90*   **Map** *3 A1*

Renovated recently, this hotel takes its name from the National Archaeological Museum at the front, and is popular with academic visitors. The rooms are up to the standards of the Best Western chain without being especially distinctive. There are also triples and quads for families. **www.bestwestern.gr**

ILISIA Airotel Alexandros
€€€

Timoléontos Vássou 8, 115 21 **Tel** *21064 30464* **Fax** *21064 41084* **Rooms** *93*   **Map** *4 F3*

The bland façade gives nothing away, but once inside the Airotel proves welcoming, with a lively bar-brasserie and designer furniture in the lobby. Rooms (some non-smoking) without a balcony are a bit larger, as are the 19 suites. **www.airotel-hotels.com**

ILISIA Hilton
€€€€€

Vassilís Sofías 46, 115 28 **Tel** *21072 81000* **Fax** *21072 81111* **Rooms** *306*   **Map** *4 D5*

For years the only five-star hotel in the city centre, the Hilton's pre-Olympics overhaul has again vaulted it into the top rank, with the rooms retaining their large balconies. The hotel's three restaurants and huge outdoor pool (open to the public for a fee) are still major meeting points. **www.athens.hilton.com**

KOLONAKI Periscope
€€€€

Charitos 22, 106 75 **Tel** *21072 97200* **Fax** *21072 97206* **Rooms** *22*   **Map** *3 B5*

Just a 5-minute walk from Kolonaki Square, this smart design hotel opened in 2005. All rooms have wooden floors and minimalist furniture in blacks, greys and whites. The luxury penthouse suite occupies the roof terrace and has an open-air Jacuzzi with stunning city views. Facilities include a gym, restaurant and cocktail bar. **www.periscope.gr**

KOLONAKI St George Lycabettus
€€€€

Kleoménous 2, 106 75 **Tel** *21072 90711* **Fax** *21072 90439* **Rooms** *157*   **Map** *3 B4*

Situated just off Platía Dexamenís halfway up Lykavittós Hill, the St George offers a rooftop pool, two well-regarded restaurants, and a bar that's a popular local hangout. The rooms are a mix of retro and modern minimalist; try to get a south-facing one with a view over the city. **www.sglycabettus.gr**

KOUKAKI Marble House
€

Alley off Anastasíou Zínni 35, 11741 **Tel** *21092 28294* **Fax** *21092 34058* **Rooms** *16*   **Map** *5 C4*

The helpful Nikoloulías family's pension has an enviable location on a quiet cul-de-sac. The simple but tidy rooms upstairs, most with bath and balcony, are complete with pine furniture and white tiles. There are two slightly larger ground floor studios. Vastly popular in season, so book well in advance. **www.marblehouse.gr**

KOUKAKI Art Gallery
€€

Erechtheíou 5, 117 42 **Tel** *21092 38376* **Fax** *21092 33025* **Rooms** *22*   **Map** *6 D4*

This family-run pension-hotel, named for the artwork on the common–area walls, recently received a make over, which meant refreshed furnishings and all new bathrooms for the parquet-floored rooms. There are two family suites and a pleasant breakfast bar (with an Acropolis-view terrace). **www.artgalleryhotel.gr**

Key to Symbols *see back cover flap*

MAKRYGIANNI Acropolis View

€€€   Map 5 C3

Webster 10, 117 42 **Tel** *21092 17303* **Fax** *21092 30705* **Rooms** *32*

Many rooms at this small hotel, located on a quiet street near the Acropolis, live up to the hotel's name, as does the popular roof garden. The white rooms are on the small side, but were redecorated with black furniture and marble baths in 2004. Wi-Fi access and unusually low rates in Jun–Aug. **www.acropolisview.gr**

MAKRYGIANNI Herodion

€€€   Map 5 D3

Rovértou Gkálli 4, 117 42 **Tel** *21092 36832* **Fax** *21092 11650* **Rooms** *90*

The Herodion has lovely common areas: the café-restaurant with patio seating shaded by wild pistachios, and the roof garden with two Jacuzzi tubs and the Acropolis a stone's throw away. Functional but fair-sized rooms, some with disabled-friendly baths and Acropolis views, have coco-fibre mattresses. **www.herodion.gr**

MAKRYGIANNI Philippos

€€€   Map 5 D3

Mitsaíon 3, 117 42 **Tel** *21092 23611* **Fax** *21092 23615* **Rooms** *50*

The Philippos, sister hotel of the Herodion around the corner, is probably better for families as there are many quad rooms; otherwise you've the same efficient service, the same stunning common areas, and a similar clientele avoiding the standard identikit mid-range hotels. As with the Herodion, book online for best prices. **www.philipposhotel.gr**

MAKRYGIANNI Divani Palace Acropolis

€€€€   Map 6 D3

Parthenónos 19–25, 117 42 **Tel** *21092 80100* **Fax** *21092 14993* **Rooms** *250*

This popular business and conference hotel has vast common facilities, though the underground restaurant is gloomily lit. Equally subterranean are exhibited sections of the Themistoklean Long Walls, discovered when the hotel was built. Rooms are a good size; there's also a small pool area and summer rooftop garden. **www.divanis.gr**

MAKRYGIANNI Hera

€€€€   Map 6 E3

Falírou 9, 117 42 **Tel** *21092 36682* **Fax** *21092 38269* **Rooms** *38*

Recently refurbished as a boutique hotel, the Hera's rooms are on the small side but lack for nothing; it's worth paying extra for fifth floor suites with bigger balconies. Further delights are the dome-lit atrium breakfast room and the year-round rooftop bar-restaurant with great views of the Acropolis. **www.herahotel.gr**

MONASTIRAKI Carolina

€€   Map 2 E5

Kolokotróni 55, 105 60 **Tel** *21032 43551* **Fax** *21032 43550* **Rooms** *34*

This budget hotel, occupying an interwar building in the heart of the bazaar, had a pre-Olympics refit which bumped prices up slightly in exchange for a better standard in the tile-floored rooms with their cheerful blue furniture. No frills in the common areas, other than a bar. **www.hotelcarolina.gr**

MONASTIRAKI Cecil

€€   Map 2 D5

Athinás 39, 105 54 **Tel** *21032 17079* **Fax** *21032 19606* **Rooms** *40*

One of the oldest buildings in central Athens, dating from the 1850s, has been restored as a good-value character hotel with soundproofed, tastefully decorated, en suite rooms. Breakfast (charged separately) is abundant, featuring homemade jams, plus there's a roof terrace. **www.cecil.gr**

NEOS KOSMOS Athenaeum Intercontinental

€€€€   Map 5 B5

Leofóros Andréa Syngroú 89–93, 117 45 **Tel** *21092 06000* **Fax** *21092 06500* **Rooms** *603*

Original artworks decorate both the sumptuous common areas and individual rooms at Athens' largest luxury hotel. Standard units are like suites elsewhere, with separate sitting area, though bathrooms are surprisingly small. Two floors of suites have their own lounge and breakfast area. Look for seasonal rates or Internet deals. **www.ichotelsgroup.com**

NEOS KOSMOS Athenian Callirhoe

€€€€   Map 6 E4

Kalliróis 32, corner Petmezá, 117 43 **Tel** *21092 15353* **Fax** *21092 15342* **Rooms** *84*

Athens' first boutique hotel, refurbished in 2004, offers three grades of designer decorated rooms (including non-smoking), with Internet acccess and double glazing. An Oriental theme bar, a small gym and a branch of the superb Corfiot-Italian restaurant Etrusco (on the roof with Acropolis views in summer) complete the profile. **www.tac.gr**

NEOS KOSMOS Ledra Marriott

€€€€   Map 5 B5

Leofóros Andréa Syngroú 115, 117 45 **Tel** *21093 00000* **Fax** *21093 58603* **Rooms** *314*

Like most other top hotels in town, the Ledra Marriott had a much needed complete overhaul before the Olympics; most standard rooms have a balcony, and there's a gym and spa. The restaurants, particularly the Polynesian-themed Kona Kai, are worth a visit. **www.marriott.com**

OMONOIA Art Athens Hotel

€€   Map 2 D2

Márnis 27/Aristotélous 16, 104 32 **Tel** *21052 40501* **Fax** *21052 43384* **Rooms** *30*

Boutique hotels are now ten a penny in Athens, but this one – occupying a converted Neo-Classical mansion – is one of the best. Light cream tones characterize the wood-floored rooms, accented by colourful original artwork. Everything is hi-tech, from lighting to voice mail to individual thermostats. Service is excellent. **www.arthotelathens.gr**

OMONOIA The Alassia

€€€   Map 2 D3

Sokrátou 50, 104 31 **Tel** *21052 74000* **Fax** *21052 74029* **Rooms** *82*

A designer hotel, deploying lots of polished metal, futuristic furniture, recessed lighting and marble surfaces in the common areas, and understated, soundproofed (if slightly small) guest rooms with Internet access. The location doesn't get much more central, but this is the least interesting corner of Omónoia. **www.thealassia.com.gr**

OMONOIA Delphi Art Hotel
€€€€
Agíou Konstantínou 27, 104 37 **Tel** 21052 44004 **Fax** 21052 39564 **Rooms** 40   **Map** 2 D3

Formerly a six-storey 1930s apartment block next to the National Theatre, this has been converted into a stylish hotel with all mod cons (including Internet access), without sacrificing original features such as bay windows and French doors opening onto balconies with wrought-iron railings. Common areas include three bar-cafés. **www.delphiarthotel.com**

PEDION ÁREOS Athens Park
€€€€
Leofóros Alexándras 10, 106 82 **Tel** 21088 94500 **Fax** 21082 38420 **Rooms** 152   **Map** 3 A1

The recent refurbishment of this classic business hotel focused on the large, comfortable if not cutting-edge rooms, the best of which face the Pédion Áreos park across the boulevard. There's a conference centre and small roof pool, but the main draw is the rooftop restaurant and bar. **www.athensparkhotel.gr**

PLAKA Phaedra
€
Chairefontos 16, corner of Adrianoú, 105 58 **Tel** 21032 38461 **Fax** 21032 27795 **Rooms** 21   **Map** 6 E2

Located at the intersection of two pedestrian lanes, the Phaedra had a thorough makeover before the Olympics and offers the best budget value in the area. Although not all tiled-floor rooms are en suite, each has an allocated bathroom and TV, while some have balconies. Pleasant ground floor breakfast room.

PLAKA Student and Travellers Inn
€
Kydathinaion 16, 105 57 **Tel** 21032 44808 **Fax** 21032 10065 **Rooms** 30   **Map** 6 E2

On a pretty pedestrian street in the heart of Pláka, this friendly, upscale hostel offers shared and individual accommodation in single, double, triple and quadruple rooms, some with en suite bathrooms. There's an internal courtyard for relaxing, plus Internet access. **www.studenttravellersinn.com**

PLAKA Acropolis House
€€
Kódrou 6–8, 105 57 **Tel** 21032 22344 **Fax** 21032 44143 **Rooms** 19   **Map** 6 E1

Athens' first mansion turned pension-hotel, Acropolis House offers a mix of en suite and basic rooms, most with high ceilings (some with murals). The academic and student clientele swap books and use the communal fridge. The Neo-Classical building's listed status prevents a much-needed facelift from occurring. **www.acropolishouse.gr**

PLAKA Kimon
€€
Apóllonos 27, 105 57 **Tel** 21033 14658 **Fax** 21032 14203 **Rooms** 14   **Map** 6 E1

Much the cheapest hotel in this part of Pláka, the Kimon – if you overlook a total lack of communal amenities – is a good option. The rooms are all en suite, painted cheerfully and come complete with mock-antique furniture (such as iron bedsteads), as well as TV and telephones.

PLAKA Central
€€€
Apóllonos 21, 105 57 **Tel** 21032 34357 **Fax** 21032 25244 **Rooms** 84   **Map** 6 E1

Italian designer furniture, marble-clad bathrooms and wooden flooring set the tone for this revamped hotel, with warm-toned soft furnishings in the comfortable, soundproofed rooms, some of which interconnect. There are four conference rooms, and a rooftop bar with a small spa and view of the Acropolis. **www.centralhotel.gr**

PLAKA Hermes
€€€€
Apóllonos 19, 105 57 **Tel** 21032 35514 **Fax** 21032 22412 **Rooms** 45   **Map** 6 E1

Part of a small group of four co-owned hotels, the Hermes has a very pleasant ground floor lounge-bar-café as well as the inevitable roof terrace. The rooms – some with balconies – vary in size, but all have polished wood floors, large, well-equipped bathrooms and designer touches. **www.hermeshotel.gr**

PLAKA Plaka
€€€€
Kapnikaréa 7, corner of Mitropóleos, 105 66 **Tel** 21032 22096 **Fax** 21032 22412 **Rooms** 67   **Map** 6 D1

A sister hotel to the Hermes, the Plaka anticipated by some years the Olympic Games renovation frenzy, and has worn well. From the leather sofas in the lobby to the striking colour schemes in the wood-floored rooms, the place is sleek and tasteful. Many nearby hotels boast of roof gardens; the Plaka's is one of the best. **www.plakahotel.gr**

PLAKA Electra Palace
€€€€€
Navárchou Nikodhímou 18–20, 105 57 **Tel** 21033 70000 **Fax** 21032 41875 **Rooms** 131   **Map** 6 E1

The only de luxe hotel in Pláka attracts attention with its Neo-Classical façade. The interior lives up to this promise, with plush rooms, antique and mock-antique decor, a wellness centre, plus plans for a rooftop pool. Rooms facing the garden are quieter. It's worth paying extra for a suite. **www.electrahotels.gr**

PSYRRI Arion
€€€€
Agíou Dimitríou 18, 105 54 **Tel** 21032 40415 **Fax** 21032 22412 **Rooms** 51   **Map** 2 D5

The Arion is yet another member of the Stathopoulos chain that also runs the Plaka and Hermes. It has a rather bland exterior without balconies, and slightly forbidding common areas, though the rooms have attractively glassed-in bathrooms. There is also a rooftop bar with Acropolis views. **www.arionhotel.gr**

PSYRRI Fresh
€€€€
Sofokléous 26 & Kleisthénous, 105 52 **Tel** 21052 48511 **Fax** 21052 48517 **Rooms** 133   **Map** 2 D4

The closest design hotel to the town centre, Fresh combines minimalist chic with shockingly vibrant colours, right down to the balcony partitions. Rooms are small but cleverly designed – you can control the blinds from your bed to reveal views of the interior rock gardens. Stylish rooftop pool and bar. Wi-Fi access. **www.freshhotel.gr**

Key to Price Guide see p264 **Key to Symbols** see back cover flap

PSYRRI Ochre & Brown 　　　　　　　　🚹 🍴 🅿️   €€€€
Leokoríou 7, 105 54 **Tel** *21033 12950* **Fax** *21033 12945* **Rooms** *10*   **Map** *1 C5*

This small, exclusive design hotel lies close to Thiseio metro station. Wood, leather and glass predominate, with splashes of orange. All the rooms have en suite marble bathrooms and Internet access. A bar-restaurant serving cocktails and Mediterranean cuisine opened in spring 2006. **www.ochreandbrown.com**

STATHMOS LARISSIS Oscar 　　　　　　🚹 🛏 🍴 🅿️   €€€
Filadélfias 25, 104 39 **Tel** *21088 34315* **Fax** *21082 16368* **Rooms** *124*   **Map** *1 C1*

The Oscar's main advantage is its position opposite the main Athens train station – ideal for late-night arrivals or early-morning departures to/from the airport or the north mainland. The common facilities, including a rooftop pool, are more than you would expect for this price, though rooms are a little dull. **www.oscar.gr**

SYNTAGMA Metropolis 　　　　　　　　🖥 🍴 🅿️   €€
Mitropóleos 46, 105 63 **Tel** *21032 17469* **Fax** *21032 17871* **Rooms** *25*   **Map** *6 D1*

This small, five-storey hotel enjoys views over its namesake, the Mitrópoli (Cathedral), and on to the Acropolis from the upper rooms. Rooms are basic, with vinyl floors and balconies, though the staff are friendly and the price is reasonable. There are no common areas, and breakfast is not provided. **www.hotelmetropolis.gr**

SYNTAGMA Athens Cypria 　　　　　　　　　🍴   €€€
Diomeías 5, 105 57 **Tel** *21032 38034* **Fax** *21032 48792* **Rooms** *71*   **Map** *6 F1*

The exterior of this hotel just off pedestrianized Ermoú is deceptively bland. Inside, earth-toned rooms with small balconies are matched by the colour scheme and stone dressing in the lobby. A disadvantage is the complete lack of common areas, other than a small café-bar with tables on the pavement. **www.athenscypria.com**

SYNTAGMA Grande Bretagne 　　　　　🚹 🛏 🍴 ♿   €€€€€
Vassiléos Georgíou 1, Plateía Syntágmatos, 105 63 **Tel** *21033 30000* **Fax** *21032 28034* **Rooms** *321*   **Map** *6 F1*

Originally built in 1842 for King Otto, the Grande Bretagne has always been Athens' most exclusive hotel. Its restaurants and bars stand out in their own right: Alexander's Bar has an 18th-century tapestry of Alexander the Great, and the brasserie and rooftop restaurant are justifiably busy. **www.grandebretagne.gr**

SYNTAGMA King George II 　　　　　　🚹 🛏 🍴 ♿   €€€€€
Vassiléos Georgíou 3, Plateía Syntágmatos, 105 64 **Tel** *21032 22210* **Fax** *21032 50504* **Rooms** *102*   **Map** *6 F1*

The 1936-founded King George is more intimate and personal than other luxury hotels in the immediate vicinity, but boasts similar antique Belle Époque decor, a small pool in the fitness centre, and a rooftop restaurant. Rooms are a good size, all unique, with handmade furniture in Second Empire style, and all mod cons. **www.grecotel.gr**

THISEIO Phidias 　　　　　　　　　　　　🖥 🍴   €€
Apostólou Pávlou 39, 118 51 **Tel** *21034 59511* **Fax** *21034 59082* **Rooms** *15*   **Map** *5 B1*

This small, quiet hotel had a light touch-up for the Olympics but prices haven't quite caught up yet. The lobby and breakfast area are 1970s relics, the rooms small but perfectly adequate, with new showers and flooring. The front eight rooms have views towards the Acropolis that most mid-town de luxe outfits envy. **www.phidias.gr**

AROUND ATHENS

KIFISIA Pentelikon 　　　　　　　　🚹 🛏 🍴 🅿️   €€€€€
Deligiánni 66, 145 62 **Tel** *21062 30650* **Fax** *21080 10314* **Rooms** *44*   **Road Map** *D4*

Built in 1929, but Belle Epoque rather than Art Deco in style, the rambling Pentelikon, set in extensive landscaped gardens, is Athens' most elegant suburban hotel. There are extensive conference and banqueting facilities, including the Michelin-starred Vardis restaurant (closed Aug). Each spacious room is individually decorated. **www.hotelpentelikon.gr**

KIFISIA Semiramis 　　　　　　　　🚹 🛏 🍴 🅿️   €€€€€
Charíláou Trikoúpi 48, 145 62 **Tel** *21062 84400* **Fax** *21062 84499* **Rooms** *52*   **Road Map** *D4*

As cutting-edge as its near neighbours in Kefalári district are retro, this design hotel isn't for everyone. The colour scheme runs to chartreuse, dark lavender and hot pink, while the contemporary furniture is intended to be looked at as much as sat on. The rooms sport every hi-tech gadget imaginable. **www.semiramisathens.com**

PIRAEUS Mistral 　　　　　　　　　　🚹 🛏 🍴   €€€
Alexándrou Papanastasíou 105, 185 33 **Tel** *21041 17150* **Fax** *21041 22096* **Rooms** *80*   **Road Map** *D4*

This mid-range hotel overlooks Mikrolímano from a good site in Kastélla district. Rooms are low-key, with sea views; the common areas are light and airy and there is a rooftop pool. An ideal place for an overnight before an early-morning ferry (though a taxi should be arranged as it's too far to walk to the port). **www.mistral.gr**

RAFINA Avra 　　　　　　　　　　　🚹 🍴 🅿️ ♿   €€€€
Arafiníon Álon 3, 190 09 **Tel** *22940 22780* **Fax** *22940 23320* **Rooms** *96*   **Road Map** *D4*

Renovated in 2006, Rafina's only hotel is well placed on the shore for a pre-ferry overnight stay. Not all of the beige and tan rooms actually overlook the sea, however, and the Avra has set its sights firmly on the conference and business trade. **www.avra-hotel.gr**

SOUNIO Grand Resort Lagonissi

🍽 🏊 🏋 📶 P ♿   €€€€€

Lagonissi, 40th klm Athens-Soúnio, 190 10 **Tel** *22910 76000* **Fax** *22910 24514* **Rooms** *346*   **Road Map** *D4*

Set on a landscaped, foot-shaped peninsula 7 km (4.3 miles) before Soúnio, this ultra-luxurious self-contained resort has several beaches and restaurants, a vast spa and its own helipad. There are four levels of rooms, bungalows and very expensive villas, the latter with their own pool and gym. Open Apr–Oct. **www.grandresort.gr**

VOULIAGMENI Astir Palace Resort

🍽 🏊 🏋 📶 P ♿   €€€€€

Apóllonos 40, 166 71 **Tel** *21089 02000* **Fax** *21089 62579* **Rooms** *570*   **Road Map** *D4*

Superbly sited on a private pine-clad peninsula 25 km (15.5 miles) from central Athens, this all-inclusive resort comprises three separate units (in ascending order of cost and modernity: Aprhodite, Nafskika, Arion). Private beaches, marinas, and every activity from jet-skiing to paragliding to yoga. Popular for international conferences. **www.astir-palace.com**

VOULIAGMENI Divani Apollon Palace & Spa

🍽 🏊 🏋 📶 P ♿   €€€€€

Agíou Nikoláou 10, corner of Ilíou, 166 71 **Tel** *21089 11100* **Fax** *21096 58010* **Rooms** *286*   **Road Map** *D4*

An ideal solution for a seaside holiday still within Greater Athens city limits, this all-inclusive resort dominates Kavoúri beach from a garden setting. Excellent sports facilities – including tennis courts and two outdoor sea water pools, two restaurants (Mythos is on the beach) and of course the thalassotherapy spa. **www.divanis.gr**

VOULIAGMENI The Margi

🍽 🏊 📶 P   €€€€€

Litoús 11, 166 71 **Tel** *21089 29000* **Fax** *21089 60229* **Rooms** *90*   **Road Map** *D4*

This boutique hotel has antiques and Persian rugs in the common areas, wood floors and tawny ochre decor in the rooms (some with hot tubs, but all with music systems and broadband), and a good buffet breakfast. There is an Oriental theme bar-café (with low divans) beside the outdoor pool. The beach is close by. **www.themargi.gr**

THE PELOPONNESE

ANCIENT CORINTH Shadow

📷 📶 P   €€

On access road to village, 200 07 **Tel/Fax** *27410 31481* **Rooms** *12*   **Road Map** *C4*

A small, friendly pension, well-placed for the ruins at Ancient Corinth and Acrocorinth, and far preferable to staying in noisy Kórinthos. The back rooms have good views out to the west. Excellent breakfasts are served in the downstairs area, which also houses a collection of rocks, crystals and natural history items. All rooms have fridges.

AREOPOLI Xenonas Lontas

🍽 📶   €€

Off Plateía Taxiarchón, 23062 **Tel** *27330 51360* **Fax** *27330 51012* **Rooms** *4*   **Road Map** *C5*

This tower-mansion has been sympathetically converted into a small, sophisticated inn by Iakovos, painter and chef, and Han Jakob. The colourful textiles and wall tones are in the best of taste. Local honey and Iakovos' marmalade is served at breakfast.

CHLEMOUTSI Katerina Lepida Apartments

📷 📶 P   €€

Loutropóleos 9, 270 50 **Tel** *26230 95224* **Fax** *26230 95444* **Rooms** *10*   **Road Map** *B4*

Conveniently situated near the centre of the village on the main through road, these self-catering units are nonetheless quiet. The rear six have magificent views over the countryside and over to the castle. A good beach is just 3 km (2 miles) downhill. Open May–Oct.

DIAKOFTO Chris-Paul

🍽 🏊 📶 P ♿   €€

Next to railway station, 250 03 **Tel** *26910 41715* **Fax** *26910 42128* **Rooms** *26*   **Road Map** *C4*

Named after the owners' children and situated a few minutes' walk from the railway station, this hotel is ideal for the Vouraikos Gorge cog-railway trip. Rooms are comfortable and well-maintained, with balconies overlooking the small pool or surrounding orchard; bathrooms are well-equipped. Bar for light meals. **www.chrispaul-hotel.gr**

DIMITSANA Xenonas Kazakou

€€€

Near the top of the village, 220 07 **Tel** *27950 31660* **Fax** *27950 31660* **Rooms** *5*   **Road Map** *C4*

Externally austere, this tastefully restored, stone and wood mansion is discreetly comfortable inside – with central heating for the chilly mountain winters. It is very quiet, apart from the Sunday church-bells. A rich traditional breakfast, including *loukomádes*, is served in the vaulted cellar. **www.xensonaskazakou.gr**

FOINIKOUNTA Porto Finissia

📷 📶   €€

Near the waterfront, 240 06 **Tel** *27230 71358* **Fax** *27230 71458* **Rooms** *27*   **Road Map** *C5*

Just a stone's throw from the central beach of Finikounta, the Porto Finissia offers comfort and convenience. Rooms have a fridge, as well as balconies with pretty ironwork railings and useful fold-out sun-canopies; most have relaxing sea views towards the island of Schíza. There is a large breakfast room and bar. Open May–Oct.

GYTHEIO Githio

📷 🏋   €€

Vassíleos Pávlou 33, 232 00 **Tel** *27330 23452* **Fax** *27330 23523* **Rooms** *7*   **Road Map** *C5*

This fine Neo-Classical building from 1864 was formerly a gentleman's club; it's now a stylishly refurbished hotel above an ice cream parlour, overlooking the seafront and harbour. Elegant, high-ceilinged rooms sleep two or three; two four-bed apartments have kitchen facilities. Breakfast is served in area carved out of the natural rock. **www.gythionhotel.gr**

Key to Price Guide *see p264* **Key to Symbols** *see back cover flap*

KALAMATA Akti Taygetos Resort
Mikrí Mantineía, south of Kalamáta, 241 00 **Tel** *27210 42000* **Fax** *27210 64501* **Rooms** *94*   **Road Map** *C5*

A well-designed low-rise complex with sweeping sea views and extensive gardens threaded by stone paths and studded with palms around a large pool. Predominantly white rooms are furnished tastefully with iron beds and marble-top tables. There's a small swimming cove just below the grounds. Open Mar–Oct. **www.aktitaygetos.gr**

KALAVRYTA Filoxenia
Ethnikís Andistáseos 10, 250 01 **Tel** *26920 22493* **Fax** *26920 23009* **Rooms** *28*   **Road Map** *C4*

With a distinct alpine ambience, wood panel decor and efficient service, the recently renovated Filoxenia caters for skiers in winter and tourists and pilgrims in summer. Rooms are well-equipped: facilities include Internet connection, hydro-massage and central heating. Balconies have mountain views. Prices rise from Dec to Apr. **www.hotelfiloxenia.gr**

KALOGRIA Kalógria Beach
North end of beach, 270 52 **Tel** *26930 31380* **Fax** *26930 31381* **Rooms** *96*   **Road Map** *B4*

Sports-oriented hotel, particularly popular with French tourists, offering tennis, volleyball and mini-golf, in addition to a wide range of water sports at the Blue Flag-awarded beach; rock-climbing pitches are nearby. After dark, the nightclub kicks in. Three main buildings, plus bungalows, set in spacious gardens. **www.peloponnestravel.gr**

KARDAMYLI Cardamili Beach
Northern end of Ritsia beach, 240 22 **Tel** *27210 73180* **Fax** *27210 73184* **Rooms** *29*   **Road Map** *C5*

Situated in a large orchard on the beachfront, and a short distance from the village, the hotel has rooms in the main building and a number of garden bungalows; some of the latter have kitchen facilities. All rooms have a fridge and views of the sea or mountains. A taverna and swimming pool on site. Open Apr–Oct.

KORONI Zaga Mylos
On the ridge overlooking the town, 240 04 **Tel** *27250 22385* **Fax** *27250 29028* **Rooms** *32*   **Road Map** *C5*

Ten minutes' walk from the castle and from lovely Zánga Beach – after which it is named – this modern hotel has a cloth-sailed windmill decoratively incorporated into its whitewashed facade. Comfortable rooms are equipped with a fridge and have sea-view balconies. Open Apr–Oct. **www.zagamiloshotel.com**

KYPARISSI Kyfanta Studios
Harbour district **Tel** *27320 53356* **Rooms** *7*   **Road Map** *B4*

Kyfanta is the ancient name of Shangri-La-like Kyparíssi, some 40 km (25 miles) north of Monemvasiá and approached via a spectacular corniche road. The spacious studios, with terracotta floor tiles and blue-green furniture, are arrayed for maximum privacy and overlook an olive grove to the sea. Managing family lives downstairs. **www.kyfantahotel.gr**

METHONI Castello
Odós Miaoúli, 240 06 **Tel** *27230 31300* **Fax** *27230 31300* **Rooms** *13*   **Road Map** *C5*

A small hotel, almost opposite the entrance to Methoni's huge fortress and a few minutes' stroll from the beach. The rooms have balconies and lovely views of the castle, sea or the town, as does the roof bar. Breakfast is available in the attractive garden. Both the garden and building overflow with potted plants. Open May–Oct. **www.castello.gr**

MONEMVASIA Malvasia
Inside the Kástro, 230 70 **Tel** *27320 61160* **Fax** *27320 61722* **Rooms** *34*   **Road Map** *C5*

Named after the malmsey wine historically grown in the area and spread over three sites in the old city, Malvasia offers sympathetically restored rooms, each different, with traditional, low-key furnishings and antique furniture, some with wooden floors, fireplaces and kitchenette facilities. Most rooms have terraces or sea views. Competitively priced.

MYKINES Belle Helene
Tsoúnta 15, 212 00 **Tel** *27510 76225* **Fax** *27510 76179* **Rooms** *5*   **Road Map** *C4*

This historical building (built in 1862) is where Heinrich Schliemann stayed for some of his excavations in the 1870s – his bed is still in use. Later visitors included Agatha Christie and Virginia Woolf. The ambience is still almost Victorian and bathrooms are not en suite, but the restaurant and hospitality are excellent.

NAFPLIO Byron
Plátonos 2, 211 00 **Tel** *27520 22351* **Fax** *27520 26338* **Rooms** *18*   **Road Map** *C4*

An elegant hotel with antique furniture, in a tastefully restored mansion above Ágios Spyrídon church. Rooms are modestly decorated in a simple but charming style, with wooden floors and rugs. Some rooms have a view or balcony. Breakfast can be taken on the patio. Internet facilities are available. **www.byronhotel.gr**

NAFPLIO King Othon 1 & 2
Farmakopoúlou 4/Spiliádou 5, 211 00 **Tel** *27520 27585* **Fax** *27520 27595* **Rooms** *20*   **Road Map** *C4*

This restored mansion, originally the Ionian Bank and retaining its spectacular curving wooden staircase, is near the old town centre. Rooms vary, some having balconies, but bathrooms are small. Breakfast is served in a flowery courtyard. Otho 2, nearby, has slightly larger rooms and suites and was renovated in 2002. **www.kingothon.gr**

NAFPLIO Grande Bretagne
Plateía Filellínon, 211 00 **Tel** *27520 96200* **Fax** *27520 96209* **Rooms** *20*   **Road Map** *C4*

This three-storey Neo-Classical building on the seafront has been transformed into an elegant hotel. All rooms feature dark hardwood furniture, high ceilings and marble-trimmed bathrooms; a few lucky ones have balconies. The restaurant here serves international cuisine. **www.grandebretagne.com.gr**

NEOS MYSTRAS Byzantion
Village centre, 231 00 **Tel** *27310 83309* **Fax** *27310 20019* **Rooms** *22*   **Road Map** *C5*

Ideally situated for exploration of the nearby Mystras site or walking in the foothills of Taygetos, the Byzantion offers quiet, spacious rooms with castle views and a pleasant pool-garden. The hotel has a bar and café, and tavernas are a few minutes stroll away. Popular with groups, so book early. **www.byzantionhotel.gr**

OLYMPIA Pelops
Varelás 2, 270 65 **Tel** *26240 22543* **Fax** *26240 22213* **Rooms** *18*   **Road Map** *B4*

Stylishly refurbished in 2004 by friendly Greek-Australian owners Theodore and Susanna, the well-equipped rooms all have balconies, and wireless Internet access is available. The hotel, where the Olympics Committee stays, is within easy walking distance of the archaeological sites. Cooking and art courses are offered. Open Mar–Oct. **www.hotelpelops.gr**

PATRA Art Primarolia
Óthonos kai Amalías 30, 262 21 **Tel** *2610 624900* **Fax** *2610 623559* **Rooms** *15*   **Road Map** *C4*

Ensconced in a converted 1930s distillery, the 15 suites of this hotel have plenty of subdued soft furnishings and art on the walls. There's more contemporary Greek art displayed in the atrium, plus a sauna and bar downstairs. There are often substantial discounts off the steep rack rates. **www.arthotel.gr**

PORTOCHELI AKS Porto Heli
Shoreline, 210 61 **Tel** *27540 53400* **Fax** *27540 51549* **Rooms** *218*   **Road Map** *D4*

A complete seaside holiday village, popular with Athenians and tourists alike, the AKS Porto Heli is set in lovely mature gardens. All conceivable diversions are offered, including sailing, water-skiing, mini-golf, tennis and a scuba centre. The rooms are large though the suites are definitely worth the extra. Open all year. **www.akshotels.com**

POULITHRA Akrogiali
Shore road, 223 00 **Tel** *27570 29106* **Fax** *27570 29108* **Rooms** *11*   **Road Map** *C4*

Family-run, stone-clad hotel in a large garden at the edge of the village, well-positioned for fabulous sunrises over the sea, just a few metres away. Spacious, comfortable rooms and apartments, the latter with a fridge and well-equipped kitchen; all have mosquito nets, and sea- or mountain-view balconies.

SPARTI Sparti Inn
Thermopylon 105–109, 231 00 **Tel** *27310 21021* **Fax** *27310 24855* **Rooms** *147*   **Road Map** *C5*

Away from Spárti's noisiest main street, but within walking distance of both the centre and main archaeological site, this large hotel provides unexciting decor but comfortable rooms with a fridge and large bathrooms. Two pools, the smaller on the rooftop with the roof-garden bar and panoramic views. Wireless Internet facilities available.

STAVRI GEROLIMENAS Tsitsiris Castle
Tsitsiris Castle, 23 071 **Tel** *27330 56297* **Fax** *27830 56296* **Rooms** *20*   **Road Map** *C5*

This two century-old complex of stone buildings and towers offers a remote, comfortable base for exploration of the Mani on foot or by car. Rooms overlook the attractive gardens; traditional furnishings and decor are in harmony with the architecture. At its heart is a cosy, vaulted breakfast-dining room.

STEMNITSA Country Club Trikolonion
Arcadia, 220 24 **Tel** *27950 29500* **Fax** *27950 81512* **Rooms** *18*   **Road Map** *C4*

Sumptuous establishment with opulent yet intimate public areas reminiscent of a gentleman's club, decorated with Greek engravings and lithographs. Bedrooms are themed in olive-green, gold or blue; the four suites feature a hearth and hydromassage shower. Internet access. Trainer-supervised gym, sauna, Jacuzzi and massage. **www.countryclub.gr**

ZACHLOROU Romantzo
Next to railway station, 250 01 **Tel** *26920 22758* **Fax** *26920 22758* **Rooms** *8*   **Road Map** *C4*

Aptly named for its romantic setting, this basic but lovely rustic wooden hotel overlooks a tiny rural rail halt on the Kalavryta cog-railway. Rooms are small but have private bathrooms and balconies. The restaurant serves hearty food at a handful of tables under streamside trees. A good base for walkers.

CENTRAL AND WESTERN GREECE

ÁGIOS IOANNIS Sofoklis
Seafront, north end, 370 12 **Tel** *24260 31230* **Fax** *24260 31021* **Rooms** *20*   **Road Map** *C3*

This professionally run hotel tries a bit harder than the competition at this beach resort. There is a century-old stone-walled ground floor lounge, oblique or direct sea views from most rooms, a tasteful breakfast terrace and an attractive pool. Unusually for this area, it's open all year. **www.sofokleshotel.pelionet.gr**

ARACHOVA Xenonas Generali
Down stair-path, below clocktower, 320 04 **Tel** *22670 31529* **Fax** *22670 32783* **Rooms** *9*   **Road Map** *C3*

This new inn offers the best standard in town. The named rather than numbered rooms are each different, though most have fireplaces and views south to the Pleistós gorge. The decor is sweet yet a little outdated, but the welcome is warm and the breakfasts are unusual. Indoor pool, spa, Turkish bath and sauna. **www.generalis-xenon.com**

Key to Price Guide *see p264* **Key to Symbols** *see back cover flap*

ARGALASTI Agamemnon
🍴 🏊 📋 €€

Village centre, 370 06 **Tel** *24230 54557* **Fax** *24230 55867* **Rooms** *11*   **Road Map** *D3*

This historic village centre mansion – where the poet Kostas Varnalis stayed while posted as a teacher here in the early 1900s – has been restored in impeccable taste as a small hotel. Antiques adorn the common areas and the bar-restaurant. The guest rooms have stone or wood floors and some have fireplaces. **www.agamemnon.gr**

DAMOUHARI Damouhari
🏊 📋 €€

Hamlet centre, on Pelion Peninsula, 370 12 **Tel/Fax** *24260 49840* **Rooms** *20*   **Road Map** *C3*

This mock village of stone-built studio cottages is arrayed under a small pool near the highest point of the sloping site. Antiques and wood trim enliven the units, while *objet-trouvé* decor dominates the Kleopatra Miramare bar. Block-booked much of the year by tour companies, but there's a waterside annexe of five state-of-the-art rooms.

DELFOI Orfeas
📋 📋 €

Ifigenías Syngroú 35, 330 54 **Tel** *22650 82077* **Fax** *22650 82079* **Rooms** *15*   **Road Map** *C3*

Guest rooms at this quietly located hotel are spacious and well maintained, and the top floor (with superb views) was recently refurbished. There's a lift – unusual in such a small hotel – and better-than-average parking on the street outside, plus a pleasant breakfast area.

DELFOI Pan
📋 📋 €

Pávlou ké Fredherikis 53, 330 54 **Tel** *22650 82294* **Fax** *22650 83244* **Rooms** *15*   **Road Map** *C3*

Most rooms here have fine views of the gulf. The best and newest rooms sleep four and are in the attic. Immediately across the street is a slightly pricier annexe, with larger rooms and bathrooms, including bathtubs, but without the views of the older building.

DELFOI Sun View
📋 📋 €

Apóllonos 84, 330 54 **Tel** *22650 82349* **Fax** *22650 82815* **Rooms** *7*   **Road Map** *C3*

At the far western end of the main commercial street, this pension offers fair sized rooms in pastel colours with original wall art, though rear-facing units are a bit dark. There's a pleasant, four table breakfast area on the ground floor, and good on-street parking adjacent. **dkalentzis@internet.gr**

GALAXIDI Galaxa
📋 📋 🅿 €€

Hirólakkas bay, west hillside, 330 52 **Tel** *22650 41620* **Fax** *22650 42053* **Rooms** *10*   **Road Map** *C3*

Management style at this superbly sited hotel might best be described as casual, but this has its advantages; your host is frequently drinking and eating with guests in the popular garden-bar, where breakfast is served. Most of the rooms have some sort of sea view, all share blue-and-white decor and miniature bathrooms.

GALAXIDI Ganimede
📋 €€

Níkou Gourgoúri 16, 330 52 **Tel** *22650 41328* **Fax** *22650 83244* **Rooms** *7*   **Road Map** *C3*

Since 2005 the Ganimede has been under the energetic management of Chrissoula Papalexi, whose family have over-hauled this much-loved 1960s inn. There are six doubles in the former captain's mansion and a family suite with loft and fireplace across the courtyard garden, where copious breakfasts are served. **www.ganimede.gr**

IGOUMENITSA (REGION) Karavostasi Beach
🍴 🏊 ♿ 📋 🅿 €€

Pérdika, 461 00 **Tel** *26650 91104* **Fax** *26650 91568* **Rooms** *47*   **Road Map** *B3*

The setting of this resort hotel – among lush gardens 140 m (460 ft) behind the best beach on the Epirot coast – is its biggest selling point. Some of the simply fuirnished, marble-clad rooms spread over four wings have sea views, while the landscaped pool-bar area makes an attractive breakfast venue. Open Easter–Oct. **www.hotel-karavostasi.gr**

IOANNINA Kastro
📋 €€

Androníkou Paleológou 57, 452 21 **Tel** *26510 22866* **Fax** *26510 22780* **Rooms** *7*   **Road Map** *B2*

This early 20th-century house inside Ioánnina's Kástro has been tastefully restored as an inn. Its rooms are mostly equipped with double iron beds. Cooler downstairs units (fans but no air con) near the breakfast room are slightly cheaper, though upstairs rooms with wooden ceilings are preferable. Limited street parking just outside. **www.epirus.com/hotel-kastro**

IOANNINA Politeia
📋 🅿 ♿ €€

Anexartisias 109, 454 44 **Tel** *26510 30090* **Fax** *26510 22235* **Rooms** *15*   **Road Map** *B2*

Built on the site of an old tradesmen's hall, this hotel is an oasis of calm in the bazaar area. It retains some period details, such as stone walls, and its original arrangement around a courtyard. Choose between standard studios at the back, or upstairs apartments that can sleep four. Breakfast available in the bar-café. **www.etip.gr**

KALAMPAKA Alsos House
📋 📋 €

Kanári 5, 422 00 **Tel** *24320 24097* **Fax** *24320 79191* **Rooms** *6*   **Road Map** *B2*

Remodelled in 2004, this small inn at the heart of Kalampáka's oldest quarter offers a mix of doubles, triples and a 4-bed family suite, all with balconies and sharing a well-equipped communal kitchen. The multilingual proprietor is a mine of information on the surrounding area. **www.kalampaka.com/alsoshouse**

KALAMPAKA Odyssion
📋 📋 🅿 €€

Patriárchou Dimitríou 30, 422 00 **Tel** *24320 22320* **Fax** *24320 75307* **Rooms** *21*   **Road Map** *B2*

Set back from the road and thus quieter than the norm for this town, this hotel offers good sized reooms with a mix of tile and parquet floors. There's a cheerful breakfast salon; plans for a pool and rear garden are pending permission from the archaeological authorities as the Odyssion backs right onto the rock formations. **www.hotelodysseon.gr**

KARPENISSI (REGION) Amadryades   €€€

Voutyro, village centre, 361 00 **Tel** *22370 80909 or 69442 46516* **Rooms** *6*   **Road Map** *C3*

This complex of two restored stone buildings comprises five wood- or tile-floored standard rooms plus one suite, all with working fireplaces and a shared balcony. Common facilities include a huge, sunny lawn with chaise lounges, and a reasonably priced café where breakfast can be taken. Open all year. **www.amadryades.gr**

KARPENISSI (REGION) Hellas Country Club   €€€€

Néo Mikró Horió, village centre, 360 75 **Tel** *22370 41570* **Fax** *22370 41577* **Rooms** *29*   **Road Map** *C3*

This is the Karpenisiotis Valley's upmarket option; an established venue for adventure activities (especially rafting and canyoning) and skiing. The best rooms have balconies facing the garden and Mt Kaliakoúdha. Extensive facilities include a gym, restaurant, conference/events hall and café. Five luxury suites. Open all year. **www.countryclub.gr**

KARYTSA Dochos   €€

At the edge of the village, 400 07 **Tel** *24950 92001* **Fax** *24950 92002* **Rooms** *9*   **Road Map** *C2*

Perched partway up the forested slope of Mt Kíssavos, with views extending from Mt Ólympos to the Sithonía peninsula, Dochos occupies one of the most spectacular sites in Greece. Huge wood-floored rooms have fireplaces and balconies facing the Thermaïc Gulf. Antique-filled common areas include a sauna-*hamam*, and bar-breakfast salon.

KASTRAKI Doupiani House   €

West of Kastráki-Metéora access road, 422 00 **Tel** *24320 77555* **Fax** *24320 24078* **Rooms** *11*   **Road Map** *B2*

The most peacefully set pension in Kastráki also has great views of the Metéora formations from most of the simple rooms. The proprietors serve breakfast in the fine hotel garden and can direct walkers to local hikes. Demand is such that an annexe is under construction. **doupiani-house@kmp.forthnet.gr**

KONITSA Grand Hotel Dentro   €€

Town access road from main road, 441 00 **Tel** *26550 29365* **Fax** *26550 29366* **Rooms** *24*   **Road Map** *B2*

While perhaps not grand, this hotel offers the best calibre of lodging for miles around. Standard doubles, some with balconies and views over the Aöös river plain, have good bathrooms. The four attic units (two suitable for families) have fireplaces and hydromassage units. Take meals here or at To Dentro taverna up the road. **www.grandhoteldentro.gr**

MAKRYNITSA Pandora   €€€€

On the slope below the central lane, 370 11 **Tel** *24280 99404* **Fax** *24280 90113* **Rooms** *7*   **Road Map** *C3*

This three-storey *archontikó* (stately mansion) may not, with its 1859 vintage, be the oldest or most imposing in the village, but it has plenty of charm in its interior staircase and fireplaces with porcelain hoods. Rooms are spacious, though bathrooms are small, owing to preservation considerations. Views of the gulf and a good breakfast are highlights.

MEGALO PAPIGKO Xenonas Kalliopi   €

On lane leading from church belfry, 440 04 **Tel** *26530 41081* **Fax** *26530 41081* **Rooms** *7*   **Road Map** *B2*

About the best-value budget accommodation in Megálo Pápigko, the Kalliopi offers en suite, soberly furnished upstairs rooms, most with fireplaces and good views. An added bonus are the filling home-made meals available at the popular courtyard taverna downstairs. Open year-round. **www.epirus.com/kalliopi**

MEGALO PAPIGKO Xenonas Papaevangelou   €€

Near the very top of the village, 440 04 **Tel** *26530 41135* **Fax** *26530 41988* **Rooms** *11*   **Road Map** *B2*

A bit hard to find, but worth the effort, this inn built in Zagorian style has large, unique, brightly lit rooms, many with views of Mt Gamíla. The best unit is a self-catering studio amid well-tended gardens. Inviting common areas include a combination breakfast salon and bar, where local snacks are served.

METSOVO Kassaros   €€

On road leading south from main square, 442 00 **Tel** *26560 41800* **Fax** *26560 41262* **Rooms** *31*   **Road Map** *B2*

All rooms at this hotel have views across the ravine to Anílio village, though the attic units are the most spacious. There is typical Metsovan folk-kitsch decor in the common areas. The management organizes summer or winter outdoor activities in the nearby mountains, providing all the necessary equipment. **www.kassaros.gr**

MIKRO PAPIGKO Xenonas Dias   €€

Village centre, 440 04 **Tel** *26530 41257* **Fax** *26530 41892* **Rooms** *12*   **Road Map** *B2*

A trekker-friendly inn, distributed over two separate buildings (the older structure has more character). Rooms are simple but wood-floored, en suite and cheerful. The two buildings span a sometimes lively restaurant which also serves as the village bar and *kafeneío*. Open all year, with seasonal courtyard seating. **www.zagori.biz/dias**

MOURESSI The Old Silk Store   €€

Village centre, opposite the bakery, 370 12 **Tel** *24260 49086* **Fax** *24260 49565* **Rooms** *6*   **Road Map** *C3*

This 19th-century mansion, lightly restored by Cornish proprietress Jill, features a lush garden with hydrangeas, distant sea views, a barbeque area and high-ceilinged rooms. There's also a self-contained, pricier studio cottage (formerly the village barbershop). Breakfasts include excellent bread and preserves. Closed Feb. **www.pelionet.gr/oldsilkstore**

NAFPAKTOS Akti   €€

Northwest end of Grímpovo beach, 303 00 **Tel** *26340 28464* **Fax** *26340 24171* **Rooms** *37*   **Road Map** *C3*

The Sakellaris brothers thoroughly updated this hotel in 2005, enlarging and modernizing its rooms – about half of which have gulf views. Rooftop suites (sleeping two to three) are palatial and worth the extra cost. An airy, cheerful breakfast salon gives a good start on the day. **akti@otenet.gr**

Key to Price Guide *see p264* **Key to Symbols** *see back cover flap*

PARGA Lichnos Beach
€€

Just south of town, 480 60 **Tel** *26840 31257* **Fax** *26840 31157* **Rooms** *98* **Road Map** *B3*

This self-contained resort makes a good-value choice for families. A mix of standard rooms and bungalows set in lush grounds are numerous enough that tours don't completely monopolise it. Tennis court, pool, and a private beach with watersport facilities compensate for somewhat dated rooms. **www.lichnosbeach.com**

PARGA Magda's Apartments
€€

North end of town, off road to Agiá village, 480 60 **Tel** *26840 31228* **Fax** *26840 31690* **Rooms** *40* **Road Map** *B3*

This complex offers either older studios or superior apartments let by the week, in a hillside garden environment with mountain and partial sea views. There's a terrace pool, small spa, good breakfasts and live musical evenings. Hospitable hosts. Book well in advance. Open Easter–late-Oct. **www.magdas-apartments.gr**

PORTARIA Kritsa
€€

Main village square, 370 11 **Tel** *24280 99121* **Fax** *24280 90006* **Rooms** *8* **Road Map** *C3*

A previously undistinguished interwar building has been transformed into some of the best-value accommodation on Pelion. There are two suites and four *plateía*-facing rooms with balconies; more attention has been paid to the room furnishings and decor than the small bathrooms. Wonderful breakfasts and very good restaurant. **www.hotel-kritsa.gr**

TRIKALA Panellinion
€€

Plateía Ríga Feraíou, 421 00 **Tel** *24310 73545* **Fax** *24310 27350* **Rooms** *18* **Road Map** *C2*

Dating from 1914, this elegant building has hosted leading Greek politicians and artists of the era, and less happily served as the local Italian and German HQ during World War II. Individual rooms, some with balconies and small tubs in the bathrooms, are parquet-floored. There's a mezzanine bar and decent restaurant. **www.panellinion.gr**

TRIKALA (REGION) Pyrgos Mantania
€€€

Tría Potamiá district, near Kalirrói village, 422 00 **Tel** *24320 87351* **Fax** *24320 87600* **Rooms** *6* **Road Map** *B2*

This stone-clad complex was only built in 2002, but you wouldn't know it, so convincing are the architectural details. Rooms vary from large designer doubles on the first floor to even bigger top floor family suites with fireplaces. There's an attractive bar-restaurant specializing in wild trout and other locally sourced products. **www.mantania-ae.gr**

TSEPELOVO Gouris
€

Easterly quarter of village, up cobbled lanes, 440 10 **Tel** *26530 81214* **Rooms** *8* **Road Map** *B2*

One of the friendlier hotels in Zagóri, run by Anthoula Gouri, widow of local tourism pioneer Alexis Gouris. She can usually be found at the traditional Kafeníou Gouri on the *plateía* (where breakfast is served). Rooms are simple but en suite. Consider half-board, as independent restaurants in Tsepélovo are unremarkable. **www.epirus.com/hotelgouris**

VYZITSA Archontiko Karagiannopoulou
€€

North of the through road, 370 10 **Tel** *24230 86717* **Fax** *24230 86878* **Rooms** *6* **Road Map** *C3*

The best maintained of Vyzítsa's half-dozen restored mansion-inns, this four-storey structure was originally built in the late 18th century. The interior features wooden staircases, carved ceiling rosettes, stained glass panels in the windows and extensive lounges on the second floor. Weather permitting, breakfast is served in the courtyard.

ZAGORA Archontiko Gayanni
€€

Near the village centre, 370 01 **Tel** *24260 23391* **Fax** *24260 22671* **Rooms** *9* **Road Map** *C3*

This gorgeous three-storey mansion dating from 1770 has Aegean views, a beautiful garden, ample parking, a genial host and copious breakfasts in a separate building that was once the family bakery. The en suite rooms have been meticulously but not overly restored, with tasteful decor and antiques in the hallways. Open all year. **www.villagayannis.gr**

NORTHERN GREECE

ALISTRATI Archontiko Voziki
€

Georgíou Stimenídi 11, 620 45 **Tel** *23240 20400* **Fax** *23240 20408* **Rooms** *9* **Road Map** *D1*

This little village between Sérres and Dráma attracts increasing numbers of visitors to the nearby Alistráti caverns, some of the largest and most spectacular in Europe. Many stay at this sensitively restored old mansion with tasteful furnishings and a swimming pool. **www.hotelboziki.gr**

AMMOULIANI ISLET, ÁTHOS Gripos
€

Between Ágios Geórgios and Megáli Ámmos beaches, 630 75 **Tel** *23770 51049* **Rooms** *6* **Road Map** *D2*

Ammouliani is Macedonia's only inhabited island, apart from Thássos. This inn, set between two of its best beaches, has terracotta-tiled rooms with copper antiques, beamed ceilings and broad balconies overlooking the pool and garden where peacocks and pheasants can be heard and a popular, good-value *ouzeri* operates.

ARNAIA Oikia Alexandrou
€€€

Platia Patriárchou Vartholomaíou tou Prótou, 630 74 **Tel/Fax** *23720 23210* **Rooms** *7* **Road Map** *D2*

This Macedonian-style mansion dating from 1812 has been lovingly restored by two architects, descendants of the original builders. The rooms (including one suite) are upstairs, most with working fireplaces and all with antique furnishings. Breakfast is served in the excellent restaurant, which is also open to non-guests. **www.oikia-alexandrou.gr**

CHALKIDIKI Gerakina Beach

🍴 🛏 🏊 📖 Ⓟ ♿   €€€

Gerakina Beach, 361 00 **Tel** *23710 52302* **Fax** *23710 52118* **Rooms** *503*   **Road Map** *D2*

Set behind its own beach, this is a better than average resort complex comprising of a high-rise wing of standard rooms and bungalows scattered across well-landscaped grounds. Common facilities include a gym, spa, two pools, two restaurants, golf and water sports. Open May–Oct. **www.gerakina-beach.gr**

DADIA Ecotourism Hostel

📝 📖 Ⓟ   €

1 km (0.5 miles) beyond Dadiá village, 684 00 **Tel** *25540 32263* **Fax** *25540 32463* **Rooms** *20*   **Road Map** *F1*

To partake in raptor-sighting at the Dadiá Forest Reserve – one of Greece's most important habitats for birds of prey – you really have to stay the night locally. The spacious, balconied, en suite rooms at this low-rise inn, all named after birds, are ideal. The café adjacent supplies drinks, breakfast and keys until 11pm; tavernas are in the village. **dadia@otenet.gr**

ÉDESSA Varosi

📝   €€

Archiepiskópou Meletíou 45–47, 582 00 **Tel** *23810 21865* **Fax** *23810 28872* **Rooms** *8*   **Road Map** *C1*

Named for the *varósi* or old quarter in which it's located, this family-run inn stands out for its warmth of welcome and copious breakfasts. The rooms have open fireplaces and period decor. Reservations are usually mandatory – book ahead to avoid disappointment. **www.varosi.gr**

FANARI Fanari

🍴 📖 Ⓟ   €

East edge of village, behind the beach, 670 63 **Tel** *25350 31300* **Fax** *25350 31388* **Rooms** *32*   **Road Map** *E1*

Hotels in nearby Xánthi tend to be noisy and overpriced, so the fishing-port and resort of Fanári provides a more attractive option. The Fanari hotel is white, modern and quietly sited; all rooms have a sea view, and fish tavernas are nearby. **www.fanari-hotel.gr**

KASTORIA Aeolis

📖 Ⓟ   €€

Agíou Athanasíou 30, 521 00 **Tel** *24670 21070* **Fax** *24670 21086* **Rooms** *14*   **Road Map** *B2*

A 1920s mansion opposite the Koursoún Tzami has become the other contender in the local bijoux hotel sweepstakes, with flawless service (including breakfast in your room on request), hydromassage tubs, minibar and ground floor cafeteria as selling points. Aeolis is open all year. **www.aiolis.gr**

KASTORIA Archontiko tou Vergoula

€€€

Aidítras 14, 521 00 **Tel** *24670 23415* **Rooms** *12*   **Road Map** *B2*

This mansion in the Doultsó hillside quarter, dating from 1857, has been meticulously and tastefully restored as one of Kastoriá's premier boutique hotels. Rooms with unimpeded lake views are pricier; those without views are less expensive. There's a breakfast salon and a wine bar that is only open at weekends. **sfinas@otenet.gr**

KAVALA Esperia

🍴 📖 Ⓟ   €€

Erythroú Stavroú 44, 654 03 **Tel** *2510 229621* **Fax** *2510 220621* **Rooms** *105*   **Road Map** *D1*

This 1970s-era building located opposite the archaeological museum was renovated in 2004 and offers decent facilities, including a breakfast terrace, good soundproofing (side or rear rooms will be quietest) and a small conference centre. **www.esperiakavala.gr**

KAVALA Imaret

🍴 🛏   €€€€

Poulídou 6, 654 03 **Tel** *2510 620151* **Fax** *2510 620156* **Rooms** *30*   **Road Map** *D1*

The Ottoman-era *imaret* or hostel for theological students has been stunningly refurbished as a five-star hotel with no detail overlooked. The former students' cells have music systems and original fireplaces; there's also a working *hamam*, wellness treatments, indoor pool and trickling fountain in the central courtyard. **www.imaret.gr**

KERKINI Oikoperiigitis

🍴 📖 Ⓟ   €€

Village centre, 620 55 **Tel** *23270 41450* **Fax** *23270 41476* **Rooms** *12*   **Road Map** *D1*

Lake Kerkíni, just 500 m (1,640 ft) from this inn, has become one of Greece's premier bird-watching venues. Oikoperiígitis organizes boating on the lake and excursions on nearby Mt Belés. The wood and stone-built inn has rooms and apartments spread over two buildings. Snacks and drinks served in the lounge/library. Open all year. **www.oikoperiigitis.gr**

LITOCHORO Villa Drosos

📝 🍴 🛏 📖 Ⓟ   €€

Archeláou 20, Ágios Geórgios district, 602 00 **Tel** *23520 84561* **Fax** *23520 84563* **Rooms** *13*   **Road Map** *C2*

The Villa Drosos may not have the unimpeded mountain views of the central-square hotels, but it does offer excellent standards in its small but balconied rooms, the best of which overlook the swimming pool and a small wood. The breakfast room has a fireplace, and the restaurant serves good grills. Open all year. **grigoris@kat.forthnet.gr**

MARONEIA Roxani Country House

📝 🍴 🛏 📖 Ⓟ   €€

Edge of village, 694 00 **Tel** *25330 21501* **Fax** *25330 21500* **Rooms** *25*   **Road Map** *E1*

Rooms at this purpose-built hotel are large, if simply furnished, with all amenities and good views. Breakfasts, served outdoors in good weather, are copious, and the enthusiastic owner arranges every conceivable local activity for guests, from archery to sea-kayaking to mountain biking. Open all year. **www.ecoexplorer.gr**

NEOS MARMARAS Kelyfos

🍴 🛏 🏊 📖 Ⓟ   €€€

North of turning for Porto Karras complex, 630 81 **Tel** *23750 72833* **Fax** *23750 72247* **Rooms** *18*   **Road Map** *D2*

On a hilltop near Néos Marmarás with sweeping sea views, this pleasant complex of buildings scattered among pines and palms comprises a mix of standard rooms, suites and studios, all spacious and tastefully appointed. Studios and suites have fireplaces and self-catering areas. The restaurant is excellent. **www.kelyfos.gr**

Key to Price Guide *see p264*   **Key to Symbols** *see back cover flap*

NYMFEO Ta Linouria   🍴 🅿   €€
At the edge of the village, 530 78 **Tel** *23860 31030* **Fax** *23860 31133* **Rooms** *6*   **Road Map** *E1*

An inn, *kafenio* and restaurant all under the same roof, Ta Linouria has warm-toned, wood-trimmed guest suites. The bar-restaurant, reliably open much of the day, year-round, serves good meals, but it's also fine just to have a refreshing drink or homemade dessert.

NYMFEO La Moara   🍴 🅿   €€€€€
Hilltop beyond Nymfeo village, 530 78 **Tel** *23860 31377* **Fax** *23105 24430* **Rooms** *8*   **Road Map** *E1*

Opened by the wine-producing Boutari family in 1993 as one of Greece's first boutique hotels, La Moara offers guest rooms with wooden floors, fine linens and state-of-the-art bathrooms. The wine cellar has over 100 varieties of foreign and domestic vintages. There are two lounges as well as a garden. Closed Mon pm–Wed am; Jul.

PRESPA LAKES Agios Achilleios   🛏 🍴   €
Ágios Achílleios islet, Mikrí Préspa lake, 530 77 **Tel** *23850 46601* **Rooms** *10*   **Road Map** *B1*

Car-free Ágios Achilleios island, ringed by reeds, is joined to the mainland by a metal pedestrian bridge, though in winter you can walk across the ice sheet to the island. The stone-clad inn comprises nine standard rooms and one attic suite, plus a ground floor restaurant featuring local specialities.

PRESPA LAKES To Petrino   🛏   €€
Near top of Ágios Germanós village, 530 77 **Tel** *23850 51344* **Fax** *23850 51854* **Rooms** *10*   **Road Map** *B1*

The largest village in the Préspa basin, Ágios Germanós offers late Byzantine churches and views of the larger lake, as well as this stone-built, wood-floored inn converted from a private dwelling, with heat provided in part by wood-burning stoves.

THESSALONIKI Orestias Castorias   🛏 🗐   €€
Agnóstou Stratiótou 14, corner Olymbou, 546 31 **Tel** *2310 276517* **Fax** *2310 276572* **Rooms** *37* **Road Map** *C2*

An unbeatable location – a quiet corner a few paces from Áyios Dimítrios basilica – and keen pricing are this hotel's main selling points. Most rooms, which lack balconies but are fairly spacious, have been converted to en suite status. There are no common areas to speak of, but complimentary coffee is always available.

THESSALONIKI Le Palace   🍴 🗐   €€€
Tsimiskí 12, 546 24 **Tel** *2310 257400* **Fax** *2310 256589* **Rooms** *54*   **Road Map** *C2*

The city's first boutique hotel is located in a 1926 Art Deco building, transformed from 1998–2002. The large, double-glazed rooms have contemporary bathrooms, while the common areas preserve some interwar touches. There's a mezzanine lounge and restaurant, which serves an outstanding buffet breakfast, and a café. **www.lepalace.gr**

THESSALONIKI Tourist   🛏 🗐   €€
Mitropóleos 21, 546 24 **Tel** *2310 270501* **Fax** *2310 226865* **Rooms** *37*   **Road Map** *C2*

One of the few surviving interwar buildings in this area, the Tourist features parquet-floored lounges, a breakfast room accessed by a period lift and irregularly shaped rooms with en suite. It's been featured in many publications on the city and has a staunchly loyal word-of-mouth clientele, so reservations are mandatory. **www.touristhotel.gr**

THESSALONIKI Capsis Bristol   🛏 🍴 🗐 ♿   €€€€€
Oplopoioú 2, corner Katoúni, 546 25 **Tel** *2310 506500* **Fax** *2310 510555* **Rooms** *20*   **Road Map** *C2*

Situated near the Ladádika nightlife district, the Capsis Bristol is Thessaloniki's second restoration hotel, in a converted 19th-century building. Breakfast is served in the central atrium, while there's a bistro-bar on-site as well as the respected Deipnosofistis restaurant. Rooms have varied colour schemes, wood floors and antique furnishings. **www.capsisbristol**

THESSALONIKI Electra Palace   🍴 🏊 🧒 🗐 ♿   €€€€€
Plateía Aristotélous 9, 546 24 **Tel** *2310 232221* **Fax** *2310 294001* **Rooms** *131*   **Road Map** *C2*

This landmark semicircular building recently underwent a refurbishment; common areas are palatially fitted with walnut and marble trim as well as chandeliers, while the wood-trimmed rooms – with every conceivable gadget – have ochre and red decor. Rooftop pool, fitness centre, English-themed bar and two restaurants. **www.electrahotels.gr**

THESSALONIKI Macedonia Palace   🍴 🏊 🧒 🗐 🅿 ♿ €€€€€
Megálou Alexándrou 2, 546 40 **Tel** *2310 897197* **Fax** *2310 897211* **Rooms** *287*   **Road Map** *C2*

The only seafront hotel in the city (though half the rooms face inland), the Macedonia Palace remains a favourite haunt of businessmen and VIPs. Accordingly, there are plenty of conference facilities and two celebrated restaurants (the Porphyra has sweeping views). There's also a gym, sauna and outdoor ground-level pool. **www.grecotel.gr**

THESSALONIKI Panorama   🍴 🗐 🅿   €€€€€
Analípseos 26, Panorama, 552 36 **Tel/Fax** *2310 344871* **Rooms** *50*   **Road Map** *C2*

If you have a car, this hotel in the southeastern hillside suburb of Panórama is an excellent choice, as parking in the city centre is nearly impossible. This 1970s structure has been renovated recently and room furnishings updated. Despite the name, only third-floor rooms have a view over the city and Thermaic Gulf. **www.hotelpanorama.gr**

VERGINA Vergina   🛏 🗐   €
Main through road, Vergína Imatheías, 590 31 **Tel** *23310 92510* **Fax** *23310 92511* **Rooms** *10*   **Road Map** *C2*

Modern Vergína village offers a quieter alternative to staying in Véria, the nearest town 16 km (10 miles) northwest, and allows an early-morning visit to the Royal Tombs before crowds appear. This block of simple but well-kept rented rooms, most with balconies, stands just a few steps from the tomb complex. A good breakfast is included in the price.

WHERE TO EAT

To eat out in Greece is to experience the democratic tradition at work. Rich and poor, young and old, all enjoy their favourite local restaurant, taverna or café. Greeks consider the best places to be where the food is fresh, plentiful and well-cooked, not necessarily where the setting or the cuisine is the fanciest. Visitors too have come to appreciate the simplicity and health of the traditional Greek kitchen – olive

A local cheese from Métsovo

oil, yoghurt, vegetables, a little meat and some wine, always shared with friends. The traditional three-hour lunch and siesta – still the daily rhythm of the countryside – is now only a fading memory for most city Greeks, who have adapted to a more Western European routine. But the combination of traditional cooking and outside influences has produced a vast range of eating places in Greece, with somewhere to suit almost everyone.

The Néon restaurant in the centre of Athens *(see p286)*

TYPES OF RESTAURANT

Often difficult to find in more developed tourist resorts, the *estiatórion,* or traditional Greek restaurant, is one of Europe's most enjoyable places to eat. Friendly, noisy and sometimes in lovely surroundings, *estiatória* are reliable purveyors of local recipes and wines, particularly if they have been owned by the same family for decades. Foreigners unfamiliar with Greek dishes may be invited into the kitchen to choose their fare. In Greece, the entire family dines together and takes plenty of time over the meal, especially at weekends.

Estiatória range from the very expensive in Athens, Thessaloníki and wealthier

suburbs, to the incredibly inexpensive *mageirió* or *koutoúki,* popular with students and workers. Here there is little choice in either wines or dishes, all of which

A sign for a taverna in Párga

will be *mageireftá* (ready-cooked). The food, however, is home made and tasty and the barrel wine is at the very least drinkable, often good, and sometimes comes from the owner's home village.

Some restaurants may specialize in a particular type of cuisine. In Thessaloníki, for example, and in the suburbs of Athens, where Asia Minor refugees settled after 1923, you may find food to be spicier than the Greek norm, with lots of red peppers and such dishes as *giogurtlú* (kebabs drenched in yoghurt and served on pitta bread) or lamb-brain salad.

The menu in a traditional restaurant tends to be short, comprising at most a dozen

mezédes (starters or snacks), perhaps eight main dishes, four or five cooked vegetable dishes or salads, plus a dessert of fresh or cooked fruit, and a selection of local and national wines.

Many hotels have restaurants open to non-residents. Smaller country hotels occasionally have excellent kitchens, and serve good local wines, so check on any that are close to where you are staying.

In the last few years a new breed of young Greek chefs has emerged in *kultúra* restaurants, developing a style of cooking that encompasses Greece's magnificent raw materials, flavours and colours. These dishes are served with the exciting new Greek wines.

Stylish Beau Brummel restaurant in Kifisia *(see p288)*

Waiter outside a restaurant in Pláka, Athens

TAVERNAS

One of the great pleasures for the traveller in Greece is the tradition of the taverna, a place to eat and drink, even if you simply snack on *mezédes* (Greeks rarely drink without eating). Traditional tavernas are open from mid-evening and stay open late; occasionally they are open for lunch as well. Menus are short and seasonal – perhaps six or eight *mezédes* and four main courses comprising casseroles and dishes cooked *tis óras* (to order), along with the usual accompaniments of vegetables, salads, fruit and wine.

Like traditional restaurants, some tavernas specialize in the foods and wines of the owner's home region, some in a particular cooking style and others in certain foods.

A *psarotavérna* is the place to find good fish dishes but, because fish is expensive, these tavernas often resemble restaurants and are patronized mainly by wealthy Greeks and tourists. In small fishing villages it is quite different and you may find the rickety tables of a *psarotavérna* literally on the beach. Close to the lapping waves the owner may serve fish that he himself caught that morning.

For delicious grills try a *psistariá*, a taverna that specializes in spit-roasts and char-grilling (*sta kárvouna*). In countryside *psistariés* lamb, kid, pork, chicken, game,

offal, lambs' heads and even testicles are char-grilled, and whole lamb is roasted on the spit. At the harbourside, fish and shellfish are grilled and served with fresh lemon juice and olive oil. Country, family-run tavernas and cafés will invariably provide simple meals, such as omelettes and salads throughout the day, but many of these places close quite early in the evening. After your meal in the taverna, follow the Greeks and enjoy a visit to the local *zacharoplasteío (see p278)* for sweets and pastries.

CAFES AND BARS

Cafes, known as *kafeneía,* are the pulse of Greek life, and even the tiniest hamlet has a place to drink coffee or wine. Equally important is the function it performs as the centre of communication – mail is collected here, telephone calls made, and newspapers read, dissected and discussed. *Kafeneía* serve Greek coffee, sometimes *frappé* (instant coffee served cold, in a tall glass), soft drinks, beer, ouzo and wine. Most also serve some kind of snack to order. All open early and remain open until late at night.

Bottle of ouzo

As the social hub of their communities, country *kafeneía,* as well as many in the city, open seven days a week.

A *galaktopoleío,* or "milk shop", has a seating area where you can enjoy fine yoghurt and honey; those around Plateía Omonoías in Athens remain open for most of the night.

A *kapileío* (wine shop with a café-bar attached) is the place to try local wines from the cask, and you may find a few bottled wines as well. The owner is invariably from a wine village or family and will often cook some simple regional specialities to accompany the wine.

In a *mezedopoleío,* or *mezés* shop, the owner will not only serve the local wine and the *mezédes* that go with it, but also ouzo and the infamous spirit, raki, both distilled from the remnants of the grape harvest. Their accompanying *mezédes* are less salty than those served with wine.

No holiday in Greece is complete without a visit to an *ouzerí.* Some of the best of these are to be found in Thessaloníki and in Athens' central arcades. You can order a dozen or more little plates of savoury meats, fish and vegetables and try the many varieties of ouzo that are served in small jugs. A jug or glass of water accompanies the ouzo to wash it down. These are traditionally inexpensive, noisy and fun places to eat and drink.

Outdoor tables on the patio at the Kritsa Hotel restaurant (see p293)

Enjoying outdoor dining in Pláka, Athens

FAST FOOD AND SNACKS

Visitors can be forgiven for thinking Greeks never stop eating, for there seem to be snack bars on every street and vendors selling sweets, nuts, rolls, and seasonal corn and chestnuts at every turn.

Although American-style fast-food outlets dominate city streets, it is easy to avoid them by trying the traditional Greek eateries. The extremely cheap *souvlatzídiko* offers chunks of meat, fish or vegetables roasted on a skewer and served with bread, while an *ovelistírio* serves *gýros* – meat from a revolving spit in a pitta bread pocket. The food is sold *sto chéri* (in the hand).

Many bakeries serve savoury pies and a variety of tasty bread rolls, and in busy city neighbourhoods you can always find a *kafeneío* serving substantial snacks and salads. Street vendors sell *koulourákia* (rolls), small pies, corn on the cob, roast chestnuts, nut brittle and candies. Snacks are often local specialities: tiny open pizza-like pies in Thessaloníki; pies of wild greens or cheese in Métsovo, and small flavourful sausages in Ioánnina.

If you have a sweet tooth you will love the *zacharoplasteío* (literally, "shop of the sugar sculptor"). The baker there makes traditional sweet breads, tiny sweet pastries and a whole variety of fragrant honey cakes.

BREAKFAST

For Greeks, this is the least important meal of the day. In traditional homes and cafés a small cup of Greek coffee accompanies *paximádia* (slices of rusk-like bread) or *koulourákia* (firm, sesame-covered or slightly sweet rolls in rings or s-shapes) or pound cakes with home-made jam. Elsewhere, and in many city *kafeneía*, this has been replaced by a large cup of brewed coffee and French-style croissants or delicious brioche-style rolls, also called *koulourákia*. In the summer, some *kafeneía* will still serve fresh figs, thick yoghurt, pungent honey and slightly sweet currant bread.

RESERVATIONS

The more expensive the restaurant, the more advisable it is to make a reservation, and it is always worth doing so at the weekend. In country areas, and in the suburbs, it is the practice to visit the restaurant or taverna earlier in the day, or the day before, and check on the dishes to be served. The proprietor will take your order and reserve any special dish that you request.

Serving *gýros* on an Athens street

WINE

Restaurateurs in Greece are only now learning to look after bottled wines. If the wine list contains the better bottles, such as Ktíma Merkoúri, Seméli or Strofiliá, the proprietor probably knows how to look after the wine and it will be safe to order a more expensive bottle. For a good-value bottle there are the nationally known Cambás or Boutári wines.

Traditional restaurants and tavernas may only stock carafe wine, which is served straight from the barrel and is always inexpensive. Carafe wines are often of the region and, among Greek wines, the rosé in particular is noted for having an unusual but pleasing flavour.

HOW TO PAY

Greece is still largely a cash society. If you need to pay by credit card, check first that the restaurant takes credit cards, and if so, that they take the card you intend to use – many proprietors accept some but not others. *Kafeneía* almost never take credit cards, and café-bars rarely, but many will be happy to take travellers' cheques. In rural areas, country tavernas, restaurants and *kafeneía* will only accept cash.

The listings in this guide indicate whether or not credit cards are accepted at each establishment.

SERVICE AND TIPPING

Greeks take plenty of time when they eat out and expect a high level of attention. This means a great deal of running around on the part of

Patrons outside a kebab restaurant in Athens

Interior patio of Ouzerí Aristotélous in Thessaloníki *(see p294)*

the waiter, but in return they receive generous tips – as much as 20 per cent if the service is good, though more often a tip is 10–15 per cent. Prices in traditional establishments do include service, but the waiters still expect a tip so always have coins ready to hand.

Western-style restaurants and tourist tavernas sometimes add a service charge to the bill; their prices can be much higher because of trimmings, such as telephones and air conditioning.

Bread ring seller, Athens

DRESS CODE

The Greeks dress quite formally when dining out. Visitors should wear whatever is comfortable, but skimpy tops and shorts and active sportswear are not acceptable, except near the beach, although it is unlikely that tourist establishments would turn custom away. Some of the most expensive city restaurants, especially those attached to hotels, request formal dress; the listings indicate which places fall into this category.

In summer, if you intend dining outside, take a jacket or sweater for the evening.

CHILDREN

Greek children become restaurant and taverna habitués at a very early age – it is an essential part of their education. Consequently, children are welcome everywhere in Greece except in

the bars. In formal restaurants children are expected to be well behaved, but in summer, when Greeks enjoy eating outside, it is perfectly acceptable for children to play and enjoy themselves too. Facilities such as highchairs are unknown except in the most considerate hotel dining rooms, but more casual restaurants and tavernas are fine for dining with children of any age.

SMOKING

Smoking is commonplace in Greece and until recently establishments maintaining a no-smoking policy have been difficult to find. However, new EU regulations make it obligatory for all restaurants to have no-smoking areas. In practice, of course, change is slow but for at least half the year you can always dine outdoors.

Drying octopus at a restaurant in Geroliménas, on the Máni peninsula *(see p199)*

WHEELCHAIR ACCESS

In country areas, where room is plentiful, there are few problems for wheelchair users. In city restaurants, however, it is a different matter, and access is often restricted. The streets themselves have uneven pavements and many restaurants have narrow doorways and possibly steps. Restaurants that do have wheelchair access are indicated in the listings pages of this guide. Also, the organizations that are listed on page 305 provide information for disabled travellers in Greece.

VEGETARIAN FOOD

Greek cuisine provides plenty of choice for vegetarians. Greeks enjoy such a variety of dishes for each course that it is easy to order just vegetable dishes for first and main courses in traditional restaurants, tavernas or *kafeneía*. Vegetable dishes are substantial, inexpensive, imaginatively prepared and satisfying.

Vegans may have more of a problem, for there are few places in Greece catering for special diets. However, as Greek cooking relies little on dairy products, it is possible to follow a vegan diet almost anywhere in Greece.

PICNICS

The best time to picnic in Greece is in spring, when the countryside is at its most beautiful and the weather is not too hot. The traditional seasonal foods, such as Lenten olive oil bread, sweet Easter bread, pies filled with wild greens, fresh cheese and new retsina wine, all make perfect fare for picnics. Summer is the ideal time for eating on the beach. The best foods for summer snacks are peaches and figs, yoghurt and cheese, and tomatoes, various breads and olives.

The Flavours of Greece

The ancient Greeks regarded cooking as both a science and an art – even a topic for philosophy. In out-of-the-way places on the mainland and on the more far-flung islands, you will still find dishes, ingredients and culinary styles untouched by time. Elsewhere, Greek cookery has been much influenced by the Ottoman Empire, with its spiced meat dishes, and filled pastries and vegetables. In the recent past, Greek cuisine was often thought of as peasant food. Today, it is that very simplicity, and its reliance on seasonal, local produce, that makes Greek food so popular with visitors.

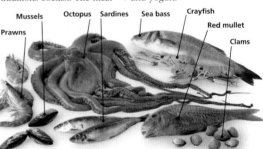
Oregano and thyme

Island fisherman returning to harbour with the day's catch

ATHENS AND THE PELOPONNESE

The capital is essentially a city of immigrants from the countryside, the islands and the shores of the eastern Mediterranean. That diversity is reflected in its markets and its cuisine. Street food is a quintessential part of Athens life. In the Peloponnese ingredients are as

varied as the terrain: fish from the sea and, from the mountains, sheep, goat and game. From the hills come several varieties of cheese, olives and honey.

CENTRAL AND NORTHERN GREECE

Mainland Greece, with its long and chequered history, is a place where regional food boundaries are blurred and a variety of cooking traditions coexist. The meat

and fruit dishes of Thessaloníki show a Jewish influence; the spices, sausages and oven cooking of Ioánnina stem from Ottoman times; while a love of sheep's cheese, pies and offal came to Métsovo and the Epirus mountains with the Vlach shepherds. The spicy food of the North is the legacy of the 1922 Greek immigrants from Asia Minor, while the Balkan influence is obvious in the use of pickles, walnuts and yogurt.

Mussels   Octopus   Sardines   Sea bass   Crayfish
Prawns   Red mullet
                                            Clams

Selection of seafood from the clear waters of Greece

REGIONAL DISHES AND SPECIALITIES

Sweets such as nougat, *pastéli* (honey-sesame candy), *loukoúmia* (yeast doughnuts in syrup) and *chalvás* (halva, or sweetmeats) have been a part of Greek street life since the days of Aristotle. They are sold in small shops or stalls. *Píttes*, or pies, are a speciality of the western Epirus region. Fillings range from game or offal to cheese and vegetables, often combined with rice or pasta. Reflecting Middle-Eastern influences, *Soutzoukákia*, a speciality of northern Thrace and Macedonia, are meat patties flavoured with coriander, pepper and cumin. *Choirinó kritikó*, the classic dish of inland Crete villages, is thick pork cutlets baked until tender, while *Sýka me tyrí* is a summer *mezés*, dessert or snack, of fresh figs with *mizthýra* cheese, made from whey.

Olives

Fakés *is a sour Peloponnese soup of green lentils, lemon juice or wine vinegar, tomatoes, herbs and olive oil.*

Produce on sale in a typical Greek market

THE ISLANDS

Each group of islands has a distinct culinary identity reflecting its geographical location and history. Many Ionian dishes are pasta based, a legacy of the era of Venetian occupation. Those of the Cyclades are intensely flavoured. The cooks of the Dodecanese and Northeast Aegean benefit from the rich harvest of the surrounding sea. Crete is unique in its long Turkish occupation and taste for highly spiced dishes, and Cretan cooking has a number of recipes unique to the island. The use of pork, a legacy of antiquity, is more popular here than anywhere else in Greece. Some lovely kitchen utensils and unusual ingredients from Minoan times have been excavated by archaeologists on Crete.

FISH AND SEAFOOD

The warm and sheltered waters of the Aegean are the migratory path for tuna and swordfish, and a feeding ground for tasty anchovies and sardines. Coves and caves around the hundreds of rocky islands shelter

Bread being baked in an outdoor communal oven

highly prized red mullet, dentex and parrot fish, while the long shoreline is home to shellfish and crustaceans. Fish are usually served with their heads on: to Greeks this is the tastiest part, and it helps to identify the variety.

OTHER PRODUCE

Greece is home to the largest variety of olives in the world. They are cured by methods used for thousands of years. The best quality olive oil, extra-virgin, is made by pressing just-ripe olives only. Greece produces sheep's, cow's and goat's cheeses, usually named by taste and texture, not place of origin.

WHAT TO DRINK

Wine has been part of Greek cultural life from the earliest times. Major wine-producing areas include Attica, Macedonia and the Peloponnese. Mavro-daphne is a fortified dessert wine from Pátra. Traditional Greek specialities include *tsípouro*, distilled from the residue of crushed grapes; retsina, a wine flavoured with pine resin *(see p147)*; and the strong, aniseed-flavoured spirit, ouzo. Coffee in Greece is traditionally made from very finely ground beans boiled up with water in a long handled *mpríki* (coffee pot) and drunk from a tiny cup. It is served in cafés rather than tavernas.

Spetzofáï, *from central Greece, is sautéed slices of spicy country sausage with herbs and vegetables.*

Barboúnia, *or red mullet, has been the most esteemed fish in Greece since antiquity. It is usually simply fried.*

Loukoumádes *are a snack of small deep-fried doughnuts soaked in honey-syrup and sprinkled with cinnamon.*

The Classic Greek Menu

The traditional first course is a selection of *mezédes*, or snacks; these can also be eaten in *ouzerís*, or bars, throughout the day. Meat or fish dishes follow next, usually served with a salad. The wine list tends to be simple, and coffee and cakes are generally consumed after the meal in a nearby pastry shop. In rural areas traditional dishes can be chosen straight from the kitchen. Bread is considered by Greeks to be the staff of life and is served at every meal. Village bakers vary the bread each day with flavourings of currants, herbs, wild greens or cheese. The many Orthodox festivals are celebrated with special breads.

Greek pitta breads

Souvlákia *are small chunks of pork, flavoured with lemon, herbs and olive oil, grilled on skewers.*

Choriátiki saláta, *Greek salad, combines tomatoes, cucumber, onions, herbs, capers and feta cheese.*

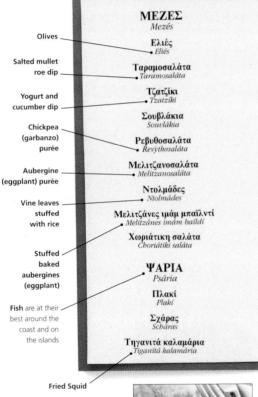

ΜΕΖΕΣ
Mezés

Olives — **Ελιές**
• *Eliés*

Salted mullet roe dip — **Ταραμοσαλάτα**
• *Taramosaláta*

Yogurt and cucumber dip — **Τζατζίκι**
• *Tzatzíki*

Σουβλάκια
Souvlákia

Chickpea (garbanzo) purée — **Ρεβυθοσαλάτα**
• *Revythosaláta*

Aubergine (eggplant) purée — **Μελιτζανοσαλάτα**
• *Melitzanosaláta*

Vine leaves stuffed with rice — **Ντολμάδες**
• *Ntolmádes*

Μελιτζάνες ιμάμ μπαϊλ.ντί
• *Melitzánes imám baïldí*

Stuffed baked aubergines (eggplant) — **Χωριάτικη σαλάτα**
Choriátiki saláta

ΨΑΡΙΑ
Psária

Fish are at their best around the coast and on the islands — **Πλακί**
Plakí

Σχάρας
Scháras

Τηγανιτά καλαμάρια
• *Tiganitá kalamária*

Fried Squid

Psária plakí *is a whole fish baked in an open dish with vegetables in a tomato and olive oil sauce.*

Scháras *means "from the grill". It can be applied to meat or fish, or even vegetables. Here, grilled swordfish has been marinated in lemon juice, olive oil and herbs before being swiftly char-grilled.*

MEZEDES

Mezédes are eaten as a first course or as a snack with wine or other drinks. *Taramosaláta* is a purée of salted mullet roe and bread-crumbs or potato. Traditionally a dish for Lent, it is now on every taverna menu. *Melitzanosaláta* and *revithosaláta* are both purées. *Melitzanosaláta* is grilled aubergines (eggplant) and herbs; *revithosaláta* is chickpeas (garbanzos), coriander and garlic. *Melitzánes imám baïldí* are aubergines filled with a purée of onions, tomatoes and herbs. *Ntolmádes* are vine leaves stuffed with currants, pine nuts and rice.

Revithosaláta

Ntolmádes

Taramosaláta

Melitzánes imám baïldí

Typical selection of mezédes

ΚΡΕΑΣ
Kréas

Μουσακάς
Mousakás

Κεφτέδες
Keftédes

Χοιρινό σουβλάκι
Choirinó souvláki

Κλέφτικο
Kléftiko

ΛΑΧΑΝΙΚΑ ΚΑΙ ΣΑΛΑΤΙΚΑ
Lachaniká kai salatiká

Μελιτζάνες και κολοκυθάκια τηγανιτά
Melitzánes kai kolokythákia tiganitá

Αγκινάρες α λα πολίτα
Agkináres a la políta

Σπαράγγια σαλάτα
Sparángia saláta

ΓΛΥΚΑ
Glyká

Φρέσκα φρούτα
Fréska froúta

Σύκα στο φούρνο με μαυροδάφνη
Sýka sto foúrno me mavrodáfni

Γιαούρτι και μέλι
Giaoúrti kai méli

Meat is more readily available on the mainland than on the islands

Moussaka (minced lamb and aubergine baked in layers)

Vegetables and salads often use wild produce

Fried aubergines (eggplant) and courgettes (zucchini)

Artichokes with potatoes, dill, lemon and oil

Asparagus salad

Desserts are simple affairs of pastry, fruit or yogurt.

Fresh fruit

Figs baked in sweet, spiced Mavrodaphne wine with orange-flower water

Keftédes *are meatballs of pork with egg and breadcrumbs, flavoured with herbs and cumin and fried in olive oil.*

Kléftiko *is usually goat meat wrapped in parchment paper and cooked so that the juices and flavours are sealed in.*

Giaoúrti kai méli *(yogurt with honey) is served in speciality "milk shops", to be eaten there or taken home.*

Sweet pastries *filled with nuts and honey, syrup-drenched cakes, pies, doughnuts and glyká (candied fruits) are mainly eaten in cafés. The most famous of all are* bakla-vas, *with layers of filo pastry and nuts, and* kataïfi, *known to tourists as "shredded wheat".*

Choosing a Restaurant

The restaurants in this guide have been selected across a wide range of price categories for their good value, traditional food and interesting location. This chart lists the restaurants by area, starting with Athens. Unless otherwise stated, the restaurants listed here are open for lunch and dinner daily.

PRICE CATEGORIES
The following price ranges are for a three-course meal for one, including a half bottle of house wine (or equivalent), tax and service.
€ under 15 euros
€€ 15–25 euros
€€€ 25–35 euros
€€€€ 35–45 euros
€€€€€ over 45 euros

ATHENS

AMPELOKIPOI Vlassis
€€
Pastér 8, off Plateia Mavíli, 115 21 **Tel** *21064 63060*
Map *4 F3*

Occupying a two-storey interwar house, Vlassis sticks to its tested formula of abundant, rich, retro cooking. Order *mezédes* like cabbage *dolmádes* from the *dískos*, and then place your order for suckling pig or grilled *thrápsalo* (giant squid). The place fills by mid-evening, so book ahead. Closed Sun dinner; Aug.

AMPELOKIPOI 48 The Restaurant
€€€€
Armatolon & Klefton 48, 115 21 **Tel** *21064 11082*
Map *4 D2*

A glamorous, image-conscious clientele, including mainstream Greek singers and actors, come here to see and be seen, and to feast on passable fusion cuisine. The polished-concrete dining area and bar look onto an internal water garden. Reservations recommended. Closed lunch; Sun.

ÁNO PETRALONA Chrysa
€€€€
Dimofóntos 81, 118 52 **Tel** *21034 12515*
Map *5 3A*

This tastefully decorated taverna is a trendy exception to the numerous traditional eateries in the area. The fare is a modern take on Greek cuisine, for example salmon, chicken and duck dishes in simple sauces, and the welcoming proprietress usually waits on you herself. Open for dinner (& lunch Sun); closed summer.

EXARCHEIA Mparmpa Giannis
€
Emmanouíl Mpenáki 94, 106 81 **Tel** *21038 24138*
Map *2 F3*

A favourite that hasn't changed much in decades, this place dishes up consistently good *mageireftá* and a handful of grills. On any given day there might be *giouvarláki* (rice & meat balls in *avgolémono*), stewed okra or baked *pérka* fish. The tables in pedestrianised Dervenion fill first in summer. Closed Sun dinner; Aug.

EXARCHEIA Cookou Food
€€
Themistokléos 66, 106 81 **Tel** *21038 31955*
Map *2 F3*

Cookou Food is a small, café-style restaurant decorated in pastel colours. The clientele is a mix of students, gays and trendy people who come for traditional dishes like meatballs in sauce and more subtle, herbally flavoured updates on Greek vegetarian recipes. Closed Sun.

EXARCHEIA Fasoli
€€
Emmanouíl Mpenáki 45, 106 81 **Tel** *21033 00010*
Map *2 F3*

Opened in 2005, Fasoli has quickly grabbed a share of the local market, thanks to excellent value at mid-range prices, and stylish decor featuring suspended lighting. The food is Greek with creative twists, such as lentil salad, *biftéki* roulade and light pasta dishes. Read the chalkboard for daily specials and desserts. Closed Sun.

EXARCHEIA Rozalia
€€
Valtetsíou 58, 106 81 **Tel** *21033 02933*
Map *2 F2*

Rozalia has become more commercialised since its garden was enclosed for all-year use, but the food – a mix of *mageireftá*, a few grills and *mezédes* – is still worthwhile. Typical winter platters include *spanakórizo* (spinach rice), *tiganiá* (pork-chunk fry-up), cabbage *dolmádes* and rabbit stew. As usual, the *mezédes* are offered on a *dískos*.

EXARCHEIA Giantes
€€€
Valtetsíou 44, 106 81 **Tel** *21033 01369*
Map *2 F3*

The modern Greek menu at Exárcheia's most upscale eatery changes by month, according to the organically produced ingredients sourced. You might be served wild greens, monkfish, lamb and sun-dried tomatoes or *tas kebab* stew. In summer dine on the tiled courtyard; in winter in the warm-toned interior.

GAZI Sardelles
€€
Persefónis 15, 104 35 **Tel** *21034 78050*

Located in a neighbourhood not generally known for inexpensive restaurants, Sardelles has carved out a niche purveying the humbler varieties of seafood like, *sardélles* (sardines). The prices may be cheap but the decor is modern enough.

Key to Symbols *see back cover flap*

GAZI Dirty Str-eat   €€€
Triptolémou 12, 104 35 **Tel** *21034 74763*

The name refers ironically to the more careful and hygienic versions of street food served: kebabs, tacos, hot dogs. There's also a wide variety of affordable seafood on offer, from fried small seasonal fish to fillets of premium cuts like sea bass. The interior has red and black decor and there is garden seating at the rear. Closed lunch; Mon.

GAZI Mamacas   €€€
Persefónis 41, 104 35 **Tel** *21034 64984*   **Map** *1 A5*

The original new wave taverna that kick-started the gentrifiction of Gázi, Mamacas is still steaming along after its 1998 opening. The fare is wholesome, updated Greek like Cretan *dákos* salad (rusks, tomato, cheese, oregano) and cuttlefish with greens. The decor is trendy and the clientele equally so. After midnight DJ sounds predominate.

GAZI Varoulko   €€€€€
Pireós 80, 104 35 **Tel** *21052 28400*   **Map** *1 C4*

Michelin-starred chef Lefteris Lazarou has diversified from the innovative fish dishes at the original Piraeus branch of Varoulko to create unlikely recipes such as goat risotto and cold tropical-fruit soup for dessert. Booking ahead is recommended despite the vast, multilevel and somewhat clinical space. Closed lunch; Sun.

KOLONAKI Il Postino   €€
Grivaíon 3, alley off Skoufá, 106 73 **Tel** *21036 41414*   **Map** *3 A4*

Cosy, genuine *osteria* with old-photo decor and equally retro music on the sound system. The unpretentious, home-made cooking, supervised by an Italian chef with an illustrious track record in Athens, comprises of pasta dishes, rabbit stew and starters like marinated anchovies. Open from lunch until the small hours.

KOLONAKI To Kioupi   €€
Platía Kolonakíou 4, 106 73 **Tel** *21036 14033*   **Map** *3 A5*

A classic basement *magereío* that had a light refit around the millennium. *Gída vrastí* (stewed goat), *gouronópoulo* (suckling pig), baked fish, *angináres ala polita* (artichokes with carrots, potatoes and dill), *chórta* and beans, plus palatable bulk wine feature on the menu. Closed Sun; Aug and summer evenings.

KOLONAKI Ouzadiko   €€€
Karneádou 25–29, 106 76 **Tel** *21072 95484*   **Map** *3 5C*

This *ouzerí* claims to offer more varieties of *ouzo* and *tsípouro* to wash down *lakérda* (white fleshed marinated bonito), *hortópitta* and *revythokeftédes* (chickpea croquettes) than anywhere else in town. Always crowded and convivial, it's a popular hangout for politicians and journalists. Closed Sun–Mon; Aug.

KOLONAKI Kiku   €€€€€
Dimokrítou 12, 106 73 **Tel** *21036 47033*   **Map** *3 A5*

An award-winning Japanese eatery, Kiku blends a contemporary minimalist interior with sushi (served at a separate bar), sashimi and tempura. There are also some less common options on offer including *udon* noodles and *yaki soba*. Closed lunch; Sun.

KOLONAKI Orizontes Lykavittou   €€€€€
Lykavittós Hill, 106 75 **Tel** *21072 27065*   **Map** *3 B4*

The views are sky-high and so are the prices (for dishes like sea bass in sauce with tagliatelle) at this spot near the summit of the hill, accessible only by the funicular or a long hike up through the pines. Seating is either in a conservatory or on a terrace.

KOUKAKI Edodi   €€€€€
Veïkoú 80, 117 42 **Tel** *21092 13013*   **Map** *5 C4*

The winner of several national awards, this intimate, eight table restaurant on the upper floor of a Neo-Classical house is tucked away in a quiet part of town. Creations such as duck in cherry sauce or smoked-goose *carpaccio* feature on the menu. Save room for the creative desserts. Good wine list. Closed lunch; Sun and summer.

MAKRYGIANNI Manimani   €€€
Falírou 10, 117 42 **Tel** *21092 18180*   **Map** *6 D3*

Discretely occupying the top storey of a 1930s house, this outfit takes its name from the Máni peninsula, but the food is in fact pan-Greek-mainland: meat, salads, *mezédes*, rare cheeses and a few desserts. Willing staff, a decent wine list and a dearth of nearby eateries mean mandatory bookings. Open Tue–Sat dinner, Sun lunch; closed Mon.

MONASTIRAKI Thanassis   €
Mitropóleos 69, 105 55 **Tel** *21032 44705*   **Map** *6 D1*

Perennial candidate for best purveyor of *souvláki* and *yíros* in town, Thanassis is always packed with Athenians queuing for a take-away or waiting for a table (you can't book ahead). It's frenetic and there's pressure to give up your seat quickly, but for a quick bite you can't beat it. The side dish of peppers is delicious.

MONASTIRAKI Café Avissynia   €€€
Kynéttou 7, off Plateía Avissynías, 105 55 **Tel** *21032 17047*   **Map** *5 C1*

Tables indoors and out are always packed at weekend lunchtimes and Friday evenings when entertainment is provided by an accordionist and singer. The food – Macedonian staples, mussel *pilaf*, baked feta – is rich and the clientele verging on the bohemian. Closed Sun dinner, Mon; summer.

MONASTIRAKI To Kouti

Adrianou 23, 105 55 **Tel** *21032 13229*   **Map** *5 C1*

On a pedestrian street skirting the ancient Agora and offering fine Acropolis views, this long-standing eatery attracts a young, arty crowd. The menu features colourful salads, pasta and inspired meat and fish dishes. A great spot for lunch while sightseeing.

NEAPOLI I Lefka

Mavromicháli 121, 114 72 **Tel** *21036 14038*   **Map** *3 B2*

Last of this district's old-style tavernas, Lefka has winter seating indoors under the retsina barrels and a summer courtyard with scuffed tables. Try the *mavromátika* (black-eyed peas), beef stew, *koukiá* (broad beans) or the baked quince dessert. Closed lunch; Sun and part of Aug.

NEAPOLI Pinaleon

Mavromicháli 152, 114 72 **Tel** *21064 40945*   **Map** *3 B2*

This well-loved winter taverna, named after the highest mountain on Chíos (from where the owner hails), has a cult following for its rich *mezédes*, meaty mains and own-made wine. It's noisy, with closely packed tables and *rebétika* music in the background. Book ahead. Closed Jun–Sep.

OMONOIA Obi

Plateia Agion Theodoron 4 & Skouleniou 2, 105 59 **Tel** *21033 14330*   **Map** *2 E5*

An informal café-restaurant in a Neo-Classical building close to Plateia Klafthmonos, just off the busy thoroughfare of Stadiou. Local business people come here for a light lunch of reasonably priced, regional Greek specialities. Closed Sun.

OMONOIA Athinaïkon

Themistokléous 2, 106 78 **Tel** *21038 38485*   **Map** *2 E3*

This busy *ouzeri* was established in 1932 but moved here in the early 1990s. It is renowned for its good service, marble tables and fresh seafood *mezédes* like mussels *saganáki*, paella and fried *gávros* (anchovy), though meat platters also appear on the menu. Decorated in wood trim, old photos and black-and-white-tiled floors. Closed Sun; Aug.

OMONOIA Bacaro

Sofokleous 1 and Aristeidou, 105 59 **Tel** *21032 11882*   **Map** *2 E4*

This smart bar-restaurant is located inside a peaceful courtyard adorned with potted olive trees. The menu features creative Mediterranean cuisine and the complex also includes an art gallery and a delicatessen stocking quality Greek products. Closed Sun dinner.

OMONOIA Ideal

Panepistimíou 46, 106 78 **Tel** *21033 03000*   **Map** *2 E3*

A city centre institution since 1922, serving international cuisine (*schnitzel* and chops) along with more exciting, and more Hellenic dishes of the day such as milk-fed veal with aubergine (eggplant) and stuffed courgettes (zucchini). Locals love both the consistent food quality and the Art Nouveau interior. Closed Sun.

OMONOIA Neon

Plateía Omonoías 1, 104 31 **Tel** *21052 36409*   **Map** *2 E3*

The menu at this self-service restaurant includes a salad bar, fresh pasta, grills and typical oven dishes; there are also good omelettes and pastries for breakfast. The decor is slightly florid Neo-Classical, lovingly refurbished after a fire in the 1990s. A less atmospheric branch with much the same fare is on Mitrópoleos, just off Syntagma.

OMONOIA Alexandreia

Metsóvou 13, corner Rethymnou, 106 82 **Tel** *21082 10004*   **Map** *2 E1*

Middle Eastern fare with Egyptian influences, as the name suggests: *koupepia* meat rissoles, *baba ghanouj* dip, *felafel* and sweets like *Om Ali* feature on the menu. Tables are either in the tiled, warmly lit interior or on a patio with potted palms and overhead fans. Booking advised at weekends. Closed lunch; Sun and Aug.

PANGRATI O Kostas

Ekális 7, 116 36 **Tel** *21070 11101*   **Map** *7 B4*

This endearing little *koutoúki* (neighbourhood local) has been in business for decades. It moved to this converted 1920s house in 2001 and preserved its original small menu featuring meatballs, sardines and bean soup, the same popular prices and the same loyal clientele. There are only 30 seats, so book ahead. Closed Sun; Aug.

PANGRATI O Vyrinis

Archimidous 11 & Arátou, 116 36 **Tel** *21070 12153*   **Map** *7 B3*

A much-loved neighbourhood taverna, now being managed by the grandsons of the founder. They've spruced up the interior, but left alone the ornamental wine barrels and the good-value fare, which includes salads, *mezédes* and creative main dishes. Popular garden in summer. Closed Sun; Aug.

PANGRATI O Karavitis

Arktínou 33 & Pafsaniou 4, 116 36 **Tel** *21072 15155*   **Map** *7 B2*

One of the last surviving 1930s tavernas, where the menu is based on baked casseroles, a few *mezédes* and grills, washed down with bulk wine, though the barrels that occupy an entire wall are now only decorative. Try one of the traditional desserts like quince or *helva*. There is outdoor seating in a lovely garden across the street. Closed lunch.

Key to Price Guide *see p284* **Key to Symbols** *see back cover flap*

PANGRATI The Sushi Bar
€€€

Plateía Varnáva, corner Stílponos, 116 36 **Tel** *21075 24354*   **Map** *7 B4*

Part of a small Athens-based chain, this outlet has a wooden-floor and high-ceiling dining area with a few tables, though they're equally geared up for take-away orders. All the sushi standards are on offer, alongside a few tempura snacks as well. Open dinner; Sat–Sun lunch.

PANGRATI Spondi
€€€€€

Pyrronos 5, 116 36 **Tel** *21075 20658*   **Map** *7 B4*

Under the command of a French chef, Michelin-starred Spondi is among the best special occasion Athens eateries. Housed in a Neo-Classical building with a stone courtyard, it offers rich cuisine that combines Continental and Pacific influences, such as herb- or truffle-flavoured duck, followed by decadent desserts. Closed lunch; Aug.

PEDION ÁREOS St'Astra
€€€€

Leofóros Alexándras 10, 106 82 **Tel** *21088 94500*   **Map** *2 F1*

This designer-furnished restaurant on the top floor of the Park Hotel enjoys enviable views of the Acropolis and Lykavitós Hill through its ample windows. The cuisine is slightly overpriced but includes such delights as duck with ginger and redcurrant sauce and terrine of *foie gras.* Closed lunch; Sun.

PLAKA O Damigos (Ta Bakalarakia)
€

Kydathinaion 41, 105 58 **Tel** *21032 25084*   **Map** *6 E2*

The last surviving basement joint in the area, O Damigos has decor that seemingly hasn't changed since the place was founded in 1865. The barrels here actually contain good *retsina,* and the cod with garlic sauce *(bakalarákia)* is the big attraction. Closed lunch; Sun and summer.

PLAKA O Kouklis (Scholarchio)
€

Tripódon 14, 105 57 **Tel** *21032 47605*   **Map** *6 E2*

Founded in 1935, this *ouzeri-mezedopoleio* with its ever-popuar terrace has managed to maintain low prices without sacrificing quality. The waiter brings 18 different platters – including flaming sausages – to choose from on the *diskos* (giant tray); wash it all down with the house wine or a carafe of *ouzo.*

PLAKA O Platanos
€

Diogénous 4, 105 57 **Tel** *21032 20666*   **Map** *6 D1*

Taking its name from the *plátanos* (plane) tree outside, this 1932-founded taverna emphasises meat-based stews and *laderá* (cooked vegetable dishes) in its repertoire. Their exceptionally good barrelled *retsina* has been profiled in Niko Manesi's *The Greek Wine Guide.* Closed Sun.

PLAKA Eden
€€

Lysiou 12, 105 56 **Tel** *21032 48858*   **Map** *6 E1*

Installed on the ground floor of a Neo-Classical dwelling, the city's only exclusively vegetarian restaurant offers a menu where beans, lentils, spinach, mushrooms and soya-based products predominate, although there are good desserts and herbal teas as well. Portions are on the small side. Closed Tue.

PLAKA Psarras (Palaia Taverna tou Psarra)
€€€

Erechthéos 16, corner Erotokritou, 105 57 **Tel** *21032 18733*   **Map** *6 D2*

In business since 1898, this classic taverna operates out of two restored old premises across from each other on a landscaped square. The standard but well-presented Greek starters are usually more accomplished than the mains (which always include fish). Celebrity patronage over the years means prices are high.

PSYRRI To Diporto
€

Sokrátous 9, 105 52 **Tel** *21032 11463*   **Map** *2 D4*

This archetypal market-traders' taverna, hidden inconspicuously in basement premises under a disused shopfront, serves just a few cooked dishes of the day like *fasoláda* (bean soup) and *revythia* (chick peas), as well as grilled sardines in season, accompanied by *retsina.* Closed Sun; public hols.

PSYRRI Tou Psyrri
€€

Eschylou 12, 105 52 **Tel** *21032 14923*   **Map** *1 C5–C6*

The first to open its doors and still one of the most popular tavernas in Pysrri, Tou Psyrri has two levels of noisy indoor seating and features all the traditional favourites in big portions. The chalkboard menu (in Greek only) is strong on fish and steam trays. Show up early to get a seat as bookings are not accepted.

PSYRRI Zeideron
€€

Taki 10–12, 105 52 **Tel** *21032 15368*   **Map** *1 C5*

Psyrri has firmly established itself as Athens' favourite nighttime playground and Zeideron is a fine place to kick off the evening. Diners feast on modern taverna fare in an old stone building with a light and airy upper-level glass extension. There are also several highly coveted tables outside on the street.

PSYRRI Kouzina
€€€

Sarri 44, 105 54 **Tel** *21032 15534*   **Map** *1 C5*

This bar-restaurant occupies a cosy, stone and wood, double-height interior space during winter, with tables moving up to the roof terrace in summer. The menu features creative Mediterranean cuisine and there's also an adjoining open air cinema from Jun–Sep.

PSYRRI Hytra
Navárchou Apostóli 7, 105 52 **Tel** *21033 16767*　　　　　　　　　　　　**Map** *1 C5*

The nouvelle Greek cuisine at this eatery matches the minimalist decor. Mains like *synagrída* fish with spinach and *mavromátika* (black-eyed peas) are followed by artisanal desserts such as yogurt and coffee mousse. There's also a set, 15 platter *mezedes* menu. Closed lunch; Sun and Jun–Sep.

THISEIO To Steki tou Ilia
Thessaloníkis 7 & Eptachálkou 5, 118 51 **Tel** *21034 22407, 21034 58052*　　　　　**Map** *1 A5*

Both premises put tables out in the street in summer and serve up little else other than the *païdákia* (lamb chops) for which they are famous (though there are also salads and a few dips). Open for dinner (and lunch on weekends); closed Mon (winter) and part of Aug.

THISEIO Filistron
Apostólou Pávlou 23, 118 51 **Tel** *21034 67554*　　　　　　　　　　　　**Map** *5 B1*

Filistron is not really a full-on taverna but more of a light-snack café/bar with *mezédes* platters, a good-quality, full Greek wine list, *tsípouro* (the north-mainland distilled spirit), *ouzo*, coffees and novelty drinks like *vinsanto* from Santorini. The big draw is the summer roof terrace with striking views of the Acropolis. Closed Mon.

THISEIO Stavlos
Iraklidón 10, 118 51 **Tel** *21034 67206*　　　　　　　　　　　　**Map** *5 B1*

Housed in what were royal stables during the 19th century, Stavlos was one of the first cafés to colonise the area in the late 1990s. There is a stone and wood trimmed bar, club, gallery and upscale restaurant. The fare is Greek with Italian influences.

THISEIO Pil Poul
Apostólou Pávlou 51corner Poulopoúlou, 118 51 **Tel** *21034 23665*　　　　　　　**Map** *5 B1*

Diners sit in tastefully decorated rooms at this former Neo-Classical mansion, with roof-terrace seating in summer. The menu offers French and Mediterranean-tinged creative cooking like fillet with truffles or grouper baked in champagne sauce, served by uniformed waiters. Open dinner; closed Mon.

AROUND ATHENS

KESSARIANI Trata O Stelios
Plateía Anagenísseos 7–9, 161 21 **Tel** *21072 91533*　　　　　　　**Road Map** *D4*

One of the best of a handful of seafood restaurants around this central square, Trata combines the virtues of fresh ingredients with efficient service, especially at crowded Sunday lunches. There's fish soup as well as the usual grilled and fried seafood. Closed Aug.

KIFISIA Monippo
Drosíni 12, 145 61 **Tel** *21062 31440*　　　　　　　　　　　**Road Map** *D4*

This genuine *ouzeri* boasts a vast range of recipes from across Greece, Asia Minor and Constantinople, served in a contemporary environment. Examples include *spétzofaï* (sausage and pepper stew), stuffed *psaronéfri* (pork medallions) and cheese turnovers. Live music Friday and Saturday nights, and also Sunday afternoon. Closed Sun dinner.

KIFISIA Beau Brummel
Agiou Dimitríou 9 corner Agíon Theodóron, 145 61 **Tel** *21062 36780*　　　　　**Road Map** *D4*

One of the most renowned restaurants in the northern suburbs, Beau Brummel offers delicious Greek cuisine with a French twist. Most ingredients are sourced from their own organic farm. Sunday brunch features a slightly more affordable buffet and there is an excellent wine list. Closed Sun dinner.

PIRAEUS Achinos
Akti Themistokléous 51, 185 34 **Tel** *21045 26944*　　　　　　　　**Road Map** *D4*

This split-level premises built against a seaside cliff is a *mezedopolio* strong on seafood, offering good value in a somewhat touristy area near the Naval Museum. If you order scaly fish you'll exceed the stated price category but you can fill up perfectly well on less expensive vegetarian and seafood platters.

PIRAEUS Kollias
Stratigoú Plastíra 3, Tamboúria district, 187 56 **Tel** *21046 29620*　　　　**Road Map** *D4*

It's worth the trek to this out of the way seafood specialist hidden behind an apartment block. Owner-chef Tassos Kollias sources shellfish and other seafood delicacies like sea urchins, oysters and barrcuda from across the country for *mezédes* to accompany more usual scaly fish. Closed Sun dinner; two weeks Aug.

PIRAEUS Vasilenas
Aitolikoú 72, 185 45 **Tel** *21046 12457*　　　　　　　　　　**Road Map** *D4*

A well-loved haunt in a less glamorous part of Piraeus, Vasilenas recently underwent a comprehensive refurbishment. Set menus are rarely good value in Greece but this one – consisting of 16 courses – is. It features meat choices in addition to the fish and seafood repertoire. Open dinner; closed Sun, part of Aug.

Key to Price Guide *see p284* **Key to Symbols** *see back cover flap*

PIRAEUS Jimmy and the Fish · €€€€

Aktí Koumoundoúrou 46, Mikrolímano, 185 33 **Tel** *21041 24417* **Road Map** *D4*

Among various waterside establishments at Mikrolímano, Jimmy and the Fish with its Hellenic blue and white decor has the best position, some of the best service and seafood, in a see-and-be-seen environment. Fish, salads, grilled octopus and steamed mussels all feature on the menu. Book ahead at weekends.

PORTO RAFTI Psaropoula-Bibikos · €€€

Léoforos Avlakíou 118, 190 09 **Tel** *22990 71292* **Road Map** *D4*

Ideally placed in this family beach resort for a tasty lunch after touring the ruins at Brauron, the long-running Psaropoula-Bibikos restaurant offers seafood *mezédes* followed by grilled fish or meat plus a few *mageireftá* dishes of the day.

RAFINA Kali Kardia · €€

Kostí Palamá 12, behind town hall, 190 09 **Tel** *22940 23856* **Road Map** *D4*

There are two rival tavernas with the same name in Rafína, both excellent. This, the more central one, excels at *biftékia*, lamb chops and *pansétta* (spare ribs), as well as a few fish dishes like baked *gávros* (fresh anchovy). Open dinner; lunch Fri–Sun.

RAFINA Ioakeim · €€€

Harbourfront, 190 09 **Tel** *22940 23431* **Road Map** *D4*

One of the best – and priciest – of several seafood tavernas around Rafína's scenic harbour, Ioakeim has been around since the 1950s. Try the grilled or fried fish garnished with leaf salads or *kritamo* (rock samphire), and the various bean-based *mezédes*. Closed Tue.

SOUNIO Syrtaki · €

2km (1 mile) north of Poseidon Temple, 195 50 **Tel** *22920 39125* **Road Map** *D4*

One of the closest non-touristy tavernas to the ancient site, this has a traditional menu featuring various *pittes* (turnovers) as *mezédes* and spit-roasted meat and grilled fish for mains. The shaded terrace has sweeping views of the sea.

VARKIZA Island · €€€€

Km 27 on Athens–Soúnio road, 166 72 **Tel** *21096 53563* **Road Map** *D4*

Island is a combination bar/restaurant/club on a clifftop, which attracts a glamorous clientele. The cuisine is modern Mediterranean, along with a tapas bar; booking is vital at weekends (seatings from 9pm on). The club, with dance floor, only gets going after midnight. Open dinner May–Oct.

THE PELOPONNESE

ANCIENT CORINTH Archontikó · €€

Paralia Lechaiou, 200 06 **Tel** *27410 27968* **Road Map** *C4*

Overlooking the coastal road, about 3.5 km (2 miles) west of town, near the Lechaion archaeological site, this taverna offers well-prepared meat dishes and *mezédes*. Specialties include *kokkinistó Archontiko*, a wine-based meat stew with mushrooms, and cockerel *kokkinistó* with pasta. Popular with locals, so book ahead. Open lunch (weekends only).

GIALOVA, NEAR PYLOS Chelonaki · €

Waterfront, 240 01 **Tel** *27230 23080* **Road Map** *B5*

The seafront 'Little Turtle' looks out over the serene waters of the Navaríno Bay, which is particularly beautiful at sunset. Home-made food, fresh fish, and a friendly, laid-back atmosphere makes it popular with unhurried locals and tourists alike. Occasional live music. Rooms are also available.

GYTHEIO Drakoulakou · €

Vasiléos Pávlou 13, 232 00 **Tel** *27330 24086* **Road Map** *C5*

An exception amongst the tourist-orientated tavernas along the waterfront, the Drakoulakou often has a small crowd at the front admiring its arresting display of fish on ice. Good traditional Greek dishes, specializing in tasty fish and seafood.

GYTHEIO Saga · €€

Odós Tzanetáki, opposite Marathonísi, 232 00 **Tel** *27330 23220* **Road Map** *C5*

From ground floor premises under the eponymous French-Greek-owned pension, this restaurant spreads tables across the narrow pavement and along the sea wall opposite. Excellent for fresh fish, with a wide choice in the chiller cabinet – including several types of sea bream – plus fish soup, shrimp *saganáki* with cheese, and charcoal-grilled octopus.

KALAMATA Kríni · €€

Evangelistrias 40, 241 00 **Tel** *27210 24474* **Road Map** *C5*

Set in the up and coming Marina neighbourhood, Kríni is a cosy taverna open most of the year and providing a good selection of fish and seafood, as well as more traditional meat grills and *maghireftá*. Good wine, service and hospitality. Closed Sun.

KORONI Kagkelários
Harbourfront, 240 04 **Tel** *27250 22648*   **Road Map** C5

Situated by a waters' edge in the small harbour of Koroni, this very popular fish taverna and *ouzeri* has fresh seafood delivered directly from the owner's small boat each evening. Specialities include small fish, lobster with pasta, and sea-urchin salad, but its signature dish is plain octopus, cooked to perfection.

KOSMAS Maleatis Apollion
Central plateía, 210 52 **Tel** *27570 31494*   **Road Map** C5

The mountain village of Kósmas, just below a pass through the Párnon range, makes an ideal lunch stop when travelling between Geráki and Náfplio. Of several tavernas on the leafy and beautifully paved square, Maleatis Apollion offers good mountain food such as bean soup and local lamb and goat. Wonderfully cool in summer.

KYPARISSI Tíris
Mitrópoli district, north side of bay, 230 52 **Tel** *27320 55260*   **Road Map** C5

A delightful family run taverna, where several relatives help out in the kitchen from noon until late. The speciality is excellent seafood and fish, but there are also meat grills and a *maghireftá* dish of the day. Friendly service and superb value.

LYGOURIO Leonídas
Village centre, 210 52 **Tel** *27530 22115*   **Road Map** C4

Leonídas offers hearty Greek dishes (grills, stews and *mageireftá*) with a home-cooked flavour, in a rustic taverna and garden. Immensely popular with both the audience and performers at the Epidaurus theatre 4 km (2.5 miles) away. The walls are decorated with photos of famous patrons – actors, presidents and prime ministers. Book ahead.

METHONI Klimatariá
Odós Miaoúli, 240 06 **Tel** *27230 31544*   **Road Map** B5

This family-run establishment is famed for its beautifully prepared and extensive range of *mezédes* and *maghireftá*, featuring both traditional dishes with a twist and exotic dishes, with plenty for vegetarians. There's a small, romantic, flowery courtyard with vine-covered pergolas. Excellent wine. Open dinner; closed Nov–Apr.

MONEMVASIA Matoúla
Inside the Kástro, 230 70 **Tel** *27320 61660*   **Road Map** C5

Opened in 1950, Matoúla is traditional inside, with old photos of Monemvasiá, however most diners gravitate towards the walled garden, which is partly shaded by trees and overlooks the sea and red-tiled roofs of Kástro. Try simple dishes such as local macaroni, *pastítsio* and fresh fish.

MONEMVASIA Skorpiós
South coast road, Géfyra district, 230 70 **Tel** *27320 62090*   **Road Map** C5

South of the bridge linking the mainland with the rock of Monemvasiá is Skorpios, with seating outside and unimpeded views towards the rock. Good *mezédes* like *tzatzíki* and *tyrokaftgrí* (spicy cheese dip) and simple small fish like marinated *gávros* and *atherina* are served. Good wine.

NAFPLIO Ómorfo Taivernáki
Vassílisis Ólgas 16, 211 00 **Tel** *27520 25944*   **Road Map** C4

This taverna on one of old Náfplio's narrower lanes is famous for its *kolokotroneïko* (pork in a wine sauce), *bekri mezé* (pork morsels in red sauce), and *spetsofáï* (sausage and pepper stew), plus grills and seafood. Cheerful decor, reliable quality and speedy service, with seating inside and on the lane. Closed Mon–Fri lunch in summer.

NAFPLIO Ta Fanária
Staïkopoulou 13 corner Soútsou, 211 00 **Tel** *27520 27141*   **Road Map** C4

This long-running restaurant offers outdoor seating under climbing vines; indoor seating is limited and for winter only. Ta Fanária is best for lunch when *maghireftá* such as *moussakás* and *soutzoukákia* emerge fresh from the oven. There's good bulk *retsina* from Mégara to wash it all down.

OLYMPIA Kladaíos
2 km (1 mile) NW of village, 270 65 **Tel** *26240 23322*   **Road Map** B4

On the west bank of the eponymous river, beyond the rail station, this small, unpretentious, rural taverna offers delicious food in relaxed surroundings. Lamb is one of the mainstays. Popular with both visitors to the site and locals. Excellent rosé house wine. Closed Nov–Mar.

PATRA Mýthos
Trión Navárhon 181, corner Ríga Feraíou, 262 22 **Tel** *26103 29984*   **Road Map** C4

Pedestrianised Trión Navárhon, linking the fishing port with Áyios Andréas basilica, is home to numerous tavernas. One of the best and oldest is Mythos, with imaginative lighting and antique furnishings. The proprietress serves up *pittes* (turnovers), salads and pasta dishes. There's a separately managed beer bar on the top floor. Open dinner.

PLAKA LEONIDIOU Bekárou (Michael & Margaret)
harbourfront, 223 00 **Tel** *27570 22379*   **Road Map** C5

Run by the Bekarou clan since 1830, this taverna is named after the current owners. It is an atmospheric, historic seafront taverna in the picturesque centre of the port. Fresh fish is on offer (though squid may be frozen). Try the sweet-tasting local *Tsakonikí* aubergines.

Key to Price Guide *see p284* **Key to Symbols** *see back cover flap*

PYLOS Gregory's €€

Odós Georgíou Krasánou, 240 01 **Tel** *27230 22621* **Road Map** *B5*

An unassuming, old-fashioned taverna hidden away on a quiet back street above the main square of Pylos, serving traditional Greek *magheireftá* – including goat and *kokkinistó* (meat stewed with wine) – plus local pasta, grilled meat and grilled fish. At the back is a pleasant garden, open to diners in the summer.

RIO Téssereis Epochés €

Somerset 64, 265 00 **Tel** *26109 94923* **Road Map** *C4*

The "Four Seasons" taverna is just 10 minutes from Pátra main train station, and offers romantic open-air dining on attractive wooden decking surrounded by colourful flowers. A good choice of *mezédes* is available, alongside some thoughtful interpretations of Mediterranean cuisine. Efficient, friendly service.

SPARTI Elysé €

Konstantínou Palaiológou 113, 231 00 **Tel** *27310 29896* **Road Map** *C5*

This elegant restaurant with pastel-pink decor offers a good range of traditional Greek casseroles and grills, made from sheep, goat and game, and seasoned well. There are also delicious vegetable and fish dishes. Dine outside in the summer.

VYTINA Ta Kókkina Pitharia €€

Town centre, 220 10 **Tel** *27950 22540* **Road Map** *C4*

Situated near the centre of town, this taverna has a cosy, stone-walled interior with an impressive fireplace. A wide range of local specialities include rabbit, hare or venison *stifádo*, roast wild boar in a claypot, *kioulmbási* (lamb with garlic and *graviera* cheese) and *argeítiko* (lamb cooked in the oven for 14 hours). Vegetarians will find plenty to eat, too.

CENTRAL AND WESTERN GREECE

ÁGIOS DIMITRIOS (PELION) Ta Pénte Platánia €

Plateía Xyróvrysi, 370·12 **Tel** *24260 32140* **Road Map** *D3*

Set on a lovely, terraced plaza in this quiet village 2 km (1 mile) above Ágios Ioánnis, this seasonal grillhouse serves up reasonably priced, simply presented chops and vegetarian *mezédes* at tables under the five plane trees for which it is named. Closed Mon–Fri late-May–Jun and Oct–mid-May.

ÁGIOS IOANNIS (PELION) Poseidónas €€

On shore road, 370 12 **Tel** *24260 31222* **Road Map** *D3*

A rarity in a resort such as Ágios Ioánnis, Poseidonas is a year-round fish taverna, the oldest one here, with a guaranteed source of fresh seafood. Fish is plainly prepared and reasonably priced. The speciality is *kakaviá* (fish soup), which should be ordered in advance.

ARACHOVA Panagióta €

Top of village, 320 04 **Tel** *22670 32735* **Road Map** *C3*

This taverna up near Ágios Geórgios church is a good place to sample local specialities in a white-tablecloth environment, away from the commercialization of the main road. Dishes include chicken soup, stewed lamb, and cheese-based recipes. Closed Mon–Fri Jul–Sep.

DIAVA (KALAMPAKA ENVIRONS) Neromylos €

Pigí Goúra, top end of Diáva village, 422 00 **Tel** *24320 25224* **Road Map** *B2*

This village taverna in a former watermill some 4 km (2.4 miles) southwest of Kalampáka is a favourite with local families. The summer terrace seating is attractive. Besides trout, high calibre ingredients include their own meat and *galotyri* as well as vegetarian *mezédhes*. Open dinner, Sun lunch; closed Mon in low season.

ELATI Sta Rizá €

Village centre, 420 32 **Tel** *26530 71550* **Road Map** *B2*

Opened in 2005, Sta Riza has quickly gained a reputation for good local cuisine, with such dishes as *zygoúri* (lamb stew) and *lachanópita* (green vegetable turnover) coming to the fore. Weather permitting, there's table seating out on the terrace with full views of the Gamíla summit-ridge. Closed Tue.

GALAXIDI Albatross €

Inland, on the road between the two churches, 330 52 **Tel** *22650 42233* **Road Map** *C3*

The cheapest and one of the best tavernas in Galaxídi offers good *mayireftá* from a brief daily menu. This might include octopus, spinach/cheese pie, rabbit stew, pale *taramosaláta* and the house speciality *samári* (pancetta in savoury sauce). Limited quantities are cooked and reservations are not taken, so get there early.

GAVROS (KARPENISSI REGION) To Spíti tou Psará €

On through road, 360 75 **Tel** *22370 41202* **Road Map** *C3*

The Fisherman's House might seem an odd name for this taverna at the bottom of the valley between Megálo Hório and Mikró Horió, but it receives top marks for its grilled trout, as well as *pittes*, dips, vegetable starters and local bulk wine. Summer seating on the rear terrace overlooks the riverside trees.

IOANNINA Bistro 1900 €€

Neoptolémou 9, near Kástro gate, 452 21 **Tel** *26510 33131* **Road Map** *B2*

Housed in an old Jewish Belle Epoque mansion and serving meals upstairs under an original painted ceiling, this upscale outfit acquits itself well at Italian-Mediterranean dishes such as *psaronéfri* (pork medallions) in plum sauce and risotto. Open dinner Oct–mid-Jun; closed Mon.

IOANNINA Fýsa Roúfa €€

Avéroff 55, 452 21 **Tel** *26510 26262* **Road Map** *B2*

Slightly elevated prices for *magheireftá* such as baked fish, suckling pig and *spetzofáï* are amply justified by the calibre of the cooking, quick service and large portions. Unusually, there's also plenty of desserts at this busy venue. Cosy loft seating for winter and decorated with old photos from Parga, the proprietor's birthplace. Open 24 hours a day.

KALAMPAKA Hoútos €

Town centre, close to City Hall, 422 00 **Tel** *24320 24754* **Road Map** *B2*

Locals know all about this grillhouse, with its superb and reasonable lamb kebab, chops, *biftéki* (rissoles) and *kokorétsi* (offal roulade) made from local lamb and pork. At peak seasons it is wise to book ahead, as the premises are relatively small. Dine on the terrace in summer.

KASTRAKI Parádeisos €

Main through road, below village centre, 422 00 **Tel** *24320 22723* **Road Map** *B2*

Most of Kastráki's dozen or so places to eat are *psistariés* (grillhouses); the best is probably Paradeisos, with fine views from its terrace. Here you can feast on *kebab* (loose chunks, not wrapped in pita), red-bean salad, red peppers and a beer.

KATIGIORGIS Flísvos €€

On the beach, 370 06 **Tel** *24230 71071* **Road Map** *D3*

Both *magheireftá* and famously fresh fish are served at tables on the sand, with only slightly bumped up prices considering the number of excursion boats that call here from Skiáthos. Dishes might be garnished with *ftéri* (fried fern) and *tsitsíravla* (marinated terebinth shoots). Closed Nov–Mar.

KIPOI Stou Miháli €

South edge of village, on through road, 440 10 **Tel** *26530 71630* **Road Map** *B2*

The only full-service taverna for quite some distance around is fortunately excellent, with an emphasis on traditional Zagorian *píttes*, game like wild boar and venison, broad beans with greens and more conventional stews, all washed down with a purplish bulk wine. Seating outdoors in summer, otherwise indoors near a fireplace.

KONITSA To Déndro €

At sharp bend in town access road from main highway, 441 00 **Tel** *26550 23982* **Road Map** *B2*

To Dendro takes its name from the enormous plane tree out the front, nurtured by the burbling fountain. The restaurant is strong on baked goat *(gástra)* or lamb, proprietor Yiannis' famous *féta psití* (baked cheese spiked with hot green chillies) and good bulk wine from Zítsa.

KORONISIA Myrtariá (Paténtas) €€

Shore road, south flank of village, 471 00 **Tel** *26810 24021* **Road Map** *B3*

On the shore of the Amvrakikós Gulf 25 km (15.5 miles) southwest of Árta, sleepy Koronisía, an island joined to the mainland by a long causeway, is a favourite destination of seafood enthusiasts. Myrtaria is the most consistently open and reliable taverna, with fair prices for impeccably prepared sole, mullet and the famous gulf-raised prawns.

LAMIA Ouzou Mélathron €

Aristotélous 3, up steps from Plateía Laoú, 351 00 **Tel** *22310 31502* **Road Map** *C3*

Housed in a building which dates back to 1891, with a stunning interior for winter seating and an alluring summer courtyard, this restaurant serves up rich Middle-Eastern and Macedonian recipes. Many dishes are cheese- or fish-based. Wash these down with Límnos bulk wine and enjoy the complimentary dessert crêpes.

MEGALO PAPIGKO Nikos & Tzoulia Tsoumánis €€

Village centre, 440 10 **Tel** *26530 41984* **Road Map** *B2*

This taverna, known simply by the names of the proprietors, stands out for both its decor and cuisine. The former is understatedly minimalist, while the menu highlights tasty soufflés, lamb platters and regional dishes. The summer terrace has stunning views of the Pyrgi formations of Astráka just across the canyon. Book ahead in peak season.

MESSOLOGGI Stin Agorá (Tou Pánou) €€

Razikótsika 7, 302 00 **Tel** *26310 51580* **Road Map** *B3*

The local speciality of Messológgi is smoked grilled eel, hunted with tridents in the nearby lagoon. Pedestrianised Razikótsika is lined with tavernas specializing in it; Stin Agora is one of the most consistent, with an up-market interior, good presentation and side dishes such as *hórta* and small fish.

MILINA (PELION) Sákis €

South end of waterfront, 370 06 **Tel** *24230 66078* **Road Map** *D3*

Sakis is a consistently good, traditional eatery with reasonable prices. You can assemble a tasty meal of seafood, plus two or three *mezédes* and bulk wine and still have change from a 20-euro note. Try *gávros* (anchovy) or *soupiés* (cuttlefish).

Key to Price Guide *see p284* **Key to Symbols** *see back cover flap*

MONASTIRAKI Iliópoulos

11 km (7 miles) east of Nafpaktos; east end of village, on gulf shore, 330 56 **Tel** *26340 52111*   **Road Map** *C3*

This, the most celebrated of a handful of tavernas in an attractive gulf-side village, has a superb selection of fish, plus a few shellfish appetizers and home-made *pittes*. For a pre- or post-prandial swim, there's a pebble beach just below the outdoor seating terrace. Closed Sun (winter).

NAFPAKTOS Papoúlis

Pedestrian zone, old port, 303 00 **Tel** *26340 21578*   **Road Map** *C3*

This popular, genuine *ouzeri*, near the mosque, offers a good mix of meat and seafood (not over-fried or oily, as is common), local wine and, of course, *ouzo*. There's seating indoors, including some tables with sea views, and outside in the pedestrian zone.

NEO MIKRO HORIO (KARPENISSI REGION) To Horiátiko

Central plateía, 360 75 **Tel** *22370 41257*   **Road Map** *C3*

To Horiátiko is a popular, reliable eatery for grilled meat that draws customers from miles around. Other dishes include *fasolákia* (French beans), sausages, *tzatzíki* and various turnovers. The staff cope well with the crowds, and it is popular for weddings and parties.

NTAMOUHARI Barba Stergios

South side of main bay, 370 12 **Tel** *24260 39207*   **Road Map** *D3*

This establishment doesn't look like much from a distance but it's an excellent source of wild (as opposed to farmed) fish, or more economical grilled meat and *magheireftá*. There are some tables on a terrace overlooking the water, and a few more in the tasteful interior for the cooler months. Good bulk wine is also available.

PARGA Golfo Beach

Behind Gólfo cove, 480 60 **Tel** *26840 32336*   **Road Map** *B3*

Kyria Evangelia is the heart and soul of one of the oldest tavernas in town, with a cult following for her sustaining, home-made *magheireftá*, encompassing all the usual stews, *dolmádes* and dips. Golfo Beach is open from breakfast (for those staying in the rooms upstairs) until 11pm. There is live music some nights.

PARGA Oskar

North waterfront, main harbour, 480 60 **Tel** *26840 31289*   **Road Map** *B3*

This tiny, friendly Italian bistro does a few things well: *plevrótous foúrnou* (baked oyster mushrooms), mountainous salads with prosciutto and sun-dried tomatoes, assorted pizzas and a range of pasta dishes, accompanied by good bulk wine. It is open all year, with takeaway service.

PARGA ENVIRONS: SARAKINIKO BAY Tou Chrístou

Sarakiniko cove, 5 km (3 miles) below Agiá village, 480 60 **Tel** *26840 35207 or 69779 82207*   **Road Map** *B3*

Only a few select vegetable dishes are cooked daily at this beach taverna, but quality is high and seafood (except for squid and octopus) is served fresh. Excellent micro-winery products and an eclectic soundtrack are added bonuses, as is the garden with a swimming pool to keep children entertained. It's advisable to book and pre-order in peak season.

PINAKATES Drosiá (Tou Papa)

Far west edge of village, 370 10 **Tel** *24230 86772*   **Road Map** *C3*

The fare at this popular hangout – including leafy *dolmádes* and *gidha lemonáti* (leMon–sauce goat) – uses local, free-range meat and poultry. Excellent *mezédes* is available (off-menu) to accompany a *karafáki* (vial) of *tsipouro* – or a jug of their deceptively potent red wine.

PORTARIA Kritsá

Central plateía, 370 11 **Tel** *24280 90006*   **Road Map** *C3*

On the ground floor of the eponymous hotel, this restaurant provides similarly high standards, with large portions, professional service, an elegant environment including table linens and specialities such as parsley-purée dip, Skópelos olive biscuit and a hearty rendition of *spetzofáï*, accompanied by excellent local wine.

PREVEZA Amvrósios

Grigoríou tou Pémptou, 481 00   **Road Map** *B3*

In the heart of Préveza's old quarter, on a lane leading east from the Venetian clocktower, is a cluster of small seafood restaurants. Amvrosios is the oldest of them, specializing in grilled fresh sardines and barrel wine – and not much else – at budget prices. Open lunch and dinner most days, but schedules can be erratic.

TRIKALA Palaiá Istoriá

Ypsilántou 3, Manávika district, 421 00 **Tel** *24310 77627*   **Road Map** *C2*

One of the best and more consistently open of the *ouzeri* in this warren of lanes, Palia Istoria displays a light touch and fair prices in dishes such as sardines, grilled portobello mushrooms and hot peppers. The interior decor features photos honouring Tríkala's favourite son, rebétika great Vassilis Tsitsanis.

TRIKALA Mezedokamómata

Ypsilántou 16–18, 421 00 **Tel** *24310 76741*   **Road Map** *C2*

Opened in 1997, Mezedokamómata was the first of many small tavernas and *tsipourádika* (the local variant of an *ouzeri*) to colonise and gentrify the old tradesmen's quarter of Manávika. It's still going strong, though the food – standard fried *ouzeri* fare – can be heavy. There's a vast, bare-brick interior for the cooler months.

VOLOS Haliambálias (Zafíris)

Orféos 8, corner Skyrou, Ágios Nikólaos district, 382 21 **Tel** *24210 20234*   **Road Map** *C3*

This inconspicuous taverna tucked inland on a pedestrianised lane is excellent for *magheireftá*. The vegetarian *tourloú* (ratatouille) and baked *pérka* fish, in particular, are delicious and appear regularly on the menu. Good bulk *retsina* as well. Closed Sun.

ZAGORA (PELION) Pétros Lándis

Plateía Agíou Georgíou, 370 01 **Tel** *24260 22666*   **Road Map** *C3*

Just off the cobbled path leading up from the square, this long-running taverna claims to be open all day every day. Portions of goat in lemon sauce, sausage, grilled meats, *chórta* and various *píttes* may be on the small side, but views over the church and its belfry to the Sporádes islands provide ample compensation.

NORTHERN GREECE

ALEXANDROUPOLI To Nissiótiko

G. Zarífi 1, 681 00 **Tel** *25510 20990*   **Road Map** *E1*

It is worth heading 400 m (quarter of a mile) west of the ferry dock and train station area, with their overpriced tavernas, to this seafood specialist with its nautical decor. Besides the usual grilled, fried and raw scaly fish and shellfish, they serve a dill-flavoured seafood risotto.

KASTORIA Krontíri

Orestiádos 13, Doultsó district, 521 00 **Tel** *24670 28358*   **Road Map** *B2*

This *mezedopoleío* would be popular just for its lakeside setting, with tables at the shoreline (as well as indoors during winter). But what draws crowds is its impeccable cuisine based largely on local recipies – such as pickled-cabbage *dolamádes*, pork and cheese in a clay pot, or veal with plums.

KASTORIA Omónoia

Mitropóleos 47, corner Plateía Omoneías, 521 00 **Tel** *24670 23964*   **Road Map** *B2*

One of the longest established tavernas in town, Omónoia is the place to go for *magheireftá*, which is brought to your table by formal, polite, uniformed staff. In fine weather the outdoor seating, on the multi-level *plateía*, is integral to the experience.

KAVALA To Athánato Neró

Poulidou 33, Panagía district, 653 02 **Tel** *25102 33477*   **Road Map** *D1*

A succession of seafood-strong *ouzerís* on this uphill street behind the Imaret has long been locals' favourite destination. To Athánato Neró is about the most popular, with a delicious dish of mussels *saganáki* (red piquant cheese sauce), other seafood titbits and palatable white wine from nearby Límnos.

KAVALA Pános Zafíra

Plateía Karaóli ke Dimitríou 20, 653 02 **Tel** *25102 27978*   **Road Map** *D1*

Tavernas on this harbourside have a reputation for being touristy and overpriced, but Pános Zafíra provides fresh fish and a wide range of casserole dishes – *pastítsio* (macaroni pie), aubergine (eggplant) recipes, stews – to discerning locals and those waiting for an afternoon or late-night ferry.

KOMOTINI Inopión

Plateía Eirínis 67, 691 00 **Tel** *25310 36082*   **Road Map** *E1*

The chef at this eatery has successfully combined local recipes with international influences, and especially delicious are the meat-based dishes. Inopión is an airy, upstairs restaurant with tasteful, low-key decor. Closed mid-Jul–Aug.

LITOCHORO Gastrodromeío en Olympo

Kentrikí Plateía, 602 00 **Tel** *23520 21300*   **Road Map** *C2*

Most tavernas in Litóchoro, used to a stream of visitors heading quickly through town en route to the mountain, don't make a special effort; Gastrodromeío does, with good renditions of suckling pig and rabbit stew, plus a decent wine list – at a price.

PRESPA REGION, PSARADES VILLAGE Syntrofia

Village centre, 530 77 **Tel** *23850 46107*   **Road Map** *B1*

Syntrofia offers home-made dishes such as *fasoláda* (bean soup) made from the famous Préspa beans, fried fish of a species found only in the lake here, and the proprietor's own wine. If you're especially taken with the place, there are simple rooms to rent upstairs.

THESSALONIKI Aristotélous

Aristotélous 8, 546 23 **Tel** *23102 33195*   **Road Map** *C2*

This is a classic, long-running *ouzeri* with two arcaded salons separated by a summer courtyard, dotted with marble-top tables. The fare is strong on seafood such as *mydopílafo* (rice with mussels), stuffed cuttlefish, and *galéos skordaliá* (small shark with garlic sauce). Closed Sun dinner; mid-Jul–mid-Aug.

Key to Price Guide *see p284* **Key to Symbols** *see back cover flap*

THESSALONIKI I Myrovólos Smýrni
Komninón 32, 546 24 **Tel** *23102 74170*
€€
Road Map *C2*

The most popular of several *ouzerís* near the west entrance of the Modiáno (covered market), I Myrovólos Smýrni serves market stallholders and manual labourers early on, office workers for lunch, and students and young people at night. Try the cheese-stuffed squid, Smyrniot meatballs or scallops, washed down with bulk *tsípouro* or wine.

THESSALONIKI Kamares
Plateía Agíou Georgíou 11 **Tel** *23102 19686*
€€
Road Map *C2*

Located close to the Roman-Byzantine *Rotónda*, this neighbourhood favourite offers salads, attractively priced seafood and a few meat grills, accompanied by white wine from Límnos. In summer Kamares has seating beside the little park.

THESSALONIKI Louloudádika
Komninón 20, 546 24 **Tel** *23102 25624*
€€
Road Map *C2*

The name comes from this *ouzerí's* location in the flower market, opposite the former Jewish women's baths. The decor is smart, with cheerfully painted walls and proper tablecloths and the fare is strong on seafood, includes cuttlefish, fresh scaly fish and humbler items such as bean soup and barrelled wine. Closed Sun.

THESSALONIKI Ta Koumparákia
Egnatía 140, 546 22 **Tel** *23102 71905*
€€
Road Map *C2*

Hiding inconspicuously in a pedestrian zone behind the Byzantine church of the Transfiguration, this little *ouzerí* offers an array of Macedonian-style cuisine, including some spicy dishes and *tursí* (pickled vegetables), as well as the more usual salads, grills and meat dishes. Closed Sun and middle of summer.

THESSALONIKI Tiffany's
Iktínou 3, 546 22 **Tel** *23102 74081 or 23102 74022*
€€
Road Map *C2*

Long-running meat specialist with a loyal local clientele drawn by the consistent quality of its classic menu, which inlcudes such favourites as t-bone steak, veal with okra and aubergine (eggplant) *bourekákia* (turnovers). There are outdoor tables in the pedestrian lane here.

THESSALONIKI To Yedí
Paparéska 13, Áno Póli **Tel** *23102 46495*
€€
Road Map *C2*

At the top of the old town, just below the Yedi Kule citadel, this popular *ouzerí* has a variable menu offering mainland dishes such as cabbage *dolmádes*, Piliot *spetzofáï* and clay-pot casseroles. House *ouzo*, *tsípouro* or *retsina* is the norm, though there is also bottled wine. Spontaneous music sessions on *bouzoúki* and *baglamás*. Open dinner.

THESSALONIKI Tsaroúchas
Olýmbou 78, 546 46 **Tel** *23102 71621*
€€
Road Map *C2*

This is one of the oldest and best of the city's *patsatzídika* (restaurants specializing in tripe-and-trotter soup – the classic Greek hangover cure). There are other choices for the squeamish, as well as Anatolian sweets such as *kazandibí* (upside-down baked pudding). Closed mid-Jul–mid-Aug.

THESSALONIKI Vrotós
Metropolítou Gennadíou 6, off Platía Áthonos, 546 30 **Tel** *23102 23958*
€€
Road Map *C2*

Around the millennium Platía Áthonos became the focus of a restaurant/*ouzerí* boom. Vrotos is one of the best and most popular, with something for everyone: vegetable dishes with or without cheese, meat, seafood, and a good wine list. Narrow indoor premises; reservations recommended in the cooler months. Closed Sun dinner and during mid summer.

THESSALONIKI Archipélagos
Kanári 1, Néa Kríni suburb **Tel** *23104 35800*
€€€
Road Map *C2*

Archipélagos sports a nautical/marine decor complete with life jackets, oars and an aquarium. Professional service delivers scaly fish, mussels and *garídes saganáki* (shrimp in piquant red cheese sauce) to the numerous indoor or (in fine weather) outdoor tables.

THESSALONIKI Ta Nisiá
Proxénou Koromilá 13, 546 23 **Tel** *23210 22447*
€€€
Road Map *C2*

Open since 1981, this upscale restaurant purveys a balanced mix of scaly fish, shellfish and meat recipes. Typical platters include *kakaviá* (fish soup), stewed octopus, roast pork in wine sauce and creative desserts. The wine list is unusually comprehensive. Pleasant interior, with island colours and decor. Closed Sun; Aug.

THESSALONIKI Zythos Dore
Tsirogiánni 7, by White Tower, 546 21 **Tel** *23102 79010*
€€€
Road Map *C2*

More or less opposite the White Tower, Zythos Dore combines retro decor – marble tables, floor tiles, ceiling fans – with contemporary Greek and continental recipes. There are lots of choices for vegetarians (vegetable soup, lentil/bean salad) as well as plenty of meat and game dishes and a wide range of bottled and barrel beer. Book ahead at weekends.

XANTHI Ta Fanarakia
Georgíou Stávrou 14, 671 00 **Tel** *25410 73606*
€€
Road Map *E1*

The student population of the local University of Thrace guarantees a wide choice of *ouzerís* in the old quarter, especially along this pedestrianised street. The menu is written in school copybooks and the stock trade is Turkish-influenced meat platters as well as *pansétta* (pork spare ribs). Occasional improvised music nights in winter.

SHOPPING IN GREECE

Shopping in Greece can be entertaining, particularly when you buy directly from the producer. There is a wide range of shops and boutiques, as well as corner stores and department stores. Markets provide a colourful shopping experience, whether you are looking for olives, sugary sweets or traditional handicrafts. In smaller villages, embroiderers, lace makers and potters can often be seen at work. Leather goods, carpets, rugs and jewellery are also widely available, as are religious icons. Most other goods in Greece have been imported and carry a heavy mark-up. For information on shopping in Athens see pages 114–17.

VAT AND TAX-FREE SHOPPING

Almost always included in the price, FPA (*Fóros Prostitheménis Axías*) – the equivalent of VAT – is about 18 per cent in Greece.

Visitors from outside the EU who stay less than three months may claim this money back on purchases over 120 euros. A "Tax-Free Cheque" form must be completed in the shop, a copy of which is then given to the customs authorities on departure. You may be asked to show your receipt or goods as proof of purchase.

Tax-free shop symbol

OPENING HOURS

Allowing for plenty of exceptions, shops and boutiques are generally open on Monday, Wednesday and Saturday from 9am to 2:30pm, and on Tuesday, Thursday and Friday from 9am to 1:30pm and 5 to 9pm. Department stores remain open Monday to Friday from 9am to 9pm and Saturday from 9am to 6pm. Supermarkets, found in all but the smallest communities, are often family-run and open long hours, typically Monday to Saturday from 8 or 9am to 8 or 9pm. Sunday shopping is possible in most tourist resorts and also in some of the suburban shopping malls in Athens. The corner *períptero* (street kiosk), found in nearly every town, is open from around 7am to 11pm or midnight, selling everything from aspirins to ice cream, as well as bus tickets and phonecards.

MARKETS

Most towns in Greece have their weekly street market (*laïkí agorá*), a colourful selection of fresh fruit and vegetables, herbs, fish, meat and poultry – often juxtaposed with shoes and underwear, fabrics, household items and sundry electronic equipment. In the larger cities, the street markets are in a different area each day, usually opening early and packing up by about 2pm, in time for the siesta. Prices are generally cheaper than in the supermarkets, and a certain amount of bargaining is also acceptable, at least for non-perishables. This guide gives market days in the information under each town entry.

In Athens, there is a famous Sunday-morning flea market that is held around Plateía Monastiríkou and its radiating streets, which should not be missed if you are in the city (*see p87*).

"Brettos" distillery and liquor store, in Athens

FOOD AND DRINK

Culinary delights to look out for in Greece include honey – the best varieties coming from the mountain villages – a wide selection of cured olives, high quality olive oil, and fresh and dried herbs and spices. A great selection of nuts is also available, including pistachios, hazelnuts and sunflower seeds.

The famous Greek feta cheese is widely available, and delicious in a salad or with rustic bread. The sweet breads and biscuits of the *zacharoplasteío* (cake and pastry shop) are another must. Sweetened with honey and syrup, Greek pastries are mouthwateringly good.

Greece is also renowned for several alcoholic drinks, including *ouzo* (an aniseed-flavoured spirit), *retsina* (a resinated wine), brandy and the firewater *tsípouro*.

Souvenir shop window in Párga, central Greece

What to Buy in Greece

Traditional handicrafts, though not particularly cheap, do offer the most genuinely Greek souvenirs. Handicrafts cover a range of items from finely wrought gold reproductions of ancient pendants to rustic pots, wooden spoons and handmade sandals. Some of the country's best ceramics can be found in the markets and shops of Athens' northern suburb, Maroúsi. Brightly coloured embroidery and wall-hangings are produced in many villages throughout Greece, where they are often seen hanging out for

Rugs for sale at Aráchova

sale, along with thick *flokáti* rugs, which are handwoven from sheep or goat's wool. These are made mainly in the Píndos Mountains and can also be found at Aráchova, near Delphi *(see p221)*. In the small, rural communities, crafts are often cottage industries, earning the family a large chunk of its annual income. Here, there is room to engage in some bartering over the price. The *Shopping in Athens* section, on pages 114–17, indicates places within the capital where traditional crafts may be bought.

Gold jewellery *is sold in larger towns or cities. Modern designs are found in jewellers such as Lalaoúnis, and reproductions of ancient designs in museum gift shops.*

Icons *are generally sold in shops and monasteries. They range from very small portraits to substantial pictures. Some of the most beautiful, and expensive, use only age-old traditional techniques and materials.*

Ornate utensils, *such as these wooden spoons, are found in traditional craft shops. As here, they are often hand-carved into the shapes of figures and produced from the rich-textured wood of the native olive tree.*

Kombolóï, *or worry beads, are a traditional sight in Greece; the beads are counted as a way to relax. They are sold in souvenir shops and jewellers.*

Kitchenware *is found in most markets and in specialist shops. This copper coffee pot (mpríki) is used for making Greek coffee.*

Leather goods *are sold throughout Greece. The bags, backpacks and sandals make useful and good-value souvenirs.*

Ornamental ceramics *come in many shapes and finishes. Traditional earthenware, often simple, functional and unglazed, is frequently for sale by the roads on the outskirts of Athens and the larger towns.*

SPECIALIST HOLIDAYS AND OUTDOOR ACTIVITIES

Many organized tours and courses cater for the special interests of visitors to Greece. You can follow in the footsteps of the apostle Paul or take a train ride through history; you can visit ancient archaeological sites with a learned academic as your guide, sample Greek wine, improve your writing skills, draw wild flowers or paint the Greek landscape. Sailing and windsurfing holidays are available, as are walking tours and botanical and birdwatching expeditions. There are also plenty of opportunities to watch sporting events. Many organized holidays include food and accommodation in the price.

White water rafting

A scenic railway journey through the Greek countryside

ARCHAEOLOGICAL TOURS

For those interested in Greece's ancient past, a tour to some of the famous archaeological sites can make a fascinating and memorable holiday. You can choose from an array of destinations and itineraries, all guided by qualified archaeologists. As well as visiting ancient ruins, many tours also take in Venetian fortresses, Byzantine churches and frescoes, museums and monasteries en route to the archaeological sites. **Filoxenia** provide tours with Minoan, Roman and medieval interests, while **Ramblers Holidays**, **ACE Study Tours**, **Andante Travels**, **Travelsphere** and **Martin Randall** all organize tours of Classical sites.

WRITING AND PAINTING

With its vivid landscape and renowned quality of light, Greece is an inspirational destination for artistic endeavour. Courses in creative writing or drawing and painting are available at all levels and are conducted by professional tutors, well established in their craft. **Filoxenia** organize a range of holidays that are centred around painting and art history.

WINE TASTING

The quality of Greek wine has increased enormously in recent years, with some vineyards winning international medals, a prospect that was unlikely a decade ago. A variety of tours of vineyards around Athens are arranged by the wine tour specialists **Arblaster and Clarke**.

RAILWAY HOLIDAYS

The rail network in Greece is not extensive, nor is it used much by visitors, who tend to prefer the country's excellent bus system. It does, however, have one of the greatest railway journeys in Europe, on the narrow-gauge track to the mountain town of Kalávryta (see p168) from Diakoftó. A trip on this railway can be arranged as part of a larger Greek tour through **Great Rail Journeys** in the UK. **Ffestiniog Travel** also arranges tailor-made rail trips around Greece, going east as far as Alexandroúpoli (see p257).

Beautiful spring wildflowers

NATURE TOURS

Much of the Greek countryside is rich in birdlife and noted for its spring flowers. The shorelines are also good for wildlife. Specialist tour operators, such as **Limosa Holidays**, **The Travelling Naturalist**, **Naturetrek** or

An archaeological guided tour

A horse-riding holiday along the azure coast

Sunbird, offer package holidays that guide visitors through the ornithology and botany of northern Greece and the Peloponnese. The **Hellenic Ornithological Society** can also be contacted for advice on birdwatching in Greece.

WALKING AND CYCLING

Greece is a paradise for walkers, particularly in the spring when the countryside is at its greenest and the wild flowers are in bloom. The best locations are in the mountain ranges of the Taÿgetos in the Peloponnese *(see p195)* and the Píndos range in central Greece *(see p206)*, where **Sherpa Expeditions** has both guided and self-guided tours. **Trekking Hellas** arranges walking holidays in these regions as well as tours to the remote mountain areas of Agrafa and Stereá, offering a harsh landscape to explore at the southern end of the Píndos range. **Waymark Holidays** offers a similar service in these and other regions, using its own hiking leaders and tour guides.

Greek Options includes walking holidays in the Mani, based in the resort of Stoúpa *(see p195)* and organized by a local travel agent. The Mani also features in the **Inntravel** programme of walking holidays, as does the Pílio peninsula *(see pp218–20)*.

Travelsphere offers a week's trekking in Chalkidikí *(see p249)*, and walking and cycling trips in and around Athens, using a local company, can be booked through **Hidden Greece**. **Bikegreece** offer coast to coast cycling tours that are suitable for all abilities and can also arrange tailor-made holidays for families.

Downhill skiing on Mount Parnassus

RIDING

The Pílio peninsula *(see pp218–20)*, home to the legendary Centaurs – half-man and half-horse – is an ideal place for a riding holiday. **Ride World Wide** offers two different riding itineraries. One follows a coastal route, while the other takes you into the lushly wooded hills of this unspoiled corner of Greece.

SKIING

There are several ski centres throughout the mainland, including some within easy reach of Athens – the closest being Mount Parnassus, near Delphi *(see p221)*. Depending on snow conditions, the season runs from the start of January to the end of April.

Costs are low compared with other European resorts, though facilities are quite basic. However, the Greek mountain resorts certainly provide an interesting alternative to the all-too-familiar names elsewhere in southern Europe.

For more information on skiing in Greece, contact the **Hellenic Skiing Federation**, or pick up a copy of the EOT's booklet entitled *Mountain Refuges and Ski Centres;* it is free from tourist offices and describes all the major ski centres.

WATERSPORTS

All along Greece's coastline, facilities for watersports are numerous. Visitors will find everything from windsurfing and water-skiing to jet-skiing and parasailing in the larger resorts, and many of the shops and beach huts that rent equipment also offer instruction. Kayaking, white-water rafting and canoeing holidays are organized by **Trekking Hellas**. Canoeing and rafting trips on the Gulf of Corinth near Pátra can also be booked through **Hidden Greece**.

Windsurfing in the Peloponnese

SNORKELLING AND SCUBA DIVING

The amazingly clear waters of the Mediterranean reveal a world of submarine life and ancient archaeological remains. Snorkelling can be enjoyed almost anywhere along the coast, though scuba diving is restricted due to many submerged ancient artifacts. Greece is highly protective of its antiquities and it is forbidden to remove them, or even to photograph them. The law was eased a little in 2006, but is still strict and you must be sure to go with a reputable company.

A list of places where oxygen equipment may be used is available from the Greek Tourist Office (EOT) *(see p306)*. The Athens-based **Aegean Dive Centre** organizes diving trips along the Attica coast, and tuition is available for those with no previous diving experience.

SAILING HOLIDAYS

Sailing holidays can be booked through charter companies either in Greece or abroad. The season runs from April to late October, and itineraries range from a few days to several weeks.

Charters fall into four main categories. Bareboat charter,

Scuba diver exploring the submarine life

without a skipper or crew, is available to anyone with sailing experience (most companies require at least two crew members to have a basic skipper's licence). Crewed charters range from the services of a paid skipper, assistant or cook to fully crewed yachts with every imaginable luxury. Chartering a yacht as part of a flotilla – typically in a group of six to 12 yachts – provides the opportunity of independent sailing with the support of a lead boat contactable by radio. **Sunsail** and **Thomas Cook** offer this kind of holiday, as well as holidays that mix cruiser sailing with shore-based dinghy sailing and windsurfing. Contact the **Hellenic Yachting Federation** for more information.

CRUISES AND BOAT TRIPS

Running from April to October, cruise options range from the luxury of a large liner or handsome tall sailing ship to inexpensive mini-cruises and boat trips. The former can be booked through the big operators such as **Swan Hellenic**, **Sunvil** or **Voyages of Discovery**, while the tall ships belong to **Star Clippers**. Mini-cruises and boat trips can be organized locally and are best booked through **Ghiolman Yachts** or at a

travel agent on the spot. For a listing of cruise companies sailing to Greece, visit the Passenger Shipping Association website (www.discover-cruises.co.uk).

A luxury cruise ship

SPAS

The Greek mainland is not as well served with spas as some of the islands, such as Crete and Santorini, but several of the resort hotels on Chalkidikí *(see p249)* do have excellent facilities. Many tour operators feature them, including **Seasons in Style** in the UK.

UNUSUAL ACTIVITIES

Not everyone wants to do a bungee-jump into the Corinth Canal, but for those who do, it can be arranged. The tour operator **Hidden Greece** specializes in finding places off the beaten track and also offers unusual activities. In addition to the bungee-jump they can book you two actor-guides in character as citizens from 460 BC to take you on a tour around Athens.

A sailboat under power along the Corinth Canal in the Peloponnese *(see p167)*

DIRECTORY

ARCHAEOLOGICAL TOURS

ACE Study Tours
Babraham, Cambridge, CB2 4AP, UK.
Tel 01223 835055.
www.study-tours.org

Andante Travels
The Old Barn, Old Road, Alderbury, Salisbury, SP5 3AR, UK.
Tel 01722 713800.
www.andantetravels.co.uk

Filoxenia
Castle Howard, York, YO60 7JU, UK.
Tel 01653 617755.
www.filoxenia.co.uk

Martin Randall
Voysey House, Barley Mow Passage, London W4 4GF, UK.
Tel 020 8742 3355.
www.martinrandall.com

Ramblers Holidays
Lemsford Mill, Lemsford Village, Welwyn Garden City, Herts, AL8 7TR, UK.
Tel 01707 331133.
www.ramblersholidays.co.uk

Travelsphere
Compass House, Rockingham Road, Market Harborough, Leicestershire, LE16 7QD, UK.
Tel 0800 191418.
www.travelsphere.co.uk

WRITING AND PAINTING

Filoxenia
See Archaeological Tours.

WINE TASTING

Arblaster and Clarke Wine Tours
Farnham Road, West Liss, Hants, GU33 6JQ, UK.
Tel 01730 893344
www.winetours.co.uk

RAILWAY HOLIDAYS

Ffestiniog Travel
Harbour Station, Porthmadog, Gwynedd, LL49 9NF, UK.
Tel 01766 512400.
www.festtravel.co.uk

Great Rail Journeys
Saviour House, 9 St Saviourgate, York, YO1 8NL, UK.
Tel 01904 521900.
www.greatrail.com

NATURE TOURS

Hellenic Ornithological Society
Vasileos Irakleion 24, 10682 Athens.
Tel 210 822 7937.

Limosa Holidays
Suffield House, Northrepps, Norfolk, NR27 0LZ, UK.
Tel 01263 578143.
www.limosaholidays.co.uk

Naturetrek
Cheriton Mill, Cheriton, Alresford, Hants, SO24 0NG, UK.
Tel 01962 733051.
www.naturetrek.co.uk

Sunbird
PO Box 76, Sandy, Bedfordshire, SG19 1DF, UK.
Tel 01767 262522.
www.sunbirdtours.co.uk

The Travelling Naturalist
PO Box 3141, Dorchester, Dorset, DT1 2XD, UK.
Tel 01305 267994.
www.naturalist.co.uk

WALKING AND CYCLING

Bikegreece
145 Kolokotroni Street, 18536 Piraeus.
Tel 210 4282 765.
www.bikegreece.com

Greek Options
26 High Street, Tring, Herts, HP23 5AH, UK.
Tel 0870 241 8668.
www.greekoptions.co.uk

Hidden Greece
10 Upper Square, Old Isleworth, TW7 7BJ, UK.
Tel 020 8758 4707.
www.hidden greece.co.uk

Inntravel
Castle Howard, York, YO60 7JU, UK.
Tel 01653 617906.
www.inntravel.co.uk

Sherpa Expeditions
131a Heston Road, Hounslow, Middlesex, TW5 0RF, UK.
Tel 020 8577 2717.
www.sherpaexpeditions.com

Travelsphere
See Archaelogical Tours.

Trekking Hellas
Filellinou 7, 10557 Athens.
Tel 210 331 0323.
www.trekking.gr

Waymark Holidays
44 Windsor Road, Slough, Berkshire, SL1 2EJ, UK.
Tel 01753 516 477.
www.waymarkholidays.com

RIDING

Ride World Wide
Staddon Farm, North Tawton, Devon, EX20 2BX, UK. *Tel 01837 82544.*
www.rideworldwide.com

SKIING

Hellenic Skiing Federation
Karagiórgi Servías 7, 10563 Athens.
Tel 210 323 4412.

WATERSPORTS

Hidden Greece
See Walking and Cycling.

Trekking Hellas
See Walking and Cycling.

SCUBA AND SNORKELLING

Aegean Dive Centre
Zamanou 53 & Pandhoras, Glyfáda.
Tel 210 894 5409.
www.adc.gr

SAILING HOLIDAYS

Hellenic Yachting Federation
Akti Possidónas 51, Moschato.
Tel 210 940 4825.
www.eio.gr

Sunsail (in UK)
Port House, Port Solent, Portsmouth, PO6 4TH, UK.
Tel 02392 222300.
www.sunsail.com

Sunsail (in USA)
Annapolis Landing Marina, 980 Awald Road, Suite 302 Annapolis, MD 21403, USA.
Tel 888 350 3568.
www.sunsail.com

Thomas Cook (in UK)
Tel 0870 750 5711.
www.thomascook.com

CRUISES AND BOAT TRIPS

Ghiolman Yachts
Filellinon 7, 10557 Athens.
Tel 210 323 0330.

Star Clippers
Crown House, Crown Street, Ipswich, Suffolk, IP1 3HS, UK.
Tel 01473 292029.
www.starclippers.co.uk

Sunvil
Upper Square, Old Isleworth, Middlesex, TW7 7BJ, UK.
Tel 020 8758 4758.
www.sunvil.co.uk

Swan Hellenic Cruises
Richmond House, Perminus Terrace, Southampton, SO14 3PN, UK.
Tel 0845 355 5111.
www.swanhellenic.com

Voyages of Discovery
Lynnem House, 1 Victoria Way, Burgess Hill, West Sussex, RH15 9NF.
Tel 0845 612 9149.
www.voyagesofdiscovery.com

SPAS

Seasons in Style
Lakeside, St David's Park, Nr Chester, CH5 3YE, UK.
Tel 01244 202000.
www.seasonsinstyle.co.uk

UNUSUAL ACTIVITIES

Hidden Greece
See Walking and Cycling.

SURVIVAL
GUIDE

PRACTICAL INFORMATION

Greece's appeal is both cultural and hedonistic. Its physical beauty, hot climate and warm seas, together with the easy-going outlook of its people, are all conducive to a relaxed holiday. It does pay, however, to know something about the nuts and bolts of Greek life to avoid unnecessary frustrations – when to visit, what to bring, how to get around and what to do if

Soldier in ceremonial dress

things go wrong. Greece is no longer the cheap holiday destination it once was, though public transport, vehicle hire, eating out and hotel accommodation are still relatively inexpensive compared with most west European countries. Tourist information is available through the many EOT offices *(see p306)*, which offer plenty of advice on the practical aspects of your stay.

WHEN TO VISIT

High season in Greece – late June to early September – is the hottest *(see p49)* and most expensive time to visit, as well as being very crowded. December to March are the coldest and wettest months everywhere, with reduced public transport, and many hotels and restaurants closed for the winter.

Skiing in Greece is possible from January to April, with around 20 mainland resorts to choose from *(see p298)*.

Spring (late April-May) is one of the loveliest times to visit – the weather is sunny but not yet debilitatingly hot, there are relatively few tourists about, and the countryside is ablaze with brightly coloured wild flowers and fresh, brilliant greenery *(see pp22–3)*.

WHAT TO BRING

Most of life's comforts are available in Greece, although it is advisable to take a good map of the area in which you intend to stay *(see p321)*, an AC adaptor for

your electrical gadgetry *(see p307)*, sunglasses and a sun hat, mosquito repellent, any medical supplies you might need and a high factor (15 and up) suntan lotion.

Apart from swimwear, light clothing is all you need for most of the year, though a sweater or light jacket for the evening is also recommended, and is essential in May and October. During winter and spring, rainwear should be taken, as well as warm clothes. Many religious buildings have dress codes that should always be adhered to *(see p307)*.

ΕΛΕΓΧΟΣ ΔΙΑΒΑΤΗΡΙΩΝ
PASSPORT CONTROL

Greek airport passport control sign

VISA REQUIREMENTS

Visitors from EU countries, the US, Canada, Australia and New Zealand need only a valid passport for entry to Greece (no visa is required), and can stay for a period of up to 90 days. For longer stays a resident's permit must be

obtained from the **Aliens' Bureau** in Athens, or the local police in remoter areas.

Any non-EU citizen planning to work or study in Greece should contact their local Greek consulate a few months in advance about visa requirements and work permits.

CUSTOMS

Visitors entering Greece from within the EU are no longer subject to any customs controls or other formalities. Limits for duty-paid goods have been similarly relaxed in recent years, though anything valuable should be recorded in your passport upon entry if it is to be re-exported. Visitors coming from non-EU countries may be subject to the occasional spot check on arrival in Greece.

However, visitors should be aware that the unauthorized export of antiquities and archaeological artifacts from Greece is treated as a serious offence, with penalties ranging from hefty fines to prison sentences.

Any prescription drugs that are brought into the country should be accompanied by a copy of the prescription for the purposes of the customs authorities *(see pp308–9)*.

On 30 June 1999, the intra-EU Duty and Tax Free Allowances, better known as Duty Free and mainly affecting such luxury items as alcohol, perfumes and tobacco, were abolished. EU residents can now import greater amounts of these goods, as long as they are for personal use.

Visitors on the beach in high summer

◁ **The attractive harbour of Paralía Astros, south of Náfplio**

A family arriving at Athens airport

TRAVELLING WITH CHILDREN

Children are much loved by the Greeks and welcomed just about everywhere. Baby-sitting facilities are provided by most hotels on request, though you should check this before you book in *(see p261)*.

Concessions of up to 50 per cent are offered on most forms of public transport for children aged 10 and under, but in some cases it is 8 and under.

Swimming in the sea is generally safe for kids, but keep a close eye on them as lifeguards are rare in Greece. Also be aware of the hazards of overexposure to the sun and dehydration.

WOMEN TRAVELLERS

Greece is a very safe country and local communities are generally welcoming. Foreign women travelling alone are usually treated with respect, especially if dressed modestly *(see p307)*. However, like elsewhere, hitchhiking alone in Greece carries potential risks and is not advisable.

STUDENT AND YOUTH TRAVELLERS

Within Greece itself, no concessions are offered on ferry, bus or train travel, except to students actually studying in Greece. However, there are plenty of deals to be had getting to Greece, especially during low season. There are scores of agencies for student and youth travel, including **STA Travel**, which has 120 offices worldwide. IYHF (International Youth Hostel Federation) membership cards are rarely asked for in Greek hostels, but to be on the safe side it is worth joining before setting off. Most state-run museums and archaeological sites are free to EU students with a valid International Student Identity Card (ISIC); non-EU students with an ISIC card are usually entitled to a 50 per cent reduction. There are no youth concessions available for these entrance fees, but occasional discounts are possible with a "Go 25" card, which can be obtained from any STA office by travellers who are under 26.

International student identity card

FACILITIES FOR THE DISABLED

There are few facilities in Greece for assisting the disabled, so careful planning is essential – sights that have wheelchair access are indicated at the beginning of each entry in this guide. Organizations such as **Holiday Care Service**, **RADAR** and **Tripscope** are worth contacting for advice. Agencies such as **Accessible Travel and Leisure** organize holidays specifically for disabled travellers.

A sign directing access for wheelchairs at a Greek airport

Holiday Essentials

The EOT's Greek tourism emblem

For a carefree holiday in Greece, it is best to adopt the philosophy *sigá, sigá* (slowly, slowly). Within this principle is the ritual of the afternoon siesta, a practice that should be taken seriously, particularly during the hottest months when it is almost a physiological necessity. Almost everything closes for a few hours after lunch, reopening later in the day when the air cools and Greece comes to life again. The shops reopen their doors, the restaurants start filling up and, at seafront locales, practically everyone partakes in the *vólta*, or evening stroll – a delightful Greek institution.

TOURIST INFORMATION

Tourist information is available in many towns and villages in Greece, either in the form of government-run **EOT** offices (Ellinikós Organismós Tourismoú, or National Tourist Organization of Greece), municipally run tourist offices, the local tourist police *(see p308)*, or privately owned travel agencies. The EOT publishes an array of tourist literature, including maps, brochures and leaflets on transport and accommodation – be aware though that not all of their information is up-to-date and reliable. The addresses and phone numbers of the EOT and municipal tourist offices, as well as the tourist police, are listed throughout this guide.

GREEK TIME

Greece is always 2 hours ahead of Britain (GMT), 1 hour ahead of European countries on Central European Time (such as France), 7 hours ahead of New York, 10 hours ahead of Los Angeles and 8 hours behind Sydney.

As Greece is now part of the EU, it follows the rule that all EU countries must put their clocks forward to summertime, and back again to wintertime, on the same days, in order to avoid any confusion when travelling between countries. This should lessen the chance of missing a ferry or flight due to confusion over the time!

Entry ticket to an archaeological site

OPENING HOURS

Opening hours tend to be vague in Greece, varying from day to day, season to season and place to place. It is therefore advisable to use the times given in this book as rough guidelines only and to check with local information centres for accurate times.

State-run museums and archaeological sites generally open from around 8:30am to 2:45pm (the major ones stay open as late as 8 or 9pm in the summer months).

Mondays and main public holidays *(see p48)* are the usual closing days for most tourist attractions. Locally run and private museums may be closed on additional public holidays and also on local festival days.

A *periptero*, or kiosk, with a wide array of papers and periodicals

Monasteries and convents are open during daylight hours, but will close for a few hours in the afternoon.

Opening times for shops are covered on page 296, pharmacies on page 309, banks on page 310, post offices on page 313 and OTE (telephone) offices on page 312.

Most shops and offices are closed on public holidays and local festival days, with the exception of some shops within tourist resorts.

The dates of major local festivals are included in the Visitors' Checklists in each main town entry in this guide.

ADMISSION CHARGES

Most state-run museums and archaeological sites charge an entrance fee of between 1.5 and 6 euros. Reductions are available, however, ranging from around 25 per cent for EU citizens aged 60 years and over (use your passport as proof of age) to 50 per cent for non-EU students armed with an international student identity card (ISIC) *(see p305)*.

Though most museums and sites are closed on public holidays, the ones that do remain open are free of charge.

EVENTS

The English-language paper *Athens News* has a What's On column, gazetting events all over the city and also those of special interest to children. The tourist office in Amalias Street has a free monthly English-language magazine, *Now in Athens*, which details cultural events and entertainment in Athens, as does the weekly Greek-language *Athinorama (see pp118–21)*.

A list of Greek festivals and cultural events is given on pages 44–8, but it is worth asking your nearest tourist office about what's happening locally. Other forms of entertainment include the outdoor cinema in summer, which is very popular with the Greeks; most films are in English with Greek subtitles. There are also

A sign about dress codes at a monastery in Metéora, central Greece

bars, discos and nightclubs in the resorts, as well as tavernas and *kafeneía* (coffee shops), found in every village and often the centre of social life.

RELIGION

Greece is almost entirely Greek Orthodox. The symbols and rituals of the religion are deeply rooted in Greek culture and are visible everywhere. Saints' days are celebrated throughout Greece *(see p48)*, sometimes on a local scale and sometimes across the entire country.

The largest religious minority are the Muslims of Thrace, though they constitute less than 2 per cent of the country's total population. Places of worship for other religions are mostly situated within Athens and its environs.

ETIQUETTE

Like anywhere else, common courtesy and respect is appreciated in Greece, so try speaking a few words of the language, even if your vocabulary only extends as far as the basics *(see pp348–52)*.

Though formal attire is rarely needed, modest clothing (trousers for men and skirts for women) is *de rigueur* for visits to churches and monasteries. Topless sunbathing is generally tolerated, but nude bathing is officially restricted to a few designated beaches.

In restaurants, the service charge is always included in the bill, but tips are still appreciated – the custom is to

leave between 10 and 15 per cent. Public toilet attendants should also be tipped. Taxi drivers do not expect a tip, but they are not averse to them either; likewise hotel porters and chambermaids.

PHOTOGRAPHY

Photographic film is readily available in Greece, though it is often quite expensive in tourist areas and close to the major sights.

Taking photographs inside churches and monasteries is officially forbidden; within museums photography is usually permitted, but flashes and tripods are often not. In most cases where a stills camera is allowed, a video camera will also be fine, but you may have to pay an extra fee.

A Greek priest

At sites, museums or religious buildings it is best to gain permission before using a camera, as rules do vary.

ELECTRICAL APPLIANCES

Two-pin adaptor, for use with all British appliances when in Greece

Greece, like other European countries, runs on 220 volts/50 Hz AC. Plugs have two round pins, or three

round pins for appliances that need to be earthed. The adaptors required for British electrical appliances are difficult to find in Greece so bring one with you. Similarly, transformers are needed for North American equipment.

CONVERSION CHART

Greece uses the metric system, with two small exceptions: sea distances are expressed in nautical miles and land is measured in *strémmata*, the equivalent of about 0.1 ha (0.25 acre).

Imperial to Metric
1 inch = 2.54 centimetres
1 foot = 30 centimetres
1 mile = 1.6 kilometres
1 ounce = 28 grams
1 pound = 454 grams
1 pint = 0.6 litres
1 gallon = 4.6 litres

Metric to Imperial
1 millimetre = 0.04 inches
1 centimetre = 0.4 inches
1 metre = 3 feet 3 inches
1 kilometre = 0.64 miles
1 gram = 0.04 ounces
1 kilogram = 2.2 pounds
1 litre = 1.8 pints

DIRECTORY

EMBASSIES IN GREECE

Australia
Thon Building, Kiasias Street & Alexandrias Avenue, Ambelokipi, 11523 Athens.
Tel 210 870 4000.

Canada
Gennadíou 4, 11521 Athens.
Tel 210 727 3400.

Republic of Ireland
Vassiléos Konstantínou 7, 10674 Athens.
Tel 210 723 2405.

New Zealand
Kifissias 268, Xalandri.
Tel 210 687 4700.

United Kingdom
Ploutárchou 1, 10675 Athens.
Tel 210 727 2600.

USA
Vasilíssis Sofías 91, 10160 Athens.
Tel 210 721 2951.

Personal Health and Security

Greece is one of the safest European countries to visit, with a time-honoured tradition of honesty that still survives despite the onslaught of mass tourism. But, like travelling anywhere else, it is still advisable to take out a comprehensive travel insurance policy. One place where danger is ever present, however, is on the road. Driving is a volatile matter in Greece, and it now has the highest accident rate in Europe. Considerable caution is recommended, for drivers and pedestrians.

Fire service emblem

too, to read the small print: not all policies, for instance, will cover you for activities of a "dangerous" nature, such as motorcycling and trekking; not all policies will pay for doctors' or hospital fees direct, and only some will cover you for ambulances and emergency flights home. Paying for your flight with a credit card such as Visa or American Express will also provide limited travel insurance, including reimbursement of your air fare if the agent happens to go bankrupt.

PERSONAL SECURITY

The crime rate in Greece is very low compared with other European countries. Nevertheless, a few precautions are worth taking, like keeping cars and hotel rooms locked, watching your handbag in public, and not keeping all your documents together in one place. If you do have anything stolen, contact the police or tourist police.

POLICE

Greece's police are split into three forces: the regular police, the port police and the tourist police. The tourist police are the most useful for holiday-makers, combining normal police duties with tourist advice. Should you suffer a theft, lose your passport or have cause to complain about shops, restaurants, tour guides or taxi drivers, your case should first be made to them. As every tourist police office claims to have at least one English speaker, they can act as interpreters if the case needs to involve the local police. Their offices also offer maps, brochures, and advice on finding accommodation.

LEGAL ASSISTANCE FOR TOURISTS

European consumers' associations together with the European Commission have created a programme, known as **EKPIZO**, to inform tourists of their rights. Its aim is specifically to help holiday-makers who experience problems with hotels, campsites, travel

A policeman giving directions to holiday-makers

agencies and so forth. They will furnish tourists with the relevant information and, if necessary, arrange legal advice from lawyers in English, French or German. Contact the main Athens branch for their local telephone numbers.

MEDICAL TREATMENT AND INSURANCE

Emergency medical care in Greece is free for all EU citizens. The European Health Insurance Card, which is available from the UK Department of Health or from a main post office, covers emergencies only; private medical insurance is needed for all other types of treatment. Be aware, however, that public health facilities are limited in Greece and private clinics are expensive. Visitors are strongly advised to take out a comprehensive travel insurance – available from travel agents, banks and insurance brokers – covering both private medical treatment and loss or theft of personal possessions. Be sure,

HEALTH PRECAUTIONS

It costs little or nothing to take a few sensible precautions when travelling abroad, and certain measures are essential if holidaying in the extreme heat of summer. The most obvious thing to avoid is overexposure to the sun, particularly for the fair skinned: wear a hat and good-quality sunglasses, as well as a high-factor suntan lotion. If you do burn, calamine lotion is soothing. Heat stroke is a real hazard for which medical attention should be sought immediately, while heat exhaustion and dehydration are also serious. Be sure to drink plenty of water, even if you don't feel thirsty, and if in any doubt invest in a packet of electrolyte tablets (a mixture of potassium salts and glucose) available at any pharmacy, to avoid dehydration and replace lost minerals.

Port policeman's uniform   **City policeman's uniform**

An ambulance with the emergency number emblazoned on its side

Fire engine

Police car

Always go prepared with an adequate supply of any medication you may need while away, as well as a copy of the prescription with the generic name of the drug – this is useful not only in case you run out, but also for the purposes of customs when you enter the country. Also be aware that codeine, a painkiller commonly found in headache tablets, is illegal in Greece.

Tap water in Greece is generally safe to drink, but in remote communities it is a good precaution to check with the locals. Bottled spring water is for sale throughout the country, and often has the advantage of being chilled.

However tempting the sea may look, swimming after a meal is not recommended for at least two hours, since stomach cramps out at sea can

Pharmacy sign

be fatal. Underwater hazards to be aware of are weaver fish, jellyfish and sea urchins. The latter are not uncommon and are extremely unpleasant if trodden on. If you do tread on one, the spine will need to be extracted using olive oil and a sterilized needle. Jellyfish stings can be relieved by vinegar, baking soda, or by various remedies sold at Greek pharmacies. Though a rare occurrence, the sand-dwelling weaver fish has a powerful sting, its poison causing extreme pain. The immediate treatment is to immerse the affected area in very hot water to dilute the venom's strength.

No inoculations are required for visitors to Greece, though tetanus and typhoid boosters may be recommended by your doctor.

PHARMACIES

Greek pharmacists are highly qualified and can not only advise on minor ailments, but also dispense medication not usually available over the counter back home. Their premises, *farmakeía*, are identified by a red or green cross on a white background. Pharmacies are open from 8:30am to 2pm, but are usually closed in the afternoon and on Saturday mornings. However, in larger towns there is usually a rota system to maintain a service from 7:30am to 2pm and from 5:30 to 10pm. Details are posted in pharmacy windows, in both Greek and English.

EMERGENCY SERVICES

In case of emergencies the appropriate services to call are listed in the directory below. For accidents or other medical emergencies, a 24-hour ambulance service operates within Athens. Outside Athens, in rural towns and on the islands, it is unlikely that ambulances will be on 24-hour call. If necessary, patients can be transferred from local ESY (Greek National Health Service) hospitals or surgeries to a main ESY hospital in Athens by ambulance or helicopter.

A complete list of ESY hospitals, private hospitals and clinics is available from the tourist police.

DIRECTORY

NATIONWIDE EMERGENCY NUMBERS

Police
Tel 100.

Ambulance
Tel 166.

Fire
Tel 199.

Road assistance
Tel 104.

Coastguard patrol
Tel 108

ATHENS EMERGENCY NUMBERS

Tourist police
Tel 171.

Doctors
Tel 1016 (2pm–7am).

Pharmacies
For information on 24-hour pharmacies:
 1434

Poison treatment centre
Tel 210 779 3777.

EKPIZO BUREAU

Athens branch
Valtetsíou 43–45,
10681 Athens.
Tel 210 330 4444.

Banking and Local Currency

Greece has now converted to the common European currency, the euro, which replaces the former drachma. Changing money from other currencies into euros is straightforward and can be done at banks or post offices. Even in small towns and resorts you can expect to find a car-hire firm or travel agency that will change travellers' cheques and cash, albeit with a sizeable commission. Larger towns and tourist centres all have the usual banking facilities, including a growing number of cash machines (ATMs), although customers should be aware this service may incur a fee.

Visitors changing money at a foreign exchange bureau

BANKING HOURS

All banks are open from 8am to 2pm Monday to Thursday, and from 8am to 1:30pm on Friday. In the larger cities and tourist resorts there is usually at least one bank that reopens its exchange desk for a few hours in the evening and on Saturday mornings during the summer season.

Cash machines, though seldom found outside the major towns and resorts, are in operation 24 hours a day. All banks are closed on public holidays (see p48) and may also be closed on any local festival days.

BANKS AND EXCHANGE FACILITIES

There are banks in all major towns and resorts, as well as exchange facilities at post offices (which tend to charge lower commissions and are found in the more remote areas of Greece), travel agents, hotels, tourist offices and car-hire agencies. Always take your passport with you when cashing travellers' cheques, and check exchange rates and commission charges beforehand, as they vary greatly. In major towns and tourist areas you may find a foreign exchange machine

Foreign exchange machine

for changing money at any time of day or night. These operate in several languages, as do the ATMs.

CARDS, CHEQUES AND EUROCHEQUES

Visa, Mastercard, American Express and Diners Club are the most widely accepted credit cards in Greece. They are the most convenient way to pay for air tickets, international ferry journeys, car hire, some hotels and larger purchases. Cheaper tavernas, shops and hotels as a rule do not accept credit cards.

You can get a cash advance on a foreign credit card at some banks, though the minimum amount is 44 euros, and you will need to take your passport with you as proof of identity. A credit card can be used for drawing local currency at cash machines. At a bank or ATM, a 1.5 per cent processing charge is usually levied for Visa, but none for other cards.

Cirrus and Plus debit card systems operate in Greece. Cash can be obtained using the Cirrus system at National Bank of Greece ATMs and the Plus system at Commercial Bank ATMs.

Travellers' cheques are the safest way to carry large sums of money. They are refundable if lost or stolen, though the process can be time-consuming. American Express and Travelex are the best-known brands of travellers' cheques in Greece. They usually incur two sets of commissions: one when you buy them (1–1.5 per cent) and another when you cash them. Rates for the latter vary considerably, so shop around

before changing your money. Travellers' cheques can be cashed at large post offices (see p313) – an important consideration if you are travelling to a rural area or remote island.

Eurocheques, available only to holders of a European bank account in the form of a chequebook, are honoured at banks and post offices throughout Greece, as well as many hotels, shops and travel agencies. There is no commission charged when cashing Eurocheques, though there is an annual fee of about £8 for holding a European account and a fee of about 2 per cent for each cheque used. All fees are debited directly from the account.

DIRECTORY

To report a lost or stolen credit card call the following numbers collect from Greece:

American Express
Tel 00 44 1273 696933.

Diners Club
Tel 00 44 1252 513500.

MasterCard
Tel 00 800 11887 0303.

Visa
Tel 00 800 11638 0304.
To report lost or stolen travellers' cheques call the following numbers from Greece:

American Express
Tel 0044 1273 571600.

Travelex
Tel 00 800 44 131411.

Visa
Tel 00 800 44 121863.

THE EURO

Introduction of the single European currency, the euro, has taken place in 12 of the 25 member states of the EU. Austria, Belgium, Finland, France, Germany, Greece, Ireland, Italy, Luxembourg, the Netherlands, Portugal and Spain chose to join the new currency; the UK, Denmark and Sweden stayed out, with an option to review their decision. The euro was introduced in the fore-mentioned 12 countries on 1 January, 2002. A transition period saw euros and local currency used simultaneously.

In Greece, euro notes and coins are now the sole legal tender. Prices, especially in restaurants, have risen, though public transport and taxis remain cheaper than in most other European countries.

Bank Notes

Euro bank notes have seven denom-inations. The 5-euro note (grey in colour) is the smallest, followed by the 10-euro note (pink), 20-euro note (blue), 50-euro note (orange), 100-euro note (green), 200-euro note (yellow) and 500-euro note (purple). All notes show the stars of the European Union.

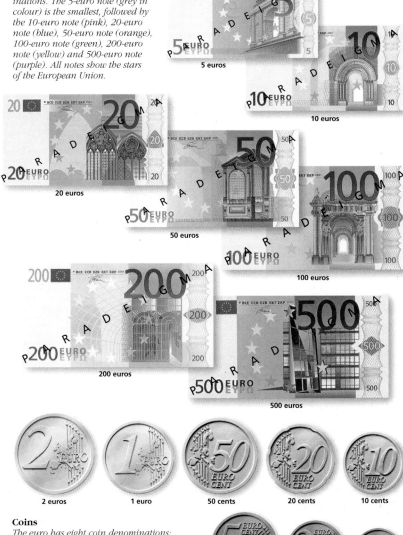

5 euros

10 euros

20 euros

50 euros

100 euros

200 euros

500 euros

2 euros

1 euro

50 cents

20 cents

10 cents

Coins

The euro has eight coin denominations: 2 euros and 1 euro (both silver-and-gold); 50 cents, 20 cents, 10 cents (all gold), 5 cents, 2 cents and 1 cent (all bronze). The reverse of each coin is the same in all Eurozone countries; the obverse is different in each country.

5 cents

2 cents

1 cent

Communications

Post office logo

The Greek national telephone company is the OTE (Organismós Tilepikoinonión Elládos). Tele-communications have improved dramatically in recent years, and now there are direct lines to all major countries. These are often better than local lines, but the rates are among the highest in Europe. Greek post is reasonably reliable and efficient, especially from the larger towns and resorts; faxes are also easy to send and receive. The Greeks are avid newspaper readers, and in addition to a vast array of Greek publications, there are also a few good English-language papers and magazines. Foreign newspapers are also available.

TELEPHONES AND FAXES

Public telephones can be found in hotel foyers and telephone booths, but as more and more people have mobile (cell) phones, the public phone booth is becoming less popular and less widely available. Long-distance calls are best made in a telephone booth using a phonecard – available at any kiosk in a variety of different values. Call charges are variable, but in general local calls are cheap, out-of-town domestic calls are surprisingly expensive, and long-distance calls are extortionate. To prevent unpleasant surprises, you can ring the operator first to find out specific rates, as well as information about peak and cheap times, which vary depending on the country you are phoning.

Ship-to-shore and shore-to-ship calls can be made through INMARSAT; for information on this service contact the marine operator from Greece on 158.

Faxes can be sent from a few city post offices, and some car-hire and travel agencies, though expect to pay a heavy surcharge wherever you go. The easiest way to receive a fax is to become friendly with your nearest car-hire or travel agency – both will usually oblige and keep faxes aside for you.

RADIO AND TV

With three state-owned radio channels and a plethora of local stations, the airwaves are positively jammed in Greece, and reception is not always dependable. There are many Greek music stations to listen to, as well as classical music stations such as ER-3, one of the three state-run channels, which can be heard on 95.6 FM. Daily news summaries are broadcast in English, French and German, and with a shortwave radio you will be able to pick up the BBC World Service in most parts of Greece. Its frequency varies, but in the Greater Athens area it can be heard on 107.1 FM. There is anoth-er 24-hour English-language station, Galaxy, which is on 92 FM.

A public phone

Greek TV is broadcast by two state-run, and several privately run, channels, plus a host of cable and satellite stations from across Europe. Most Greek stations cater to popular taste, with a mix of dubbed foreign soap operas, game shows, sport and films. Fortunately for visitors, foreign language films tend to be subtitled rather than dubbed. Satellite stations CNN and Euronews televise internation-al news in English as it breaks around the clock. Guides that give details of the coming week's television programmes are published in all the English-language papers.

USING A PHONECARD TELEPHONE IN GREECE

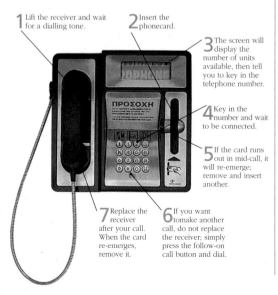

1 Lift the receiver and wait for a dialling tone.

2 Insert the phonecard.

3 The screen will display the number of units available, then tell you to key in the telephone number.

4 Key in the number and wait to be connected.

5 If the card runs out in mid-call, it will re-emerge; remove and insert another.

6 If you want to make another call, do not replace the receiver; simply press the follow-on call button and dial.

7 Replace the receiver after your call. When the card re-emerges, remove it.

A pictorial telephone card

The standard bright yellow post box

NEWSPAPERS AND MAGAZINES

The trusty corner *períptera* (kiosks), bookshops in larger towns and tourist shops in the resorts often sell day-old foreign newspapers and magazines, though the mark-up is substantial. A much cheaper, and also widely available option, is the English-language paper published in Athens, *Athens News*, which is printed weekly and issued on Fridays. The *Odyssey*, a bi-monthly, glossy magazine, is available in most resorts as well as the capital. These two publications are excellent sources of information on local entertainment, festivals and other cultural goings-on, while also providing decent coverage of domestic and international news events. The most popular Greek language newspapers are *Eleftherotypía, Eléftheros Týpos* and *Kathemeriní*.

POST

Greek post offices *(tachydromeía)* are generally open from 7:30am to 2pm Monday to Friday, with some main branches, especially in larger towns or cities, staying open as late as 8pm (main branches occasionally open for a few hours at weekends). All post offices are closed on public holidays *(see p48)*. Those with an "Exchange" sign will change money in addition to the usual services.

Post boxes are usually bright yellow; those with two slots are marked *esoterikó*, meaning domestic, and *exoterikó*, meaning overseas. Bright red post boxes are reserved for express mail, both domestic and overseas. Express is a little more expensive, but cuts delivery time by a few days.

Stamps *(grammatósima)* can be bought over the counter at post offices and also at *períptera*, the latter usually charging a 10 per cent commission. Airmail letters to most European countries take three to six days, and anywhere from five days to a week or more to North America, Australia and New Zealand. If you are sending postcards allow additional time for reaching any destination.

The poste restante system – whereby mail can be sent to, and picked up from, a post office – is widely used in Greece. Mail should be clearly marked "Poste Restante", with the recipient's surname underlined so that it gets filed in the right place. A passport, or some other proof of identity, is needed when collecting the post, which is kept for a maximum of 30 days before being returned to the sender.

If you are sending a parcel from Greece to a non-EU country, do not seal it before going to the post office. The contents will need to be inspected by security before it is sent, and if the package is sealed they will unwrap it.

The main post offices in the centre of Athens are indicated on the Street Finder map *(see pp122–35)* at Plateía Omonoías, Plateía Syntágmatos and on Aiólou.

DIRECTORY

Domestic Calls

Tel 151 (domestic operator).

Tel 131 (directory assistance for local calls anywhere in Greece).

International Calls

Tel 139 (international operator and directory assistance).

International Calls from Greece

Dial 00, the country code (a list is given below), the local area code (minus the initial 0) and then the number itself.

Australia *61*.

Ireland *353*.

New Zealand *64*.

UK *44*.

USA & Canada *1*.

International Calls to Greece from Abroad

Dial the international access code (a list is given below), 30 (country code), the area code then the number itself.

Australia *0011*.

Ireland, UK & New Zealand *00*.

USA & Canada *011*.

Athenians reading newspapers on a clothes line at a street kiosk

TRAVEL INFORMATION

Reliably hot, sunny weather makes Greece an extremely popular destination for holiday-makers, particularly from the colder parts of northern Europe. During high season (May to October) there are countless flights, bringing millions to the shores of Greece. For those with more time, it is also possible to reach Greece by car, rail and coach. Travelling on the Greek mainland is easy enough. There is an extensive bus network reaching even the tiniest communities, with frequent services

Olympic Airlines passenger aeroplane

on all major routes. Greece's rail network is skeletal by comparison and, aside from the intercity expresses, service is much slower. Travelling around by car offers the most flexibility, allowing the visitor to dictate the pace, and to reach places that are not accessible by public transport. However, road conditions are variable, and in remoter parts can be rough, pot-holed and dangerous (see p322). Some of the larger centres and popular tourist destinations can also be visited by plane from Athens and Thessaloníki.

GETTING TO GREECE BY AIR

The main airlines operating direct scheduled flights from London to Athens and Thessaloníki are **Olympic Airlines** (the Greek national airline) and **British Airways**. Athens now has a new airport, Elefthérios Venizélos, which handles all international and domestic flights. The old airport (Hellinikon) is no longer used.

From Europe, there are around 20 international airports in Greece that can be reached directly. On the mainland, only Athens and Thessaloníki handle scheduled flights. The other mainland international airports – Préveza, Kalamáta and Kavála – can be reached directly only by charter flights. From outside Europe, all

Travellers with airport shopping

scheduled flights to Greece arrive in Athens, although only a few airlines offer direct flights – most will require changing planes, and often airlines, at a connecting European city. There are direct flights daily from New York operated by Olympic and **Delta**.

From Australia, Olympic Airways operates flights out of Sydney, Brisbane and Melbourne. These generally necessitate a stop-off in Southeast Asia or Europe, but there are two direct flights a week from Australia, which leave from Melbourne and Sydney. Flights from New Zealand are also via Melbourne or Sydney. Other carriers with services from Australasian cities to Athens include **Singapore Airlines** and **KLM**.

Athens' new international airport

Check-in desks at Athens' new Elefthérios Venizélos Airport

CHARTERS AND PACKAGE DEALS

Charter flights to Greece are nearly all from within Europe, and mostly operate between May and October. Tickets are sold by travel agencies either as part of an all-inclusive package holiday or as a flight-only deal.

Although they tend to be the cheapest flights available, charters do carry certain restrictions: departure dates cannot be changed once booked and there are usually minimum and maximum limits to one's stay (typically between three days and a month). And if you plan to visit Turkey from Greece, bear in mind that charter passengers can only do so for a day trip; staying any longer will forfeit the return ticket for your flight home from Greece.

Booking agency in Athens

FLIGHT TIMES

Flying to Athens from London or Amsterdam takes about 3.5 hours; the journey time from Paris and Berlin is around 3 hours – the trip from Berlin being a little quicker. From Madrid it takes just over 4 hours and from Rome a little under 2 hours. There are direct flights to Athens from New York, which take 10 hours, although a non-direct flight can take more than 12. From Los Angeles the flight's duration is from 17 to 19 hours, depending on the European connection. From Sydney, via Bangkok, it is a 19-hour flight.

AIR FARES

Fares to Greece are generally at their highest from June to September, but how much you pay will depend more on the type of ticket you decide to purchase. Charters are usually the cheapest option during peak season, though discounted scheduled flights are also common and worth considering for longer visits or during the low season, when there are few charters available. Reasonable savings can also be made by booking an APEX (Advance Purchase Excursion) ticket well in advance but, like charters, these are subject to minimum and maximum limits to one's stay and other

restrictions. Budget travellers can often pick up bargains through agents advertising in the national press, and cheap last-minute deals are also advertised on Teletext and Ceefax in the UK. Whoever you book through, be sure that the company is a fully bonded and licensed member of ABTA (the Association of British Travel Agents) or an equivalent authority – this will ensure that you can get home should the company go bankrupt during your stay; it also should ensure that you receive compensation. Note that domestic flights in Greece are subject to an airport tax *(see p316)*.

ATHENS' AIRPORT

Greece's largest and most prestigious infrastructure development project for the millennium opened to air traffic in 2001. Located at Spata, 27 km (17 miles) north-east of the city centre, Athens' airport now handles all the city's passenger and cargo flights. It has two runways, designed for simultaneous, round-the-clock operation, and a Main Terminal Building for all arrivals and departures. Arrivals are located on the ground floor (level 1) and departures on the first floor (level 2). The smaller Satellite Building is accessed along an underground corridor with moving walkways. The airport has been designed to allow for a 45-minute connection time between two scheduled flights.

Departure gate symbol

The airport's modern business and service facilities include a shopping mall, restaurants and cafés in the Main Terminal Building and a four-star hotel in the airport complex. Car-rental firms, banks, bureaux de change and travel agencies are in the arrivals area.

TRANSPORT FROM ATHENS AIRPORT

A six-lane highway links the airport to the Athens City Ring Road, while metro line 3

Light, space and accessibility are features of Athens' airport

now runs from Sýntagma to the airport. From the airport, the E95 bus runs to and from Plateía Syntágmatos in the city centre every 15 minutes with a journey time of about one hour. Bus E96 runs to and from Piraeus every 20 minutes, taking about 100 minutes. Tickets for both journeys cost 2.90 euros. These tickets are in effect one-day travel cards and can also be used to travel around the city *(see p327)*. A taxi-ride into town costs 25–30 euros.

One of the smaller planes in Olympic's fleet, for short-haul flights

Athens' new airport, designed in the blue and white national colours

FLIGHT CONNECTIONS IN GREECE

As well as having the largest number of international flights in Greece, Athens also has the most connecting air services to other parts of the country. Both international and domestic flights now arrive at and depart from the main terminal at the city's Elefthérios Venizélos airport. Thessaloníki also handles scheduled flights, but only from within Europe. Greece's other international airports are served by charters only, mostly from the UK, Germany, the Netherlands and Scandinavia.

DOMESTIC FLIGHTS

Greece's domestic airline network is extensive. **Olympic Airlines** operate most internal flights, though there are also a number of private companies, such as **Aegean Airlines**, providing services between Athens and the major island destinations. Fares for domestic flights are at least double the equivalent bus journey or deck-class ferry trip. Tickets and timetables for Olympic flights are available from any Olympic Airlines office in Greece or abroad, as well as from most major travel agencies. Reservations are essential in peak season.

Olympic Airlines operates direct flights from Athens to eight mainland towns, including Thessaloníki, Ioánnina and Alexandroúpoli, and to over two dozen islands. A number of inter-island services operate during the summer, and about a dozen of these fly year round (*see p315*).

A small airport departure tax is charged on domestic flights of between 62 and 466 air miles. For "international" flights (that is, those over 466 air miles) the tax is doubled.

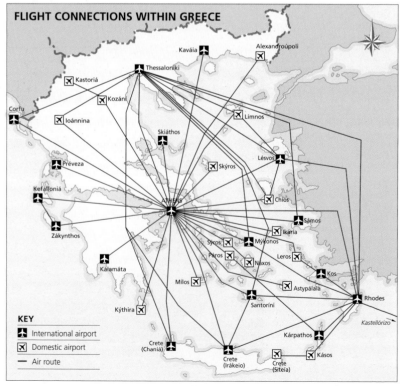

FLIGHT CONNECTIONS WITHIN GREECE

Kaváia
Alexandroúpoli
Thessaloníki
Kastoriá
Kozáni
Corfu
Ioánnina
Limnos
Skiáthos
Préveza
Skýros
Lésvos
Kefalloniá
Chíos
ATHENS
Sámos
Zákynthos
Ikaría
Sýros
Mýkonos
Páros
Leros
Naxos
Kos
Kalamáta
Astypálaia
Milos
Rhodes
Santoríni
Kýthira
Kastellórizo
Kárpathos
Crete (Chaniá)
Crete (Irákeio)
Crete (Siteía)
Kásos

KEY
✈ International airport
☒ Domestic airport
— Air route

ISLAND	DISTANCE	FLYING TIME	ISLAND	DISTANCE	FLYING TIME
Corfu	381 km (237 miles)	40 minutes	Crete (Chaniá)	318 km (198 miles)	45 minutes
Rhodes	426 km (265 miles)	45 minutes	Santoríni	228 km (142 miles)	40 minutes
Skýros	128 km (80 miles)	40 minutes	Kos	324 km (201 miles)	45 minutes
Skiáthos	135 km (84 miles)	30 minutes	Mtkonos	153 km (95 miles)	30 minutes
Límnos	252 km (157 miles)	45 minutes	Páros	157 km (98 miles)	35 minutes

DIRECTORY

ATHENS AIRPORT

Elefthérios Venizélos – Athens International Airport
5th km Spata-Loutsa Ave.,
10904 Spata.
Tel 210 353 0000.
Fax 210 369 8883.
www.aia.gr

OLYMPIC AIRLINES

Arrivals and Departures
Tel 210 353 0000.
🆔 *1440.*

Athens Office
Syngroú 96,
11741 Athens.
Tel 210 926 9111.

Thessaloníki Office
Kountouriótou 3,
Thessaloníki.
Tel 2310 368 311.
www.olympic-airlines.com

OTHER AIRLINES

Aegean Airlines
Viltanoti 31,
14561 Athens.
Tel 801 112 0000.
www.aegeanair.com

Air Canada
Syngroú 5,
11743 Athens.
Tel 210 900 6081.
www.aircanada.ca

Air France
Leof. Vouliagménis 18,
16674 Athens.
Tel 210 960 1100.
www.airfrance.com

British Airways
Themistokleous 1,
16674 Athens.
Tel 801 115 6000.
(Phone for details of Qantas Airline services).
www.british-airways.com

Delta Airlines
Athens Airport.
Tel 00800 4412 9506.
www.delta.com

Easyjet
Tel 210 353 0300.
www.easyjet.com

KLM
Vouliagménis 41,
16675 Athens.
Tel 210 911 0000.
www.klm.com

Singapore Airlines
Xenofóntos 9,
10557 Athens.
Tel 210 372 8000.
www.singaporeair.com

United Airlines
Syngroú 5,
11743 Athens.
Tel 210 924 2645.
www.ual.com
(reservations)

TRAVEL AGENCIES IN ATHENS

American Express Travel Services
Mesogion 318,
Ag. Paraskevi,
11527 Athens.
Tel 210 324 4975.

Blue Star Ferries
Amalias 30, 10558
Athens.
Tel 210 891 9800.

Himalaya Student Travel
Filellinon 4,
10225 Athens.
Tel 210 322 5159.
www.himalayatravel.gr

Oxygen Travel
Eslin 4,
Athens.
Tel 210 641 0881.
www.oxygentravel.gr

Superfast Ferries
Amalias 30, 10558
Athens.
Tel 210 891 9130.

OLYMPIC AIRLINES OFFICES ABROAD

Australia
37–49 Pitt Street,
Suite 303,
Level 3,
Underwood House,
Royal Exchange,
Sydney,
NSW 2001.
Tel (02) 9251 1047.

Canada
80 Bloor Street,
Suite 502,
Toronto,
Ontario
M5S F2V1.
Tel (416) 964 2720.

UK
11 Conduit Street,
London
W1R OLP.
Tel (020) 7629 9891.
Tel 0870 606 0460
(reservations).

USA
Satellite Airlines Terminal,
125 Park Avenue,
New York, NY 10017.
Tel (718) 269–2200.

Travelling by Train

Greece's rail network is limited to the mainland, and the system is fairly skeletal by European standards. With the exception of intercity express trains, service tends to be slow. In compensation, non-express tickets are very inexpensive (much less than coaches in fact) and some lines are pleasurable in themselves, travelling as they do through rugged and beautiful countryside. Fast and efficient intercity trains operate on some of the major lines, though tickets for these trains are more expensive. An overnight sleeper service is also available on the Athens–Thessaloníki and Thessaloníki–Alexandroúpoli routes.

Greek railway's OSE logo

continues to Budapest, via Belgrade; the line via Alexandroúpoli splits, going to Sofia and Istanbul; and the line to Flórina continues to Skopje. Intercity express trains run from Athens to Thessaloníki, Alexandroúpoli, Vólos and Kozáni; and from Pireaus to Pátra, Kyparissía and Thessaloníki. From Thessaloníki express trains run to Kozáni, Alexandroúpoli and Vólos.

TRAIN TICKETS

Train tickets can be bought at any OSE office or railway station, plus some authorized travel agencies. It is worth getting your ticket – and reserving a seat at no extra charge – several days in advance, especially in summer. A 50 per cent surcharge is levied for tickets issued on the train.

There are three basic types of ticket: first class, second class and intercity express. The first two are at least half the price of the equivalent coach journey, though service tends to be slower; tickets for intercity express trains are more costly but worth it for the time they save. A 20 per cent reduction is offered on all return journeys, and a 30 per cent discount for groups of six or more. In addition, a Greek Rail Pass is available which allows the user 3 or 5 days of unlimited rail travel in one month on first class trains, anywhere in Greece. The only exclusion with this pass is travel on the intercity express trains, which is not included in

First- and second-class carriages of a non-express train

TRAVELLING TO GREECE BY TRAIN

Travelling to Greece by train is expensive, but may be useful if you wish to make stopovers en route. From London to Athens, the main route takes around three and a half days. The journey is through France, Switzerland and Italy, then by ferry from the Adriatic ports of Ancona, Bari or Brindisi, via the Greek island of Corfu, to the port of Pátra, and finally on to Athens.

The other route is through the region of the former Yugoslavia, and does not necessitate a ferry crossing. The train travels overland via Budapest in Hungary, on to Belgrade and Skopje to arrive in Greece at Thessaloníki.

TRAVELLING AROUND GREECE BY TRAIN

Greece's rail network is run by the state-owned **OSE** (Organismós Sidirodrómon Elládos), and Athens forms the hub of the system. A northbound line from Laríssis station links Athens and Thessaloníki, with branch lines to Chalkída (Evvoia); Vólos; Kardítsa,

Tríkala and Kalampáka; and Edessa and Kozáni. Trains to the Peloponnese depart from either Athens' Anargyroi or Laríssis station (Peloponnísou station is currently closed) on the Proastiakos network to Corinth, and from Corinth to further destinations with Hellenic Railways. Some routes are extremely picturesque, two of the best being the rack-and-pinion line between Diakoftó and Kalávryta in the Peloponnese *(see p168)*, and the elevated section of line between Leivadiá and Lamía in central Greece.

From Thessaloníki there are three lines. The Polýkastro line

Athens' Lárissis station, for trains to northern Greece

Train station ticket window

the fixed price. InterRail and Eurail passes are both honoured in Greece, though supplements are payable on some lines. The passes also allow reductions on some ferries between Italy and Greece.

TRAIN STATIONS IN ATHENS

Athens has two main stations, virtually next door to each other, about a 15-minute walk northwest of Plateía Omonoías. Laríssis station, on Deligiánni, serves northern Greece (Thessaloníki, Vólos and Lárisa), the Balkans, Turkey and western Europe. Additionally, tickets for OSE coaches abroad are sold here, and there are baggage storage facilities. Peloponnísou station is currently closed; trains for the Peloponnese, including Pátra which is the main port for ferries to Italy, now depart from the small Anargyroi station or Laríssis station. Laríssis station is served by the metro, and by trolleybus No. 1 from Plateía Syntágmatos. Alternatively, taxis are abundant and inexpensive compared to other European cities.

The distinctive front end of an intercity express train

GREEK RAIL NETWORK

Sofia
Kastaniés
Istánbul
Sofia
Belgrade
Skopje
Sidirókastro
Sérres
Xánthi
Dráma
Komotiní
Féres
Polýkastro
Kilkís
Alexandroúpoli
Flórina
Amýntaio
Edessa
Véroia
Thessaloníki
Kozáni
Kateríni
Litóchoro
Kalampáka
Lárisa
Trikala
Kardítsa
Vólos
Stilída
Lamía
Leivadiá
Chalkída
Algio
Pátra
Diakoftó
Thebes
Kyllíni
Kalávryta
Xylókastro
ATHENS
Corinth
Piraeus
Spata
Olympía
Argos
Pýrgos
Trípoli
Náfplio
Kyparissía
Megalópoli
Messini
Kalamáta

KEY

— Principal rail routes

0 kilometres   200
0 miles   100

Travelling by Road

Road sign to port

Travelling around Greece by car gives you the flexibility to explore at your own pace. There are express highways between Athens, Thessaloníki, Vólos and Pátra, which are very fast, though tolls are charged for their use. The maps in this guide categorize the roads into four groups, from the express routes in blue to non-asphalt roads in yellow *(see back flap)*. The road system is continually being upgraded, and most routes are now surfaced.

An express recovery vehicle

You have priority	**You have right of way**

Do not use car horn	**Wild animals crossing**

Hairpin bend ahead	**Roundabout ahead**

TRAVELLING TO GREECE BY CAR

Owing to political upheaval in the former Yugoslavia, the most direct overland routes to Greece are currently not recommended. The **AA** and **RAC** can supply up-to-date information on the advisability of routes and, for a small fee, will compile individual itineraries. It is worth asking their advice on insurance needs and on any special driving regulations for those countries en route.

In order to drive in Greece, you will need to take a full, valid national driving licence, and have insurance cover (at least third party is compulsory). **ELPA** (the Automobile and Touring Club of Greece) also offer useful information on driving in Greece.

RULES OF THE ROAD

Driving is on the right in Greece and road signs conform to European norms. There may be exceptions on small rural back roads, where the names of villages are often signposted in Greek only.

The speed limit on national highways is 120 km/h (75 mph) for cars; on country roads it is 90 km/h (55 mph) and in towns 50 km/h (30 mph). The speed limit on national highways for motorbikes up to 100 cc is 70 km/h (45 mph), and 90 km/h (55 mph) for larger motorbikes.

Although usually ignored, the use of seatbelts in cars is required by law, and children under the age of ten are not allowed to sit in the front seat. Parking and speeding tickets must be paid at the local police station or your car-hire agency.

CAR HIRE

There are scores of car-hire agencies in every tourist resort and major town, offering a full range of cars and four-wheel-drive vehicles.

Sign for car hire

A line of mopeds for hire

International companies such as **Budget**, **Avis**, **Hertz** and **Sixt** tend to be more expensive than their local counterparts, though the latter are generally as reliable.

The car-hire agency should have an agreement with an emergency recovery company, such as **Express**, **Hellas** or the **InterAmerican Towing Company** in the event of a vehicle breakdown. Also, be sure to check the insurance policy cover: third party is required by law, but personal accident insurance is strongly recommended. A valid national driving licence that has been held for at least one year is needed, and there is a minimum age requirement, ranging from 21 to 25 years.

MOTORBIKE, MOPED AND BICYCLE HIRE

Motorbikes and mopeds are readily available for hire in all the tourist resorts. Mopeds are ideal for short distances on fairly flat terrain, but for travel in more remote or mountainous areas a motorbike is essential.

Whatever you decide to hire, make sure that the vehicle is in good condition before you set out, and that you have adequate insurance cover; also check whether your own travel insurance covers you for motorbike accidents (many do not).

Speeding in Greece is penalized by fines, drink-driving laws are strict and helmets are compulsory.

Though less widely available, bicycles can be hired in some tourist resorts.

Rack of bicycles for hire at a coastal resort

The hot weather and tough terrain make cycling extremely hard work but, on the positive side, bikes can be transported free on most Greek ferries and buses, and for a small fee on trains.

PETROL STATIONS

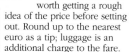
Unleaded and super petrol

Petrol stations are plentiful in towns, though in rural areas they are few and far between – always set out with a full tank to be on the safe side. Fuel is sold by the litre, and the price is comparable to most other European countries. There are usually either three or four grades available: super (95 octane), unleaded, super unleaded and diesel, which is confusingly called *petrélaio* in Greece.

Filling stations set their own working hours in Greece. Generally they are open seven days a week, from around 7am or 8am to between 7pm and 9pm. Some stations in the larger towns remain open 24 hours a day.

TAXIS

Taxis provide a reasonably priced way of making short trips around Greece. All taxis are metered, but for longer journeys a price can usually be negotiated per diem, or per trip. Also, drivers are generally amenable to

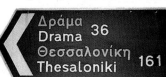
Dual-language road sign, found on most routes

dropping you off somewhere and returning to pick you up a few hours later.

In Athens taxis are plentiful and can simply be hailed. In smaller towns it is best to find one at a taxi rank, which is likely to be either in the centre or by the bus or train station. Most rural villages have at least one taxi, and the best place to arrange for one is at the local *kafeneío* (café). In Greece taxis are often shared with other passengers; each pays for their part of the journey. Although taxis are metered, it is worth getting a rough idea of the price before setting out. Round up to the nearest euro as a tip; luggage is an additional charge to the fare.

HITCHHIKING

Greece is a relatively safe place for hitchhiking but, like anywhere else, there are potential risks. Women especially are advised against hitching alone.

If you do hitchhike, finding a lift is usually easier in the less populated, rural areas, than on busy roads heading out from major towns and cities.

MAPS

Not too much reliance should be given to maps issued by local travel agents and car-hire agencies. Visitors intending to do much motoring are advised to bring with them the GeoCenter regional road maps (1:300,000 range), the single-sheet Freytag & Berndt maps (1:650,000), or to buy regional Road Editions maps when in Greece.

Travelling by Coach and Bus

Greece's bus system is operated by KTEL (Koinó Tameío Eispráxeon Leoforeíon), a syndicate of privately run companies. The network is comprehensive in that it provides every community with services of some sort. In rural villages this may be once a day or, in remoter places, once or twice a week. Services between the larger centres are frequent and efficient. Time permitting, bus travel is a good way of experiencing the country.

International coaches also connect Greece with the rest of Europe, though fares do not compare well with charter bargains during the summer holiday season.

EUROPEAN COACH SERVICES TO GREECE

Coach journeys from London to Athens take many days and are not as cheap as a bargain air fare. However, if you are not in a hurry, it is cheaper than taking the train.

Eurolines is a very reliable company, with a huge network of European destinations. Its coaches have reclining seats, toilets and washing facilities, and there are frequent short stops en route. Tickets can be booked in person, or by telephone using a credit card. Eurolines coaches depart once a week from London's Victoria coach station to Ancona in Italy, from where you can then take the ferry across to Greece.

Top Deck is an adventure tour operator used mainly by young travellers. Tours to Greece take about 20 days, and include many stops on the way.

UK COACH OFFICES

Eurolines
52 Grosvenor Gardens, Victoria,
London SW1.
Tel 020-7730 8235.
www.eurolines.com

Top Deck
William House, 14 Worple St,
Wimbledon, London SW19 4DD.
Tel 020-8879 6789.
www.topdecktours.co.uk

TRAVELLING IN GREECE BY COACH AND BUS

The Greek coach and bus system is extensive, with services to even the remotest destinations and frequent

Domestic coach, run by KTEL

express coaches on all the major routes. Large centres, such as Athens, usually have more than one terminal, and each serves a different set of destinations.

Ticket sales are computerized for all major routes, with reserved seating on modern, air-conditioned coaches. It pays to buy your ticket at least 20 minutes before the coach is scheduled to depart, as seats often get sold out on popular routes, and Greek coaches have a habit of leaving a few minutes early.

In the villages of the countryside, the local *kafeneío* (café) often serves as the bus and coach station. You can usually buy your ticket from the proprietor of the *kafeneío*, who may also have a timetable. Otherwise it is possible to buy a ticket when you board.

KTEL logo

COACH TOURS

In the resort areas, travel agents offer a wide range of excursions on air-conditioned coaches accompanied by qualified guides. These include trips to major archaeological and historical sites, other towns and seaside resorts, popular beaches and specially organized events. Depending on the destination, some coach tours leave very early in the morning, so they are best booked a day in advance.

COACH SERVICES FROM ATHENS

From Athens there are frequent coach services to all the larger mainland towns, apart from those in Thrace, which are served by coaches from Thessaloníki. Athens' Terminal A is situated 4 km (2 miles) northeast of the city centre at Kifisoú 10 *(see p327)*. The terminal serves Epirus, Macedonia, the Peloponnese and the Ionian islands of Corfu, Kefalloniá, Lefkáda and Zákynthos (ferry crossings are included in the price of the ticket). It takes 7.5 hours to Thessaloníki, and 7 hours to the port of Párga.

Terminal B is at Liosíon 260, north of Agios Nikólaos metro station, but most easily reached by taxi. It serves most destinations in central Greece, including Delphi, which takes 3 hours, and Vólos, which takes 6. Coaches to destinations around Attica, including Soúnio, Lávrio, Rafína and Marathónas, leave from the Mavrommataíon coach terminal in Athens, a short walk north from the National Archaeological Museum on the corner of Leofóros Alexándras and 28 Oktovríou (Patisíon).

Eurolines international coach

Travelling by Sea

Greek catamaran

Greece has always been a nation of seafarers and, with its hundreds of islands and thousands of miles of coastline, the sea plays an important part in the life and history of the country.

Today, it is a major source of revenue for Greece, with millions of tourists descending each year for seaside holidays in the Mediterranean and Aegean. The Greek mainland and islands are linked by a vast network of ferries, hydrofoils and catamarans.

TRAVELLING TO GREECE BY SEA

There are regular year-round ferry crossings from the Italian ports of Ancona, Bari, Brindisi and Venice to the

Passengers on the walkways of a car ferry leaving dock

Greek ports of Igoumenítsa in Epirus and Pátra in the Peloponnese. Journey times and fares vary greatly, depending on time of year, point of embarkation, ferry company, type of ticket and reductions (for young people, students or rail-card holders). Several shipping lines cover the Italy–Greece routes, so it is best to shop around. In summer, reservations are advisable, especially if you have a car or want a cabin.

GREEK FERRY SERVICE

The government is implementing stricter checks on ferries, which should result in higher safety standards. However, ferry service schedules and departure times are

MINOAN LINES

Minoan Lines logo

notoriously flexible. From the smaller ports, your only concern will be getting a ferry that leaves on the day and for the destination that you want. Check the timetable on arrival for frequency and times of services, as schedules are changed each week.

Matters get more complicated from Piraeus, Greece's busiest port. Each of the many competing companies have agents at the quayside. Tickets and bookings (essential in high season) should be made through them, or at a travel agency.

Greece also has a network of hydrofoils and catamarans. They are twice as fast as ferries, though twice as expensive. As well as serving the islands, many stop at ports along the mainland coast. Most depart from Rafína, but those going to the Peloponnese coast leave from Piraeus, nearly all from Zéa port. Advanced booking is usually essential.

The Greek tourist office's weekly schedules can serve as a useful guideline for all departures, and some of the English-language papers also print summer sailings.

If you are travelling out of season, expect all services to be significantly reduced and some routes to be suspended.

PIRAEUS PORT MAP

This shows where you are likely to find ferries to various destinations.

Piraeus Port Authority:
Tel 01 422 6000.
Coastal Services Timetables:
Tel 1440.

KEY TO DEPARTURE POINTS

- Argo-Saronic islands
- Northeast Aegean islands
- Dodecanese
- Cyclades
- Crete
- International ferries
- Hydrofoils and catamarans

Key to symbols *see back flap*

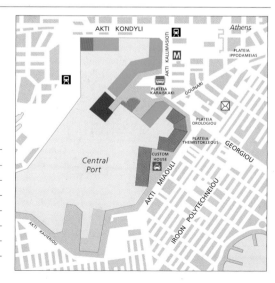

Getting Around Athens

Trolleybus stop sign

The sights of Athens' city centre are closely packed, and almost everything of interest can be reached on foot. This is the best way of sightseeing, especially in view of the appalling traffic congestion, which can make both public and private transport slow and inefficient. The expansion of the metro system, though not yet complete, already provides a good alternative to the roads for some journeys. However, the bus and trolleybus network still provides the majority of public transport in the capital for Athenians and visitors alike. Taxis are a useful alternative and, with the lowest tariffs of any EU capital, are worth considering even for longer journeys.

Orange and white regional bus for the Attica area

One of the fleet of yellow, blue and white buses

BUS SERVICES IN ATHENS

Athens is served by an extensive bus network. Bus journeys are inexpensive, but can be slow and uncomfortably crowded, particularly in the city centre and during rush hours; the worst times are from 7am to 8:30am, 2pm to 3:30pm and 7:30pm to 9pm.

Tickets can be bought individually or in a book of ten, but either way, they must be purchased in advance from a *períptero* (street kiosk), a transport booth, or certain other designated places. The brown, red and white logo, with the words *eisitíria edó*, indicates where you can buy bus tickets. The same ticket can be used on any bus or trolleybus, and must be stamped in a ticket machine to validate it when you board. There is a penalty fine for not stamping your ticket and tourists who are unfamiliar with this system are often caught out when inspectors board buses to carry out random checks. Tickets are valid for one ride only, regardless of the distance and, within the central area, are not transferable from one vehicle to another.

Athens bus ticket booth

USEFUL ROUTES IN ATHENS

Work continues on the Metro extension to Kerameikós. The metro station for the site will be Botanikós and it is due to be in operation by 2007.

Ⓜ◯ Botanikós (open 2007)

Plateía Omonoías Ⓜ

National Archaeological Museum

National Historical Museum ◯

National Gallery of Art ◯

Monastiráki Ⓜ◯

Plateía Syntágmatos Ⓜ

KEY

— Bus A5

— Bus 230

⋯ Trolleybus 1

— Trolleybus 3

— Trolleybus 7

⋯ Trolleybus 8

— Trolleybus 9

Ⓜ Metro

Acropolis Ⓜ

Benáki Museum

Museum of Cycladic Art

Pláka

ΜΟΝΑΣΤΗΡΙΟΝ
Monastirion

Monastiráki metro sign

ATHENS BUS NETWORKS

There are three principal bus networks serving greater Athens and the Attica region. They are colour coded blue, yellow and white; orange and white; and green. Blue, yellow and white buses cover an extensive network of over 300 routes in greater Athens, connecting districts to each other and to central Athens. In order to reduce Athens' smog, some of these are being replaced with green and white "ecological" buses running on natural gas.

Orange and white buses serve the Attica area (see pp142–3). On these you pay the conductor and, as distances are greater, fares are also more expensive. The two terminals for orange and white buses are both situated on Mavrommataión, by Pedío tou Areos (Areos Park). Though you can board at any designated orange stop, usually you cannot get off until you are outside the city area. These buses are less frequent than the blue, yellow and white service, and on some routes stop running in the early evening.

Green express buses, the fourth category, travel between central Athens and Piraeus. Numbers 040 and 049 are very frequent – about every 6 minutes – running from Athinas, by Plateía Omonoías, to various stops in Piraeus, including Plateía Karaïskáki, at the main harbour.

TROLLEYBUSES IN ATHENS

Athens has a good network of trolleybuses, which are purple and yellow in colour. There are over 20 routes that criss-cross the city. They provide a good way of getting around the central sights. All routes pass the Pláka area. Route 3 is useful for visiting the National Archaeological Museum from Plateía Syntágmatos, and route 1 links Lárissis railway station with Plateía Omonoías and Plateía Syntágmatos.

An Athens trolleybus

ATHENS' METRO

The metro, which has three lines, is a fast and reliable means of transport in Athens.

Line 1, the original line, runs from Kifissiá in the north to Piraeus in the south, with central stations at Thiseío, Monastiráki, Omónoia and Victoria. The majority of the line is overland and only runs underground between Attikí and Monastiráki stations through the city centre. The line is used mainly by commuters, but offers visitors a useful alternative means of reaching Piraeus (see p327).

Lines 2 and 3 form part of a huge expansion of the system, most of which was completed in time for the 2004 Olympic Games. The new lines have been built 20 m (66 ft) underground in order to avoid material of archaeological interest. Sýntagma and Acropolis stations have displays of archaeological finds.

Line 2 now runs from Agios Antónios in northwest Athens to Agios Dimitrios in the southeast. Line 3 runs from Monastiráki to D. Plakentias in the northeast with some, but not all, trains continuing to Eleftheríos Venizélos airport.

One ticket allows travel on any of the three lines and is valid for 90 minutes in one direction. You cannot exit a station, then go back to continue your journey with the same ticket. A cheaper ticket is sold for single journeys on Line 1. Tickets can be bought at any metro station and must be validated before entering the train – use the machines at the entrances to all platforms. Trains run every five minutes from 5am to 12:30am on Line 1, and from 5:30am to 12:30am on Lines 2 and 3.

Archaeological remains on display at Sýntagma metro station

DRIVING IN ATHENS

Driving in Athens can be a nerve-racking experience, especially if you are not accustomed to Greek road habits. Many streets in the centre are pedestrianized and there are also plenty of one-way streets, so you need to plan routes carefully. Finding a parking space can also be very difficult. Despite appearances to the contrary, parking in front of a no-parking sign or on a single yellow line is illegal. There are pay-and-display machines for legal on-street parking, as well as underground car parks, though these usually fill up quickly.

In an attempt to reduce dangerously high air pollution levels, there is an "odd-even" driving system in force. Cars that have an odd number at the end of their licence plates can enter the central grid, also called the *daktýlios,* only on dates with an odd number, and cars with an even number at the end of their plates are allowed into it only on dates with an even number. To avoid this, some people have two cars – with an odd and even plate. The rule does not apply to foreign cars but, if possible, avoid taking your car into the city centre.

No parking on odd-numbered days of the month

No parking on even-numbered days of the month

Yellow Athens Taxi

ATHENIAN TAXIS

Swarms of yellow taxis can be seen cruising around Athens at most times of the day or night. However, trying to persuade one to stop for you can be difficult, especially between 2pm and 3pm when taxi drivers usually change shifts. Then, they will only pick you up if you happen to be going in a direction that is convenient for them.

To hail a taxi, stand on the edge of the pavement and shout out your destination to any cab that slows down. If a cab's "TAXI" sign is lit up, then it is definitely for hire (but often a taxi is also for hire when the sign is not lit). It is also common practice for drivers to pick up extra passengers along the way, so do not ignore the occupied cabs. If you are not the first passenger, take note of the meter reading immediately: there is no fare-sharing, so you should be charged for your portion of the journey only, (or the minimum fare of 1.70 euros, whichever is greater).

Athenian taxis are extremely cheap by European standards – depending on traffic, you should not have to pay more than 3 euros to go anywhere in the downtown area, and between 4.5 and 7.5 euros from the centre to Piraeus. Higher tariffs come into effect between midnight and 5am, and for journeys that exceed certain distances from the city centre. Fares to the airport, which is out of town at Spata, are between 25 and 30 euros. There are also small surcharges for extra pieces of luggage weighing over 10 kg (22 lbs), and for journeys from the ferry or railway terminals. Taxi fares are increased during holiday periods, such as Christmas and Easter.

For an extra charge, (1–2.5 euros), you can make a phone call to a radio taxi company and arrange for a car to pick you up at an appointed place and time. Radio taxis are plentiful in the Athens area. Listed below are the telephone numbers of a few companies:

Athina 1
Tel 210 921 7942.
Ermis
Tel 210 411 5200.
Hellas
Tel 210 645 7000.

WALKING

The centre of Athens is very compact, and almost all major sights and museums are to be found within a 20- or 25-minute walk of Plateía Syntágmatos, which is generally regarded as the city's centre. This is worth bearing in mind, particularly when traffic is congested, all buses are full, and no taxi will stop. Athens is still one of the safest European cities in which to walk around, though, as in any sizable metropolis, it pays to be vigilant, especially at night.

Sign for a pedestrianized area

Visitors to Athens, walking up Areopagos hill

ATHENS TRANSPORT LINKS

The hub of Athens' city transport is the area around Plateía Syntágmatos and Plateía Omonoías. From this central area trolleybuses or buses can be taken to the airport, the sea port at Piraeus, Athens' two train stations, and its domestic and international coach terminals. In addition, three new tram lines connect the city centre with the Attic coast.

Bus E95 runs between the airport and Syntágma and bus E96 between the airport and Piraeus *(see p315)*.

Buses 040 and 049 link Piraeus harbour with Syntágma and Omonoías in the city centre. The metro also extends to Piraeus harbour and the journey from the city centre to the harbour takes about half an hour.

Trolleybus route 1 goes past Lárissis metro station, as well as Lárissis train station, with the Peloponnísou station *(see p318)* a short walk away from them. Bus 024 goes to coach terminal B, on Liosíon, and bus 051 to coach terminal A, on Kifisoú *(see p322)*.

Tram line 1 (T1) runs from Syntágma to Néo Fáliro on the coast; T2 runs from Néo Fáliro to the Athens suburb of Glyfáda; T3 runs from Glyfáda to Syntágma.

Though more expensive than public transport, the most convenient way of getting to and from any of these destinations is by taxi. The journey times vary greatly but, if traffic is free-flowing, from the city centre to the airport takes about 40 minutes; the journey from the city centre to the port of Piraeus takes around 40 minutes; and the journey from Piraeus to the airport takes about 90 minutes. Taxis are abundant in Athens and are relatively inexpensive compared with most other European cities.

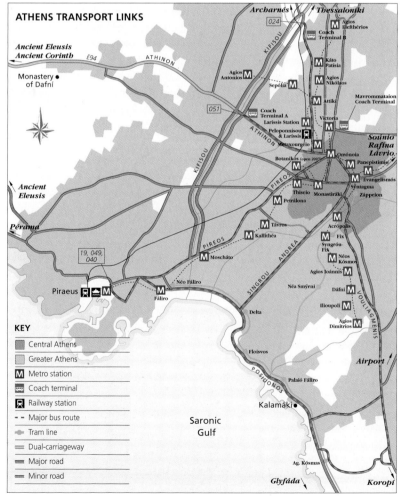

ATHENS TRANSPORT LINKS

KEY

- ■ Central Athens
- ■ Greater Athens
- Ⓜ Metro station
- 🚌 Coach terminal
- 🚉 Railway station
- - - Major bus route
- Tram line
- Dual-carriageway
- Major road
- Minor road

General Index

Acknowledgments

Dorling Kindersley would like to thank the following people whose contributions and assistance have made the preparation of this book possible.

Main Contributors

Marc Dubin is an American expatriate who divides his time between London and Sámos. Since 1978 he has travelled in every province of Greece. He has written or contributed to numerous guides to Greece.

Mike Gerrard is a travel writer and broadcaster who has written several guides to various parts of Greece, which he has been visiting annually since 1964.

Andy Harris is a travel and food journalist based in Athens. He is the author of *A Taste of the Aegean*.

Tanya Tsikas is a Canadian writer and travel guide editor. Married to a Greek, she has spent time in Crete and currently lives in Oxford.

DEPUTY EDITORIAL DIRECTOR Douglas Amrine

DEPUTY ART DIRECTOR Gillian Allan

MANAGING EDITOR Georgina Matthews

MANAGING ART EDITOR Annette Jacobs

Additional Illustrations

Richard Bonson, Louise Boulton, Gary Cross, Kevin Goold, Roger Hutchins, Claire Littlejohn.

Design and Editorial Assistance

Hilary Bird, Julie Bond, Elspeth Collier, Michelle Crane, Catherine Day, Jim Evoy, Emily Green, Emily Hatchwell, Leanne Hogbin, Kim Inglis, Lorien Kite, Esther Labi, Felicity Laughton, Andreas Michael, Rebecca Milner, Ella Milroy, Lisa Minsky, Robert Mitchell, Adam Moore, Jennifer Mussett, Tamsin Pender, Marianne Petrou, Jake Reimann, Simon Ryder, Collette Sadler, Rita Selvaggio, Ellie Smith, Claire Stewart, Claire Tennant-Scull, Amanda Tomeh, Helen Townsend.

Dorling Kindersley would also like to thank the following for their assistance: The Greek Wine Bureau, Odysea.

Additional Research

Anna Antoniou, Garifalia Boussiopoulou, Anastasia Caramanis, Michele Crawford, Magda Dimouti, Shirley Durant, Jane Foster, Panos Gotsi, Zoi Groummouti, Peter Millett, Eva Petrou, Ellen Root, Tasos Schizas, Linda Theodora, Garifalia Tsiola, Veronica Wood.

Additional Photography

Stephen Bere, John Heseltine, Ian O'Leary, Steven Ling, Clive Streeter, Jerry Young.

Artwork Reference

Ideal Photo S.A., The Image Bank, Tony Stone Worldwide.

Photography Permissions

Dorling Kindersley would like to thank the following for their assistance and kind permission to photograph at their establishments:

Ali Pasha Museum, Ioannina; City of Athens Museum; Museum of Greek Folk Art, Athens; V Kyriazopoulos Ceramic Collection; Kavala Modern Art Gallery; National Gallery of Art, Athens; National War Museum, Athens; Nicholas P Goulandris Foundation Museum of Cycladic and Ancient Art, Athens; Theatrical Museum, Athens; University of Athens Museum; Polygnotos Vagis Museum, Thassos. Also all other cathedrals, churches, museums, hotels, restaurants, shops, galleries, and sights too numerous to thank individually.

Picture Credits

t = top; tl = top left; tlc = top left centre; tc = top centre; trc = top right centre; tr = top right; cla = centre left above; ca = centre above; cra = centre right above; cl = centre left; c = centre; cr = centre right; clb = centre left below; cb = centre below; crb = centre right below; bl = bottom left; b = bottom; bc = bottom centre; bcl = bottom centre left; br = bottom right; bottom right above = bra; bottom right below = brb; d= detail.

Works of art have been reproduced with the permission of the following copyright holders: Vorres Museum *Water Nymph* (1995) Apostolos Petridis 150t.

The publisher would like to thank the following individuals, companies and picture libraries for permission to reproduce their photographs:

ALAMY IMAGES: CW Images/ Chris Warren 298bl; FAN Travelstock/Katja Kreder 278tl; GreekSportStock 299c; Andrew Holt 298cl; Peter Horree 10br, 11cl, 281tl; Werner Otto 298crb; Picpics 299br; picturescolourlibrary.com 11br; Robert Harding Picture Library Ltd/ Robert Harding World Imagery 281c; AISA ARCHIVO ICONGRAFICO, Barcelona: Museo Archeologique Bari 57tr; Museo Archeologique Florence 54tl, 54bl; CAKG, London: 173t, 259; Antiquario Palatino 53bl; *Bilder aus dem Altherthume*, Heinrich Leutemann 228c; British Museum 95br; Edward Dodwell 87cr; Erich Lessing Akademie der Bildenden Künste, Vienna 54c; Musée du Louvre 53tl; National Archeological Museum, Athens 26–7(d), 27t; Staatliche Kunstsammlungen, Albertinum,

Wilson 237cr; Nature Photographers: S C Bisserot 236c; Brinsley Burbridge 23clb, 23br; N A Callow 22b; Andrew Cleave 23bc, 237b; Peter Craig Cooper 237cl; Paul Sterry 23t, 23cra, 225cr; Antonis Nicolopoulos: 299t.

Octopus Sea Trips: Peter Nicolaides 300tr; Olympic Airways: 314t; Oronoz Archivo Fotografico: 211b; Biblioteca National Madrid *Invasions Bulgares Historia Matriksiscronica FIIIV* 36cb(d); Charlotten-berg, Berlin 54tr; El Escorial, Madrid *Battle Lepanto Cambiaso Luca* 38cr(d); Museo Julia 53c(d); Musee Louvre 60b; Museo Vaticano 61bl, 221tr.

Romylos Parisis: 14t, 104b, 136–7, 218b; City of Athens Museum 40cb; Pictures: 12, 14b, 44crb, 298c; Popperfoto: 42crb, 43cra, 43br, 98b, 180t, 262t; Michalis Pornalis: 218c, 219cb, 219b; Private Collections: 5t, 216t, 217t, 217b.

Ride World Wide: 299tl; Rex Features: 17c; Argyropoulos/Sipa 48t; Sipa/C.Brown 43tr.

Scala, Florence: Gallerie degli Uffizi 28b; Museo Archeologico, Firenze 29t; Museo Mandralisca Cefalu 30ca; Museo Nationale Tarquinia 61br; Museo de Villa Giulia 28–9, 60tr; Spathario Shadow Theatre Museum: 151c; Spectrum Colour Library: 244b; Maria Stefossi: 118b; Theodoros-Patroklos Stellakis: 154b; Carmel Stewart: 279c; Tony Stone Images: Aperion 152tl(d); Sunvil: 300bl; Swan Hellenic: 300cr.

Tap Service Archaeological Receipts Fund Hellenic Republic Ministry of Culture: A Epharat of Antiquities 5b, 43cb, 58b, 94bl, 94br, 95t, 95c, 96b, 98c, 99cr, 100t, 100c; Acropolis Museum 96t, 97t, 97c; Ancient Corinth Archaeological Museum 166c; B Epharat of Antiquities 82, 141b, 144 all, 146c, 146bl, 146br, 147tl, 147c, 148c, 148b; Byzantine Museum, Athens 67t, 76 all; D Epharat of Antiquities 139c, 139bl, 162–3 all, 164–5, 167bl, 177b, 178t, 179t, 179b, 180c, 181c; Delphi Archaeological Museum 50–1, 228t, 230tl, 231t, 231b; E Epharat of Antiquities 174cb; Elefis Archaeological Museum 156b; 11th Epharat of Byzantine Antiquities 237tr; 5th Epharat of Byzantine Antiquities 21tl, 21cl, 37c,

190–1, 192t, 192b; 1st Epharat of Byzantine Antiquities 139cra, 152c, 153cb, 222–3 all; I Epharat of Antiquities 138ca, 205t, 226–7, 228b, 229c, 230tr, 230b; IB Epharat of Antiquities 211t, 212c; IO Epharat of Antiquities 256c; IST Epharat of Antiquities 241c; Keramikos Archaeological Muscum 89t, 89cr, 89br, 91t, 91car; Marathon Archaeological Museum 145c; National Archeological Museum, Athens 3c, 26t, 28tr, 65tl, 68t, 68c, 68b, 69t, 69c, 69b, 70–1 all, 99t, 155t, 157cr; 9th Epharat of Byzantine Antiquities 248c, 248b; Pireaus Archaeological Museum 155t; 2nd Epharat of Byzantine Antiquities 21tr; 6th Epharat of Byzantine Antiquities 13t, 21cr; 7th Epharat of Byzantine Antiquities 21bl, 218tl, 219ca; Thebes Archaeological Museum 221t; Thessaloníki Archaeological Museum 31t, 139t, 233t, 242b(d), 244t, 246t, 246ca, 246b, 247 all; I Epharat of Antiquities 88c, 88b, 89cl, 89bl, 90t, 90b, 91t, 91cla, 91cb, 91b, 156t, 156c, 157cl, 157bl, 157bc; Z Epharat of Antiquities 138cb, 170c, 170b, 171t, 171b, 172 all, 201c, 201b, 298c; Trekking Hellas: 298tc; Trip Photographic Library: Marc Dubin 250–1; Yannis Tsarouhis Foundation: Private Collection *Barber Shop in Marousi* (1947) 42tr.

Wadsworth Atheneum, Hartford Connecticut: T Pierpont Morgan Collection 189b; Werner Forman Archive: 36t; Alan Williams: 49t; Peter Wilson: 59bl, 92–3, 94t, 100b, 106–7, 214–5, 216c; Woodfin Camp & Associates: John Marmaras 254t; Adam Woolfitt 45clb.

Front Endpaper: all special photography except Rt Ideal Photo SA: T Dassios and Rbl Kostos Kontos (d).

Jacket
Front – Corbis: Free Agents Limited/Dallas and John Heaton main image; DK Images © The Trustees of the British Museum/Philip Nicholls clb. Back – Alamy Images: Frank Chmura cla; DK Images: Rob Reichenfeld bl; Peter Wilson tl, clb. Spine – Corbis: Free Agents Limited/Dallas and John Heaton t; DK Images: Rob Reichenfeld b.

All other images © Dorling Kindersley. For further information see: www.dkimages.com

---

Phrase Book

There is no universally accepted system for representing the modern Greek language in the Roman alphabet. The system of transliteration adopted in this guide is the one used by the Greek Government. Though not yet fully applied throughout Greece, most of the street and place names have been transliterated according to this system. For Classical names this guide uses the k, os, on and f spelling, in keeping with the modern system of transliteration. In a few cases, such as Socrates, the more familiar Latin form has been used. Classical names do not have accents. Where a well-known English form of a name exists, such as Athens or Corfu, this has been used. Variations in transliteration are given in the index.

GUIDELINES FOR PRONUNCIATION

The accent over Greek and transliterated words indicates the stressed syllable. In this guide the accent is not written over capital letters nor over monosyllables, except for question words and the conjunction ή (meaning "or"). In the right-hand "Pronunciation" column below, the syllable to stress is given in bold type.

On the following pages, the English is given in the left-hand column with the Greek and its transliteration in the middle column. The right-hand column provides a literal system of pronunciation and indicates the stressed syllable in bold.

THE GREEK ALPHABET

Α α	A a	**a**rm
Β β	V v	**v**ote
Γ γ	G g	**y**ear (when followed by e and i sounds) **n**o (when followed by ξ or γ)
Δ δ	D d	**th**at
Ε ε	E e	**e**gg
Ζ ζ	Z z	**z**oo
Η η	I i	bel**ie**ve
Θ θ	Th th	**th**ink
Ι ι	I i	bel**ie**ve
Κ κ	K k	**k**id
Λ λ	L l	**l**and
Μ μ	M m	**m**an
Ν ν	N n	**n**o
Ξ ξ	X x	ta**x**i
Ο ο	O o	**fo**x
Π π	P p	**p**ort
Ρ ρ	R r	**r**oom
Σ σ	S s	**s**orry (zero when followed by μ)
ς	s	(used at end of word)
Τ τ	T t	**t**ea
Υ υ	Y y	bel**ie**ve
Φ φ	F f	**f**ish
Χ χ	Ch ch	lo**ch** in most cases, but **h**e when followed by a, e or ι sounds
Ψ ψ	Ps ps	ma**ps**
Ω ω	O o	f**o**x

COMBINATIONS OF LETTERS

In Greek there are two-letter vowels that are pronounced as one sound:

Αι αι	Ai ai	**e**gg
Ει ει	Ei ei	bel**ie**ve
Οι οι	Oi oi	bel**ie**ve
Ου ου	Ou ou	l**u**te

There are also some two-letter consonants that are pronounced as one sound:

Μπ μπ	Mp mp	**b**ut, sometimes nu**mb**er in the middle of a word
Ντ ντ	Nt nt	**d**esk, sometimes u**nd**er in the middle of a word
Γκ γκ	Gk gk	**g**o, sometimes bi**ng**o in the middle of a word
Γξ γξ	nx	a**nx**iety
Τζ τζ	Tz tz	ha**nds**
Τσ τσ	Ts ts	it**'s**
Γγ γγ	Gg gg	bi**ng**o

In an Emergency

Help!	Βοήθεια! / Voíthia	vo-**ee**-theea
Stop!	Σταματήστε! / Stamatíste	sta-ma-**tee**-steh
Call a doctor!	Φωνάξτε ένα γιατρό / Fonáxte éna giatró	fo-**nak**-steh **e**-na ya-tro
Call an ambulance/ the police/the fire brigade!	Καλέστε το ασθενοφόρο/την αστυνομία/την πυροσβεστική / Kaléste to asthenofóro/tin astynomía/tin pyrosvestikí	ka-**le**-steh to as-the-no-**fo**-ro/teen a-sti-no-**mia**/teen pee-ro-zve-stee-**kee**
Where is the nearest telephone/hospital/ pharmacy?	Πού είναι το πλησιέστερο τήλεφωνο/νοσοκο-μείο/φαρμακείο; / Poú eínai to plisiés-tero tiléfono/nosoko-meío/farmakeío?	poo **ee**-ne to plee-see-**e**-ste-ro tee-**le**-pho-no/no-so-ko-**mee**-o/far-ma-**kee**-o?

Communication Essentials

Yes	Ναι / Nai	neh
No	Οχι / Ochi	**o**-chee
Please	Παρακαλώ / Parakaló	pa-ra-ka-**lo**
Thank you	Ευχαριστώ / Efcharistó	ef-cha-ree-**sto**
You are welcome	Παρακαλώ / Parakaló	pa-ra-ka-**lo**
OK/alright	Εντάξει / Entáxei	en-**dak**-zee
Excuse me	Με συγχωρείτε / Me synchoreíte	me seen-cho-**ree**-teh
Hello	Γειά σας / Geiá sas	yeea sas
Goodbye	Αντίο / Antío	an-**dee**-o
Good morning	Καλημέρα / Kaliméra	ka-lee-**me**-ra
Good night	Καληνύχτα / Kalinýchta	ka-lee-**neech**-ta
Morning	Πρωί / Proí	pro-**ee**
Afternoon	Απόγευμα / Apógevma	a-**po**-yev-ma
Evening	Βράδυ / Vrádi	vrath-i
This morning	Σήμερα το πρωί / Símera to proí	**see**-me-ra to pro-**ee**
Yesterday	Χθές / Chthés	chthes
Today	Σήμερα / Símera	**see**-me-ra
Tomorrow	Αύριο / Avrio	**av**-ree-o
Here	Εδώ / Edó	ed-**o**
There	Εκεί / Ekeí	e-**kee**
What?	Τί; / Tí?	tee?
Why?	Γιατί; / Giatí?	ya-**tee**?
Where?	Πού; / Poú?	poo?
How?	Πώς; / Pós?	pos?
Wait!	Περίμενε! / Perímene!	pe-**ree**-me-neh

Useful Phrases

How are you?	Τί κάνεις; Τί κάάνεις?	tee ka-nees
Very well, thank you	Πολύ καλά, ευχαριστώ Poly kalá, efcharistó	po-lee ka-la, ef-cha-ree-sto
How do you do?	Πώς είστε; Pós eíste?	pos ees-te?
Pleased to meet you	Χαίρω πολύ Chaíro polý	che-ro po-lee
What is your name?	Πώς λέγεστε; Pós légeste?	pos le-ye-ste?
Where is/are...?	Πού είναι; Poú eínai?	poo ee-ne?
How far is it to...?	Πόσο απέχει...; Póso apéchei...?	po-so a-pe-chee?
How do I get to?	Πώς μπορώ να πάω...; Pós mporó na ráo...?	pos bo-ro-na pa-o?
Do you speak English?	Μιλάτε Αγγλικά; Miláte Angliká?	mee-la-te an-glee-ka?
I understand	Καταλαβαίνω Katalavaíno	ka-ta-la-ve-no
I don't understand	Δεν καταλαβαίνω Den katalavaíno	then ka-ta-la-ve-no
Could you speak slowly?	Μιλάτε λίγο πιο αργά παρακαλώ; Miláte lígo pio argá parakaló?	mee-la-te lee-go pyo ar-ga pa-ra-ka-lo?
I'm sorry	Με συγχωρείτε Me synchoreíte	me seen-cho-ree teh
Does anyone have a key?	Έχει κανένας κλειδί; Echei kanénas kleidí?	e-chee ka-ne-nas klee-dee?

Useful Words

big	Μεγάλο Megálo	me-ga-lo
small	Μικρό Mikró	mi-kro
hot	Ζεστό Zestó	zes-to
cold	Κρύο Krýo	kree-o
good	Καλό Kaló	ka-lo
bad	Κακό Kakó	ka-ko
enough	Αρκετά Arketá	ar-ke-ta
well	Καλά Kalá	ka-la
open	Ανοιχτά Anoichtá	a-neech-ta
closed	Κλειστά Kleistá	klee-sta
left	Αριστερά Aristerá	a-ree-ste-ra
right	Δεξιά Dexiá	dek-see-a
straight on	Ευθεία Eftheía	ef-thee-a
between	Ανάμεσα / Μεταξύ Anámesa / Metaxý	a-na-me-sa/me-tak-see
on the corner of....	Στη γωνία του... Sti gonía tou...	stee go-nee-a too
near	Κοντά Kontá	kon-da
far	Μακριά Makriá	ma-kree-a
up	Επάνω Epáno	e-pa-no
down	Κάτω Káto	ka-to
early	Νωρίς Norís	no-rees
late	Αργά Argá	ar-ga
entrance	Η είσοδος I eísodos	ee ee-so-thos
exit	Η έξοδος I éxodos	eee-kso-dos
toilet	Οι τουαλέτες /WC Oi toualétes / WC	ee-too-a-le-tes
occupied/engaged	Κατειλημμένη Kateiliméni	ka-tee-lee-me-nee

unoccupied/vacant	Ελεύθερη Eléftheri	e-lef-the-ree
free/no charge	Δωρεάν Doreán	tho-re-an
in/out	Μέσα /Έξω Mésa/ Exo	me-sa/ek-so

Making a Telephone Call

Where is the nearest public telephone ?	Πού βρίσκεται ο πλησιέστερος τηλεφωνικός θάλαμος; Poú vrísketai o plisiésteros tilefonikós thálamos?	poo vrees-ke-teh o plee-see-e-ste-ros tee-le-fo-ni-kos tha-la-mos?
I would like to place a long-distance call	Θα ήθελα να κάνω ένα υπεραστικό τηλεφώνημα Tha íthela na káno éna yperastikó tilefónima	tha ee-the-la na ka-no e-na ee-pe-ra-sti-ko tee-le-fo-nee-ma
I would like to reverse the charges	Θα ήθελα να χρεώσω το τηλεφώνημα στον παραλήπτη Tha íthela na chreóso to tilefónima ston paralípti	tha ee-the-la na chre-o-so to tee-le-fo-nee-ma ston pa-ra-lep-tee
I will try again later	Θα ξαναπηλεφωνήσω αργότερα Tha xanatilefoníso argótera	tha ksa-na-tee-le-fo-ni-so ar-go-te-ra
Can I leave a message?	Μπορείτε να του αφήσετε ένα μήνυμα; Mporeíte na tou afisete éna mínyma?	bo-ree-te na too a-fee-se-teh e-na mee-nee-ma?
Could you speak up a little please?	Μιλάτε δυνατότερα, παρακαλώ; Miláte dynatótera, parakaló	mee-la-teh dee-na-to-te-ra, pa-ra-ka-lo
Local call	Τοπικό τηλεφώνημα Topikó tilefónima	to-pi-ko tee-le-fo-nee-ma
Hold on	Περιμένετε Periménete	pe-ri-me-ne-teh
OTE telephone office	Ο ΟΤΕ / Το τηλεφωνείο Ο ΟΤΕ / Το tilefoneío	o O-TE / To tee-le-fo-nee-o
Phone box/kiosk	Ο τηλεφωνικός θάλαμος Ο tilefonikós thálamos	o tee-le-fo-ni-kos tha-la-mos
Phone card	Η τηλεκάρτα I tilekárta	ee tee-le-kar-ta

Shopping

How much does this cost?	Πόσο κάνει; Póso kánei?	po-so ka-nee?
I would like....	Θα ήθελα... Tha íthela	tha ee-the-la...
Do you have....?	Έχετε...; Echete...?	e-che-teh
I am just looking	Απλώς κοιτάω Aplós koitáo	a-plos kee-ta-o
Do you take credit cards/travellers' cheques?	Δέχεστε πιστωτικές κάρτες/ travellers' cheques; Décheste pistotikés kártes/travellers' cheques?	the-ches-teh pee-sto-tee-kes kar-tes/ travellers' cheques?
What time do you open/close?	Ποτέ ανοίγετε/ κλείνετε; Póte anoígete/ kleínete?	po-teh a-nee-ye-teh/ klee-ne-teh?
Can you ship this overseas?	Μπορείτε να το στείλετε στο εξωτερικό; Mporeíte na to steílete sto exoterikó?	bo-ree-teh na to stee-le-teh sto e-xo-te-ree ko?
This one	Αυτό εδώ Aftó edó	af-to e-do
That one	Εκείνο Ekeíno	e-kee-no

expensive	Ακριβό Akrivó	a-kree-**vo**
cheap	Φθηνό Fthinó	fthee-**no**
size	Το μέγεθος To mégethos	to **me**-ge-thos
white	Λευκό Lefkó	lef-**ko**
black	Μαύρο Mávro	mav-ro
red	Κόκκινο Kókkino	ko-kee-no
yellow	Κίτρινο Kítrino	kee-tree-no
green	Πράσινο Prásino	pra-see-no
blue	Μπλε Mple	bleh

Types of Shop

antique shop	Μαγαζί με αντίκες Magazí me antíkes	ma-ga-**zee** me an-dee-kes
bakery	Ο φούρνος O foúrnos	o foor-nos
bank	Η τράπεζα I trápeza	ee tra-pe-za
bazaar	Το παζάρι To pazári	to pa-**za**-ree
bookshop	Το βιβλιοπωλείο To vivliopoleío	to vee-vlee-o-po-lee-o
butcher	Το κρεοπωλείο To kreopoleío	to kre-o-po-lee-o
cake shop	Το ζαχαροπλαστείο To zacharoplasteío	to za-cha-ro-pla-stee-o
cheese shop	Μαγαζί με αλλαντικά Magazí me allantiká	ma-ga-zee me a-lan-dee-**ka**
department store	Πολυκάταστημα Polykatástima	Po-lee-ka-**ta**-stee-ma
fishmarket	Το ιχθυοπωλείο/ ψαράδικο To ichthyopoleío/ psarádiko	to eech-thee-o-po-lee-o /psa-rá-dee-ko
greengrocer	Το μανάβικο To manáviko	to ma-**na**-vee-ko
hairdresser	Το κομμωτήριο To kommotírio	to ko-mo-**tee**-ree-o
kiosk	Το περίπτερο To períptero	to pe-**reep**-te-ro
leather shop	Μαγαζί με δερμάτινα είδη Magazí me dermátina eídi	ma-ga-**zee** me ther-ma-tee-na ee-thee
street market	Η λαϊκή αγορά I laïkí agorá	ee la-ee-**kee** a-go-**ra**
newsagent	Ο εφημεριδοπώλης O efimeridopólis	O e-fee-mee-ree-tho-po-lees
pharmacy	Το φαρμακείο To farmakeío	to far-ma-**kee**-o
post office	Το ταχυδρομείο To tachydromeío	to ta-chee-thro-**mee**-o
shoe shop	Κατάστημα υποδημάτων Katástima ypodimáton	ka-**ta**-stee-ma ee-po-dee-**ma**-ton
souvenir shop	Μαγαζί με "souvenir" Magazí me "souvenir"	ma-ga-**zee** meh "souvenir"
supermarket	Σουπερμάρκετ/ Υπεραγορά "Supermarket"/ Yperagorá	"Supermarket" / ee-per-a-go-**ra**
tobacconist	Είδη καπνιστού Eídi kapnistoú	Ee-thee kap-nees
travel agent	Το ταξειδιωτικό γραφείο To taxeidiotikó grafeío	to tak-see-thy-o-tee-**ko** gra-**fee**-o

Sightseeing

tourist information	Ο ΕΟΤ O EOT	o E-OT
tourist police	Η τουριστική αστυνομία I touristikí astynomía	ee too-rees-tee-**kee** a-stee-no-**mee**-a
archaeological	αρχαιολογικός archaiologikós	ar-che-o-lo-yee-**kos**

art gallery	Η γκαλερί I gkalerí	ee ga-le-**ree**
beach	Η παραλία I paralía	ee pa-ra-lee-a
Byzantine	βυζαντινός vyzantinós	vee-zan-dee-**nos**
castle	Το κάστρο To kástro	to **ka**-stro
cathedral	Η μητρόπολη I mitrópoli	ee mee-**tro**-po-lee
cave	Το σπήλαιο To spílaio	to spee-le-o
church	Η εκκλησία I ekklisía	ee e-klee-see-a
folk art	λαϊκή τέχνη laïkí téchni	la-ee-**kee** tech-nee
fountain	Το συντριβάνι To syntriváni	to seen-dree-**va**-nee
hill	Ο λόφος O lófos	o **lo**-fos
historical	ιστορικός istorikós	ee-sto-ree-**kos**
island	Το νησί To nisí	to nee-**see**
lake	Η λίμνη I límni	ee leem-nee
library	Η βιβλιοθήκη I vivliothíki	ee veev-lee-o-thee-kee
mansion	Η έπαυλις I épavlis	**ee**e-pav-lees
monastery	Μονή moní	mo-**ni**
mountain	Το βουνό To vounó	to voo-**no**
municipal	δημοτικός dimotikós	thee-mo-tee-**kos**
museum	Το μουσείο To mouseío	to moo-see-o
national	εθνικός ethnikós	eth-nee-**kos**
park	Το πάρκο To párko	to par-ko
garden	Ο κήπος O kípos	o kee-pos
gorge	Το φαράγγι To farángi	to fa-**ran**-gee
grave of....	Ο τάφος του... O táfos tou...	o ta-fos too
river	Το ποτάμι To potámi	to po-**ta**-mee
road	Ο δρόμος O drómos	o thro-mos
saint	άγιος/αγιον/αγία /αγίες ágios/ágioi/agía/agíes	**a**-yee-os/**a**-yee-ee/a-yee-a/a-yee-es
spring	Η πηγή I pigí	ee pee-yee
square	Η πλατεία I plateía	ee pla-tee-a
stadium	Το στάδιο To stádio	to sta-thee-o
statue	Το άγαλμα To ágalma	to **a**-gal-ma
theatre	Το θέατρο To théatro	to the-a-tro
town hall	Το δημαρχείο To dimarcheío	To thee-mar-**chee**-o
closed on public holidays	κλειστό τις αργίες kleistó tis argíes	klee-sto tees ar-yee-es

Transport

When does the .... leave?	Πότε φεύγει το ....; Póte févgei to...?	po-teh fev-yee to...?
Where is the bus stop?	Πού είναι η στάση του λεωφορείο υ; Poú eínai i stási tou leoforeíou?	poo ee-neh ee sta-see too le-o-fo-ree-oo?
Is there a bus to...?	Υπάρχει λεωφορείο για....; Ypárchei leoforeío gia...?	ee-**par**-chee le-o-fo-ree-o yia...?
ticket office	Εκδοτήρια εισιτηρίων Ekdotíria eisitírion	Ek-tho-tee-reea ee-see-tee-ree-on
return ticket	Εισιτήριο με επιστροφή Eisitírio me epistrofí	ee-see-tee-ree-o meh e-pee-stro-**fee**
single journey	Απλό εισιτήριο Apló eisitírio	a-**plo** ee-see-tee-reeo

bus station	Ο σταθμός λεωφορείων O stathmós leoforeíon	o stath-mos leo-fo-ree-on
bus ticket	Εισιτήριο λεωφορείου Eisitírio leoforeíou	ee-see-tee-ree-o leo-fo-ree-oo
trolley bus	Το τρόλλεϋ To trólley	to tro-le-ee
port	Το λιμάνι To limáni	to lee-ma-nee
train/metro	Το τρένο To tréno	to tre-no
railway station	σιδηροδρομικός σταθμός sidirodromikós stathmós	see-thee-ro-thro-mee-kos stath-mos
moped	Το μοτοποδήλατο / το μηχανάκι To motopodílato / To michanáki	to mo-to-po-thee-la-to/to mee-cha-na-kee
bicycle	Το ποδήλατο To podílato	to po-thee-la-to
taxi	Το ταξί To taxí	to tak-see
airport	Το αεροδρόμιο To aerodrómio	to a-e-ro-thro-mee-o
ferry	Το φερυμπότ To "ferry-boat"	to fe-ree-bot
hydrofoil	Το δελφίνι / Το υδροπτέρυγο To delfini / To ydroptérygo	to del-fee-nee / To ee-throp-te-ree-go
catamaran	Το καταμαράν To katamarán	to catamaran
for hire	Ενοικιάζονται Enoikiázontai	e-nee-kya-zon-deh

Staying in a Hotel

Do you have a vacant room?	Έχετε δωμάτια; Echete domátia?	e-che-teh tho-ma-tee-a?
double room with double bed	Δίκλινο με διπλό κρεβάτι Díklino me dipló kreváti	thee-klee-no meh thee-plo kre-va-tee
twin room	Δίκλινο με μονά κρεβάτια Díklino me moná krevátia	thee-klee-no mo-na kre-vat-ya
single room	Μονόκλινο Monóklino	mo-no-klee-no
room with a bath	Δωμάτιο με μπάνιο Domátio me mpánio	tho-ma-tee-o meh ban-yo
shower	Το ντους To douz	To dooz
porter	Ο πορτιέρης O portiéris	o por-tye-rees
key	Το κλειδί To kleidí	to klee-dee
I have a reservation	Έχω κάνει κράτηση Echo kánei krátisi	e-cho ka-nee kra-tee-see
room with a sea view/balcony	Δωμάτιο με θέα στη θάλασσα/μπαλκόνι Domátio me théa sti thálassa/mpalkóni	tho-ma-tee-o meh the-a stee tha-la-sa/bal- ko-nee
Does the price include breakfast?	Το πρωινό συμπεριλαμβάνεται στην τιμή; To proinó symperi-lamvánetai stin timí?	to pro-ee-no seem-be-ree-lam-va-ne-teh steen tee-mee?

Eating Out

Have you got a table?	Έχετε τραπέζι; Echete trapézi?	e-che-te tra-pe-zee?
I want to reserve a table	Θέλω να κρατήσω ένα τραπέζι Thélo na kratíso éna trapézi	the-lo na kra-tee-so e-na tra-pe-zee
The bill, please	Τον λογαριασμό, παρακαλώ Ton logariazmó parakaló	ton lo-gar-yas-mo pa-ra-ka-lo
I am a vegetarian	Είμαι χορτοφάγος Eímai chortofágos	ee-meh chor-to-fa-gos
What is fresh today?	Τί φρέσκο έχετε σήμερα; Tí frésko échete símera?	tee fres-ko e-che-teh see-me-ra?

waiter/waitress	Κύριε / Γκαρσόν / Κυρία (female) Kýrie/Garson°/Kyría	Kee-ree-eh/Gar-son/Kee-ree-a
menu	Ο κατάλογος O katálogos	o ka-ta-lo-gos
cover charge	Το κουβέρ To "couvert"	to koo-ver
wine list	Ο κατάλογος με τα οινοπνευματώδη O katálogos me ta oinopnevmatódi	o ka-ta-lo-gos meh ta ee-no-pnev-ma-to-thee
glass	Το ποτήρι To potíri	to po-tee-ree
bottle	Το μπουκάλι To mpoukáli	to bou-ka-lee
knife	Το μαχαίρι To machaíri	to ma-che-ree
fork	Το πηρούνι To piroúni	to pee-roo-nee
spoon	Το κουτάλι To koutáli	to koo-ta-lee
breakfast	Το πρωινό To proïnó	to pro-ee-no
lunch	Το μεσημεριανό To mesimerianó	to me-see-mer-ya-no
dinner	Το δείπνο To deípno	to theep-no
main course	Το κυρίως γεύμα To kyríos gévma	to kee-ree-os yev-ma
starter/first course	Τα ορεκτικά Ta orektiká	ta o-rek-tee-ka
dessert	Το γλυκό To glykó	to ylee-ko
dish of the day	Το πιάτο της ημέρας To piáto tis iméras	to pya-to tees ee-me-ras
bar	Το μπαρ To "bar"	To bar
taverna	Η ταβέρνα I tavérna	ee ta-ver-na
café	Το καφενείο To kafeneío	to ka-fe-nee-o
fish taverna	Η ψαροταβέρνα I psarotavérna	ee psa-ro-ta-ver-na
grill house	Η ψησταριά I psistariá	ee psee-sta-rya
wine shop	Το οινοπωλείο To oinopoleío	to ee-no-po-lee-o
dairy shop	Το γαλακτοπωλείο To galaktopoleío	to ga-lak-to-po-lee-o
restaurant	Το εστιατόριο To estiatório	to e-stee-a-to-ree-o
ouzeri	Το ουζερί To ouzerí	to oo-ze-ree
meze shop	Το μεζεδοπωλείο To mezedopoleío	To me-ze-do-po-lee-o
take away kebabs	Το σουβλατζίδικο To souvlatzídiko	To soo-vlat-zee-dee-ko
rare	Ελάχιστα ψημένο Eláchista psiméno	e-lach-ees-ta psee-me-no
medium	Μέτρια ψημένο Métria psiméno	met-ree-a psee-me-no
well done	Καλοψημένο Kalopsiméno	ka-lo-psee-me-no

Basic Food and Drink

coffee	Ο καφές O Kafés	o ka-fes
with milk	με γάλα me gála	me ga-la
black coffee	σκέτος skétos	ske-tos
without sugar	χωρίς ζάχαρη chorís záchari	cho-rees za-cha-ree
medium sweet	μέτριος métrios	me-tree-os
very sweet	γλυκύς glykýs	glee-kees
tea	τσάι tsái	tsa-ee
hot chocolate	ζεστή σοκολάτα zestí sokoláta	ze-stee so-ko-la-ta
wine	κρασί krasí	kra-see
red	κόκκινο kókkino	ko-kee-no
white	λευκό lefkó	lef-ko
rosé	ροζέ rozé	ro-ze

raki	Το ρακί Το rakí	to ra-kee
ouzo	Το ούζο Το oúzo	to oo-zo
retsina	Η ρετσίνα I retsína	ee ret-see-na
water	Το νερό Το neró	to ne-ro
octopus	Το χταπόδι Το chtapódi	to chta-po-dee
fish	Το ψάρι Το psári	to psa-ree
cheese	Το τυρί Το tyrí	to tee-ree
halloumi	Το χαλούμι Το chaloúmi	to cha-loo-mee
feta	Η φέτα I féta	ee fe-ta
bread	Το ψωμί Το psomí	to pso-mee
bean soup	Η φασολάδα I fasoláda	ee fa-so-la-da
houmous	Το χούμους Το houmous	to choo-moos
halva	Ο χαλβάς Ο chalvás	o chal-vas
meat kebabs	Ο γύρος Ο gýros	o yee-ros
Turkish delight	Το λουκούμι Το loukoúmi	to loo-koo-mee
baklava	Ο μπακλαβάς Ο mpaklavás	o bak-la-vas
klephtiko	Το κλέφτικο Το kléftiko	to klef-tee-ko

Numbers

1	ένα éna	e-na
2	δύο dýo	thee-o
3	τρία tría	tree-a
4	τέσσερα téssera	te-se-ra
5	πέντε pénte	pen-deh
6	έξι éxi	ek-si
7	επτά eptá	ep-ta
8	οχτώ ochtó	och-to
9	εννέα ennéa	e-ne-a
10	δέκα déka	the-ka
11	έντεκα énteka	en-de-ka
12	δώδεκα dódeka	tho-the-ka
13	δεκατρία dekatría	de-ka-tree-a
14	δεκατέσσερα dekatéssera	the-ka-tes-se-ra
15	δεκαπέντε dekapénte	the-ka-pen-de
16	δεκαέξι dekaéxi	the-ka-ek-si
17	δεκαεπτά dekaeptá	the-ka-ep-ta
18	δεκαοχτώ dekaochtó	the-ka-och-to
19	δεκαεννέα dekaennéa	the-ka-e-ne-a
20	είκοσι eíkosi	ee-ko-see
21	εικοσιένα eikosiéna	ee-ko-see-e-na
30	τριάντα triánta	tree-an-da
40	σαράντα saránta	sa-ran-da
50	πενήντα penínta	pe-neen-da
60	εξήντα exínta	ek-seen-da
70	εβδομήντα evdomínta	ev-tho-meen-da

80	ογδόντα ogdónta	og-thon-da
90	ενενήντα enenínta	e-ne-neen-da
100	εκατό ekató	e-ka-to
200	διακόσια diakósia	thya-kos-ya
1,000	χίλια chília	cheel-ya
2,000	δύο χιλιάδες dýo chiliádes	thee-o cheel-ya-thes
1,000,000	ένα εκατομμύριο éna ekatommýrio	e-na e-ka-to-mee-ree-o

Time, Days and Dates

one minute	ένα λεπτό éna leptó	e-na lep-to
one hour	μία ώρα mía óra	mee-a o-ra
half an hour	μισή ώρα misí óra	mee-see o-ra
quarter of an hour	ένα τέταρτο éna tétarto	e-na te-tar-to
half past one	μία και μισή mía kai misí	mee-a keh mee-see
quarter past one	μία και τέταρτο mía kai tétarto	mee-a keh te-tar-to
ten past one	μία και δέκα mía kai déka	mee-a keh the-ka
quarter to two	δύο παρά τέταρτο dýo pará tétarto	thee-o pa-ra te-tar-to
ten to two	δύο παρά δέκα dýo pará déka	thee-o pa-ra the-ka
a day	μία μέρα mía méra	mee-a me-ra
a week	μία εβδομάδα mía evdomáda	mee-a ev-tho-ma-tha
a month	ένας μήνας énas mínas	e-nas mee-nas
a year	ένας χρόνος énas chrónos	e-nas chro-nos
Monday	Δευτέρα Deftéra	thef-te-ra
Tuesday	Τρίτη Tríti	tree-tee
Wednesday	Τετάρτη Tetárti	te-tar-tee
Thursday	Πέμπτη Pémpti	pemp-tee
Friday	Παρασκευή Paraskeví	pa-ras-ke-vee
Saturday	Σάββατο Sávvato	sa-va-to
Sunday	Κυριακή Kyriakí	keer-ee-a-kee
January	Ιανουάριος Ianouários	ee-a-noo-a-ree-os
February	Φεβρουάριος Fevrouários	fev-roo-a-ree-os
March	Μάρτιος Mártios	mar-tee-os
April	Απρίλιος Aprílios	a-pree-lee-os
May	Μάιος Máios	ma-ee-os
June	Ιούνιος Ioúnios	ee-oo-nee-os
July	Ιούλιος Ioúlios	ee-oo-lee-os
August	Αύγουστος Avgoustos	av-goo-stos
September	Σεπτέμβριος Septémvrios	sep-tem-vree-os
October	Οκτώβριος Októvrios	ok-to-vree-os
November	Νοέμβριος Noémvrios	no-em-vree-os
December	Δεκέμβριος Dekémvrios	the-kem-vree-os

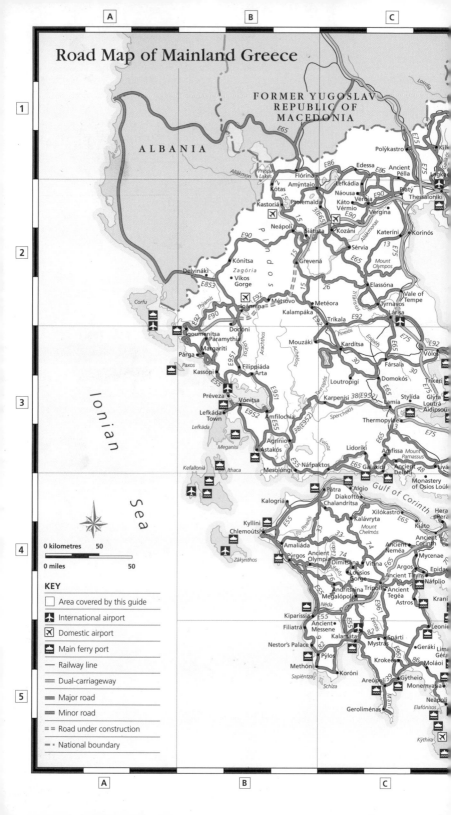